TERATOLOGIES

Sto— —ess
of— —ed
liv— —ns,
ca— —ple
wh— —eir
co— —ed;
it— —*cer*
in— —l in
co— —of,
an— —gly
po—

m— —elp
at— —ok
co— —ese
of— —ing
ar— —ons
hi— —the
th— —and
—ety.
—ret-
ic— —the
cu— —ness
u— —onal
st—

Ja —ural
S—

TERATOLOGIES

A cultural study of cancer

Jackie Stacey

London and New York

First published 1997
by Routledge
11 New Fetter Lane, London EC4P 4EE

Simultaneously published in the USA and Canada
by Routledge
29 West 35th Street, New York, NY 10001

Typeset in Baskerville and Frutiger by
Ponting–Green Publishing Services,
Chesham, Buckinghamshire

Printed in Great Britain by
Butler & Tanner, Frome, Somerset

British Library Cataloguing in Publication Data
A catalogue record for this book is available from the
British Library

Library of Congress Cataloguing in Publication Data
Stacey, Jackie.
Teratologies: a cultural study of cancer / by Jackie Stacey.
Includes bibliographical references and index.
1. Cancer – Social aspects.   2. Medical literature.
I. Title.
RC262.S79   1997
362.1'96994 – dc21   96–37055
CIP

ISBN 0–415–14959–2 (hbk)
ISBN 0–415–14960–6 (pbk)

For Dr H.

teratologies

teras *(med.)* *n.* a monstrosity:
teratogeny, *n.* the production of monsters:
teratology, *n.* the study of malformations or abnormal growths, animal
or vegetable; a tale of marvels:
teratoma, a tumour, containing tissue from all three germ layers:
[Gr. *teras, -atos,* a monster.]

(*Chambers Dictionary*, 1973)

CONTENTS

FIGURES

Plates courtesy of:

Munksgaard Publishers, Copenhagen, Denmark (2.1–2.4, 3.2, 3.3); Metro Pictures (3.1); Denoyer-Geppart Science Company, Chicgao 60640, USA (4.1 and 4.2); W. H. Freeman and Company, New York, USA (5.3 and 5.4); Nature's Sunshine Products Inc., UK and Ireland (5.5–5.7); The Jo Spence Memorial Archive (7.1 and 7.2); and Maggie Murray (7.3).

ACKNOWLEDGEMENTS

Expressing my appreciation for support with writing a book that crosses the boundaries between the personal and the academic, the auto-biographical and the theoretical is a particularly difficult task. It would be impossible to mention everyone who has helped me through the illness *and* with the writing of the book, and yet in many cases the two are inseparable.

I would like to thank Lancaster University for its generous institutional support during my illness (and especially John Urry and Nicholas Abercrombie for facilitating this), and colleagues in the Department of Sociology and in Women's Studies for all their hard work covering for me during this period, most importantly Sarah Franklin, Celia Lury and Lynne Pearce. I am also grateful to the Department, and to the University, for granting me a sabbatical in 1993 that enabled me to carry out the research for this book and to begin drafting some of the main ideas in it.

Earlier versions of some of the chapters were given as papers at the 'Identity and Cultural Change' seminar and the Sociology Departmental seminar at Lancaster University in 1993/4 and at the Women's Studies seminar and the Lesbian and Gay Studies Annual Conference, 'Queer Bodies', at the University of Warwick in 1995. I am grateful for many fruitful and informative discussions with colleagues at these events. The international conference, 'Encounters with Cancer', at Rosendal in Norway in 1996, offered a unique opportunity to consider my own work in relation to that of other academics writing about experiences of cancer. Meeting Arthur Frank and reading his work at this event had an important, if rather belated, impact on my thinking in this area. I have appreciated his generous assistance with my project and hope to engage further with his work in future publications.

The Centre for the Study of Women and Gender at the University of Warwick offered me considerable support during the redrafting of parts of this book in 1994/5 and I am grateful to colleagues there and elsewhere in the University for discussions of ideas and arguments in progress. In particular, I would like to thank Aylish Wood for helping to bridge the gaps between scientific discourse and cultural theory in Chapter 2, Kate Chedgzoy and John Fletcher for illuminating exchanges about 'queer theory' that informed Chapter 3, Hilary Graham for her detailed commentary on the sociological implications of changing ideas about medical responsibility discussed in Chapter 7, and Adrian Heathfield for suggesting ways to approach the subject of the interface between writing and mortality which helped shape the final chapter.

I would also like to thank the following people for reading and commenting on earlier drafts of some of the chapters of *Teratologies* and/or for pointing me in the right direction at the early stages of the research: Anne Butterfield, Tom Cahill, Erica Carter, Claudia Castañeda, Rowena Clayton, Robin Grove-White, Keith Harvey, Sylvia Harvey, Flis Henwood, Annette Kuhn, Mark Levins, Phil Macnaghten, Maureen McNeil, Hazel Platzer, Andrew Quick, Gillian Rose, Bron Szerszynski, Mo White and Sue Wiseman. Two anonymous readers also gave me extremely constructive guidance at the final stages of rewriting, as did Mari Shullaw from Routledge whose editorial engagement with the project has stretched beyond the call of duty. I am grateful to her and to John Urry, the Series Editor of the International Library of Sociology, for their confidence in the sociological pertinence of this kind of research. My thanks also go to Wendy Langford for all her hard work on the bibliography.

I would like to thank Aganetha Dyck, who very kindly gave me permission to use her *Beework* for the cover of this book. Permission to reproduce an extract from 'Hairball', *Wilderness Tips* (1991), by Margaret Atwood, was granted by Bloomsbury Publishing. Permission to reproduce an extract from *Written on the Body*, by Jeanette Winterson (Jonathan Cape, 1992) was granted by the author. An earlier version of Chapter 1 appeared in Patricia Duncker and Vicky Wilson (eds) *Cancer: through the eyes of ten women*, Pandora (1996).

During the last five years, colleagues at Lancaster University have offered their usual generosities in the collaborative spirit that typifies academic work here. Staff and students in the Department of Sociology, the Centre for Women's Studies, the Cultural Change Research Group and the Centre for the Study of Environmental Change have all contributed to the stimulating intellectual context that has substantially influenced this project. Celia Lury, Lynne Pearce, Beverley Skeggs, Alison Young and most especially Sarah Franklin have all read, and sometimes reread, earlier drafts of parts of this book. Their feedback and encouragement have been central to the development of many of the arguments found throughout. The combination of social and intellectual exchanges, and the balance between critical interrogation and enthusiastic engagement amongst these friends and colleagues have produced an exceptionally valuable working environment which I continue to appreciate.

I am also indebted to the numerous people who helped me through some very gruelling cancer treatments in 1991/2. Maureen McNeil was an extraordinarily dedicated visitor to the chemotherapy ward; Richard Dyer, Joyce Canaan, Geraldine Wilkins, Helen Docherty and Bernie Keenan all provided regular culinary support; Anne Butterfield, Sarah Franklin, Michèle Fuirer, Joan O'Hagan, Keith Harvey, Flis Henwood, Diana Wallace, Keiko, Erika and Dai Ishimaru, Lottie Rawicz-Szczerbo, Phil Levy, Angela Lloyd, Jac Matthews, Lynne Pearce, Kathryn Perry, Rosi Roper, Deborah Steinberg, Tony and Tina Stacey and Jayne Warburton all offered care and domestic help, often travelling some distance to do so. Friends who had experiences of cancer themselves were a great source of support and advice, including Meg Stacey and Jennifer Lorch, Marie and Sahra Gibbon, and Susan Franklin who offered long-distance empathy. My acupuncturist, Angie Hughes, treated me in and out of hospital and often provided the only source of relief from the sickness. Malcolm Gibb, Jo Li and Richard Dyer offered spectacular hospitality for the party to celebrate the end of the treatment. I am grateful to all these friends and relatives, and to many, many others, for their thoughtfulness, kindness and hard work which did not go unnoticed. I would also like to thank my parents, Daphne and Leslie Stacey, for their confidence and trust in me during my illness and since. I hope this book, in its attempt to address a rather broader audience than most academic writing, succeeds in speaking to them in part, if not in its entirety.

Finally, my deepest gratitude goes to Hilary Hinds, who cared for me during the time of the illness with her usual unassuming generosity and calm sensitivity. A constant presence at each stage of the treatment, she witnessed the terrors without being engulfed by the fear. In addition to the physical and emotional work of caring, she has maintained a high degree of intellectual engagement with the ideas in this book during the past four years. Her conviction in the purpose of its more ambitious dimensions inspired me to keep writing and rewriting until a satisfactory sense of completion had been achieved.

1

HEROES

Books about cancer always tell stories. Those who write them offer recognisable narratives of diagnosis, of treatment and of prognosis. Those who read them often do so in search of the comforting hope of survival. Faced with a sudden change in the story of their lives following a cancer diagnosis, many rehearse the possible trajectories which now present themselves through the accounts of those who have been there before them.

There are books written by doctors about 'the facts' you need to know; they tell of the different types of cancer, the typical prognoses and the likely treatments and their side-effects.[1] There are books written by alternative practitioners encouraging a holistic approach to the disease, advising on diet, therapy and a change of lifestyle.[2] There are books written by spiritual evangelists who write of cancer as an opportunity for salvation.[3]

There are also, of course, books written by patients, or their friends and relatives, which offer personal accounts of the experience of living with cancer. If the person with cancer has lived to tell the tale, the story is often of a heroic struggle against adversity. Pitting life against death and drawing on all possible resources, the patient moves from victim to survivor and 'triumphs over the tragedy' that has unexpectedly threatened their life. These are often the stories of transformation in which the negative physical affliction becomes a positive source of self-knowledge. The person who has faced death and yet still lives, who has recognised the inevitability of human mortality, now benefits from a new-found wisdom. Accepting the fragility of life itself, the cancer survivor sees things others are not brave enough to face (or so the story goes). Cancer offers the chance to reassess. It allows the person to pause and to re-evaluate their life: having cancer teaches us that life may be shorter than we thought and that it may be time to decide to live it differently.[4] These are the kinds of wisdoms which are told and retold in books about cancer.

If, on the other hand, the person with cancer dies, the story told is one of loss and of pain, but also tends to be a celebration of their courage and dignity. It may be written by friends, lovers or relatives. Stories of pointlessly shortened lives, lost opportunities, or of medical or industrial malpractice and ineptitude, warn others to try to avoid a similar fate. The late diagnosis, the misread X-ray or the high levels of radiation near nuclear power stations are some of the motivations for authors to tell their stories.[5] But few write (or publish) accounts which tell only of disaster and depression, suffering and unbearable loss. For there is always room for heroism in tragedy and many such stories offer accounts of stoicism and of a fighting spirit. They document the triumphs along the way, even in the event of death.[6]

The market for books about cancer is enormous. Amongst the expanding health and fitness/self-development/New Age and spirituality sections of highstreet bookstores and the increasing number of publications for sale in health food shops, books about cancer are not hard to find; in fact, they are hard to avoid. Once the news has been broken, books about cancer surface from all directions: they are on every friend's bookshelf, in every shop window. A veritable 'cancer subculture' proves to have been thriving, but, like so many others, it remains invisible until it becomes relevant and then, as if by magic, it seems suddenly all-pervasive. For many people with cancer these books are the starting point of coming to terms with the diagnosis. They are read in the hope of finding a story that fits, of finding a story that offers hope, of even finding a story that ends happily. They are also read for information about the disease or about the treatment: some offer the chance to learn the language of oncology, to understand the principles of chemotherapy or radiotherapy; others educate their readers on the workings of the immune system, the anti-cancer diet or the negative effects of stress on the body. Read all of them and you can become an expert in your field, an expert on your particular disease and an expert on yourself.

Given the changes in health cultures in 1990s Britain, the proliferation of this market of 'self-health' cancer books is hardly surprising. As the government cuts in public health provision become the source of endless stories in everday life (patients returned home prematurely after surgery, beds not available for emergencies, newly equipped wards standing empty because there's no money to staff them, nurses' threats of unprecedented industrial action signalling intense desperation and frustration), people are increasingly encouraged to look elsewhere for reassurance. The introduction of internal markets into the National Health Service in Britain through the National Health Service and Community Care Act (implemented on 1 April 1991) fundamentally changed its principles of organisation and management, placing health

firmly within a world of competition and consumerism.[7] In these
emergent health cultures, where the language of the market has come
to dominate ideas about health provision, the scope for appealing to
individuals to take charge of their health is ever-widening. As the
National Health Service no longer guarantees to provide the patient
care necessary, the responsibility increasingly shifts elsewhere. As well
as expecting families (read women) to do more unpaid caring, there is
also a growing imperative for individuals to take responsibility for their
own health.[8] This is perhaps the most glaring overlap between some
alternative approaches to health and the Thatcherite legacy of the
cult of the individual. In the marketisation of public sector areas
such as health, there has been a shift in responsibility, and thus
funding, that encourages us to heal ourselves. The market for cancer
books thus expands as beliefs about self-health more generally capture
our imaginations.

My own response to being diagnosed with cancer was to read as much
as I could about the subject. I borrowed and bought as many books as
possible – biomedical, self-health and personal narratives. I sent off to
cancer charities for leaflets and phoned helplines for advice. I spent
days and weeks, and eventually months, reading about cancer and how
to get rid of it. In a characteristically academic way, my response to the
illness was to turn it into a research project. While I was still in hospital,
friends researched the details of the rare kind of cancer I had, since it
did not appear in many of the standard accounts. What characterised
this type of cancer and how did it spread, what were my chances and
what treatments should I expect? Medical libraries were consulted and
bookshops searched to find the maximum amount of information for
my purpose.

This desire for knowledge was clearly a bid for control at the very
moment it had been taken away from me. It was also an instrumental
use of the academic skills of my world and a way of making the
alienating medical world, in which I had suddenly found myself, more
familiar and more manageable. Unlike many other people with cancer,
who do not have my educational advantages, I did have a powerful set
of resources to draw upon. Turning the disease into a research project
channelled my otherwise overwhelming fear and panic. The desire for
information, and the confidence to access it, is often the privilege
of those with certain educational histories and race and class back-
grounds, but also belongs to a new generation of what I call 'participatory patients'. On the whole, my parents' generation, for example,
have far less inclination to be put in the picture. They are happier to
leave it to the medical experts and to avoid the burdens and responsibilities such knowledge might demand. But those of us who have been
influenced by the information cultures of the last twenty years are more

susceptible to the desire to know and to the fantasies of knowledge as power. We are encouraged to seek out information about ourselves with an obsessive curiosity. In my own case, in the context of complete ignorance about my illness, I welcomed any new explanations.

But the information proved to be inseparable from the stories: other people's stories, and then very quickly, my own. As the pieces fitted together, a story began to take shape. First the cancer was named. I had had (and possibly still had) a teratoma: more specifically an endodermal sinus tumour, a malignant growth originating in the yolk sac of an egg cell. Then the tumour type was described: large (the size of a melon), fast-growing, usually mono-lateral (one-sided). With this information, memory traces of a transformed body are rearranged to produce a retrospective account of the illness. Passing sensations that barely registered at the time now took on enormous significance as signs of a life-threatening disease which had been quietly present in my body. The narrative that emerged gradually organised physical sensations into a temporal sequence with a causative effect. Looking back, the abdominal bloating seemed more obvious, the pressure on the bladder at night an unquestionable symptom. These almost negligible manifestations were reread as the crucial early signs of the disease. The subsequent and much more dramatic physical symptoms were then also rationalised within this pathological trajectory: I was told that the abdominal pain had been caused by the tumour rupturing and bleeding into the abdominal cavity, resulting in peritonitis. The puzzling events of those last few days are given narrative coherence, and conversations and advice take on new meaning in the light of the seriousness of the diagnosis. The doctor who did not insist on immediate surgery now looks to have been somewhat negligent; his permission to wait, which seemed a godsend at the time, is condemned as incompetent. His female superior, who finally made a correct diagnosis and insisted on emergency surgery on a Sunday, becomes an angel rescuing me from imminent danger.

The narrative of my body continued to be rewritten at each stage. As I lay recovering from surgery, I tried to find out what had been removed apart from the tumour. The surgeon had taken out the tumour and also the fallopian tube and the ovary on the right side. Overnight my identity was reinvented: I was now a cancer patient; or was I? I was told the disease may or may not still be present in my body. It may or may not return. Since the tumour had ruptured, some malignant cells may have been left behind and therefore chemotherapy might be necessary. Weekly tests would tell. It soon became a story of uncertainty, impossible to predict the future, because the present situation might change at any moment. Next year might be beyond reach. Next month I might be back at work or in hospital having chemotherapy. According to the statistics,

I reminded myself, I had an 80 per cent to 90 per cent chance of recovery. A hopeful prognosis by all accounts.

Illnesses become narratives very rapidly. Some sense is sought of time and sequence, sense for others and for oneself. The past confusion is explained; the present situation requires a story (I struggle to offer a coherent answer to the question, 'What has happened?'); and the future presents the possibility of terrifying resolutions (What are my chances of survival?). Only a little information is necessary and the narrative structuring begins: linearity, cause and effect and possible closures present themselves almost automatically. Decide on the name of the disease, explain a few symptoms, predict the outcome and the story is practically written. Indeed, the genres of medical knowledge are organised around just such temporal trajectories: diagnosis, treatment and prognosis are in some ways just other names for the different stages of the story.

The usual temporal sequencing is both disrupted and reimposed in the search for order, reason and predictability. The past must now be reimagined and rescripted. Life, it has turned out, was not what it seemed. The present is not the imagined future it once was. And as for the future, it is suddenly compressed into the most frightening of time scales, previously unimaginable. In the light of the diagnosis, the recent past must be reexamined for clues of this newly revealed deception. The body becomes the site of a narrative teleology that demands a retelling.

Given the demands of this new bodily evidence, I found myself inventing stories about myself. If such an illness had been present the whole summer (perhaps longer) what sense can be made of the memories of those idyllic months? 'But you looked so well', became the incredulous refrain of friends and family. Perhaps these memories themselves were simply the nostalgic product of the loss of good health. Were those remembered weeks in which I had felt better than I had for years simply a retrospective reinvention at a time of danger and threat? Feelings of a golden age emerge in the face of mortality. The old narratives struggle against the pressures of the new, whose authority have the advantage of immediacy, physical presence and, indeed, medical emergency. The body tells a new story and so demands a reinterpretation of recent life history. Is it no longer to be trusted? Why has it withheld such crucial evidence? Whose side is it on anyway?

In the light of a cancer diagnosis, these new narratives of the body rescript the story of my life with ruthless editorial authority. While the mind had been full of stories of life, the body had been planning another story: the threat of death. How should my life be imagined in such an unexpected context? Can the self be reinvented to cope with the shock? What kind of person does not know they have cancer? What kind of body hides the evidence so effectively? And what kind of disease could disguise itself so skilfully? I had thought I was aware of my body and its complaints. I had assumed that I could read the corporeal codes. I was body-literate. I could see the signs. I knew if protest was taking place. I had learnt to 'listen to my body'. But the shock of this diagnosis suggested that all was not what it seemed: the healthy body that hosted deadly disease, the smooth surface that concealed a malignant tumour. My energy for life that summer had been matched by another: the prolific growth of a malignant tumour. How could they have pulled in such opposite directions with the same enthusiasms? Competing agendas and conflicting trajectories: whose authority would win out? I had to find new ways of writing the story of my life given the sudden change of agendas. I had to consider the story of my death with an unprecedented urgency.

Before my diagnosis I had harboured the hackneyed (though barely articulated) fantasy that I would live until my early eighties and would die suddenly, but peacefully, in my armchair. Not that I spent much time planning that far ahead, but with such a diagnosis many semiconscious projections that have informed our sense of selves surface and take a more definite shape. Moreover, the shock of the diagnosis not only produced a rapid series of renarrativisations, but also illuminated the extent to which all kinds of narratives had quietly structured my imagination previously, almost without my knowledge. When I was first diagnosed with cancer, my initial shock placed me outside the narrative of my own life, watching it as if it were on film (a predictable visual manifestation of the cliché 'and her life flashed before her' for someone who teaches film studies). I felt as if someone had got the story wrong: this was not how it was supposed to go. The first reel of the film had finished and the rest of my life, already recorded on the second reel of film which lay next to the projector, ready and waiting to be screened, had been forgotten. The whole episode felt as if it was someone else's script, not mine. The denial of powerlessness produced a cinematic trope which seemed to offer a guarantee of narrative certainty and predictability: there should be a whole second half still to show.

At the next stage chemotherapy did in fact prove necessary: four doses of it over the course of three months. It seemed to work. It was followed by weekly, then monthly, then quarterly and then six-monthly tests. But there are few real certainties with cancer narratives, and so many possible complications that it is rare to be able to breathe that sigh of relief that says 'it's over'. Until recently (now four years later) my experience of having had cancer felt firmly in the past. I had finally become confident enough to speak about it in the past tense. For many months I had used the present perfect tense to describe my situation: 'I have had cancer'; it started in the past and may be continuing in the present (as the grammar books put it). To have used the present tense, 'I have cancer', seemed too pessimistic, since I hoped I did not any more; the past tense, 'I had cancer', seemed to deny the possibility of its return. But during the rewriting of this book, I had a letter following my annual scan telling me that a report had been sent to my consultant warning that 'the uterus looks bulky and there's a suggestion of a cyst on the other ovary'. With further investigation this proved to be a false alarm and I was reassured to be told that the radiologist had 'overread the image'. There was nothing to worry about. Thus, although when I first drafted this introduction I felt as if this particular cancer story was almost over, this more recent episode only serves to underline the ways in which cancer narratives refuse to offer the reassurances of complete resolution.

Few cancers are considered completely curable and consultants hedge around such absolutes in their conversations with patients. I am much more fortunate than many, in so far as there is a five-year threshold for teratoma patients, the crossing of which at least promises the all-clear. I'm still subject to annual tests, but I am told that I am on much safer ground these days. But there are so many variables with cancer and its treatments. Some chemotherapy can cause long-term side-effects. In my case, while the teratoma may remain banished, I was told that the chemotherapy may cause leukaemia in fifteen or twenty years' time, though it may not, of course. Added to such prospects are the litany of so-called side-effects from chemotherapy which continue to change self-image, aspirations and the stories I tell myself and others about my life and the kind of person I am in the world.

As the distance between the initial diagnosis and my present state of relatively good health grows, my memories of the experience become more muddled, but the narrativisation of certain events increasingly solidifies. As the stories have taken shape a new teleology has been produced. Present self has begun to connect to past and future selves through narrative structures that have placed a meaning where there had suddenly been only confusion. I now have my own stories of diagnosis, of treatments, of prognosis and, indeed, of survival. The narrative follows one of the typical trajectories: crisis, rescue and recovery. Despite resistance to the absolutes of closure, I push my particular story in that desirable direction. Although it is not yet over, the whole episode can now be represented in a series of narratives. When people ask about the experience, there are plenty of stories to tell. I have my favourites, of course. And many of them are retold in this book.

II

Cultural narratives in general offer reassuring accounts of problems which have resolutions. Be it in self-health accounts of cancer, Hollywood cinema, opera or Shakespeare's plays, narratives move from problem to resolution with some sense of predictability and comforting repetition. There may be hold-ups, detours or unexpected twists along the way (indeed, the more dramatic the hold-ups, the more gratifying the resolution), but on the whole the stories that surround us are those whose riddles are solved, whose enigmas are understood, whose villains are destroyed and whose lost orders are restored. Narrative offers a way of ordering events and assigning roles; it gives temporal continuity and spatial coherence. The term 'narrative' draws attention to the story as convention and highlights the cultural forms of its typical patterns.[9] The repeated use of particular structures across a range of genres suggests that narratives offer fantasies of the triumph of good over evil and of order over confusion. Thus a common formula in popular culture is as follows: the stasis of a character, a community or a nation is threatened by corruption or invasion from outside (or from an enemy within); this produces chaos and yet offers the chance to explore the threat to its limits before it is eradicated; the reassuring narrative closure reestablishes order; this is often a new and better order than that disrupted in the first place.[10]

In popular cultural narratives it is usually the *male* protagonist who takes a number of risks in the name of truth, justice, morality or love and, in overcoming the negative forces in favour of these principles, he (or sometimes she) achieves a heroic stature which we might all admire or even aspire to. These masculine heroes offer fantasies of invincibility. They are the larger-than-life ego-ideals who shape our hopes. Their bodies are impenetrable and their boundaries are immutable. Their force is indestructible and their certainty unshakeable. Being on their side, we might imagine ourselves to be the agents of history; identifying with their power, we believe ourselves to control our destinies. These are the heroes who enable us to trust ourselves, to trust our judgement, to know we are right. We too can be omnipotent; we can take charge. These have been the (enviable?) forms of masculine heroism that have been challenged by recent feminist cultural criticism. Those of us engaged in such debates may become aware of the power of such fantasies of transcendence at precisely the moments in our lives when we are forced to reshape our own self-narrativisations.

Stories about illness are an intensification of the way in which we generally understand our lives through narrative. The experience of cancer may bring these narrative processes into particularly sharp focus, but in many ways it only makes explicit the importance of narratives in the construction of the self in contemporary culture.[11] We have stories about our childhood, a mixture of our memories and the family favourites we have heard repeatedly. We tell stories about our relationships, both successful and otherwise. We relate our (public and private) stories about who we are and what makes us special or different from the next person.[12] We have projected stories about who we might become in the future through romance and love, paid work, parenthood, sports and leisure activities and so on. When something unexpected occurs, such as illness, the scripts need rewriting, but normally the shock of the experience can be partly absorbed by the telling of a new story. The clash with the previous stories gradually loses its impact as it is integrated as a narrative feature in its own right. Life before and after illness; life before and after a baby; life before and after (a) death.

In contemporary Western culture, we are encouraged to think of our lives as coherent stories of success, progress and movement. Loss and failure have their place but only as part of a broader picture of ascendance. The steady upward curve is the favoured contour. Different relationships to material and psychic privileges offer inequitable resources for the fulfilment of plans and ambitions, and for some, dreams may seem more realisable than for others. But in a society so obsessed with its own progress and improvement it is almost impossible for us to avoid the pull of such narratives. In the face of crisis, another story begins and with the power of retrospection the past is rewritten for the exigencies of the present and the future.

But the power of narrative is not always enough to pull us through. With its demand for spatial and temporal coherence, for linear sequence and for closure and resolution, conventional narrative structure cannot necessarily contain the demands of a changing world. Autobiographical accounts of HIV and AIDS, for example, have begun to reshape the contours of narrative.[13] What sense can be made of the temporal continuity that characterises the autobiographical form for the writer with AIDS whose only imaginable future promises bodily decline? And what kind of new spatial dimensions need to be invented to accommodate the imagined identities of those living with the insecurities of 'borrowed time'? AIDS narratives might thus be said to have put pressure on the structures of conventional genres of storytelling. For some, it is argued, there is now a general anxiety about the narrative meaning of time in a culture where knowledge about AIDS has thrown into question conventional temporal securities and predictable trajectories of self-development.[14]

Cancer, too, threatens to rob us of our dreams of the future. But the uncertainties it generates are typically transformed into the hope of a return to familiar narrative structures. For some, the diagnosis of cancer may be as final as the diagnosis of being HIV positive (though the possibility of a cure for both may nevertheless perform a 'hope function'). For other people with cancer, however, the triumph-over-tragedy story offers a structure for an imagined future. Cancer and AIDS both have highly unpredictable prognostic patterns, but at the moment at least, some forms of cancer are considered curable if caught at early enough stages. The temporal expectations of the person with cancer are thus thrown into question, but not necessarily radically fractured as they are said to be for those writing about their experiences of HIV and AIDS. Having had cancer, one wonders when it will be safe to start planning again (if ever). At what point will the apparently healthy appearance of someone who has had cancer be anything other than of troubling significance? Should we trust the stories our bodies seem to tell us after treatment? How capable are we of reading the signs? These disturbances to temporality and self-perception ('falling out of time') that result from illness produce a desire for predictable trajectories and guaranteed survival.[15] They generate fantasies of heroic recoveries and miracle cures. These are the *teratologies*: the tales of monsters and marvels that pervade the popular imaginary of cancer subcultures.

Cancer never really invades the body as such, but rather reproduces itself from within. Malignant growths secretly proliferate. Like the monster of screen horror, it threatens bodily order and takes over its regulating systems. Horror films often tell tales of the conquering of monsters. Invaders from outside (and increasingly from inside) threaten the order of human society and must be exterminated in the name of civilisation.[16] More often than not, the monstrous threat invades the body. Occupied by an alien force or physical presence, the innocent human victims lose control of the body and its functions.[17] Be it vampires, ghouls or monsters from outer space, the horror narrative explores the boundaries between human and non-human, between life and death and between self and other. Its resolution requires the expulsion of the alien from the physical and social body it threatens, and the reestablishment of human order and stability. The heroes (the good scientists, the decent citizens, the protective fathers and husbands – and very occasionally the Sigourney Weavers) fight the monster to its death and return the rule of law to its rightful supremacy.[18]

Stories of surviving cancer fit easily into these patterns of a journey from chaos to control.[19] They combine the masculine heroics of such adventure narratives with the feminine suffering and sacrifice of melodramas. The narrative structure lends itself well to such masculine heroic epics combined with the emotional intensity of the more feminine 'triumph-over-tragedy' genre. There is the meta-narrative of the fight against cancer in general, accompanied by the micro-narratives of the emotional episodes along the way. While the books I read varied a great deal, stories of heroes, victims and villains were never far away.

The crisis–rescue–recovery formulation pits the hero against the disease in a life-and-death battle. The hero usually has truth, goodness and the pursuit of knowledge on his/her side. People who survive cancer are transformed from *feminised victim* to *masculinised hero* in the narrative retelling of individual triumph.

The narrativisation of the struggle against cancer is not only present in accounts of the personal experience, it pervades all representations of the disease. In the biomedical accounts, it is scientific progress that is heroised: science will produce the cure for cancer (eventually). So often it is the heroic men of medicine who are represented as victors; and so often they save women from the horrors of their bodies. Cancer is commonly seen as the cells in chaos, the body out of control, governed only by the rules of outlaws. Medical science, personified in the figure of the doctor, brings the chance of rationalisation, the promise of order. Cancer is a disease against which Western science has long waged battle. We are told it is winning.[20] Through the progress of scientific discovery and the pursuit of more and more knowledge, the fantasy of ultimate control is offered; with enough time and money, cures will be found. Each new discovery offers the chance of cracking the code, of solving the cancerous riddle which has brought death to so many. Genetics, the information science, is the latest in a long line of disciplinary developments which promises to stretch the limits of knowledge and give us the power to defy the disease. We now read of the oncogene: the final frontier? If the gene can be isolated, surely a cure is in sight?[21]

In my own research on the teratoma, I read about how it used to be one of the most fatal cancers, killing its victims within eighteen months, its unusually fast-growing cells spreading through the body like wildfire. In the 1990s, however, it is one of the most treatable cancers; the new discovery of a particular chemotherapy cocktail, which acts effectively on such rapidly dividing cells, has brought an *almost* guaranteed promise of a cure. Bleomycin, etoposide and cisplatinum provide the magic formula in most cases. From the worst to the best kind of cancer in fifteen years. Thank God for scientific discovery; I could feel myself inclining towards hero-worship. Faced with a teratoma which might devour my body within the next year, medical science became the welcome rescuer. The medical accounts of the teratoma exemplified the success of the scientific project, of the steady upward curve, the ever-expanding boundaries of scientific knowledge. Medical science had discovered a cure and I might be – *would* be – saved.

The appeal of the masculine hero narratives of science cannot be overestimated. Trust the doctors, they know best. Your body becomes the battleground between good science and bad disease. If you give yourself up to their wisdom and follow their instructions, you stand the best chance. Many (though by no means all) medical staff show little tolerance for patients who do otherwise. Indeed, some warn that you ignore their instructions at your peril. One woman's account of breast cancer treatment claims that she was labelled a 'non-cooperator' and a 'militant' by hospital staff and warned of the consequences.[22] Medical experts are there to make the decisions for you and we can hope they will shoulder the responsibility for the narrative outcome, for it is their job to do so. Of course, even the most conventional of biomedics would agree that a positive patient is preferable, but beyond this the patient has little determining effect on the direction of the story. They alone are the narrators, perhaps even the authors.

In the alternative and self-health medical accounts, by contrast, it is the patient, with the help of the practitioner or therapist, who becomes the hero. With the correct guidance, the cancer patient can discover a new self, a true self, an Ur-self (or original self); you are invited to 'become who you are', or rather to 'become who you should have been'. With suitable monitoring, this can be maintained as a 'defended self': the fantasy of masculine invincibility surfaces again.[23] Although the patient is positioned differently in these accounts, the structure of the narrative is very similar to those found within biomedical discourses. The typical story is of the patient who is unexpectedly diagnosed as having cancer, who plummets to the depths of despair, who reassesses their values and the meaning of their life and who rises phoenix-like from the experience a new and better person. Having given them the chance for a new start in life, cancer in retrospect feels like a blessing in disguise. Indeed, with the wisdom of hindsight, the person who has now overcome the threat of cancer in their life is able to see how the cancer was an integral part of their previous follies which they have now abandoned. Cancer is interpreted as a metaphor for the self-destructive lifestyle that has since been rejected. The tumour eating away at the body is seen as a sign of unhappiness, distress or, indeed, dis-ease. Through diet, relaxation, emotional expression and various kinds of alternative medicine, patients can cure themselves of cancer and go on to lead a happier life than before. And, moreover, they live to tell the tale.

Cancer is thus constructed as a monstrous physical manifestation of other problems: these may be the problems of modernity (pollution, workaholism, chemicals and so on); or they may be the problems of a repressive and repressed culture which cannot deal with emotional life and prefers instead to be governed by rationality and intellect. In both respects, masculine values *seem* to be under attack. The question debated in this book is to what extent the so-called alternatives to such a masculinised culture really introduce new ways of thinking and of conceptualising the self in society. In particular, the forms of individualism produced within these alternative accounts are interrogated for their gendered appeal, not to mention their potential complicity with emergent and established forms of enterprise culture.[24] My own ambivalence towards alternative and self-health approaches to cancer is the starting point for a detailed analysis of the discourses which form the basis for their 'truth claims'.

The narrative structure of many of these alternative accounts follows the traditional pattern of the hero fighting an unexpected or unwelcome enemy. The shock of this disruption, however, is followed by the relief of the successful battle against it and the restoration of order following its exclusion. Conflict between good and evil is thus still at the heart of this cancer narrative. The person with cancer is offered the opportunity to achieve heroism through bravery, fortitude and strength of will-power. Having faced death and survived, the hero of this narrative is good and wise and true to themselves. Social identities, such as race, class or gender are barely mentioned and instead the focus is on the extraordinary qualities of the individual hero: their exceptionalism. Indeed, it is often precisely individuality that is at stake in the healing process. Through the experience of the disease and the fight against it, these people become heroes by discovering their uniqueness and individuality. This is the true value of the trauma: the chance to find oneself.

III

It is impossible to have cancer and not be seduced by the power of such cultural narratives. Part of the appeal of books about cancer is their promise of a compelling narrative. The key elements are bound to be present: life and death, a conflict, heroism, and the heightened emotional intensity that characterises the best of all stories. It is tempting to write such a story here, and it would be easy to do. Linearity imposes order. Cause and effect produce a rationality. Closure offers reassurance. I could start it:

> On 3 September 1991, as I sat at my desk trying to finish writing my PhD, I suddenly felt the most unfamiliar abdominal pain. I was troubled, but so intent on my thesis writing that I tried to ignore it. The next day the pain was more acute and I could ignore it no longer . . .

And then what happened? What other symptoms were there? What did the doctor say? How long before the surgery? Why was chemotherapy necessary and what was it like? Was I very sick? Were there other side-effects? Am I all right now? Am I sure? How have I changed? Do I feel wiser? Are my values different? Am I more or less afraid of death? Am

I a better person now? The narrative questions are endless. And many of them are answered throughout this book, but not in the usual sequence, not with the typical reassurances and not simply through story-telling. Instead they are explored alongside discussion of more analytical material about the cultural meanings of health and illness. Theoretical discussions about the changing significance of diseases such as cancer interrupt and indeed investigate the narrative flow of my particular story.

So why refuse the reader these conventional narrative pleasures, which I myself sought when I was at my most anxious and uncertain? After all, I desired a narrative by which to organise the newly imposed chaos and confusion. I read other people's accounts of their experience of cancer partly to break the isolation and to find out information, but most of all to find narratives which offered a future. I wanted to read stories of how other people had come through the experience; I wanted to be inspired by accounts of courage and bravery. In particular, I sought an intensity which might match my own heightened emotional state, a drama to fit the excitement and the terror of this extraordinary situation which had presented itself out of the blue. I read one cancer narrative after another, looking for clues of what might be in store for me, trying desperately to map out my own trajectory, savouring the moments of experiential overlap between myself and the author. I sought the relief of recognition, affirmation and reassurance in these accounts, as I am sure these authors had done before me.

Perhaps some readers of this book are similarly seeking the re-assurances of a story of my heroic triumph over cancer and of how I fought my way back to health. I could include all the ingredients of the classic 'triumph-over-tragedy' genre: starting at the beginning, there was the shock of it all – so young for cancer and so fit (or so we thought); moving through the numerous twists in the middle – the 'misdiagnosis', the suspense of the weekly tests, twelve weeks of improvement followed by a relapse, the horror of the treatment, the relief when it ended; and moving finally towards the available closures – the hair growing back, returning to work, coming to terms with my new physical limits, crossing the two-year threshold, having survived. I could write the story of a hero's successful struggle and you could read about it. It might satisfy my need for recognition, for external validation, or for the experience to become a distant narrative in the well-crafted and finished story of an illness; it might satisfy some readers' curiosity to know about it from a distance, to be glad it was not their fate, or, for those who have been there too (or who fear they may be next), it might offer the chance to compare notes or to prepare themselves.

But what remains untold in these heroic narratives? What does linearity exclude? What can not be restored with closure? Where is the

14

continued chaos and disorder in such accounts? Where is the forgotten pain? Stories of progress and rationality are tempting, but perpetuate the illusion of life as a steady upward learning curve in which all crises have a profound meaning and show that 'God is working his purpose out'. Such mythologies encourage us to believe that suffering makes us wiser and serve to heroise those who suffer the most. They leave no room for the futility of the pain and the arbitrariness of disease, the unbearable pointlessness of suffering. They cover up the absences, the amnesia and the gaps in the story. They iron out the competing accounts, the multiple meanings, the lack of meaning. They offer the promise of delivering the truth about the illness, the essence of self and the essence of the disease brought together in a tightly structured account. They offer fantasies of power and control through the narrative rationalisations of progress and improvement. The universality of human goodness and the transcendence of the suffering cancer patient fit easily into familiar narrative structures of good triumphing over evil.

Heroic cancer narratives also reproduce the conventional privileging of the triumphs of a few at the expense of the majority. The lucky ones (though they are never called that) are celebrated while the rest suffer defeat. The heroes of cancer are represented as special people, as unique individuals, as better than the rest. Isn't she brave? Isn't he wonderful? They were supposed to have died five years ago but have since climbed every mountain; they did not notice the treatment and kept working while others fell around them; they fought until the end but then died gracefully. And what of the others? What of those who declined rapidly, who cried with fear and terror in the face of death, who live haunted by the threat of cancer returning or for whom there is no hope? What of those who do not smile bravely? In the success/ failure binarisms of hero narratives these people can only be seen as the failures. Sadly, they did not rise to heroic status. They may not feel wiser now, but more confused, bitter, cheated. Theirs may not have been the story of discovering the generosity of the human spirit, of the bountiful goodness of friends and family. Perhaps they discovered new depths to loneliness and depression, or felt betrayed and abandoned by those they relied upon. What if everyone around them was not so wonderful? And what if there was not anyone around, wonderful or not? In the heroic cancer narratives written in so many books, these stories are left untold.[25]

I thus return again and again to the political questions raised by cultural narratives. The dangers of the success story hover above me as I write, and yet narration is impossible to avoid and brings irreplaceable comforts to many. Is narrative possible without these dubious forms of heroism? Might we rescue some aspects of story-telling from their more conservative tendencies? Or should we even consider the more positive dimensions of heroism itself: can it not also inspire and lead the way? After all, it offers structure and purpose to a sense of self shattered by fear and panic. If I found comfort in the processes of narration and if these gave my overwhelming fear a direction, why seek to deny others such solace? Is not the process of telling one's story and of being heard a significant and restorative effect of testimony?

Indeed, much writing about trauma more generally has confirmed the immeasurable significance of the process of 'witnessing' for the subject who feels haunted, even possessed, by the memories of traumatic events.[26] Accounts by survivors of the unthinkable traumas of war, of concentration camps and of nuclear attack have provided the basis for much discussion of the patterns of recovery from such traumatic events. But witnessing and testimony are by no means straightforward processes. For many, the traumatic events can never be fully known or remembered, either because of the numbing effect of the shock or because of the latency in the experience itself: the now commonplace Freudian idea of the delayed reaction.[27] The testimony of the traumatic event might thus involve a retelling not of its truth or essence, but of its enigma, and the witnessing might require the acknowledgement of the impossibility of recapturing that original moment.[28] The remembering at stake might be a route out of, not into, the experience. The survivor thus might move on from the trauma through a witnessing of the distance from the event, rather than a return to it.

These theories of trauma, event and memory are based on cases of survivors of public events of historical horror, such as Hiroshima and the Holocaust. Recovery from more private and everyday traumas, such as cancer and chemotherapy, may be of a different proportion and a different order, but some of the patterns may be familiar, if much less severe.[29] The feeling of isolation imposed by the trauma generates a desire for others to bear witness to the impact of the shock. The repetition of the narrative functions to rehearse that sense of disbelief, but also to return to the moment of impact before the temporal delay occurred. For many cancer patients, relating their stories is integral to their recovery. Thus, cancer narratives function not only to differentiate (the heroes from the failures), but also to confirm similarity between patients, even if that similarity is not in the recapturing of the events, but rather in the need to relate them as narratives. In this sense, narrative might be seen more positively as an important mechanism for recognition and, for many, for sanity.

Cancer (and other) support groups testify to the powers of affirmation and witnessing.[30] The feeling that 'someone has heard my story', and that it's legitimate to want to tell that story, calms the psyche. It can offer the necessary reassurance at a time of crisis or trauma, or the route out of it retrospectively. The feeling of not being alone that is offered by narrative identifications has increasingly become a central component of cancer-patient culture. Informal networks of people eager to share their stories and to hear those of others have sprung up all over the country. There are literally hundreds of such groups. While the person with cancer is ill, their peers are likely to be at school or at work and life goes on with its routine freneticism. Often, there is only one child in a class with leukaemia, only one lecturer with a teratoma (though for women in their fifties with breast cancer, for example, they may find many friends and colleagues in the same boat). In this context, then, relating one's story may offer support, comfort and reassurance. It may help people live through the trauma of the illness and the treatment and may help people who are recovering to begin to put the experience into the past tense.

In my own case, this sense of isolation seemed especially acute as the cancer I had was so rare. There had been only one other case in the last five years at the second largest cancer centre in England where I was being treated. I was constantly told how unusual I was. I was unlikely to meet anyone with the same disease. In addition, my response to the chemotherapy was so acute that I developed endless side-effects which seemed to make me an even more unusual case. A teratoma patient had rarely had quite so many side-effects or had those particular side-effects so badly, I was told. For a whole host of reasons, I stood out as different. Others on my ward were much older than I was. Support groups were typically for an older age group. I was not married with children. I was having a relationship with a woman. I was using a number of alternative treatments against cancer as well as the conventional ones. I did not wear a wig, the only one on the ward without one. So not only did I feel cut off from friends who, for all their generous support, continued in their busy schedules of work and play (as I would have done in their position), but I felt separate from the cancer cultures I found myself unwillingly inhabiting. In this context my story had a certain freakish ring to it; no one else seemed to have been here before.

IV

We had chosen the holiday as an end-of-chemotherapy treat. More expensive than we could really afford, but that was part of its appeal. We spent days choosing from hundreds of options: France, Italy, Greece; self-catering, hotel or taverna; the week after the final treatment or later than that? How could you plan a holiday when there were so many variables? The story of the treatment kept changing: five doses, then four; postponed because of side-effects; postponed because of bed shortages. When would I be finished and well enough to travel? No one knew. If the final treatment had not been cancelled, we'd have had to have changed the dates. If I'd readmitted myself when the vomiting wouldn't stop after the fourth treatment, they may have urged me to wait longer. In the midst of this uncertainty, we plumped for a date: we would go on 14 April, for two weeks. Such indulgence. Booked in February as an incentive to get me through it. It helped with visualisation: I was on a Greek island in the warmth of the sun, and with the sound of waves to comfort me. I memorised the description of 'Olive Tree Cottages' from the holiday brochure:

> As the road climbs towards the gorge, you can just catch a glimpse of the tiled roofs of the cottage below you, peeping out between green olive trees on the far side of the river bed and framed by the endless blue vistas of the Libyan Sea . . . Hidden away round the corner from the main cottage, this studio . . . has french windows from the sleeping area [which] lead out to a cloistered little patio facing west with a shady olive tree to one side. Beyond the patio with its fringe of flowers, shrubs and a knarled old carob tree, the land drops away to the dried-up river bed, where trees grow in profusion and birds sing joyfully in the sunshine.

This place was chosen because it was away from the main village. If I wanted to, I could hide away from the usual people-watching of holiday chic and enjoy the privacy of seclusion. And yet there was more people-watching than usual, of course. As I walked down the main street of Paleachora in Crete, people stared. They always stare, but on this holiday they stared a lot. Not surprising really. I had lost eyebrows, eyelashes and hair, and that does give a person an unusual look. I wore a scarf or a hat in public, but I did look different. Certainly no one else looked like me. That is, until two women walked towards me, one of whom wore a pale blue headscarf wound round in a recognisable turban style. She also had that rather uncannily naked look of someone with no eyebrows or eyelashes. She looked completely familiar and yet totally unfamiliar at the same time. Did I do a double-take, or do I just imagine I did? How obvious was the shock in my expression? In a typically English way, we passed each other without acknowledgement, our concern for each other's privacy overriding our desire to speak to each other. Despite the bodily visibility of our recent histories, we walked on politely.

A youngish woman (in her twenties?) who bore a strange resemblance to me had suddenly appeared as my mirror image in a street in a small Greek village. I could not wait to get back to the flat and tell all. I wished I had spoken to her but what would I have said? 'Excuse me, are you English and have you had chemotherapy? That's strange, so have I.' It seemed absurd, but also foolish not to. Passing by in silence left me with a yearning, a longing for the might-have-been of recognition, but it also protected me from disappointment: we may not have spoken the same language; she may have had alopecia; I may have disliked her. Having let this opportunity slip, I assumed we would not see each other again: she was probably on a day trip, or staying in a large hotel far away. Instead of these more likely scenarios, however, I saw the same two women again, this time not in the public thoroughfare of the village, but in the relative privacy of the entrance to Olive Tree Cottages. Obviously returning from a mountain hike they went in through the front door of the other self-catering studio flat. There were only three apartments in this terrace, and between us we occupied two of them. Next-door-but-one: this was too much to bear; I had to go and speak to them. My whole body buzzed with the excitement of coincidence.

Keen to reclaim my body again after months of sickness, I was driven by a desire to get fit like never before. Walking in the mountains had been my main aim in coming to southern Crete. It seemed as if it had also been hers. It provided a point of connection to our neighbours and a good excuse to go and talk to them. Could they recommend any walks, I wondered? There were plenty of choices. Were they strenuous walks, as I had to be careful – I was convalescing. So was she, but, no, they were fine. I was recovering from chemotherapy. So was she. Trying to hide my voracious appetite for her story, on the point of leaving but never quite making it, I asked more questions and she followed suit. What kind of cancer have you had? (I never know which tense to use. Nor do I.). Well, it's very rare. So is mine. It's called a teratoma. A teratoma? So was mine. You had it removed, and an ovary too? So did I. And chemotherapy? Bleomycin, etoposide and cisplatinum. Me too. I've got these strange scratch marks on my skin as a side-effect. So have I. I'm having AFP tests every week. So am I. My tests are clear so far. So are mine. I've been taking high dose vitamins. So have I. I've tried all the alternative medicines. So have I. I've been seeing a healer. So have I. They offered me a wig, but I refused. So did I. I've read all the cancer books. So have I. But I've never met anyone else. . . Nor have I.

I wanted to say, 'Tell me everything and tell me now. Here on the doorstep.' I could hardly bear the suspense. I was torn between a desire to stay forever and to compare all the details of our stories, and my sense that we had only just met, we did not know each other and this exchange might at any moment become an intrusion. After all, we might not like each other. Having had cancer is no guarantee of friendship. And it would be hard to draw back after such confidences had been shared. But caution lost out as the pleasures of recognition drew me in. The insurmountable relief of recognition. The physical relaxation of the emotional connection. The same cancer, the same surgery, the same treatment. Some of the same side-effects. Someone else had indeed been there before, or, rather, at exactly the same time. And now, we were both here. Of all possible places, at all possible times, we had both decided to recover in that particular village in that particular week in April. More than a coincidence. A magical meeting indeed. When I got back to my flat, I wept with relief. I awoke the next day with the childlike excitement of a 6-year-old on Christmas morning.

When I returned to England and recounted this incredible narrative-of-narratives, everyone had the same response. Stranger than fiction. If you put it in a novel or a film, no one would believe it were true. Too fictional to ever hope for, yet too coincidental to belong in good fiction. It was a million-to-one encounter that defied the odds. Not only the coincidence of our meeting, but the literal coincidence of the timing of the disease and the treatment, not to mention the holiday. Our narratives told almost identical stories and we stood side by side, poised on the threshold of recovery.

For me, this encounter is the story of my re-entry into the social world after weeks of claustrophobic internality in my physical body. There had been others around, significant others, and I had never completely lost touch with life as I had known it. But the isolation of the suffering and the impossibility of articulating its enormity had left me feeling like a stranger surrounded by familiarity. The presence of another (similar but not the same, like me but not me) enabled me to make a crucial transition out of the frozen shock of the treatment and into the world of narrative exchange. Her story made sense of mine. And my story gained substance as she listened. Unbeknown to each of us, there had been a travelling companion on this terrifying journey, and this offered retrospective comfort. The whole narrative could now be retold in the light of this knowledge. The similarities continued to mount as we found our common concerns extended beyond the illness to intellectual, political and cultural allegiances. I looked forward to sharing the narrative closure we both hoped for in our respective cancer stories. We would stay in touch and confirm each other's recovery as the AFP levels stayed obediently below normal.[31]

But then the pleasure of the discovery of our shared fate began to dissolve. Our paths suddenly diverged when her AFP levels went up again. We had rehearsed another story, but it escaped our control. Couldn't the power of our shared narrative pull her back towards recovery? I refused to believe that our joint physical embodiment of the survival narrative wouldn't make us immutable: surely we were now protected by the doubling effect of our encounter? But to my horror, she soon embodied another narrative. Our difference was cruelly underlined as her teratoma refused to be defeated. It came back again and again. More surgery and it still came back. More chemotherapy and it came back again. Surgery, intensive chemotherapy, radiotherapy. And on and on. Until finally, it had gone. Now four years later, I almost dare not say that we might both be in the clear. We still have tests. To suggest a closure at this point may tempt fate. And we don't have a shared narrative any longer. My nightmares faded into the past as hers accumulated new horrors from week to week and month to month. Now we stand on the terrain of recovery together but I don't imagine that we survived the journey together; I'd be kidding myself if I thought I knew what she'd been through now. The pain of separation after such blissful narrative convergence had been too much to bear. As I had gone back to work, she had gone back to hospital. As I passed my one-year threshold, she got weaker and sicker. As I had begun to gain some distance, she had become more deeply immersed. As I had had moments of forgetting, she had had constant reminders. How to keep hoping when the stories won't oblige? What should we tell ourselves for comfort? Did she wish she were me? Did I wish she were me? Both recovering together it had been meant to be. But if one goes down, what should the other do? The dangers of narrative trajectories which promise closures of certainty. What disappointments and pain they may bring instead.

V

There are stories about cancer in this book, then, but they are told with caution. They are told but often untold in the analysis that follows them. The stories in this book carry a health warning: beware the certainties they promise; beware the subjects they construct; beware the truths they guarantee; and beware the closures that seem inevitable. There are variables beyond our prediction and influences beyond our control that disrupt the easy linearity of the classic triumph-over-tragedy cancer narrative. They may take us by surprise even at the moments when we feel most sure of their closures. They may change the course of the story even as the end appears to be in sight. I may have wished to write a triumph-over-tragedy story at certain moments, and some readers may want to read one (perhaps despite themselves). But I see such projects not only as disappointing to (and even condemning of) the person who does not make it, but also as potentially very worrying in terms of the cultural ideals they promise: those fantasies of omnipotence, of masculine invincibility, of individual effect.

This is not to say that we should not tell and write the stories of our illnesses. For most people who suffer with cancer and other life-threatening diseases, their stories have a much smaller circulation, if they are even heard at all. So few have the opportunity to have their accounts turned into print. Instead, their stories circulate informally, among friends, family and support groups. There are many forms of public recognition, but publication bestows status in a very different way: it can be a form of empowerment. Academics like myself, along with other kinds of writers, have the unusual privilege to tell our stories if we wish, and to expect others to read them and even respond to them. But we should not be seduced by the power of authorship into thinking that we *alone* can determine the script of our lives. Part of the project of this book is to open up critical debate on precisely the fantasies around cancer which give rise to such aspirations. What is the particular appeal of these cancer narratives in contemporary culture? How do the different medical knowledges and practices which people with cancer may come across offer the patient particular ways of constructing stories about themselves and their illnesses?

21

My use of personal narratives is thus interspersed in what follows with a study of the cultures of health that I encountered during the course of my illness. These include both the cultures of biomedicine and those of alternative therapies; indeed, I aim to challenge aspects of each, while also identifying some of the emergent overlaps between them. With a few notable exceptions, both sides claim legitimacy for their truths, both sides promise progress and a better future, and both sides are fiercely reluctant to reflect upon the kinds of knowledge they produce and their significance for people with illnesses. While I am certainly not interested in proposing a wholesale dismissal of either biomedicine or its alternative counterparts, I have found that both can be frustratingly resistant to self-scrutiny and patronising to those wishing to question their assumptions and theories. Alternative medicines may be less traditionally professionalised, but they too have their institutions, doctrines and concepts that are jealously and, sometimes, rather stubbornly guarded.[32] Thus, while I would caution against sweeping critical judgements of these health cultures, I do nevertheless argue that there is an urgent need for more rigorous analysis of many of their taken-for-granted categories. My aim is broadly to suggest the need for greater analytical self-reflection on both sides of the bio/ alternative medical divide and for the location of such an analysis within an understanding of cultural changes more generally.

My account of each of these health cultures is, of course, heavily dependent on my very specific experience of them through face-to-face encounters as well as through books and other printed material. The knowledge contained in this book is partial, contextual and thus very much a product of a specific set of circumstances. It is possible, for example, that if I had had a misogynist consultant, I may have written more fiercely about the patriarchal character of the medical profession (though that critique is there, in Chapters 4 and 6). It may also be true that if the chemotherapy had not worked, or if I had had to have any more of it, I might have written more critically about the limits of medical knowledge. It may also be the case that had I gone to different alternative therapists I might have had less to say about some of the more conservative elements of the 'self-health' cultures of alternative medicine. Or perhaps, had I not lived through fifteen years of Thatcherite and post-Thatcherite 'hyper-individualism', in which the rhetoric of individual achievement seduces while denying such basic rights and freedoms to so many, my concern about self-health cultures might have been less urgent.

Like many academics in the postmodern 1990s, I do not claim universal representativeness (though obviously I believe I have presented issues that are of general concern). Indeed, the biomedical account suggests that mine was a highly unusual case. In particular, I believe my experience of chemotherapy was especially severe; some patients around me in hospital sat up in bed eating, drinking and enjoying visits from friends and relatives during their treatments. For those readers who may be facing chemotherapy, I would caution against automatic fear and panic in response to my account, for the only certainty is the *unpredictability* of the effects of these treatments. Similarly, my stories of alternative and self-health therapies do not necessarily predict other such encounters: alternative medicines and their practitioners vary enormously. Indeed, my own experience of such practices has been highly diverse; as well as those of which I have been more critical in the book, I have had considerable support and highly effective treatment from many alternative approaches – for example, acupuncture proved to be the only really helpful treatment against the nausea and vomiting during chemotherapy.

While much academic knowledge is heavily autobiographical (even if only implicitly or motivationally so), this particular book is clearly more directly so than most. My interest in writing it stemmed primarily from my experience of having cancer and my overwhelming feeling that what was happening to me was not only horrible and terrifying, but also intellectually intriguing. I found the constructions of cancer (and of teratomas in particular) fascinating from the point of view of my academic 'training' in cultural studies, women's studies and sociology. My virtual submergence within these competing health cultures provided so much 'data' that I could have written several books. As well as the genuine intellectual interest, I have also needed to reflect upon my own psychic desire to write about the subject: perhaps this has helped me to externalise the experience, place it as firmly in the past as possible, and even (despite my own cautions) to enjoy a fantasy of regained control. Or perhaps it has enabled me to 'forget' in some senses. For remembrance itself can also be a form of forgetting. These interpretations point towards the idea of writing as restoration and, indeed, there are those who have celebrated the idea that writing can somehow heal the wounds of life.[33] But this belief in the 'restorative powers of writing' has also been attacked for being part of a more general 'culture of redemption' that characterises the twentieth-century reliance on art to cure the ills of history.[34]

Religious metaphors abound in characterisations of the function of writing: writing as redemption, as confession, as transcendence and as sacrament.[35] All suggest the significance of the symbolic place of writing in this culture's sense of itself. Each indicates something rather different about the complicated relationship between 'lived experience' and the process of writing – a relationship that has been much theorised by those concerned with the politics of representation.[36] Without rehearsing these debates here, I want to make it clear that I do not believe that my writing can straightforwardly capture the traumatic experience of having cancer for myself or for the reader. Neither do I assume that I myself have direct access to my past experience: the accounts that we produce are structured by the formations of memory and the conventions of narrative, as I have tried to indicate. Much of the experience has been produced and reproduced through oral (and now written) story-telling. However, since my motivation to write this book *did* emerge out of my experience of illness, and the connections, tenuous as they may be, between the experience and the writing continue to inform its production, I want to stress that I *am* interested in combining different modes or 'registers' of writing: personal, political and theoretical.[37] In particular, I want to use my experience as a series of textual 'rhetorics of the self' that connect competing forms of knowledge, and indeed allow me to interrogate the very formations of these different knowledges.[38]

Thus, while this book does not promise to disclose the 'truth of my experience' of cancer (nor indeed the essence of its author's self), neither does it seek an objectivity predicated on the banishment of the self as a guarantee of the author's anonymity or neutrality. So, while I am well aware of the problematic and fragile connections between physical, emotional and intellectual experiences and the processes of writing (not to mention reading), I am nevertheless concerned to overcome some of the usual boundaries between academic and other forms of writing which have conventionally separated the personal from the intellectual. It is difficult to label these modes of personal writing: do they draw on autobiography, memoir, confession or testimony?[39] Each of these produces a slightly different version of the 'self': put crudely, we might say they promise respectively to reveal the self, to situate the self, to absolve the self or to qualify the self.[40] My use of the notion of 'rhetorics of the self' seeks to introduce the idea that the stories presented here are highly motivated and strategic as well as textual. Part of my motivation for telling the stories contained in this book has doubtless been to take revenge on the illness. In the retrospective recounting, the power relations appear to be reversed. Perhaps the writing is a way of bringing the self back to life, or reinstating oneself after an absence from the social world of work. It is connected not only to life but also to death; perhaps I feel safer with a text between the two. Perhaps I fantasise that the text might be more permanent than the body and it is reassuring to think of it outlasting its author (immortality after all?). Or perhaps it's an insurance against the return of the disease: at least a textual trace of me will be left behind if I do end up dying of cancer. To publish this book may thus both acknowledge and deny my mortality.[41]

With all the above provisos, the issues raised in this book concern more than my very specific story of having cancer. Through the retelling and the analysis, I connect aspects of my particular encounters to broader cultural issues. Indeed, the structure moves towards increasing generality. It has its own narrative trajectory moving from the personal to the political, from the individual account to the social and cultural implications. In moving between my stories of having cancer and an academic commentary on the meaning of health and illness in contemporary Western societies, this book can be located within highly interdisciplinary territory. Drawing on work from history, sociology, film and cultural studies, and feminist theory, I offer a commentary on the meanings attributed to cancer in today's changing health cultures, each chapter focusing on one specific dimension of the cancer cultures that I encountered during my illness.

What does your cancer symbolise to you? Time and time again I was faced with questions such as this. I was urged to find a range of metaphorical meanings embedded in, and embodied by, my cancer. Was it a corporeal sign of my stressful lifestyle? Did it symbolise the genetic malfunctions of a post-nuclear age? Were my repressed desires finally expressing themselves? This has led me, in Chapter 2, to question the use of metaphors to explain cancer as a disease, and to consider the danger (as well as the appeal) of seeing illnesses as metaphors more generally. How has cancer been understood as a sign of degeneration, corruption and decay and how have these interpretations been attributed to the cancer patient as indicative of their inner weakness and self-destructiveness?

Whatever you do, don't say cancer. What is so unspeakable about cancer? Why does it have the power to evoke such horror in people, compared with other illnesses such as heart disease? The answers to these questions are closely connected to the ways in which cultural taboos have constructed cancer as a stigmatised illness, and these are the subject of Chapter 3. In particular, how is the monstrousness of cancer to be understood in relation to cultural fears about the body and its desires? Drawing on my own accounts of cancer as a taboo illness, I look at the connections between different medical and sexual 'abject states' that produce a sense of dread and revulsion. In that chapter I explore the parallels between taboos surrounding sexuality and those surrounding cancer, and ask why the C word and the L word produce such high anxiety in so many people.

Healthy mind, healthy body. This cliché dogged my encounters with a range of different medical and therapeutic practices during my illness. A positive attitude makes recovery more likely; mind over matter will conquer the disease; listen to your cancer, it may have something to tell you. Chapter 4 looks at how cancer is conceptualised in a culture in which mind and body are increasingly believed to be mutually dependent. The controversial issue of the mind–body relationship lies at the heart of changing ideas about health and illness. While there are well-rehearsed criticisms of the biomedical 'mechanical' view of the body, I found myself also questioning some of the more recent models of the mind–body relationship employed within self-health cancer books. Looking at the genesis of some of these theories of cancer, I highlight the ways in which these changing understandings of the body as a text of the psyche are not restricted to such accounts, or indeed to alternative medical thinking, but are in fact increasingly permeating biomedical discourses.

Close your eyes and imagine yourself healthy. In following this practice, I attempted to visualise my way back to good health. Like thousands of others with cancer I imagined the destruction of the disease and the recovery of a healthy immune system. This belief in the power of vision in the healing process is characteristic not only of alternative approaches to cancer treatment, but also of biomedical methods. Chapter 5 investigates the cultural imperative to delve deeper into the recesses of the body through innovations in medical imaging techniques: X-ray, ultrasound, CT scans, MRIs. Through these new techniques the much-discussed masculine 'medical gaze', with its desire to see, to know and to conquer, has vastly extended its scope. How might forms of visualising cancer be understood within these histories of ways of seeing the body and its interiors?

Become an expert on yourself. In participating in my own recovery from cancer I found myself required to learn about nutrition, relaxation, drug treatments, emotional expression, dream analysis, cell behaviour and my immune system. As a cancer patient, a constant monitoring of physical and emotional reactions is expected: is the IV drip running evenly? Does the urine measurement indicate good kidney function? Have I processed the shock of the diagnosis? Are the chest pains dangerous? Why have my hands and feet gone numb? Did I have an unhappy childhood? Have I faced up to my own mortality? Chapter 6 considers what imperatives of self-knowledge circulate around the person with cancer in this age of information cultures. In this context I look at how cancer is often represented as a disease in which the cells of the body are microcosms of the self which betray their host for no good reason. Instead of protecting us from harm, the body's cells become the source of a life-threatening disease that will destroy the system which generates and supports them. This chapter is concerned with the impact of systems theory on both conventional and alternative medical practices. How is the self conceptualised as a system within these accounts of cancer and what new imperatives of the care of the self do these models evoke?

We are all 100 per cent responsible for everything that happens to us. Like so many other cancer patients in the 1990s, I participated fully in decisions about my care and treatments, sometimes willingly, sometimes unwillingly, often with great ambivalence. I wanted to be kept informed by medical professionals, but many decisions that fell to me, or to those caring for me, were alarmingly daunting: should I return to hospital for surgery having been told the problem was not urgent? Should I take a final fifth dose of chemotherapy? On a continuum with these worrying responsibilities offered to cancer patients by biomedicine were the claims within alternative approaches to cancer treatment that we can all heal ourselves. Again, I felt ambivalent about the chance to participate in my own recovery, a task that brings with it such intense satisfactions and disappointments, depending on the outcome. These experiences led me to pose the central question addressed in Chapter 7: whose responsibility is health? Are people increasingly suspicious of conventional medicine and science and have they begun to reject its previously reassuring promises of progress and liberation? And if so, should the rapid growth in the popularity of alternative medicines and therapies be seen as a radical departure from the monolithic paternalism of Western science and medicine, or as the sign of an unwelcome fantasy of omnipotent individualism in the wake of a declining Welfare State? These questions are looked at in the context of shifts in the so-called foundational beliefs of modernity, and are discussed in terms of the privatisation of health and the New Right emphasis on individual responsibility in contemporary Britain.

'Am I going to die, doctor?' 'We all have to die sometime.' When I overheard this exchange between doctor and patient on my chemotherapy ward I was struck by the incongruity between the personal terror of death on the one hand, and the professional reduction of mortality to an inevitable mundanity on the other. The doctor's refusal to engage with the patient on anything other than routine terms seemed to me typical of the ways in which biomedicine responds to death so inadequately and yet, surely, so frequently. Within a system that seeks to control life, death can only be recorded as a failure, and as such must be minimised in terms of its significance. Some seek a contrast to such biomedical 'inhumanity' in alternative health practices. And many have found solace in approaches where patients are expected to have powerful emotional responses to death. But even here, I found much evidence

of a flight from mortality in the models of self-healing that promised the individual total control of their medical destiny. If the mind can control the body, then we may indulge in fantasies of invincibility and immortality. Chapter 8 discusses just such issues. In it, I consider the feminist criticisms of the fear of death that permeate the models of self, knowledge and power within biomedical and alternative approaches to cancer. I then finish with some final reflections upon my own relationship to death through a consideration of my motivations for writing this book: is writing one way of dealing with, deferring or, indeed, of denying mortality?

These questions go far beyond the concerns with narrative discussed in this chapter; they transport this book into the arena of the cultural study of health and illness more generally. And yet many of them return us on occasion to the problems of narrative raised here: problems of truth and of certainty; problems of the meanings of identity; problems of how cultures define diseases. This book explores some of the ways in which a person with cancer is subject to, if not bombarded with, powerful and contradictory discourses about the nature of their illness. Confusion and panic are likely responses to such a proliferation and range of theories of cancer and how to treat it. As well as coping with the trauma and discomfort/pain of the illness, the person with cancer confronts a host of beliefs and practices which compete to define the meaning of the illness: its prevalent metaphorical manifestations; the connections between body and psyche; constructions of the healthy and the diseased self; and questions of duty and responsibility. They all offer the promise of different solutions. Some threaten recurrence if theirs is not chosen. Part of the experience of cancer in today's culture is suddenly confronting this excess of opinion about the meaning of the disease and the logic of the cure.

The path through the maze of information, mythology and fantasy varies according to a multitude of factors. Mine was that of an academic: highly sceptical, obsessively self-reflective and with a sense of entitlement that feminism had added to what my class and ethnicity (middle class and White) had promised. My experience of the illness was continually inflected by the interplay of intellectual, emotional and political identifications and allegiances. At times I felt completely dependent upon medical science to save my life, while noticing (and cringing at) the heroic status I was tempted to bestow upon it. At other times I was fully engaged in alternative therapies, diets, spiritual healing, meditation and acupuncture, accompanied by a critical analysis of their appeal. As I swallowed my vitamins every three hours, I reflected upon the profits of these renewed self-health industries (and resented my own burgeoning overdraft). As I meditated twice a day, visualising myself cured (or even 'healed'), I wondered about the emergent pervasiveness and persuasiveness of the 'healthy mind, healthy body' philosophy which surrounded me. This book offers a critical account of the story of an illness.

2

METAPHORS

A cancer diagnosis brings a person into a highly contested arena: competing definitions and explanations of the disease and how to treat it circulate widely in professional and popular contexts. Different expert knowledges wrestle for the power to determine exactly what cancer is. In some ways, of course, it is a meaningless term, including so many different diseases and treatments that any generalisations are rendered redundant (Rose, 1995). Biomedical information about cancer tends to be divided according to the origin of the malignancy, and patients who wish to know more about their cancer need to consult quite specialised textbooks in order to obtain a really detailed account of what is likely to happen to them. Shortly after my diagnosis, I found myself engaging with two opposing accounts of my disease: on the one hand, I read medical textbooks about teratomas, and endodermal sinus tumours in particular; on the other, I began what proved to be the first of many encounters with alternative medical approaches to cancer which offered very different readings of my condition.

ENDODERMAL SINUS TUMOUR

Definition

The endodermal sinus tumour is a rare, and highly malignant, tumour of the germ cell (egg cell or sperm cell). Germ cell tumours comprise about 20 per cent of all ovarian neoplasms in North America and Europe. Incidence of malignancy among ovarian tumours is 5 per cent (in contrast to 99 per cent among testicular tumours with which they are otherwise homologous) (Talerman, 1985). Associated with other germ cell tumours (teratomas), the endodermal sinus tumour is a very distinct histopathological entity. It 'grows rapidly, invades locally, and metastasises [spreads] early via the lymphatics to the regional lymph nodes and also by the hematogenous route to the lungs, liver and other organs' (Talerman, 1985: 80). It is also known as a yolk sac tumour (since it is composed of functioning yolk sac tissue), immature mesonephroma, embryonal carcinoma, extra-embryonal teratoma, mesoblastoma vitellinum and Teilum tumour (named after Teilum who published a series of articles on these tumours in 1959, 1965, 1978 and who ultimately named it 'endodermal sinus tumour'). Derived from 'endo' (in composition, 'inside' as opposed to ecto, 'outside'), the endoderm is described as 'a close-set sheath, one cell thick, enclosing the central cylinder in plants'; the sinus can be understood as an 'indentation, a notch, a cavity, a bend or a fold' (*Chambers Dictionary*, 1973). There is a resemblance to the endodermal sinuses of Duval in the yolk sac of the rat placenta. The close relationship to the yolk sac is further underlined through the production of elevated serum levels of alpha fetoprotein (henceforth AFP) during tumour growth. AFP is produced by foetal liver cells and by some hepatomata. Testing for the presence of AFP is used for diagnosis and after surgery to monitor recurrence. These proteins are also present in the blood during pregnancy.

Incidence

In two studies in the United States, patients ranged from 14 months to 45 years and from 7 to 37 years; in both cases the median age was 19 years.[1] Another study suggests it occurs most frequently in the second and third decades of a patient's life and is extremely rare after menopause (Talerman, 1985). No accurate estimate exists of the occurrence of this tumour. Between 1953 and 1975 in the Manchester area in Britain, forty-six ovarian tumours were seen in children under 16 and four of these were endodermal sinus tumours. The majority of these tumours have been found in White girls, but these tumours have also been recorded in Asian, Black, and South American girls and young women (Fox and Langley, 1976:197).

Clinical profile

Symptoms include abdominal enlargement or pain, vaginal bleeding and fever. These occur over a period of between two days and six months. The preoperative diagnoses of these tumours have been appendicitis and ectopic pregnancy.

Operative findings

The tumour usually occurs unilaterally, but neither left nor right side are more typical sites for growth. Tumour rupture has been found in between 27 per cent and 37 per cent of cases, most often intraoperatively

31

rather than preoperatively. Rupture of the tumour presents problems for the containment of the malignant cells. In over half the cases in each study cited above, the tumour was discovered at Stage 1 (early in the disease process).

Pathology

The tumour is round or oval and varies in size in its greatest diameter from 7 to 28 cms, and from 9 to 40 cms, giving a médian of 15 and 17 cms respectively in each of the two studies referred to above. The tumours are usually 'smooth, encapsulated and lobulated, with a glistening surface' and 'the cut surface is usually tan to gray-yellow with a variegated appearance, with cystic and solid areas and extensive areas of hemorrhage and necrosis [dead cells]' (Gershenson and Rutledge, 1987:226). The surface of the tumour has been described as 'slimy or mucoid' (Talerman, 1985).

Some of the most common varieties of histologic patterns in these tumours are described as:

> the reticular [netted] pattern, characterised by a meshwork of empty vacuoles lined by flattened cells . . . The festoon [garland suspended between two points] or endodermal sinus pattern consists of undulating epithelial cells often associated with Schiller-Duval bodies. The polyvesicular vitelline pattern is rare; it is composed of numerous cysts or vesicles surrounded by dense fibroblastic stroma. The solid pattern is composed of undifferentiated embryonal cells.
>
> (Gershenson and Rutledge, 1987:226–7)

In addition, hyaline (glassy, transparent) bodies are commonly found in the tumour. Multiple patterns exist in most tumours with one or two predominating in each.

Another description concurs with some of the basic components:

> large encapsulated tumours . . . having a rubbery, semifluctuant consistency. The outer surface is smooth, sometimes nodular, and grey or pinkish grey. The cut surface is usually variegated and areas of necrosis and haemorrhage are often present together with gelatinous cysts. Sometimes adhesions to adjacent structures may occur.
>
> (Fox and Langley, 1976:197)

Its microscopic appearence is characterised by a 'vacuolated network containing microcysts lined by flattened cells' and between these networks:

mingling with them, are groups and sheets of stellate cells of definite character . . . In about three-quarters of our tumours labyrinthine formations are present, consisting of elongated, inter-communicating channels lined in part by cuboidal or hob-nail cells, but elsewhere by flattened cells . . . Perivascular formations . . . project into a sinusoidal space communicating with the labyrinthine formations.

(Fox and Langley, 1976:197–8)

Studies have also identified what they call the 'ultrastructure' of an ovarian endodermal sinus tumour. Key characteristics include the composition of the connections between the stellate cells, the presence of lysosomes with granular material and deposits of electron-dense substance, the irregular nucleoli, and the form of the lining of the capillary in the centre of the endodermal sinus. In addition, the 'basement membrane of the capillaries was incomplete' and 'epithelium investing the capillary was separated from the vessel by an irregular space containing amorphous electron-dense material' (Fox and Langley, 1976:199–200). This ultrastructure of the endodermal sinus tumour is also observed to resemble that of the rat yolk sac.

Treatment and survival

Surgical removal of a tumour is usually followed by combination chemotherapy. During surgery, biopsies are taken of surrounding high-risk tissue (ovary, bowel and so on). Treatment varies according to staging. With surgery alone, only a small percentage of patients survive; for example, of fifty-one patients with an endodermal sinus tumour treated by surgery alone, seven (14 per cent) were alive two years later (Gallion et al., 1979, quoted in Gershenson and Rutledge, 1987). In another study of fifty-five cases, the longest survival was only 19 months (Fox and Langley, 1976).

Since the mid-1960s, combination chemotherapy has been used in the treatment of endodermal sinus tumours. These treatments were refined and improved during the 1970s and 1980s and now have high success rates. From being one of the most rapidly spreading malignancies, with which patients typically survived for about 18 months, this tumour has now become one of the most successfully treatable (80–95 per cent success rate). Typical regimes include vinblastine, bleomycin and cisplatin (VBP) which are administered in 3–4 week cycles (Gershenson and Rutledge, 1987). The use of bleomycin, etoposide and cisplatin (BEP) has now become a common treatment of this tumour. Two cycles are usually administered after the AFP levels have dropped below normal.

Epidemiology

There are no detailed studies of the epidemiology of this particular tumour as it accounts for less than 1 per cent of all ovarian tumours (Talerman, 1985). However, accounts of ovarian cancer more generally do exist (Beral, 1987). Ovarian cancer is the most common malignancy of the female genital tract in most Western countries. There are about 4,500 women who develop ovarian cancer in England and Wales, which results in 3,700 deaths annually. In 1983, of the 4,500 new cases of ovarian cancer, only 25 per cent survived after five years. The death rate has doubled in England and Wales over the last seventy years (Beral, 1987). These statistics are misleading in the cases of germ cell tumours, which, although they are often classified as ovarian tumours, have a much better survival rate, as detailed above.

Ovarian cancer is a malignancy of Western countries, having low incidence rates in Asia, Africa and Latin America (Sharp and Soutter, 1987). The risk of ovarian cancer is increased in nulliparous (childless) and infertile women; indeed, the more children a woman has, the lower her risk of ovarian cancer. There is also an apparent reduction in risk associated with female sterilisation and hysterectomy.

The above account of the endodermal sinus tumour offers a summary of the typical medical literature on the subject. The focus is on the physical body: organs, tissue and cells. The symptoms given in the clinical profile are those of perceivable abnormality such as swelling and reported pain. The organs affected are isolated (ovary, liver, lungs) and the 'progress' of the disease through the lymph system is detailed. The pathology offers a vivid account of the appearance (as opposed to the smell or the feel, for example) of the tumour at both macroscopic and microscopic levels of visibility. The colour, shape and differing compositional elements of the mass are outlined; it has a 'glistening surface'. The cell patterning and its variations are given in their precise specificity; diagnosis of the correct type of germ cell tumour is made through *visual identification* of these distinct cell formations (see Figures 2.1 to 2.4). Treatment is outlined in quantitative measures (grammes of chemicals for units of time) and survival rates are given as percentages whose improvements have been measured over time.

The biomedical discourses thus present the disease as a statistical, quantifiable and observable phenomenon. Above all, correct diagnosis, and thereby treatment, is made through an identification of the tumour type which relies almost exclusively on *visual* criteria. In the case of the endodermal sinus tumour, the detection of AFPs in the blood is a clear indicator of its presence in the body (even at the microscopic level of cell division); however, the medical literature primarily focuses on the

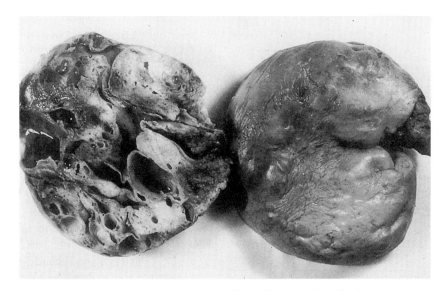

Figure 2.1 Ovarian tumour from the Schiller collection described as a mesonephroma. The tumour shows typical appearance of yolk sac tumour and this
has been confirmed histologically
Source: Jacobsen and Talerman, 1989:92

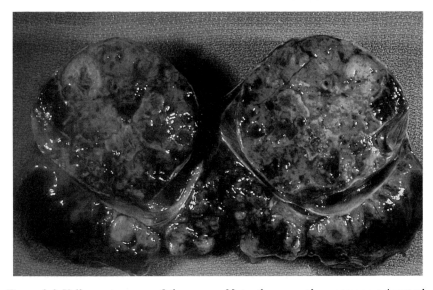

Figure 2.2 Yolk sac tumour of the ovary. Note the smooth contour, variegated
appearance and presence of tumour deposits outside the ovary
Source: Jacobsen and Talerman, 1989:92

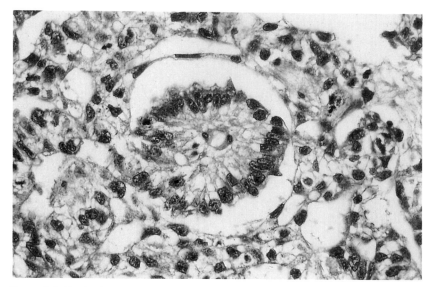

Figure 2.3 Typical perivascular formation, endodermal sinus or Schiller-Duval body, present within yolk sac tumour. The perivascular formation contains a blood vessel in the centre and projects into a space lined by flattened cells
Source: Jacobsen and Talerman, 1989:105

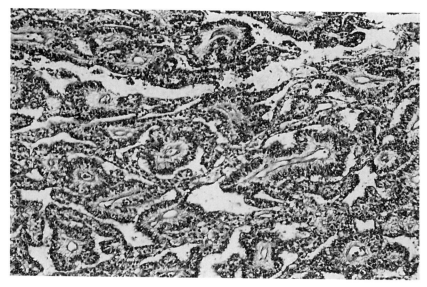

Figure 2.4 Yolk sac tumour showing endodermal sinus pattern. It is composed of numerous perivascular formations cut both transversely and longitudinally
Source: Jacobsen and Talerman, 1989:105

observable specificities of the cell formations in the tumour once it has been removed from the body and dissected under a microscope.

These biomedical discourses of visuality and physicality could not be more different, in some respects, from those of certain kinds of alternative medicine operating outside conventional hospital culture. To explore these differences, I offer the following account of a treatment I had with a Reiki practitioner shortly after leaving hospital. Having had surgery to remove the tumour, I was given the opportunity to wait a few weeks to see if the AFP levels would drop without chemotherapy. These levels were at 16,000 (they remain in the blood after the tumour is removed) and needed to drop to under ten to be safe. They would halve each week if the disease was no longer present. But if cell division began again they would double on a weekly basis. A reprieve, therefore, and a challenge. Could my body get rid of any remaining malignant cells without further medical intervention? My urgent (and, looking back, rather indiscriminate) embarkation upon numerous forms of self-health almost immediately upon being discharged from hospital took place in the context of a 'countdown narrative'. Avoiding chemotherapy, with its damaging side-effects and increased risk of other cancers (such as leukaemia) in later life was the main aim.

THE REIKI STORY

A few days out of hospital, in September 1991, still raw from surgery and diagnosis, I made an appointment to see a woman who did Reiki healing. I went with little idea of what Reiki was or how it worked; I had simply heard that she was good, and was up from London for a couple of days that week. I knew there was a chance that there were still cancer cells multiplying in my body as a result of the spillage from the tumour during surgery, and my oncologist had decided to wait and see if chemotherapy would be necessary by monitoring the development of these cells weekly. Thus, each day felt significant in my attempt to do everything possible to avoid chemotherapy. At this stage, whatever might help my body get rid of any remaining cancer cells (if there were any) seemed a definite bonus: after all, it couldn't do any harm, I thought.

The Reiki practitioner welcomed me calmly and took some initial details (the work I did, where I lived, what surgery I had had). I then lay on a treatment couch and revealed the wound from the surgery. I was asked to close my eyes. As the practitioner hovered over my body, she began her commentary.

Imagine yourself in the space where the ovary used to be. Go down into that space and experience it. How does it feel?

You have lost an ovary, which was the sign of your femininity, what does that feel like?

37

What does it mean to you that you have had cancer of the ovary?

Try not to be be so analytical. You're an academic, this means the rational, masculine side of yourself has been developed at the expense of the more emotional, feminine side. When I ask you questions, try to give your gut response; don't think, just speak. Do you find it hard to express your emotions? Do you think you lack femininity in your life?

Are you loved and nurtured?

Oh, your partner is female.

Do you feel a lack of the masculine in your life?

Have you heard of Louise Hay? She believes that illnesses are a result of emotional distress.

What would you say if I suggested to you that her writing makes you angry because it touches something deep inside you? Perhaps you know she is right, but don't want to admit it?

The 'communication' ceased for a while and, peeping from under my eyelids, I could see her doing what I immediately thought of as a passable imitation of a police officer directing traffic, one hand raised, palm outward, in front of her, while the other waved in the oncoming energies from her right. This was Reiki (or a Westernised version of it): the redirection of the energy field surrounding my body, a Japanese healing art that was already, through the ministries of this practitioner, proving far from restorative. I had come with an 'open mind', I reminded myself. Maybe this would help, but I was rapidly getting to the stage where I doubted it.

Finally, she told me I needed to relax more. (Who doesn't?) But I agreed to try. Had I learnt to meditate, she asked me. Transcendental meditation was no good, much too cerebral, she advised. I should try 'gibberish meditation'. She demonstrated. Holding her hands out in front of her and flexing her fingers, closing her eyes, contorting her face, she made noises like someone talking gibberish . . . bleh rah blah, mnur blee blur. Amazed, I watched this practice for a minute. This gets deeper into your unconscious, she told me. Using language interrupts that possibility.

If you come and see me twice a week I'm sure I can help you avoid chemotherapy. I fully support your reluctance to have it and to pursue alternatives.

I couldn't get out of the door fast enough. I was furious. There I was, fresh from the alienating experience of conventional medicine, expecting something better from its alternative counterparts. I would have welcomed someone treating me as a person and not a set of symptoms, which is what we usually expect from alternative medicine. But I found this experience equally patronising and insulting. Was I missing the feminine or the masculine in my life? I suppose there's a fifty-fifty chance, but to try both seemed an over-blatant clutching at straws.

As I walked home I rehearsed the arguments in my mind (no doubt contributing further to my imbalance). I wondered if other forms of alternative treatment were going to be so normative. Not only had this Reiki healer introduced new orthodoxies, but she had also reinforced certain very traditional ideas about essences, about woman and nature, and about sexuality and reproduction. Being in a relationship with a woman might cause imbalance in my life – a lack of masculinity – which might in turn have produced a lop-sided growth on one of my ovaries; this was even more insulting than the repeated biomedical inisistence that I might be pregnant despite my certainty to the contrary. Perhaps my academic job meant that I had an over-abundance of masculinity, which, in turn, might have caused my ovary to cry out for help, for recognition, to take revenge on me for my professional ambition and my rejection of my (and its) nurturing, life-giving function. Surely these two imbalances might cancel each other out within this logic? Might academic lesbians be confident of achieving the perfect balance? Apparently not. A double risk was involved, it seemed.

This retrospective narrativisation was written some time after the event. Like other stories in this book it has been told many times orally, and has thus crystallised into a certain form through time. Particular moments, phrases and feelings have been selected and have come to represent this past experience. A series of metonymic processes have shaped its gradual solidification into this particular narrative: the event itself stands in for a whole series of similar experiences, of which this is the most acute; certain aspects of this encounter are foregrounded because they epitomise my wider concerns about the politics of self-health. It is a narrative which enables me, retrospectively, to enjoy the privileges of authorial power, to assert the rational voice of authority and thus to reverse the power dynamics of the encounter which I remember as humiliating and infuriating. The 'victim' becomes the narrator and the retelling becomes a form of revenge.

But perhaps it is too easy to mock such alternative belief systems about health; after all, how wedded am I to the rational biomedical discourse from which position the alternatives seem so laughable? Other forms of alternative healing which could be presented in such terms escape such ridicule here; for example, acupuncture has a whole language of elemental metaphors (earth, water, fire; or heat and damp) which refer to the body and its imbalances and which could strike an unfamiliar patient as rather ludicrous, and yet I accept such terminology these days without so much as a smile. My choice of Reiki as the subject of this story is not based on a desire to attack this form of healing in particular, but rather is used here to exemplify the problems with certain practices, especially the abuse of power between patient and practitioner that can occur even in the alternative domain. One of the most important challenges of alternative medical approaches to cancer has supposedly been their more 'democratic' exchanges between expert (doctor/practitioner) and patient. However, there was certainly no sense of 'partnership' in this incident, and this is not an isolated exception.[2]

This story also functions here to present a very different account of my illness from the biomedical discourses. What might be deduced from this account is that the physical symptoms of an illness (in my case a tumour on the ovary, stemming from the germ cell) are not to be taken at face value: they are signs to be decoded. The tumour is read as a indication of imbalance and neglect in my life. The desirable state is one of harmony, wholeness, and equilibrium of left and right, masculine and feminine, intellect and emotion; the correction of a disturbance in my natural balance. The treatment therefore focuses on the emotional, rather than the physical, dimensions of the illness: what feelings did that part of my body contain? What did my ovaries symbolise? And what was my body trying to tell me about my life more generally by producing this disease? The conclusions drawn *for me* by the healer in this context were that the balance between right and left had been disrupted; that my work as an academic had meant that I was out of touch with my emotions; and that my lesbian relationship and lifestyle meant that I had denied myself the 'natural' harmony between masculine and feminine guaranteed by heterosexuality. Unlike other differences, gender is consitituted here as complementary. It is un-imaginable that the absence of 'race' or class differences in one's relationships might be suggested to have produced a disequilibrium and ultimately a disease such as cancer.

In contrast to the biomedical discourses, the size, the appearance and the cell composition of the tumour were of no interest to the Reiki healer; neither was the information that the tumour originated in the egg, rather than the ovary tissue – a very significant distinction within medical oncology in terms of treatment success and survival rates (and thus, not an uninteresting distinction for me at that time either). Indeed, the observable characteristics of the disease, detailed in the macroscopic and microscopic accounts of the tumour, entirely misdirect our attention, according to the Reiki diagnosis. It was the 'invisible' energies outside the physical body which needed to be rechannelled and which the Reiki healer worked upon during the session. The oppositions between these two systems is emphasised in the above accounts: the former, biomedicine, works exclusively with the physical disease as represented in the textbooks through microscopic *visual evidence*; the latter, Reiki healing, sees the original tumour only as a sign of other imbalances and works upon '*invisible*' and unquanti-fiable energies which cannot be seen through macro- or microscopic vision (although some healers claim to see auratic energies which surround the body). The cure, for the former, is the eradication of the physical disease; healing, for the latter, goes beyond cure, requiring the patient to make some kind of quantum leap, undergo some kind of sea-change in lifestyle, beliefs and emotional patterns. Thus, in contrast to the former where the patient is acted upon, Reiki healing supposedly involves the active participation of patients in their own recovery.

THIS METAPHOR CHANGES LIVES

The Reiki story is only one example of the metaphorisation of illness I experienced during this time. In the alternative medical literature on cancer I was to read in the coming months, in my attempt to avoid chemotherapy, I encountered other versions of this discourse. Louise Hay, the writer mentioned by the Reiki healer above, has written a number of books on health and healing. She runs her own healing centre and trains teachers in her beliefs who now run healing work-shops outside the United States (in Britain and elsewhere). Her ideas have become increasingly popular, as evidenced by the growth in visibility of 'Louise Hay-style workshops' advertised locally, nationally and internationally. According to Hay's model of illness, the physical disease is simply a manifestation of a negative psychological pattern. Any physical problems we experience, from colds to cancer, are, Hay asserts, a sign of destructive inner feelings and thoughts:

> I believe we create every so called 'illness' in our body. The body, like everything else in life, is a mirror of our inner thoughts and beliefs. The body is always talking to us, if we will only take the time to listen. Every cell within your body responds to every single thought you think and every word you speak.
>
> (Hay, 1988:127)

Hay sets out a table in her 'Little Blue Book' *Heal Your Body* (1989), as well as in the longer version of her writing on illness, *Heal Your Life* (1988). A schema of illness, cause and cure is set out in a chart headed by three categories: *Problem*; *Probable Cause*; *New Thought Pattern*. Thus, readers can look up their physical problems, such as 'Athlete's Foot' (which I happened to be suffering from after the confinement of surgical stockings), to find the probable cause: 'Frustrated at not being accepted, inability to move forward with ease'; and apply the recom-mended new thought pattern: 'I love and approve of myself, I give myself permission to go ahead, it's safe to move'. It's not quite as straightforward as that, however, as you are also told to identify the origin of the negative thought pattern in order to replace it firmly with the new one: for example, 'lack of self-love' might originate in 'trying to win Daddy's approval' (Hay, 1988:32).

In relation to cancer, Hay offers the following analysis:

Problem	Probable Cause	New Thought Pattern
Cancer	Deep Hurt. Longstanding resentment. Deep secret or grief eating away at the self. Carrying hatreds. What's the use.	I lovingly forgive and release all of the past. I choose to fill my world with joy. I love and approve of myself.

(Hay, 1988:159)

The metaphorical interpretation of the illness functions through the attribution of cause to a characteristic of the illness in common-sense terms: cancer is a secret. The metaphor of the secret applies both to the way the disease develops and to the cultural meaning ascribed to it: cancer can grow 'secretly' inside the body for years without a person having any knowledge of its existence (sometimes for between five and ten years); and cancer has traditionally been 'kept a secret' from both patients and their friends and relatives because of its association with suffering and death.

Similarly, Hay employs a metaphorical rhetoric in her diagnosis of HIV/AIDS. She identifies the 'probable cause' of AIDS as: 'Feeling defenceless and hopeless. Nobody cares. A strong belief in not being good enough. Denial of the self. Sexual guilt' (Hay, 1989:11). Here the popular beliefs about how the disease progresses, through gradual destruction of the body's immunological defences, and possible feelings resulting from the cultural experience of the illness, such as sexual guilt or loneliness and abandonment, are given causative agency. Thus, Hay's philosophy offers the reader a likely identification, and hence the potency and the danger of her model. Apart from the fact that her analyses are so general that anyone would recognise themselves (who doesn't need to 'love and accept themselves' more, wasn't 'hurt in their childhood' and isn't 'lonely' sometimes?), Hay also invites recognition through metaphorical attribution of *cause* to *effect*. Thus, whether you felt a 'deep secret or grief eating away at you' or a 'defencelessness' before you were ill, you are likely to feel some of Hay's so-called 'probable causes' after the diagnosis of either cancer or AIDS since they are derived from the stigmas and taboos associated with these particular diseases in this culture at present.

Hay's writing on HIV/AIDS is especially insidious (and may even have been modified as a result of the criticisms of her work since those publications). In suggesting that the possible effects or manifestations of the disease are its probable *causes*, Hay reinforces vicious homophobic myths about the gay community having brought the AIDS epidemic upon itself. According to Hay, members of the gay community have to deal with 'much of society pointing their fingers at them saying, "Bad!" Usually, their own mothers and father are also saying, "You're bad". This is a heavy load to carry. So gay men created a disease called AIDS . . . which can even be fatal [sic]' (Hay, 1988:137). Not the divine retribution of Christian fundamentalists, nor the social punishment of the permissive society by New Right politics, rather Hay's model is one of HIV/AIDS as the physical metaphor for gay men's internalised self-hatred and self-induced sense of failure:

> gay men . . . have created a culture that places tremendous emphasis on youth and beauty. While everyone is young to start with, only a few fit the standard of beauty. So much emphasis has been placed on the physical appearance of the body that the feelings inside have been totally disregarded . . . The person does not count; only the body counts.
>
> Because of the ways gay people often treat other gays, for many gay men the experience of getting old is something to dread. It is almost better to die than to get old. And AIDS is a disease that often kills . . .
>
> While it is often deplorable the way straights treat gays, it is *tragic* the way many gays treat other gays.
>
> (Hay, 1988:139)

The problems with such claims hardly need spelling out in detail. Suffice it to say that it is difficult to explain why heterosexual women did not 'create AIDS', according to Hay's spurious argument, since they are clearly the most pressurised group in terms of the production of bodily youth and beauty; and, furthermore, it is impossible to explain why heterosexual men and women have increasingly contracted HIV/AIDS if it is 'caused' by gay men's negative self-image. This vicious 'blame the victim' philosophy is all too familiar to lesbian and gay communities and serves to fuel the antagonism expressed towards them by the wider homophobic culture.[3]

Hay's analysis of why women develop cancer is equally individualising and depoliticising: the individual's inability to create a positive sense of self is blamed for the disease, while power dynamics and social inequalities are simply accepted as a given, almost natural and inevitable context.[4] Hay's model relies on the recognition of bodily metaphors. Her story of her own cancer is read as a metaphoric expression of the pain she had stored in her body for years as a result of her childhood experience of sexual abuse:

> Then one day I was diagnosed as having cancer.
>
> With my background of being raped at five and having been a battered child, it was no wonder I manifested cancer in the vaginal area . . . I knew I had to clear the patterns of resentment I had

been holding since childhood. It was imperative to let go of the blame ... Yes, I had had a very difficult childhood with a lot of abuse – mental, physical, sexual. But that was many years ago and it was no excuse for the way I was treating myself now. I was literally eating my own body with cancerous growth because I had not forgiven.

(Hay, 1988: 200–1)

Indeed, Hay argues that the reason women have so many tumours in the uterine area is that they hold on to the damage that they have received: 'they take emotional hurt, a blow to their femininity, and nurse it. I call this the "He done me wrong syndrome"' (Hay, 1988:146). The tumour is thus not wrongly programmed cell growth, but rather 'a false growth ... an old hurt' which we nurse and 'keep pulling the scab off' (Hay, 1988:146).

The approaches of both Hay and the Reiki healer are symptomatic of a much wider phenomenon, which, in various forms and to differing degrees, places the meaning of illness firmly within the domain of the metaphorical: the physical signs are symptoms of other disturbances – emotional trauma, unmet needs, imbalanced lifestyles. Illness is simply the language of the psyche writ large on the body. While these two examples demonstrate the crudest oversimplifications of the metaphorisation of illness, they nevertheless condense a whole cluster of more general beliefs about the meaning of illness in contemporary culture. My experience of cancer was circumscribed by this powerful (and potentially very persuasive) 'textual body' discourse which draws upon some centrally shared, and increasingly common-sense, cultural beliefs. While rejecting Hay's explanation of cancer, or HIV/AIDS, for example, many of us (myself included) share other beliefs on a continuum with this philosophy: we are more likely to get colds or 'flu when we are run down or over-worked; headaches are often caused by stress; some people get emotional needs met through being ill; contemporary society literally makes people 'worried sick', and so on.[5] Few readers, I suspect, would reject *all* of the above assumptions about the significance of the onset of illnesses at particular times in their lives, even if, like many critics, they might be wary of straightforward readings of illness as metaphor.

'AGAINST INTERPRETATION'

I want to describe, not what it is really like to emigrate to the kingdom of the ill and to live there, but the punitive or sentimental fantasies concocted about that situation: not real geography, but stereotypes of national character. My subject is not

44

physical illness itself but the uses of illness as a figure or metaphor. My point is that illness is *not* a metaphor, and that the most truthful way of regarding illness – and the healthiest way of being ill – is one most purified of, most resistant to, metaphoric thinking. Yet it is hardly possible to take up one's residence in the kingdom of the ill unprejudiced by the lurid metaphors with which it has been landscaped.

(Sontag, 1977:3)

Thus begins Susan Sontag's eloquent plea against metaphorical thinking in matters medical, *Illness as Metaphor.* Motivated by her own experience as a cancer patient, Sontag offers a persuasive polemic against precisely the kinds of interpretations of cancer discussed so far in this chapter. As Sontag argues, it is virtually impossible to have cancer and to avoid these tropic readings of the disease. Even for patients outside the culture of alternative and self-health medicines, the cultural taboos surrounding cancer continue to reproduce a sense of blame and shame with considerable potency.

According to Sontag, the roots of this cultural potency are firmly embedded in the historical accumulation of the meanings attributed to particular diseases. In order to draw attention to the *constructedness* and *relativity* of contemporary ideas about cancer, Sontag uses a comparative method through which she documents beliefs about TB current in the nineteenth century that seem almost laughable today. TB and cancer have shared the status of the metaphorical diseases of the nineteenth and twentieth centuries respectively; until, that is, the AIDS epidemic of the 1980s and 1990s which in turn shifted the status of cancer as a disease, crystallising, as it has done, cultural anxieties about sexuality and morbidity.[6] Introducing her critique of *AIDS and its Metaphors,* Sontag writes: 'In recent years some of the onus on cancer has been lifted by the emergence of a disease whose charge of stigmatisation, whose capacity to create spoiled identities, is far greater' (Sontag, 1988:101).

The focus for her critique of metaphors of cancer is not the alternative 'heal yourself of cancer' industry, although this is mentioned (LeShan, 1977, quoted in Sontag, 1977:52), but rather the more widely shared cultural assumptions about illness, the self and suffering which function intertextually across literature and medicine. TB and cancer are both diseases which have been steeped in metaphoric meanings in these contexts. The reason for their acquisition of such status is the lack of knowledge about their cause and thus their cure, Sontag argues:

Now it is cancer's turn to be the disease that doesn't knock before it enters, cancer fills the role of an illness experienced as a ruthless, secret invasion – a role it will keep until, one day, its etiology becomes as clear and its treatment as effective as those of TB have become.

(Sontag, 1977:5)

This lack of etiological knowledge has resulted in a cultural displacement of bodily disease on to psychology, Sontag suggests. Here TB and cancer have shared the attributions of causation to the patient's disposition, or personality:

> However much TB was blamed on poverty and insalubrious surroundings, it was still thought that a certain inner disposition was needed in order to contract the disease. Doctors and laity believed in a TB character type – as now the belief in a cancer-prone character type, far from being confined to the back yard of folk superstition, passes for the most advanced medical thinking. In contrast to the modern bogey of the cancer-prone character – someone unemotional, inhibited, repressed – the TB-prone character that haunted imaginations in the nineteenth century was an amalgam of two different fantasies: someone both passionate and repressed.

(Sontag, 1977:40)

Of course there were other stigmatised diseases in the nineteenth century, such a syphilis, which aroused fear of death, anxiety about infection and moral judgements about sexual practice. However, their known causation meant that a psychological attribution to the patient was spared: 'TB, once so mysterious – as cancer is now – suggested judgements of a deeper kind, both moral and psychological, about the ill' (Sontag, 1977:40).

Not only was TB considered to be the disease of people with heightened, yet unfulfilled, sensitivities, it was also associated with a certain artistic temperament. 'The tubercular' became romanticised as a tragic figure whose suffering was identified with creative potential. TB was thus seen as 'the artists' disease': 'So well established was the cliché which connected TB and creativity that at the end of the century one critic suggested that it was the progressive disappearance of TB which accounted for the current decline of literature and the arts' (Sontag, 1977:33). Furthermore, certain tubercular qualities became chic: looking sickly, thin and pale became a sign of glamour. Indeed, the look associated with TB became fashionable and interesting: 'Gradually, the tubercular look, which symbolized an appealing vulnerability, a superior sensitivity, became more and more the ideal look for women' (Sontag, 1977:30).

The aestheticisation of sickness is not something which has been carried over from TB to cancer. Rather, cancer has become the repository for the 'agonies that can't be romanticized', Sontag argues (Sontag, 1977:36). The metaphorisation of cancer, unlike that of TB, conveys a moralism in which not only suffering, but punishment, are at stake:

> Given the romantic values in use for judging character and disease, some glamor attaches to having a disease thought to come from being full of passion. But there is mostly shame attached to a disease thought to stem from the repression of emotion . . . The view of cancer as a disease of the failure of expressiveness condemns the cancer patient: expresses pity but also conveys contempt.
>
> (Sontag, 1977:49)

It is the potential damage of these discourses which blame the patient for their illness that Sontag seeks to challenge (see also Chapter 7). Metaphors are dangerous, according to Sontag, because they, wrongly, make the individual responsible for the cause and cure of their own disease, and thus add a psychological burden to the already unpleasant and painful physical one. Resistance to such metaphorical explanations is felt by Sontag to be empowering in the face of such victimising rhetoric. Indeed, her enquiry is dedicated to our 'liberation from such metaphors'. Their obsolescence, she foresees, will come about with the discovery of new, more effective forms of medical treatment of cancer. Sontag's faith in medical science thus brings her narrative to resolution. For her, science is the hero who will rescue cancer patients from their stigmatised status, their scapegoated role for the crises of modernity and their isolated location in the contemporary cultural landscape.

Like DiGiacomo (1992), I share Sontag's desire to challenge the 'stigmatization of cancer sufferers' and her rage at the 'intepretive mode that ultimately blames victims for their own suffering', but am left perplexed at Sontag's 'extraordinary argument against interpretation' (DiGiacomo, 1992:117–18).[7] As DiGiacomo and Scheper-Hughes and Lock (1986) argue, Sontag's solution seems to be 'a retreat into the radical materialism of biomedicine'. Liberation from these 'excesses of meaning' will only come when we begin to see cancer as *just* a disease (Sontag, 1988:100), and, as DiGiacomo argues, 'no one ever experiences cancer as the uncontrollable proliferation of abnormal cells' (DiGiacomo, 1992:117). DiGiacomo goes on to demonstrate how all illnesses are inseparable from the meanings ascribed to them within their specific cultural location. Western biomedicine is no exception; it is not immune to the metaphorical. 'Science' may gain credence from its aspirations to objectivity and neutrality, but feminist and other cultural critics have long since demonstrated the ways in which values and power relations are embedded in the knowledge production and practice of both biology and medicine.[8] In the light of these challenges, Sontag's solution seems to offer an idealisation of the medical profession and ignores the politics of its cultural values, and, indeed, of its own metaphorical dependencies.[9]

Although in her later writing she acknowledges that 'one cannot think without metaphors', and that 'saying a thing is or is like something-it-is-not is a mental operation as old as philosophy and poetry, and the spawning ground of most kinds of understanding, including scientific understanding, and expressiveness' (Sontag, 1988:91), Sontag nevertheless asserts the 'truth value' of science over other discourses. While she modifies the claims made in her earlier text that 'illness is not a metaphor' to an assertion that just because all 'thinking is interpretation' this does not mean 'it isn't sometimes correct to be "against" interpretation' (Sontag, 1988:91), Sontag's faith in biomedicine remains uncritical. The aim of her earlier polemic, she says, was to highlight the ways that myths and metaphors kill: 'they make people irrationally fearful of effective measures such as chemotherapy, and foster credence in thoroughly useless remedies such as diets and psychotherapy'. Furthermore, she hoped to persuade people who were ill to 'consult doctors . . . Get the doctors to tell you the truth; be an informed, active patient; find yourself good treatment, because good treatment does exist (amid the widespread ineptitude)' (Sontag, 1988:100).

Of course, receiving successful biomedical treatment for cancer is likely to increase one's confidence in the profession and its knowledge. This is as true for me as it was for Sontag. However, what Sontag leaves intact, despite her later 'revisions', is the belief that science can be value-free and literal or non-metaphorical; her aim seems to be to achieve a 'science of the concrete' (Hawkes, 1972:83). There is in fact a long history of debates about the role of metaphor in the production of scientific knowledge. Whether arguing for the 'constitutive' function of metaphor, as well as the 'exegetical', or exploring the role of metaphor in 'theory change', philosophers of science have rarely ignored the highly metaphorical character of scientific language (see Boyd, 1979, and Kuhn, 1979, quoted in Ortony, 1979:356–419). Even Sontag's re-reading of *Illness as Metaphor* does little to undermine its powerful polemic against metaphorical thinking in relation to illness and the concomitant assumption that scientific constructions are somehow free from metaphorical corruption. Her later position that 'all thinking is metaphorical, but some metaphors are better than others', with which it is hard to disagree, thus needs rigorous further elaboration.

BEYOND METAPHOR?

What is at stake in the debates detailed above is the meaning of the term metaphor. Sontag refers back to Aristotle's definition: 'Metaphor . . . consists in giving the thing a name that belongs to something else' (Aristotle, quoted in Sontag, 1988:91); in other words, it is a process of substitution. The term originally comes from Greek *metaphora* (*meta*, meaning 'over', and *pherein*, 'to carry') and is a form of figurative language which has been scrutinised and widely debated. All forms of tropes, or figurative language, involve some kind of 'turn', 'conversion' or 'deviation'. The metaphor is the most common trope; others, such as simile, synecdoche and metonymy tend to be seen as derived from metaphor. These can be defined and illustrated as follows:

She was pregnant with death
Metaphor: the use of a word or expression 'which in literal usage denotes one kind of thing or action [but] is applied to a distinctly different kind of thing or action, without asserting a comparison' (Abrams, 1988:65).

The tumour was as big as a melon
Simile: 'a comparison between two distinctly different things' (Abrams, 1988:64).

This is the endodermal sinus tumour I told you about
Synecdoche: '(Greek for "taking together"), a part of something is used to signify the whole, or more rarely, the whole is used to signify a part' (Abrams, 1988:67).

She'd got the big C
Metonymy: '(Greek for "a change of name"), the literal term for one thing is applied to another with which it has become closely associated' (Abrams, 1988:66)

Sontag's reference to Aristotle is significant because his conceptualisation of metaphor is much narrower than many later models. Since his founding work there has been a fundamental shift in how metaphor has been theorised, and, indeed, in the ways in which language and meaning systems more generally have been conceptualised. The *classical* (Aristotelian) view of metaphor as a device which can be employed in order to achieve certain effects, and thus as something separate from it, has been gradually, if unevenly, replaced by a model of metaphor as integral to language itself (Hawkes, 1972). Increasingly, it is 'the grammatical structure of the metaphor' which is of interest, not merely 'its content or relationship to reality' (Hawkes, 1972:68). As one linguist put it: 'Metaphor is not merely the perception of similarity in dissimilarity, it is the changing of words by one another, and syntax is rich

49

in methods of doing this' (Brooke-Rose, quoted in Hawkes, 1972:68).

Instead of the classical model of metaphor, then, many studies of metaphor have emphasised the pervasiveness of tropic thinking in the structures of language. Anticipating many of the claims of post-structuralists in the 1970s and 1980s, critics have claimed that 'metaphors make us' rather than the other way around. Hawkes sums up many twentieth-century theorists of metaphor when he claims that:

> *All* language, by the very nature of its 'transferring' relation to 'reality' ... is fundamentally metaphorical ... Metaphor is a function of *language*, not of picture-making ... it is the 'omni-present principle' of all language. Indeed, all languages contain deeply embedded metaphorical structures which covertly influence overt meaning. A language cannot be 'cleared' of meaning without using a metaphor in the verb 'to clear'.
>
> (Hawkes, 1972:60)

In their classic study *Metaphors We Live By* (1980), Lakoff and Johnson argue that 'most of our ordinary conceptual system is metaphorical in nature', and that 'metaphor is not just a matter of language ... of mere words ... [O]n the contrary, human *thought processes* are largely metaphorical ... the human conceptual system is metaphorically saturated and defined' (Lakoff and Johnson, 1980:6). They illustrate their claims by examining the diversity of different kinds of metaphors – structural, orientational, ontological and so on. Highlighting the systematicity of metaphorical conceptualisation, their claims move us firmly away from the idea of metaphor as language play and into the domain of cultural meaning-systems more generally.

Ricoeur (1986) extends this elaboration further. Instead of the usual account of the history of metaphor shifting from an Aristotelian 'rhetoric of metaphor', which focuses on the word, to more con-temporary accounts of language systems, he offers a new model which combines elements of each. Ricoeur is not advocating the abandonment of the traditional rhetorical definition of metaphor as 'transposition of the name', since the word, he argues, 'remains the carrier of the effect of metaphorical meaning', but rather he aims to show how metaphor 'focuses on the word' (Ricoeur, 1986:4). He then traces the transition from the 'semantic' to the hermeneutical level. In so doing, he identifies metaphor as a trope of resemblance, as a figure, in which it constitutes a displacement and an extension of the meaning of words; 'its explanation is grounded in a theory of substitution' (Ricoeur, 1986:3). Finally, he places metaphor within 'tension theory' which looks at the production of the metaphor in the sentence as a whole (Ricoeur, 1986:4). Metaphor, he concludes:

is the rhetorical process by which discourse unleashes the power that certain fictions have to redescribe reality ... From this conjuncture of fiction and redescription I conclude that the 'place' of metaphor, its most intimate and ultimate abode, is neither the name, nor the sentence, nor even discourse, but the copula of the verb *to be*. The metaphorical 'is' at once signifies both 'is not' and 'is like'. If this is so, we are allowed to speak of metaphorical truth, but in an equally 'tensive' sense of the word 'truth'.

(Ricoeur, 1986:7)

What Ricoeur highlights is the extent to which meaning is metaphorical, not simply at the level of analogy or comparison (resemblance or substitution), but in the conjugation of the basic units of ontology.

All these theorists of metaphor share a concern to convey the depth and the pervasiveness of metaphorical tropes in contemporary culture: 'metaphors we live by' (Lakoff and Johnson, 1980), we conceptualise and communicate with (Hawkes, 1972), we exist through (Ricoeur, 1986). How then might we think of something like an illness as non-metaphorical? Within any of these post-Aristotelian models of metaphor it is impossible to think of experiencing an illness such as cancer outside the metaphorical, as Sontag (1977) advocates. Indeed, as I shall go on to show, according to some cultural critics, it is not only the experience of the illness that inevitably occurs in the domain of the metaphorical, but scientific and medical knowledge itself which is constituted according to certain metaphorical conventions.

'THE SPACE IN WHICH BODIES AND EYES MEET'[10]

Two specific forms of metaphor identified by Lakoff and Johnson (1980) are particularly pertinent to the consideration of the metaphorical character of medical knowledge: spatial and visual metaphors. The former belongs to the more general category of 'orientational' metaphors which 'give a concept a spatial orientation' (Lakoff and Johnson, 1980:14), the latter to the genre of 'ontological metaphors' through which the 'visual field' is constituted (Lakoff and Johnson, 1980:30). Both these metaphors are central to the construction of contemporary scientific knowledge and the emergence of biomedicine. Metaphors of the spatial and the visual, and indeed their relationship to each other, are fundamental to arguments about the ways in which the clinical gaze has conceptualised the human body in biomedicine.

In his significantly titled study of modern medicine, *The Birth of the Clinic: An Archaeology of Medical Perception* (1973), Michel Foucault examines these specific processes of knowledge production in the

51

development of modern medicine. Tracing the mechanisms by which
'illness . . . came to light . . . in the visible . . . but accessible space
of the human body' (Foucault, 1973:195), Foucault examines the
reorganisation of medical perception during the late eighteenth and
early nineteenth centuries. During this period, what had previously
been the invisible illness now came under the scrutiny of the medical
gaze: 'the abyss beneath illness, which was illness itself, has emerged
into the light of language' (Foucault, 1973:195).

In order to explain the ways in which modern biomedicine is indeed
highly metaphorical while effectively covering its figurative tracks, I
want to trace some of the shifts in the history of medical thought
through Foucault's account of the transition from 'classificatory medicine' to what he calls 'clinico-anatomical medicine' which has shaped
the familiar forms of biomedicine today. The patterns of the conceptualisation of illness, disease, the body, the doctor and the patient have
become 'second nature' to our contemporary Western culture, and are
integral to its fundamental discourses of rationality, objectivity and
positivism. Thus, in order to unpick these conventions and the specificity of their formation, it is necessary to pursue Foucault's account in
some detail. His argument requires us not simply to take a step back
from our common-sense medical perceptions of our (sick and healthy)
bodies, but to take several complex detours into the history of medicine
before returning to reconsider our own clinical practice and the forms
of knowledge upon which it is based.

In the transition from classificatory medicine (of seventeenth- and
eighteenth-century Europe) to the 'birth of the clinic' at the end of the
eighteenth and the beginning of the nineteenth century, there is,
according to Foucault, a fundamental 'reorganization of the elements
that make up the pathological phenomenon' in which 'a grammar of
signs . . . replaced a botany of symptoms' (Foucault, 1973:xviii). At
the heart of this transition, he argues, is a different formal, spatial
organisation of disease and of the patient's body. This might be
summed up as follows:

> the exact superposition of the 'body' of the disease and the body
> of the sick man [sic] is no more than a historical, temporary
> datum. Their encounter is self-evident only for us, or, rather, we
> are only just beginning to detach ourselves from it. The space of
> configuration of the disease and the space of localization of the
> illness in the body have been superimposed, in medical ex-
> perience, for only a relatively short period of time – the period
> that coincides with nineteenth-century medicine and the privil-
> eges accorded to pathological anatomy.
>
> (Foucault, 1973:3–4)

Such a claim only begins to make sense when the clinical model of disease is contrasted with its classificatory antecedent. According to Foucault, in classificatory medicine the patient and the disease are conceptually separable from each other. This highly counterintuitive statement for those of us brought up with contemporary Western medicine can be illustrated through a number of instances. The classificatory rules of medicine from the late eighteenth century, for example, define diseases in terms of species, kinships and genera. Following the logic of natural history and botany, different diseases can be grouped together because of their resemblances: for example, discharges link catarrh in the throat and dysentery in the intestine; bleeding connects a nosebleed with cerebral haemorrhage. A cure for the disease depends on knowledge of disease, not knowledge of the body. In classificatory medicine, doctors believe diseases must not be treated too soon before all the symptoms have manifested themselves fully.

Indeed, the automony of the disease can be seen in the belief that symptoms may move around the body and from one body to another but still be considered the same disease. The same spasmodic malady, for example, may move around the body causing dyspepsia in the lower abdomen, palpitations in the chest and epileptic convulsions in the head (Foucault, 1973:10). Thus, the 'space of the body and space of the disease possess enough latitude to slide away from one another' (Foucault, 1973:10). Not only are the patient and the disease not synonymous, but the patient is even thought to interfere with the knowledge of the disease and with its correct course (Foucault, 1973:14). Doctors are advised to subtract the individual from the disease in order to classify it correctly. Groups of disease are treated together by doctors so that all people with bleeding will be treated in one way and all those who need a change of air another (Foucault, 1973:15).

The spatial metaphors in classificatory medicine are not concerned with the location of the disease in the depths of the human body, but rather with a more two-dimensional spatial metaphor of the disease in which 'formal similarities define the interest in vicinity'. The definition of the disease is concerned with the non-spatial category of the quality of elements: of fibres, fluids and vessels. This earlier medicine defined 'a fundamental system of relations involving envelopments, subordinations, divisions, resemblances' (Foucault, 1973:5). This space involves not the interior of the human body, but the conceptualisation of disease through vertical divisions of heat and cold, and horizontal ones of subdivisions of the spasms (Foucault, 1973:5). There *is* a spatial metaphor operating here when the configuration of the disease is conceptualised, but it is not the space of the body, and is not the same as the internal space of the ill person. Instead, the classificatory gaze is sensitive to surface divisions, and vicinity is not defined by measurable distances, but by formal similarities between diseases (Foucault, 1973:6–7). In this botanical model of medicine the doctor finds essences of diseases which are considered to belong to an order which 'equals a "carbon copy" of the world' (Foucault, 1973:7). Thus, the disease is not embodied in the same way as it is in clinico-pathology, and patient and disease remain distinct (Foucault, 1973:8).

With the beginnings of pathological medicine at the end of the eighteenth century, Foucault identifies a move away from a concern with the place of disease in a *family* of diseases towards a belief about its location in the *organism*. Rather than the categorisation of diseases according to the 'table of nosological species' detailing general morbid entities that grouped symptoms together, 'the clinic appears . . . as a new distribution of the discrete elements of corporal space . . . a reorganization of the elements that make up the pathological phenomenon . . . a definition of the linear series of morbid events . . . *and a welding of the disease onto the organism*'; this change signified the replacement of a classification of these morbid entities 'by a local status that *situates the being of the disease with its causes and effects in a three-dimensional space*' (Foucault, 1973: xviii; my emphasis).

What characterises this new mode of medical thinking about disease for Foucault is this reorganisation of spatial metaphors through which a bodily depth enters the field and in which the disease becomes an integral part of the organism and thus of the patient. Foucault's detailed history thus maps the medical journey through three spatial metaphors. In 'primary spatialization', no significance is given to the individual patient, and the species of the disease is situated in 'an area of homologies'. In 'secondary spatialization', the individual patient is treated separately from the group and the disease species, and the increasingly 'penetrative medical gaze' brings the the doctor and patient into an ever more intimate relationship. In 'tertiary spatialization', 'the disease *is isolated, divided up into closed privileged regions of the body*' (Foucault, 1973:15–16; my emphasis). This new structure is indicated in the change in the doctor's question from 'what's the matter with you?' to 'where does it hurt?' in which Foucault claims 'we recognize the operation and the principle of the clinic and the principle of its entire discourse' (Foucault, 1973: xviii).

Foucault traces the connection between this reconfiguration of bodily space in relation to the centring of metaphors of the visible within these medical discourses. This medical revolution meant that:

> not only the names of diseases, not only the grouping of systems were not the same; but the fundamental perceptual codes that were applied to patients' bodies, the field of objects to which

observation addressed itself, the surfaces and depths traversed by the doctor's gaze, the whole system of orientation of this gaze also varied.

(Foucault, 1973:54)

The clinical gaze, which is taken for granted in contemporary Western culture, is not the inevitable outcome of scientific progress or technological invention, but rather originated in a very specific medical culture in which the discourse of *visibility* became central. The clinic is a place primarily of vision and observation: doctors learn to see, to isolate, to recognise, to compare and thus to match (or not), to scrutinise and then to intervene. As well as its interest in formal arrangements, such as size, number and structure, which had been the focus of the botanical gaze of natural history from the seventeenth century onwards, the clinical gaze 'could and should grasp colours, variations, tiny anomalies, always receptive to the deviant' (Foucault, 1973:89).

This reconceptualisation of disease is inextricable from the different ways in which it is recognised by doctors. Increasingly the 'prognostic sign' becomes the basis for the recognition of the disease and its essence presented in the visible (Foucault, 1973:91). Diseases are no longer classified in terms of homologous symptoms, but rather in their visible signs, which come to designate the 'truth of the disease'; thus the 'perceptual act' becomes the fundamental relation of doctor and patient in the arena of the clinic (Foucault, 1973:95). The recognition of the disease is no longer organised through kinship metaphors, but rather through an '*isomorphism of relations between elements*' in which symptoms are seen as signs of other dysfunctions. Thus the system of analogy used in the clinic is of quite a different order; the analogy here is between related elements in one individual, not between different diseases (Foucault, 1973:104). Within this reconfigured medical field of vision, the doctor's job increasingly became one of prediction, forecast and conjecture (Foucault, 1973:105). In foreseeing the path of the patient's illness, the doctor enters a new domain of mapping the questions of risk, chance and frequency (Foucault, 1973:105).

The metaphors of visibility become increasingly significant to the 'nature' of medical knowledge: 'what was fundamentally invisible is suddenly offered to the brightness of the gaze, in a movement of appearance so simple, so immediate, that it seems to be a natural consequence of a more highly developed experience' (Foucault, 1973:195). With the development of pathology, in which doctors 'opened up a few corpses', the clinical gaze combines with the anatomical one and dedicates itself to making visible and knowable the previously invisible interiors of the human body (Foucault, 1973:136).

Foucault describes the change in structures of perception at the end of the eighteenth century in which seeing no longer meant rendering visible through light but rather 'the truth of seeing' is in the 'slowness of the gaze . . . all light has now passed over into the thin flame of the eye' (Foucault, 1973:xiv). In the desire of the eye to bring truth to light, 'medical rationality plunges into the marvelous density of perception, offering the grain of things as the first face of truth, with their colours, their spots, their hardness, their adherence' (Foucault, 1973:xiii). This clinical gaze carves up the body in a different way; it sees discrete elements of corporeal space: for example, the paradox of the 'internal surface' is constituted through the isolation of body tissue (Foucault, 1973:xviii). A medicine emerges of 'organs, sites and causes' which is based upon pathological anatomy (Foucault, 1973:122).

The importance of this new centrality of the visible in medical discourse is not only the sense of depth and distinctiveness it confers on the elements of the body's interior, but also in the ways in which knowledge itself is restructured. The fusing of seeing and believing, of the visible and the legible, of the perceivable and the expressible, are all central to this new medical epistemology. The detailed pathological account offers a synthesis of visibility and expressibility and with it the guarantee of the 'faithful description' (Foucault, 1973:113). A new relationship between words and things is forged as medical perception begins to say and to show what it sees. In this new alliance, saying and seeing become one (Foucault, 1973:xi).[11]

We can thus now appreciate the complex ways in which contemporary medical knowledge appears to be the very opposite of metaphorical through its accumulated credibility as a neutral and objective science. Through the fusion of the illness with its perception a new and enduring empiricism is born. What Foucault offers is an account of how medical knowledge has been able to cover its figurative tracks and naturalise its use of spatial and visual metaphors in such a way as to present the clinical gaze as the inevitable conduit of the truth of the disease. Thus:

> the anato-clinical method – constitutes the historical condition of a medicine that is given and accepted as positive . . . Disease breaks away from the metaphysic of evil . . . this positive medicine marked, at the empirical level, the beginning of that fundamental relation that binds modern man [sic] to his original finitude . . . health replaces salvation.
>
> (Foucault, 1973:196–8)

The tendency to consider medicine as a literal and empirical science, according to Foucault has its roots in the last years of the eighteenth century when 'European culture outlined a structure that has not yet been unraveled' (Foucault, 1973:199). We might therefore situate Foucault's account of the invasion of the 'dark' mysteries of the body by science in the context of an aggressive colonial desire to dominate and control not only the unknown territory of the human body, but also that of non-European cultures (Turner, 1984, 1987).

The main reason for introducing Foucault's controversial history of science and medicine is to foreground the ways in which biomedicine is not only figurative, but so ingeniously appears not to be. While operating within the laws of objectivity and positivism, indeed being their greatest ambassador, biomedicine, in Foucauldian terms, can be seen to be highly metaphorical.[12] The contrast to previous medical systems, such as the classificatory, or indeed, many forms of contemporary medicine such as acupuncture, highlights the specificity of the rules of medical knowledge. In acupuncture, for example, the laws of heat and damp are central, discharges, rashes and sweats are grouped as symptoms, and the location of pain may or may not be of significance to diagnosis (see Chapter 4). The common sense of seeing, knowing and naming in biomedicine is, therefore, an acquired one. Its logic, however, is so familiar to many of us brought up in the biomedical culture that some detailing of alternative ways of seeing and, more importantly, ways of knowing in medicine seems necessary.[13] What is most significant here is the way in which the metaphorical quality of medical knowledge is highlighted. It is through this lens, as it were, that I now wish to return to the 'faithful medical descriptions' of the endodermal sinus tumour with which I began this chapter.

REREADING THE ENDODERMAL SINUS TUMOUR

Rereading the medical accounts of the endodermal sinus tumour which appear at the beginning of this chapter, having taken this Foucauldian detour through medical history, their apparently literal mode of observation appears in a rather different light. Cancer is a disease very definitely 'mapped onto the organism'. It is isolated and then divided up into sub-categories which are organised around particular organs – 'privileged regions of the body'; these organs are used adjectivally to describe different types of cancer, such as breast cancer, ovarian cancer, bowel cancer, as opposed to being grouped around treatments ('cisplatin cancers') or symptoms ('bleeding cancers'). Ovarian cancers are subdivided into finer and finer sub-categories. Chapter headings, for example, include: 'Germ Cell Tumours and Mixed Germ Cell-Sex Cord-Stromal Tumours of the Ovary' (Talerman, 1985), 'Endodermal Sinus Tumour and Embryonal Carcinoma of the Ovary' (Gershenson and Rutledge, 1987), and 'Germ Cell Tumours with Predominantly Extra-Embryonic Development' (Fox and Langley, 1976).

The medical textbooks typically conform to a similar pattern in their disease descriptions: definition, incidence, pathology (macroscopic, microscopic), clinical presentation, operative findings, treatment and survivial. The detailed observation by the medical gaze is thus followed by the task of prediction and ratings of 'risks' and 'chances'. The privileging of pathology is striking in all the accounts: it is in pathology that it is possible to distinguish one kind of tumour from another. The endodermal sinus tumour is then represented in detail, often in contra-distinction to others in its group of germ cell cancers. Many of these details, which function for the purposes of 'distinction', are repres-ented through the spatial and visual metaphors characteristic of the modern medical gaze. This gaze, however, is not only the 'thin flame of the eye' but is now also the technologised gaze of scans, X-rays and microscopes, which facilitate the detailed description of the tumours (see Chapter 5).[14] The symptoms of the endodermal sinus tumour tell the doctors very little, and may, in fact, be misleading and produce a misdiagnosis. The other diseases with which it is grouped on a sympto-matic basis are ectopic pregnancy or appendicitis. It is only by looking, first inside the body and then under the microscope, that the correct disease classification can be made. Cancers are defined through the appearance of a tumour which is described in terms of its size, shape, colour, pattern, grain, surface and texture. In identifying the correct type of tumour, then, the disease is named.

If we look at the detail of the representation of the tumour type its metaphorical reliances abound. The histologic patterns define the specificities and variations in different kinds of tumours. Indeed, in the quotations used at the beginning of this chapter, there is barely a phrase characterising the endodermal sinus tumour which does not rely on spatial and visual metaphors. One refers to 'the *reticular pattern*, charac-terised by a *meshwork* of empty vacuoles lined by flattened cells . . .', and then the '*festoon* or endodermal sinus pattern consists of *undulating* epithelial cells often associated with Shiller-Duval bodies' (Gershenon and Rutledge, 1987:226–7, my emphasis). The cell pattern is named 'endodermal sinus' or 'festoon'; thus the name of the cancer is itself synonymous with a metaphorical structure meaning a 'garland sus-pended between two points'. The structure, shape and visual patterning are thus the defining characteristics of the tumour. Further: 'The polyvesicular vitelline pattern is rare; it is composed of numerous cysts or vesicles *surrounded by* dense fibroblastic stroma. *The solid pattern* is composed of undifferentiated embryonal cells' (Gershenon and Rutledge, 1987:226–7; my emphasis). Attention is thus paid to de-viations and 'tiny anomalies' in the general grain, texture and cell organisation of the tumour.

In another example, the representation relies heavily on communication system metaphors (see Chapter 6): 'vacuolated network contain-ing microcysts' characterise the microscopic appearance of the tumour, and between them and 'mingling with them' are 'groups of sheets of stellate cells of definite character'; 'in about three-quarters of our tumours labyrinthine formations are present, consisting of elongated, intercommunicating channels . . . Perivascular formations . . . project into a sinussoidal space communicating with the labyrinthine forma-tions' (Fox and Langley, 1976:197–8). This language of information and communication technology is fóllowed by further structural meta-phors of space through which the 'ultrastructure' of the tumour is defined as having a 'basement membrane'. Deviation is highlighted (for example, in the tumours' 'irregular nucleoli') and analogy is frequently employed to synthesise a similarity in spatial organisation: the ultra-structure of the endodermal sinus tumour is also observed to resemble that of the rat yolk sac (Fox and Langley, 1976:199–200).

Thus, figurative language is heavily relied upon to produce the pathological picture, and modern biomedical discourse, far from being a literal description, is instead littered with a heavy use of metaphor. Given how much debate has taken place within scientific communities about the use of metaphorical language in the development of ideas and concepts in all fields of research, Sontag's appeal to biomedicine as the guarantor against metaphor can only be viewed as polemical. This belief in the 'literal illness', and its faithful description in biomedicine, ignores the ways in which science and medicine are themselves full of metaphorical representations which follow certain spatial and visual conventions; furthermore, as Foucault demonstrates, the model of the 'literal illness' is itself a culturally and historically specific belief. Indeed, the above textual analysis demonstrates what Boyd (1979) and more recently Tauber (1994) have claimed about the role of metaphor in the formation of scientific knowledge:

> concepts are not defined solely in terms of their inherent proper-ties or an implicit comparison, but rather emerge from their interactional properties, arising from experience in an open-ended fashion, with the important caveat that they may be based on similarities derived from cultural values. Thus metaphor may create new meaning and serves as a means of structuring our conceptual system.
>
> (Tauber, 1994:137)

MONSTROUS METAPHORS

It was thus not just the discourses of alternative and self-health therapies, criticised earlier in this chapter, that encouraged meta-phorical readings of my cancer; biomedical accounts of teratomas also invited such interpretations. Wary as I might have been of the politics of such questions, I found it impossible to avoid asking: what would it mean for me to see the tumour I had in the light of metaphor? For me, the imperatives of alternative and biomedicine combined with the cultural horrors surrounding teratomas to give my cancer a particularly monstrous metaphorical charge.

Although the endodermal sinus tumour is not ovarian cancer in the strict sense of the term, mine had nevertheless presented itself in the form of an ovarian cyst. Ovarian cysts have a bad reputation. Not just because they can be malignant (in about 5 per cent of cases), but because they belong to a set of medical mythologies which are retold almost as urban myths in order to disgust and fascinate. One of their characteristics is their size: ovarian cysts can be enormous. Nurses on my surgical ward delighted in comparing notes on the biggest one they had heard about: one had been 'as big as football'; 'No!'; 'Yes'. She'd seen it; the size of a baby, yes really, some women had thought they were pregnant; and have you heard about the one that weighed five stone and the woman had to be craned up on to the operating table for surgery? She arrived at the hospital a very large woman and left a very small one. My tumour, I was told, was big. It was the size of that fruit bowl, said someone who'd seen it, pointing at the large bowl full of grapes and other fruit which stood on the hospital table next to my bed. It was the size of a melon, said another; a large aubergine, another.

The second unappealing, yet fascinating, characateristic of ovarian cysts, benign or malignant, is that they can contain other bodily parts: teeth, hair, nails, bones (even bowel, my consultant informed me with a hint of glee when I enquired about this several months after my treatment). The germ cell tumours, in particular, can produce all kinds of bodily tissue because the tumours originate from the egg cell whose function it is in pregnancy to produce differentiated cells that form other body parts. The cysts are likely to contain organs (in part or whole) with fast-growing cells in particular, like hair and nails. 'Oh yes, they have been seen covered in hair and full of teeth', I was told.

Story after story of monstrous growths haunted me as I found out more about teratomas. The iconography of science fiction and horror films provided a rich set of images to fuel my imagination further. The cancer I had seemed to me to belong to the genre of what film studies scholars have identified as the 'body horror' typical of late twentieth-century Hollywood cinema: *The Fly*, *The Incredible Hulk*, *Rosemary's Baby* and the *Alien* trilogy.[15] These films explore the compelling themes of the boundaries between the human and the non-human, between the normal and the abnormal and between the inside and the outside of the body. The disgust expressed at these monstrous creations/mutations is accompanied by a sense of voyeuristic intrigue that keep audiences coming back for more.

Given the popular mythologies surrounding ovarian cysts, I found it almost impossible *not* to consider them within their metaphorical histories. A teratoma has particularly grotesque connotations, I discovered:

> **teras** *(med.)* *n.* a monstrosity; – **teratogen,** an agent that raises the incidence of congenital malformations; – *n.* **teratology,** the study of malformations or abnormal growths, animal or vegetable: a tale of marvels; **teratoma,** a tumour, containing tissue from all three germ layers; – *adj.* **teratomatous.** [Gr. *teras*, a monster.]
>
> (*Chambers Dictionary*, 1973:1392)

Had I produced a monstrous birth, as the dictionary definition suggested? Indeed, the birth analogies are endless. The tumour had begun with egg (albeit unfertilised egg) cell division, like the beginning of foetal development. Its growth released alpha fetoproteins into the blood, like a pregnancy. The doctors at the hospital where I was first tested asked me again and again if I might be pregnant. Was I sure? What kind of contraception did I use? After surgery I was informed that they had removed the ovary and the fallopian tube as well as the tumour because 'they had all got a bit tangled up'. A common diagnosis before surgery is ectopic pregancy (where the fertilised egg begins to develop in the fallopian tube). The tumour was big enough to be a baby. And at the time I wondered if it had hair, teeth, bones, as a foetus would have (later, I discovered that it had not). The original diagnosis of an ovarian cyst had been made after an ultrasound scan revealed a 'large complex mass' in my abdomen; the same test is used during certain stages of pregnancy. The surgeons had cut open my abdomen and taken out a large growth, not dissimilar, except from the length and angle of the incision, to that of a caesarean delivery. Furthermore, after surgery, having lost one ovary and with the threat of chemotherapy, I was informed of the possibility of my infertility. What more obvious interpretation than that this tumour symbolised my unrealised desire to have a child and be a mother which I had repressed in favour of developing my professional (masculine) identity? No wonder the Reiki practitioner had had a field day.

Indeed, the birth metaphors can be extended further. The tumour 'presented' three weeks before the deadline for the submission of my PhD. My supervisor's reassuring words to me at the end of our last supervision rang in my head: 'I have no doubt that you will submit by the deadline.' Doctoral students frequently feel that when they finish their thesis they have given birth; they cannot let go and they feel bereft when they do. Why had I produced a malignant tumour just before the end of the long gestation of my thesis? Was there a part of me that could not let myself complete? Perhaps it was merely a classic example of feminine self-sabotage, that shadow of patriarchal culture which anticipates women's failure at every juncture; that tap on the shoulder that we all dread; the fear that we struggle to overcome, but never quite manage to banish entirely. Instead of the healthy birth of a PhD thesis, delivered into the academic world, ensuring my future within it, had I produced a malignant tumour, about the same weight, which contained another kind of knowledge, revealed a deeper truth? Had my 'masculine' ambition battled with my residual 'feminine' insecurities to create this unnatural and twisted offspring? Once again the woman's body speaks its unconscious yearnings and dreads.

According to contemporary biomedical discourse, a malignant tumour is the result of abnormal cell development; according to the metaphorical interpretations of my encounter with the Reiki practitioner, it might be read as indicative of other deviant developments, such as those connected with gender and sexuality. Body metaphors here produce evidence of deviant medical and sexual states (see Chapter 3). The monstrous birth metaphor can thus be extended further to a reading of the tumour in the light of my 'deviant' sexuality: the just deserts of the unnatural notion of the lesbian mother? This category is legislated against and held in the highest contempt: how could such a mannish identity desire such womanly rewards? The unnaturalness of the sexual, as well as of the reproductive, perversion had combined to produce a double insult to 'Mother nature'. Had I stayed on the straight and narrow, and not been led astray by the temptations of lesbianism in my twenties, perhaps I would not have been punished with this potentially deadly birth. In the absence of a punishing God, our internalised sense of guilt has bodily repercussions and makes our transgressions visible for all the world to see. After all, who could produce such a monstrous birth? Only an unnatural woman. Such a reading is reiterated in definitional terms by cross-referencing of 'teratogenesis' and 'lesbianism' in Roget's *Thesaurus*. Under 'nonconformity' we find:

> *abnormality*, aberration *deviation*; mutation *variant*; abortion, monstrous birth, terata, teratogenisis, monstrosity, monster; sexual abnormality, bisexuality, homosexuality, lesbianism, Sapphism; necrophilia.
>
> (Roget's *Thesaurus*, 1982:56–7)

THE POWER OF METAPHOR

In the light of these accounts, the possible tropic readings of cancer are endless. Cancer is the *self* at war with the *self*. Thus, surely one's identity is at stake (on trial?) with the onset of such a disease. As the classic 'system breakdown' disease in which cells go berserk and attack their 'host' body, cancer lends itself particularly well to metaphoric manoeuvrings which introduce one's duty to oneself into the healing equation. Indeed, according to one medical anthropologist, metaphorical thinking about illness receives its 'most extensive elaboration in the case of cancer' (DiGiacomo, 1992:118). But what cautions might we introduce against such free-associative readings? Are these metaphorical interpretations across the cancer patient's body helpful and instructive in any way? Do they really reveal the truth about oneself? Why was it almost impossible for me to banish such constructions of the disease from my own imagination? The pervasiveness of such a mode of interpretation cannot be underestimated. The power of this discourse derives from its successful condensation of so many deep-rooted beliefs about the body in contemporary culture, in particular fears about the limits and acceptability of its desires.

It is thus not metaphor of which we should be wary *per se*, but the cultural uses to which its heightened applications may be put. If, as I have argued, metaphorical readings of illness are inevitable because of the ways in which language works, what we need to focus on in careful detail is how metaphors might serve the purposes of constructing particular illnesses as shameful. To remain sceptical about the possibility of ever understanding illness beyond metaphor is not to abandon entirely Sontag's important attack on the popular tropes through which TB, then cancer, and now HIV/AIDS have been subject to a whole culture's projected anxieties, pity and contempt. In both her essays (1977, 1988), Sontag identifies the damage caused by the stigmatisation of particular illnesses.[16] 'The very names of such diseases', she writes, 'are felt to have a magic power . . . As long as a particular disease is treated as an evil, invincible, predator, not just a disease, most people with cancer will indeed be demoralized by learning what disease they have' (Sontag, 1977:7). Such stigmatised illnesses are vulnerable to a heightened metaphorical designation. It is in the challenge to the perpetuation of such *stigmatisation* that I wish to extend and build on Sontag's critical investigation of the metaphorical function.

The high degree of anxiety about cancer has ensured a continued charge to the metaphors generated around this disease. Fear produces a desire to avoid and deny and most particularly to transform. The fear which the naming of cancer engenders fuels the desire to seek linguistic reassurance: perhaps cancer does not have to be confronted if we do not speak its name. Metaphors rush to the rescue of the subject whose terror is otherwise uncontainable. Metaphors provide the necessary balm for the psychic pain of the unbearable knowledge. Metaphors enable us to detour around undesirable subjects. If metaphor involves the transformation of one thing into another, then the stigmatised category can be displaced effectively through such manoeuvrings. But is metaphorical sublimation ever fully effective? Does metaphor always transform the object into something else, or is there a way in which both terms coexist despite a metaphorical renaming?[17] In moving towards a critical consideration of stigmatisation we are thus returned to the distinction between metaphor and metonymy. For Peggy Phelan this is a crucial distinction:

> Metaphor works to secure a vertical hierarchy of value and is reproductive; it works by erasing dissimilarity and negative difference; *it turns two into one.* Metonymy is additive and associative; it works to secure a horizontal axis of contiguity and displacement.
>
> (Phelan, 1993:150)

According to this view, metaphor might be more suited to the banishment of impossible knowledge, since it is more fully transformative than metonymy. But the 'magical power' of stigmatisation insists on contiguity. Like a ghostly presence it continues to haunt the subjects who desire its absence. In this sense, the stigmatised illness might be transformed into metaphor, but its powerful impact extends in excess of such containment. It is not just that there is 'a surplus of meaning', but rather that there is 'an excess over meaning' (Readings, 1991:31).

The power of metaphor in the case of cancer makes the silence speak (or at least whisper) the forbidden word, the banished category. As the subject is avoided, it enters everyone's mind. Sitting somewhere between metaphor and metonymy, the stigmatised category produces the desire for complete transformation and yet its lingering presence ensures only partial displacement. What remains is the subject of the next chapter.

3

MONSTERS

THE C WORD AND THE L WORD

Whatever you do, don't say 'cancer'. The unspoken word, written on everyone's lips, must not be voiced. Frozen in its previous associations with inevitable death, cancer is still an illness which even hospital staff endeavour to avoid. Even after my diagnosis no one on the surgical ward says the word cancer to me. The nurses' rounds, which previously involved introducing the patients to the new shift by explaining the nature of their illness or surgery, suddenly have a different format; my case, the C word, is whispered about in the office before the round, and not mentioned when they pass my bed twice a day. Instead of pausing to introduce me as they had done previously, by name and then by medical problem, 'This is Jackie and she's had a right laparotomy', they introduce me by name, 'This is Jackie . . .', followed by an awkward smile which fills the place of the second half of the naming ritual. In my imagination, and I am sure in theirs too, an anonymous voice whispers 'and she has cancer'. This non-naming ritual is repeated twice a day at every shift change until I leave the ward and come under the treatment of an oncologist who feels more relaxed about naming his specialism more openly.

Shortly before I leave hospital one of the more sociable nurses sits on a patient's bed down the row from mine and chats about her work. What are her ambitions, one of the patients asks her. She would love to work in oncology, she replies. Suddenly catching sight of me, she blushes with embarrassment. Unaware of the reason for this mood change, the patient asks her what oncology is. The whole ward falls silent. 'It's . . .' she glances nervously in my direction, hesitates, and never finishes her sentence. She had better get on with her tasks, she announces. Have I a disease so unspeakable, I wonder to myself?

My experience of the cancer diagnosis and its aftermath felt very familiar. I had definitely been here before. Although the context and the content were different, many of the rules were the same. Certain feelings fitted emotional and bodily memories that I recognised: the ways in which other people's fears were condensed in particular kinds of language practices and behaviour rituals. These frequently exceeded

65

their conscious control and ruptured the usual cultural conventions of communication and interaction. They were symptomatic of pervasive forms of cultural anxiety.

This prohibition on speaking the C word reminded me of my experience of the L word. Albeit for very different reasons, I have always been struck by the depth of people's anxieties about saying the word 'lesbian'. The censorship and self-censorship which operate around this cultural category prohibit speaking it aloud, especially in public places. Lesbians and gay men are repeatedly told that if they must lead the lives they do they shouldn't keep 'ramming it down everyone else's throats'. Any visibility, any open expression of affection, any desire for recognition is perceived as excessive: two lesbians are a crowd; seeking acknowledgement of one's relationship is pushy. The central message continues to be that it's safer, and nicer, to remain silent and keep it hidden.

When, and if, the silence is broken, all kinds of euphemisms are used to speak about these categories without saying the L word or the C word. In the case of deviant sexualities euphemisms are commonplace.[1] Euphemisms are deployed both by those in homophobic culture who seek to ignore the existence of homosexuality and lesbianism, and by lesbians and gay men themselves who seek the protection of a code or a cover. For some, there is almost a physical inability to say the word 'lesbian' at all, even to describe themselves.[2] Anything would seem preferable. Desexualising language is often substituted: lovers become friends, best friends, special friends; lesbians are single, spinsters or even gay. And this is not to mention the derogatory labels given to lesbians and gay men by homophobic culture, some of which have been reclaimed, such as 'queer'. Euphemisms are also central to lesbian and gay cultures; sometimes used strategically, sometimes fearfully, sometimes ironically, there are probably hundreds of words that have been used to substitute for the categories of lesbian and gay. Like a secret language or code between lovers, euphemisms for the words 'lesbian' and 'gay' are continuously reinvented and adapted. They function as part of the self-reflexive and campy subcultures, such as 'he's a friend of Dorothy's' or 'she has DDP', but also as a way to talk about lesbian and gay sexualities in crowded public places, such as restaurants, bars or on public transport.[3] Moreover, many use these euphemisms for private discourse with irony and humour as a means to articulate the specificity of cultural marginality, drawing attention to the absurdity of such strategies through exaggeration (such as 's/he shops at Safeways or Tescos' as a way of marking out 'sexual preference').

Cancer, too, is spoken about through euphemism. If possible, some other word, phrase or reference might be employed in order to make the speaker and the listener feel more comfortable: something nasty, a malignancy, the big C, the cruel C. In my case, when I was diagnosed the medical staff told me: I might need more treatment, the cyst might be nasty, three months' chemotherapy might be necessary, the tumour was being tested in case it was malignant, and finally that Dr M would answer all my questions (see Chapter 4 for a full acount of this story). Thus, the disease was euphemised through the treatment and even the doctor, and it was left to me to name it myself. For me, the euphemisation of the disease added to the problems of being a 'cancer patient'. The inability of the medical staff to say the word cancer in front of me conveyed a sense of embarrassment which added a feeling of shame to the already intense emotional charge of having this life-threatening disease. No doubt some of the medical profession consider these euphemisms to be preferable from the patient's point of view, and in some cases this may be correct. There is, however, rarely an attempt to find out the patient's preference. For the most part, the widespread use of euphemisms bears witness to the unease of the medical staff rather than to a concern for the wishes of the patient.

Another parallel in my experience of the C word and the L word is the constant negotiation of 'passing'. Once you know, can others tell? Or can you pass? And do you want to pass? Would lesbians prefer to be thought of as heterosexual, and cancer patients as healthy individuals? What does it mean to pass successfully? Passing operates in a variety of ways in the lives of people with cancer. At the early stages of cancer, of course, no one can tell, not even the person her/himself. That's often part of the problem. A tumour might be growing for years without detection. People's fear of cancer is often expressed as a fear of something secretly growing inside the body. Once it has been diagnosed, passing may be a preferable option for many. In certain circumstances, people with cancer may want to hide their illness. Even though I was open about my own diagnosis, I also made strategic decisions about disclosure. I was delighted, for example, when I passed as healthy to my bank manager on requesting an overdraft; I explained to him I'd had extra expenses recently due to medical problems for which I had been seeing a number of alternative practitioners. He granted the loan, declaring that I looked perfectly healthy to him. On the other hand, the pressure to pass as healthy can be a burden for the person with cancer. Concealing the illness, the effects of treatments, the distress of the diagnosis often contribute to the stress of the whole experience. Don't upset this friend or relative, hide it at work, keep it from your children. The cultural imperatives of secrecy and disguise are a constant reminder of the price of living with a stigmatised illness.[4]

Passing is similarly a constant part of everyday life in relation to sexualities designated as deviant. The heterosexual assumption operates prescriptively almost on a daily basis, whether through humour, modes of address, innocent questioning or sexual harassment. 'Coming out', as has been said before, is not something one does once, but is a process of continual negotiation and on-the-spot decision-making: do I correct the assumption, do I answer the question directly, do I name names or speak of ungendered 'persons'?[5] To pass or not to pass has been an integral part of lesbian histories and subcultures which are full of secret loves, double lives, cross-dressing, gender and sexual disguise and closeted relationships.

When I first began to write about the parallels between my experiences of the C word and the L word I felt sure that this was more than just the anomalous coincidence of someone who happened to have come up against the impact of two unconnected stigmatised cultural categories. For my experience of people's reactions to my having cancer brought such a profound emotional echo of previous encounters that I felt something more significant must be at stake. And my experiences of the cultural associations between the C word and L word continued after I left hospital, as the Reiki story in Chapter 2 exemplifies. On embarking on various alternative therapeutic approaches to cancer, I found myself subject to the patholigisation of my sexuality by a Reiki practitioner. In trying to read the tumour on my ovary as a metaphor for the general imbalances in my life, she suggested that my lesbian relationship was a sign both of too much femininity and too much masculinity, and in any case a repression of my maternal instinct. With the licence that such a metaphorical reading allows, she slipped from disease to desire and back again with the greatest of ease.

Despite my growing conviction that the connections between the C word and the L word required exploration, I was also aware that this was dangerous territory. There seemed to be many good reasons not to draw people's attention to these parallels. What important differences between the two categories might my analogies obscure? Why single out these two and ignore other equally important stigmatised categories? What kind of readings could be provoked by highlighting such connections? Might I be in danger of reinforcing many of the more unpleasant associations of 'deviant sexuality' with disease and death that it is important to challenge? Given that this culture has attempted to construct lesbian sexuality as pathological, unnatural and even malignant, bringing it under the same lens as cancer might seem to many to be imprudent to say the least.

These connections between sexuality and disease have become further entrenched in the contemporary context of HIV and AIDS (Richardson, 1987; Carter and Watney, 1989; Boffin and Gupta, 1990; Patton, 1990). During the last decade, homosexual desires have been reinscribed as deathly within the popular imagination through the widespread deployment of a renewed pathological discourse. In a homophobic culture keen to distance itself from the implications of the 'AIDS crisis', popular representations of HIV and AIDS have associated it specifically with gay male communities and have then blamed them for the irresponsible spread of the disease to 'the rest of society' (Watney, 1987). Given how rapidly and how fiercely these homophobic constructions have woven together death and desire in their depictions of HIV and AIDS, there may be an imperative to shatter the mythologies reproduced by such analogies. But in many ways, living in a culture where deviant sexualities are being repathologised through HIV and AIDS discourse has made me more, rather than less, inclined to pursue my questions about the parallels between the C word and the L word. Although not typically associated in everyday discourse perhaps, the overlaps I experienced were no doubt fuelled by the renewed phobias circulating around constructions of both sexuality and disease more generally; avoiding such constructions (for fear of being misread) will not make them go away. Instead, I wanted to investigate the cultural implications of this coincidence of phobias, and to theorise what might lie behind some of the patterns of behaviour and response I had encountered. What might my previous experiences of homophobia tell me about the cultural construction of cancer; and how might this confrontation with the dread surrounding cancer reflect upon the regulation of sexuality in this culture? As I began to explore these issues theoretically, rather than just anecdotally, I became more and more interested in what this overlap might reveal about the deep-rootedness of certain cultural anxieties.

HIGH ANXIETY

The denial, avoidance and displacement of the C word and the L word serves to withhold the kind of external confirmation which takes place routinely around other cultural categories.[6] Those whose experiences include them within these unspeakable categories live out their meanings in the absence of such a public recognition, but in relation to the expectation of its presence. What marks such moments is the emotional charge of the unspoken term leaving a tangible anxiety hanging in the air. These are dialogic exchanges, not only between self and other, but between the projections of their mutual perceptions. In an endless cultural relay of dialogic fantasies, the relationality and intersubjectivity of identities are acted out; the importance of recognition from another is given emotional shape (Benjamin, J. 1990). Such exchanges have become commonplace in our day-to-day lives and only become visible by means of their absence. Part of the feeling that we belong to a culture occurs in the moments when such recognitions bestow a legitimate sense of place on us. When no such place appears on the horizon, even as a distant promise, its absence marks the subject as other, as outsider, as alone. This surfaces here through the repeated negotiations of the responses of others. Once (or if) the stigmatised category has been named, it has to be continuously reiterated as the lesbian 'comes out' (if she decides to) and the person with cancer 'breaks the news' to friends, family and colleagues. How will this news on both counts change one's relationships? As the news travels, other people's responses demand attention. The shock effect can be felt afresh each time as the next outsider gains insider knowledge. A complex interchange of projection and protection is at play in this process of sharing the news. Has so-and-so heard? How did they react? And through *their* shocked reaction your own sense of discrepancy between who-you-thought-you-were and who-you-must-be-now is repeatedly rehearsed.

Despite the therapy culture of the late twentieth-century Western world, in which the cure-all for everything is *apparently* to talk about it openly, cancer nevertheless remains something people find difficult, if not impossible, to discuss and to respond to. Although this varies from country to country, place to place and even hospital to hospital, few people with cancer in Britain in the 1990s tell stories of direct discussions with doctors about death and dying, or even about the disease and its treatment. So while one in three people in Britain get some form of cancer, making it almost inevitable that we will all come into contact with the disease at some point in our lives, cancer still invokes the dread of the unknown in our imaginations.[7] How can something so commonplace have the emotional impact of something almost unthinkable? To have cancer is to inhabit a world designated for the unfortunate few. For the person diagnosed with cancer, a culture once saturated with information about how to avoid carcinogenic influences is transformed into one which is unable even to name the disease. We read everywhere of cancer's increasing prevalence and yet are deeply shocked when it does not pass us by. Cancer has a ubiquitous presence in everyday culture and yet the person with cancer is nevertheless confronted by a striking silence that reminds them they have entered stigmatised territory.

But this silence is not one which ensures the absence of the source of anxiety, rather, it affirms its presence. Thinking about this contradiction in the context of sexuality in the discourse of the closet, Eve Sedgwick suggests that 'among the striking aspects of considering closetedness in this framework, for instance, is that the speech act in question is a series of silences!' (Sedgwick, 1994:11). The avoidance of speaking certain words, or naming particular sexualities or illnesses, and attempting to remain silent on certain subjects, requires a series of linguistic tropes which might be seen as 'performative acts', according to Sedgwick.[8] It is not only in articulating something that 'the action is named' but also in certain non-articulations. Thus, silence, as well as speech, construct the status of particular cultural categories. In writing about her experience of breast cancer, Sedgwick discusses the ways in which the 'formal and folk ideologies around breast cancer not only construct it as a secret, but construct it as the secret whose sharing defines women as such' (Sedgwick, 1994:262). Sexual and gender identities are reproduced through the rituals surrounding breast cancer in which femininity is (literally and symbolically) reconstituted: 'with the proper toning exercise, make-up, wigs and a well-fitting prosthesis, we could feel just as feminine as we ever had and no one (i.e. no man) need ever know that anything had happened' (Sedgwick, 1994:262). To keep one's femininity intact requires elaborate efforts on the part of the woman with cancer: above all, energy should be directed into covering up the signs of this stigmatised disease and the effects of its treatments.

Thus, perhaps the terms 'denial, avoidance and displacement' are misleading in some ways. The inability to say the words 'cancer' or 'lesbian', the euphemisms that are then resorted to with relief and the tricky negotiations around passing that I describe above all refer to the production of cultural categories, as much as to their containment. In fact, these two are inseparable, they occur in the same move. As I suggested at the end of Chapter 2, far from ensuring successful banishment of these categories, these linguistic manoeuvres guarantee them a lingering presence, if a highly undesirable one. The L word and the C word are constituted here as stigmatised categories in the classic 'I know, but nevertheless . . .' move described by psychoanalysis as disavowal; they are 'affirmed in the same gesture as [they are] denied' (Wright, 1992:114). A layering of *cultural disavowals* erases the categories in question but simultaneously confirms their significance. The concept of disavowal refers to the ways in which the attempted banishment of undesirable subjects is never fully successful and indeed may be a way of reiterating their existence. While the force of people's fear may require that these categories be euphemised, displaced or substituted, the necessity of such strategies leads directly back to the prohibitive imperatives of that fear. This apparent unutterability of the C word and the L word regenerates the powerful stigma of these categories. It is not that these silences prevent them from coming into being, but rather that they are produced as unspeakable through this heightened anxiety.[9]

CULTURAL TABOOS

Both the C word and the L word are constituted as taboo categories through these processes of disavowal. The notion of taboo extends the

71

social shaming processes described by the concept of stigmatisation to refer to their emotional impact that draws upon unconscious investments for its force. While I am aware that taboo is a much debated term, I use it here to investigate the compelling grip that the C word and the L word have on our psyches in contemporary culture.[10] In the following section I map some of the manifestations of the powerful terrors that surround these categories and trace the contours of the dread that inform their taboo status.[11] In order to explore how and why these two apparently unrelated categories might overlap in their figuring as cultural taboo, I return to the realm of the metaphorical, to the tropes, imagery and associative connotations that the C word and the L word have been ascribed within the popular imagination.[12] In so doing I rehearse the thoughts and feelings that serve to construct my otherness and deviancy so as to come to grips with their persuasiveness. Indicative of the power of their cultural purchase is the fluency with which I can recite their scripts, for the discourses by which one is othered are always so familiar to those who suffer their effects.[13]

To witness responses to the C word and/or the L word, temporarily or more permanently, is to be confronted by a deep sense of the horrific. In being so rigorously disavowed, both are constituted in relation to psychic revulsion. Each signifies something quite monstrous. Each touches on something unbearable. Such responses point to the limits of the tolerable. The fear and loathing directed towards lesbians, and the terror directed towards people with cancer are signs of their taboo status, despite their very different manifestations. What disturbs so deeply in both cases is something which goes beyond rational or conscious reponses, something which threatens most profoundly. We are haunted by the constancy of its tormenting presence and horrified by its particular manifestations.

Cancer is one of the most feared diseases. Other diseases kill, other diseases are painful and humiliating and other diseases have treatments with horrible side-effects, but few fill people with such a feeling of inexpressible dread. HIV and AIDS, of course, as Sontag points out, have also acquired the power of that intense cultural anxiety, once the preserve of cancer and before that TB (see Chapter 2). Seen as symbolic of the contamination of contemporary society with the promiscuous values of the infamous 1960s, HIV and AIDS have been viciously represented as a punishment from God, the just deserts of flamboyant liberationism and the pitiful fate of nonconformists. People with AIDS have to confront many of the feelings I describe here which escalate around the subject of cancer.[14] Alongside HIV and AIDS, cancer is the disease which so many dare not contemplate (though some may secretly believe it will be their fate).

The power of cancer's horror is partly due to its association with death. A diagnosis is taken to be a death sentence. But many diseases share this association. Why should the dread of cancer haunt our imaginations so particularly? Why should cancer disturb the subject so profoundly on a psychic level? Perhaps because cancer deceives. It silently makes itself at home and waits. The body which appears healthy hides the imminent truth of its mortality. Recovery is possible, but is not dared to be hoped for. Better to face the worst; if not now, then sometime. The pretence of immortality, through health and fitness, workaholism, control, supremacy, productivity and reproduction will no longer provide their former comforts. Once diagnosed, death becomes part of life and refuses to be banished. It becomes a constant companion. A new certainty. The only certainty. Chemotherapy and radiotherapy evoke a further sense of dread. The vomiting, the hair loss, the burns. And perhaps all for nothing. So many have been through this and died anyway. Might it just prolong the agony? Why poison yourself with no guarantees? Why submit yourself to radiation, which our collective memories associate with destruction – or even with more cancer? The stories of radiation in the postwar period involve the production of cancer, not its extinction. The treatments are profoundly counter-intuitive.

The force of homophobia in this culture suggests that lesbianism has also been ascribed the power to horrify. It goes against nature, we are told. Refusing the connection between sexuality and reproduction, lesbianism is seen as fundamentally unnatural. Deviant and perverse, the lesbian is represented as freakish and shocking – the vampire, the predator, the most unnatural of women.[15] In a culture obsessed with marking the boundaries of sexual difference, lesbians threaten nature's guarantee of order and difference. A reproductive telos has come to mark out sexual difference as complementary.[16] When the animals 'went in two by two' the binary organisation of sexual difference preserved future generations. The reproduction of difference is the reproduction of life itself, we are told. Seen as non-reproductive, lesbians threaten the future of the planet, the future of the human race; when they die, who will carry on our great journey to perfection? If everyone chose 'sameness' there would be no future. Only extinction. The mythic status of natural difference and natural selection ensures that the only place for lesbians within nature is as its freaks. Lesbians are represented as the necessary exception that proves the rule, the margins that define the centre, the deviants that define the normal.

Lesbianism is figured in the popular imagination as both asexual and hypersexual. The endless source of masculine heterosexual fantasy, lesbians are erotic and compelling. Yet they are really awaiting the right man, since without him they remain regressive, immature, the victims of arrested development. They have failed to progress to adult heterosexuality. Trapped in the childish pursuits of midnight feasts and sleeping over with best friends, fantasies of these schoolgirl antics are seen as cloyingly repellent. Lesbians cannot be real women, but neither are they innocent girls. On the other hand, lesbians are seen only in terms of sex. They never stop having sex. They are predatory and desire every woman they come into contact with. They are after your wife, your girlfriend and your daughter. They are like men; and we all know what they are like. Lesbianism is thus constructed both as asexual girls' play and as testosterone-crazed insatiability. Each unnatural in its own way; both refusals of natural femininity.

Desire between women in the homophobic imagination is more than troubling; it can disturb at a fundamental level. Public humiliation of the deviant offenders is a reassuring defence. For lesbians and gay men it is a constant threat. For many, self-censorship has become a way of life. Negotiating the risks of retribution is second nature: 'it comes with the territory'.[17] Either scapegoats or objects of projected desire, lesbians (and indeed gay men) have been made into the enemy within.[18] Either perceived as fundamentally different and thus a safe bet as a scapegoat, or as threateningly similar and thus a reassuring sign of denial, these sexual deviants must be constantly shamed. And years of practice make the shaming easy, almost automatic. Those who come out unscarred have escaped lightly.

Both the C word and the L word cut deep. They meet with profoundly felt responses, sometimes beyond volition, sometimes quite in its accordance. Shame runs across each category in different ways but with a common refrain which relies upon deep-rooted and heartfelt conventions and customs. But can this really explain all the fuss? Are these reasons sufficient to account for the power of these taboos? What is it that has this ability to provoke such an intense dread, such a strong desire to repel, such a complete revulsion? In order to extend my analysis further I want to address the physicality of these emotional responses I have been exploring. For these responses are often accompanied by an almost visible physical shudder: the stomach turns, the shock travels down the body, the flesh creeps, the skin heats up, the cheeks flush. The taboo category may evoke a thud of bodily recognition. The C word and the L word are not only taboo categories heightened by anxiety or fear, but there is also a *physical disgust* that marks their impact. This bodily manifestation of psychic dread gives these taboo categories the full force of their cultural horror.

But the horror is only half the story. As others have suggested, the 'powers of horror' lie precisely in the ways in which they are accompanied by a kind of fascination, a sense of intrigue, a desire to take another look, to know more of the awful truth (Douglas, 1966; Kristeva, 1982, and see below). In an unfortunate way the subject of taboo is special, different, other, and as such attracts a certain compelling, even illicit, attention. To pursue the connections between the fascination and the horror of these two categories further, and to delve deeper into the physicality of their power, I shall consider the taboos around the body and its boundaries in relation to Kristeva's theory of abjection.[19]

ABJECT BODIES

Investigating cultural taboos raises the question of what is sacred and how it is protected, of what is abominable and how it is to be avoided, and of what is defiled and how it might be purified (Freud, 1913–14; Douglas, 1966). As we have seen, the maintenance of cultural taboos serves a regulatory function which facilitates the ritual exclusion of matter/objects/people from that which is considered in need of pre-servation. Rituals of cleanliness and purification fulfil a symbolic func-tion of ordering: as Mary Douglas has argued, 'dirt is essentially disorder. There is no such thing as absolute dirt: it exists in the eye of the beholder . . . Eliminating it is not a negative movement, but a positive effort to organise the environment' (Douglas, 1966:2). Cultural taboos, according to this view, are reproduced in order to secure distinctions. Douglas claims that 'ideas about separating, purifying, demarcating and punishing transgressions have as their main function to impose system on inherently untidy experience' (Douglas, 1966:4). Ideas about pollution operate in accordance with certain *boundaries* and imagined spaces beyond those boundaries where jettisoned objects can be placed: 'the potency of pollution is therefore not an inherent one; it is proportional to the potency of the prohibition that founds it' (Kristeva, 1982:69).

In relation to these anxieties about pollution, the body has been understood to be constituted within and through a system of bound-aries which are integral to wider beliefs about defilement and purifica-tion. The boundaries of the body are invested with feelings of danger and thus passage across them is repeatedly and scrupulously monitored and regulated. The 'jettisoned objects' from the body's interior are expelled to the other side of those boundaries, to the margins, and it is this marginality which remains crucial to the regulation of certain bodily states. Douglas argues that:

> Matter issuing from . . . [the orifices of the body] is marginal stuff of the most obvious kind. Spittle, blood, milk, urine, faeces or tears by simply issuing forth have traversed the boundary of the body . . . The mistake is to treat the bodily margins in isolation from all other margins.
>
> (Douglas, 1966, quoted in Kristeva, 1982:69)

The fixing of the boundaries of the body and the ascription of matter as appropriate to its interior and its exterior contributes to the legitimation of certain subjects over others.

Neither subject nor object, the abject is that which makes us feel 'beside ourselves'. It reminds us of the impossibility of fixing permanent or immutable boundaries between self and other, and of the temporary character of our banishment of undesirable objects. The abject haunts the subject long after it has been banished. The abject:

> signals the fading or disappearance, the absolute mortality and vulnerability of the subject's relation to, and dependence upon, the object. The abject is the impossible object, still part of the subject: an object the subject strives to expel but which is ineliminable. In ingesting objects into itself, or expelling objects from itself, the subject can never be distinct from these objects. The ingested/expelled 'objects' are neither part of the body, nor separate from it.
>
> (Grosz, 1992:198)

The abject, then, is both separate from, and yet part of, the subject. It is that which we want to exclude, but which threatens to re-enter. As such, it is a constant reminder of the mutability of our borders and the vulnerability of the subject.

So how might we extend the implications of Douglas' work on taboo and Kristeva's theories of abjection to 'understand the boundaries of the body as the limits of the socially *hegemonic*' (Butler, 1990:131)? This question demands an argument that extends beyond the details of the individual to consider collective categories. Constructions of groups of abject bodies might thus be considered within a broader set of power relations. For example, Sander Gilman has documented the colonial fascination with Black bodies. He argues that White culture's fascinated disgust with the 'Hotentot Venus' exemplifies its need to construct the Black body as other to the norms of White culture (Gilman, 1992:178–9). Iris Young has also used theories of abjection to analyse how 'the repudiation of bodies for their sex, sexuality, and/or color is an "expulsion" followed by a "repulsion" that founds and consolidates culturally hegemonic identities along sex/race/sexuality axes of differentiation' (Butler, 1990:133).

The instituting of boundaries of inner and outer, of self and other can thus be read in relation to cultural practices that constitute identities as 'Other' and in need of regulation through expulsion. Here, the processes of the foundation of bodily subjectivity are not merely metaphors for the social, but are integral to forms of social regulation and control. Thus the force of social othering derives from the cultural ascription of the bodies of these 'Others' as abject.

Lesbians, for example, have been seen as 'polluted' and their bodily exchanges as 'dangerous' (Butler, 1990:132). These 'powers of horror' operate within the establishment of certain categories as 'uninhabitable', categories which generate the response: *I would rather die than do or be that* (Laplanche and Pontalis, 1967, quoted in Butler, 1993:243; my emphasis). This sense of 'dreaded identification' is articulated repeatedly in relation to those 'abject zones within sociality' which 'threaten the cohesion and the integrity of the subject' (Butler, 1993:243). It is in the context of such explorations of 'dreaded identifications' that I want to consider the ways in which the cultural categories of the C word and the L word might be shot through with fear of what Kristeva has called the abject[20]. As such, both categories generate anxieties about the certainty of the boundaries between subject and object, between normal and abnormal or deviant, between inside and outside, between sameness and difference and between life and death.

> Normal life processes are often directly illuminated by study of the abnormal. This book is another testament to the accuracy of that research adage; for the understanding it will record begins not with the beauties of living form, but with cancer, one of nature's aberrations. The fingers of a newborn child or the pattern of a butterfly's wing represent what we normally admire in biological systems: form; control; a unity of design and function that favors the survival of the organism. In cancer, all of these virtues are lost. *Cancer cells divide without restraint, cross boundaries they were meant to respect,* and fail to display the characteristics of the cell lineage from which they were derived.
>
> (Varmus and Weinberg, 1993:1; my emphasis)

The distinction between the normal and the abnormal is analogised here as that between the life-giving cell and its deathly counterpart. In this opening to *Genes and the Biology of Cancer*, its authors demarcate the significance of controlled cell division (as opposed to promiscuous proliferation) and adherence to tradition (as opposed to foolish youthful experimentation) for the healthy body.

The malignant cell of the cancer tumour is not an invader, an outsider, like a virus or a bacterium; rather, it is produced by the body, it is of the body, and yet it is a threat to the body. Neither self nor other, it is both the same as and different from its host. It is misrecognised as one of the body's normal cells, but it is a deviant cell in innocent disguise. Its deviancy is not immediately detectable, since new cells are produced by the body all the time; indeed, we are told, all cells have proto-oncogenes.[21] The cancer cell is just a self-serving replicant with no duties. It should be an expelled object, but it remains part of the system, travelling incognito. Its facility for self-replication brings it more allies until they outnumber the cells of the organs which house them. The tumour which these rogue cells come to form is part of the body and yet separate from it. It is produced by bodily matter but its redundancy can kill. When it takes hold it can enlarge organs and protrude from the body. It can even transgress bodily boundaries and break through the skin, bringing the inside to the outside. If only it came out immediately and could be routinely cut off like an unruly shoot, perhaps survival might stay within sight. But it hides inside instead, to protect itself until its roots prevent pragmatic amputation. It impersonates the subject long enough to establish the power of its real difference, often until it can overpower its host body.

The figure of the lesbian also features in the homophobic imagination as ignorant of the imperative of difference and desire. To desire another who is perceived as the same troubles the law of difference. If difference and desire are always sure bedfellows, who dares risk a preference for sameness? Too much a part of the subject and yet also an object. Permissible in infancy, perhaps, when merging and sameness were part of nature's harmony, but in later life it is sadly regressive. A return to the blending of self and other. Sexual amorphism that should have been expelled. It will lead to the dissolution of self, to psychosis (Butler, 1990:84). If only we would see that difference is best. The other should be clearly marked. It is reassuringly in balance. Two halves of a whole. 'Adam and Eve, not Adam and Steve' (or Ada and Eve).[22] After all, the male and female body fit so perfectly; we were made that way. Isn't something lacking otherwise? Doubly lacking? Pitifully lacking? Both subject and object of desire, the doubling of femininity confuses the boundaries of desire and identification. Both the same and different, each cannot take its rightful place.

For Kristeva, 'it is thus not lack of cleanliness or health that causes abjection but what disturbs identity, system, order. What does not respect borders, positions, rules. The in-between, the ambiguous, the composite' (Kristeva, 1982:4). If 'abjection is the horror of not knowing the boundaries of distinguishing "me" from "not me"', then this pertains to both the C word and the L word as they have been constructed in the popular imagination of this culture (Chisholm, 1992: 439). The disease characterised by the body's inability to expel the other; the sexuality characterised by the subject's inability to desire the other. Both signify sameness, an excess of sameness that goes against the natural order. Deviant cells and deviant desires both generate a horror of (as well as a fascination with) the presence of the *undifferentiated* that 'must be repelled for fear of self-annihilation' (Creed, 1993:10). In both cases the boundaries between subject and object, self and other, me and not-me are perceived to be murky. Where does one end and the other begin? How can the difference be properly recognised? If that alone could be clarified, order might be maintained. Once believed to be suitably excluded, the abject refuses to let go. Instead it haunts the subject with stories from the borders of the self, both guaranteeing its existence and yet affirming its end. It both summons and repels the subject, it both attracts and horrifies: 'what is *abject* . . . the jettisoned object, is radically excluded and draws me into a place where meaning collapses' (Kristeva, 1982:2). The abject can never be fully rejected: 'while releasing a hold, it does not radically cut off the subject from what threatens it – on the contrary, abjection acknowledges it to be in perpetual danger' (Kristeva, 1982, in Creed, 1993:8).

THE BOUNDARIES BETWEEN LIFE AND DEATH

The end of the subject and of meaning is surely promised by death. Perhaps fear of death is at the root of these cultural anxieties. But it is more than a desire to deny mortality that fuels these fears, although that is also there. Rather, abjection is 'immoral, sinister, scheming and shady: a terror that dissembles, a hatred that smiles, a passion that uses the body for barter instead of inflaming it, a debtor who sells you up, a friend who stabs you' (Kristeva, 1982:4). Indeed, for Kristeva the utmost abjection is not to be found in death itself, but in '*death infecting life*' (Kristeva, 1982:4; my emphasis).

Cells are the kernels of life, the basic units of the body, according to contemporary biological discourse. Life itself, we read, begins with cell division.[23] Cell growth continues throughout our lives. New cells replace old ones, and the cycle of life continues. Cells are formed by division: one becomes two becomes four. The sign of life, cell division promises renewal. Biological textbooks describe how the organism is formed out of a basic pattern of cell division. 'By successive divisions, the zygote [fertilised egg] ultimately gives rise to a large number of descendants that form a complete organism. The cell division of these somatic (nongerm) cells through the process of mitosis ensure the transfer of the entire complement of chromosomes' (Varmus and Weinberg, 1993:5). Continued cell division is necessary throughout life as the cells die and are replaced by new ones, formed through division. Compensating for the loss of the old cells, 'primitive, undifferentiated' cells are continually dividing; as they develop, 'these recently differentiated cells then replace their predecessors' (Varmus and Weinberg, 1993:28).

Cancer is widely understood as a disease of uncontrolled cell growth. The first signs of life are indistinguishable from the first signs of death. Cancer invites an unwelcome visitor into the land of the living. By exaggerating the reproduction of life, cancer introduces the threat of death. Too much life; too many cells; the work of a deadly enthusiast. The body's natural processes of regeneration miss a beat and turn into their opposite. Cancer thus not only promises death but it promises death by the means of life, death by reproduction. Cancer is 'death infecting life' by the means of life itself. By reproducing life, it reproduces death. The source of life that destroys, cancer echoes the horrors of abjection.

But what is distinctive about the malignant cell, as opposed to the benign one? If division is necessary for the regeneration of life, how does it come to be the source of death? The fatal flaw seems to reside in differentiation, or the lack of it. It is often the 'undifferentiated cells' that are blamed for threatening uncontrolled growth, leading to tumour formation. The language of 'differentiation', 'dedifferentiation' and 'redifferentiation' pervades biomedical explanations of cancer. According to some, '*by definition* there is no such thing as undifferentiated cells' since they all 'exhibit certain morphological features and perform certain functions' (Schjeide and de Vellis, 1970:2). A more accurate term might be 'uncommitted' in the sense that some cells are capable of further differentiation (Schjeide and de Vellis, 1970:2). For others, the 'origin of undifferentiated cells' is important in the basic understanding of how cancer cells work (Varmus and Weinberg, 1993:38); indeed, in this model 'the more undifferentiated and atypical the cells ... the greater the potential danger of their continued proliferation' (Varmus and Weinberg, 1993:28–9). Cancer cells are thus designated as lacking 'the differentiated, specialized traits of their ancestors' (Varmus and Weinberg, 1993:38). At worst, they form a 'fully undifferentiated jumble of cells' and do not 'respect territorial boundaries', generating growth in other organs (Varmus and Weinberg, 1993:29).[24]

If only the body could be relied upon to recognise the difference between self and other, then deviant cell replication might be nipped in the bud. The failure to identify the malignant cell as a threat puts the body at risk from an internal outsider. But how did this masquerading traitor gain acceptance? Like the kiss of Judas, its generosity masks a desire to destroy its keeper. 'Abjection is elaborated through a failure to recognize its kin; nothing is familiar, not even a shadow of a memory' (Kristeva, 1982:5); cancer is a disease of misrecognition of legitimate familial members. The dread of betrayal is finally confirmed. Loyalties can no longer be relied upon. In these representations of the human body it fails to differentiate itself from an alien presence. Abjection works 'as a means of separating out the human from the non-human and the fully constituted subject from the partially formed subject' (Creed 1993:8). The malignant growth threatens to cross the borders between the normal and the deviant and expose their mutability. Cancer is a poor imitation of the self, mimicking cell division but without sufficient differentiation and with potentially deathly consequences: 'this loss of differentiated traits often signals the presence of what is termed a high-grade, aggressive tumour' (Varmus and Weinberg, 1993:38).

The treatments for cancer extend this confusion further; radiotherapy destroys as it heals, chemotherapy pollutes as it cleanses. To kill the cancer cells the body is pumped full of poison. As pint after pint of liquid enters intravenously, cells are destroyed in their millions. The veins offer convenient transport for the 'alien' fluids. Each chemical damages different parts of the body which are left in shock. All fast-growing cells must die, benign and malignant, regardless of origin, regardless of purpose. The only hope is to wipe out the lot. The faster growing the tumour, the greater its vulnerability to such attack. The quicker it can kill you, the more likely you are to outlive it. The cocktail of chemicals, as they call it, is especially effective; mutually reinforcing, three drugs work better than one. But they have trouble spotting the enemy; all rapid cell growth is a potential threat, hair or tumour, skin or tumour, stomach lining or tumour. The damage is regrettable, but unavoidable. There is no time for choice. The poisons rush in and wipe out originals and replicants alike. Neither the body's defences nor the medical cure can recognise the disease for what it is.

In threatening death, cancer echoes the beginnings of life, for the malignant cells resemble those of embryonic development: 'the relatively undifferentiated state of certain tumour cells is reminiscent of the state of embryonic cells prior to their specialization during development' (Varmus and Weinberg, 1993:38). Malignant cells are seen to be regressive, adopting inappropriately immature behaviour for adult cells; they are described as reverting 'to a more primitive state of differentiation' and evolving 'backward, shedding many of its attributes and specialized functions that it and its forebears acquired during embryonic development' (Varmus and Weinberg, 1993:38). This process of what is often called 'dedifferentiation' leads to excessive cell division, we are told, since 'most fully differentiated cells have lost their ability to divide' (Varmus and Weinberg, 1993:39).

Unnatural by virtue of its separation from reproduction, lesbian sexuality is seen to refuse the sacred connection between love and life. Homophobic discourse constitutes lesbian sexuality not as deadly in any literal sense perhaps, but certainly as non-life-giving. Most sexual encounters aren't life-giving, of course, but the idea that they might be, or could, or would be, still matters. Reproductionless sex tastes of death in a culture governed by the heterosexual imperative. The rhetorical devices commonly used to ridicule and devalue lesbianism become tedious refrains: where are the future generations to come from?

Wherein lies the guarantee against extinction? Not in sexual acts between women certainly. Instead, we are told, they offer but a shallow mockery of the life-giving act, a futile and narcissistic act of pleasure. Mere self-indulgence. Autoeroticism is bad enough, but with another such self it is simply irresponsible. This barren mirroring reeks of futility. What can two barren spinsters possibly reproduce that is of use to future generations? Cancer may be generative of death, but lesbianism is generative of emptiness. Fundamentally sterile, it cannot even generate itself. These vicious reproaches are reiterated in different forms in the discourses of compulsory heterosexuality that pervade contemporary anxieties about sexual deviancy.[25]

REVOLTING BODIES

It is the crossing of the border between I/other and between inside and outside that truly disgusts; not death, then, but that which must be eradicated in order to live:

> A wound with blood and pus, or the sickly, acrid smell of sweat, of decay, does not *signify* death. In the presence of signified death – a flat encephalograph, for instance – I would understand, react, or accept. No, as in true theatre, without makeup or masks, refuse and corpses *show me* what I permanently thrust aside in order to live. These bodily fluids, this defilement, this shit are what life withstands, hardly and with difficulty on the part of death. There I am at the border of my condition as a living being. My body extricates itself, as being alive, from that border.
>
> (Kristeva, 1982:3)

There are times when such an extrication proves more than difficult. Cancer may bring such times closer. The abject bodily wastes of 'blood, shit, vomit, saliva, sweat, tears' become the currency of everyday life. What did you do today? Cleared up vomit, measured urine, wiped away tears, gave more blood, inserted suppositories; what about you? The abject is that which is hidden through these rituals of purification.

Bodily revulsion is the sign of abjection. 'Food loathing is perhaps the most elementary and archaic form of abjection; like the skin on warmed milk, it is refused with complete aversion' (Kristeva, 1982:2). Nausea accompanies such refusals: 'I experience a gagging sensation, and still further down, spasms in the stomach, the belly; and all the organs shrivel up the body, provoke tears and bile, increase the heartbeat, cause forehead and hands to perspire' (Kristeva, 1982:3).

The abject dimensions of the body and connected matter is the subject of Cindy Sherman's 'disgust pictures' of the late 1980s. In these, Sherman offers a troubled exploration of the monstrousness of the 'ruined' body. She stages the other side of the 'cosmetic facade' of femininity (see 'Untitled' nos 190 and 239 in Krauss, 1993:156 and 149 respectively): 'the interior of the female body is projected as a kind of lining of bodily disgust – of blood, of excreta, of mucous membranes' (Krauss, 1993:192). Not the smooth glossy surfaces of the perfect, youthful, desirable body, but rather we see the hidden corporeal processes in need of exclusion to achieve such effects (Mulvey, 1991). In 'Untitled no. 190' the sticky mass has engulfed the face of grotesque proportions: the raw and the digested, the internal and the external intermingle. Brought into view from behind the usual screens, we see 'sexual detritus, decaying food, vomit, slime, menstrual blood and hair' (Mulvey, 1991:148). It is hard to distinguish human from non-human, self from other, use from waste and life from death. Exploring the limits around what is acceptably representable, Sherman shows those things hidden from the public display of the desirable body. The wastes usually banished from view are shown here, sometimes in plastic close-up, sometimes buried in an abject jumble; either way, the spectator is invited to explore their horrified intrigue, their fascinated disgust.

To survive, we strive to move beyond these corporeal reminders of our origin and our fate. We banish the fear which such matter-out-of-place represents:

> that word 'fear' – a fluid haze, an elusive clamminess – no sooner has it cropped up than it shades off like a mirage and permeates all words of the language with nonexistence, with a hallucinatory, ghostly glimmer. Thus fear having been bracketed, discourse will seem tenable only if it ceaselessly confronts that otherness, a burden both repellent and repelled, a deep well of memory that is unapproachable and intimate.
>
> (Kristeva, 1982:6)

But these are times when fear lingers longer than usual and banishment to the borders feels less and less likely. Cancer and its treatment may intervene in the reassuring rituals of purification which keep the body in its rightful place.

Chemotherapy disturbs the conventional flows of the body and its fluids. The chemicals that race through the micro-system of veins in the body produce a violent reaction. The regulation of corporeal boundaries quickly becomes impossible. The stomach is turned inside out, its lining destroyed, its fast-growing cells of necessity wiped out. Nausea becomes a way of life. It ebbs to a permanent tightness in the back of the throat and flows to waves of vomiting which, unlike childhood vomiting, bring no relief. On the arrival of another dose, the vomiting increases to several times a day, or several times an hour, with monotonous regularity, until only bile is left. And still the vomiting continues. Retching until watering eyes turn to tears. Vomit, tears and mucous mix in the bowl for immediate inspection. But the nauseous stomach also longs for food. Like the pregnant woman, the chemotherapy patient craves sugar and carbohydrates. Steroids increase this desire to excess. An incongruously insatiable appetite accompanies the constant nausea. A hungry tapeworm sits eagerly in wait, ready to devour. But food calms the burning stomach only to be regurgitated. The inside of the body is desperate to escape. It surges towards all possible exits. But the bladder and the colon nerves are also under siege and cannot function. Choked by the poisons, the deadened nerves do not respond to the urgency of the desired escape from within. Sometimes days and days of numbness are followed by such long and sharp pain when the nerves come alive. Until then the only chance is up the oesophagus, to be vomited to freedom. The body's flows are set in reverse: where food should enter, vomit exits; where waste should exit, suppositories enter.

Then the hair dies. Sitting on the head like the nylon wig promised for the future, it changes texture, shape and tone. Dead hair, but still attached, mimicking its former living self. Part of the live body, yet a sign of decline. It dies first and then falls. The first handful is an alarming relief. Then more and more. So much dead hair. It fills the bed, it covers pillows and sheets. Every day the bed must be swept. It fills the bath. It forms a thick, dark matted layer on the bath water. But it refuses to separate when the water cools and the body moves to go. Separate but clinging onto the body in a desperate attempt not to be left behind. The hair must be removed in a sieve before the body can abandon it as waste. Finally free, the body surfaces more naked than before, having lost another layer of protection. The head sweats constantly with no layer of hair to absorb it; the body chills quickly with no hair to warm it.

As the hair on the rest of the body slowly falls too, all borders between inside and outside are laid bare. The loss of pubic hair reveals what has remained hidden for years. Returned to pre-adolescence and yet prefiguring an aged body, time has nothing to tell. The nose runs intermittently with nothing to stop it. Without the tiny nostril hairs, no warning is sensed. Adults with 'runny noses'. Sweat runs into the eyes without eyebrows or eyelashes to catch it. Ears are tunnels for flies and insects to enter at their ease. Only half darkness is possible without the eyelashes to block out the light. The hairless body is uncannily silky smooth to touch. A familar and yet strange state. A return to childhood and yet an inevitable ageing. A big bald baby but with adult organs.

The skin is overburdened.[26] It represents the interface between inside and outside and is the body's ambassador: it meets the world. Without its protective covering of hair it is exposed. It must work harder. But the drugs rush outward towards the edges of the body and nothing is spared. The skin develops rashes, red and itching. Wild scratching becomes a vicious cycle. The nails try to scrape away the irritant. Another drug brings relief, but the scratch marks become scars and stay, a permanent reminder. As far as the hands could reach, long marks bear witness to the allergic reaction and continue to do so. Dermographia. Skin drawing. The hot flushes rush to fill the rest of the body. The burning heat rises from the stomach until the upper body is coloured in with red. Sweat pours. The heat tingles. Menopausal foreshadowings. They have no sense of occasion and appear at random. A sign of hormonal disturbance for all to see.

Trapped inside the body in revolt, there is no escape. The body becomes the only reality. Its limits are no longer visible. To think would be a relief, to speak a rebellion, to move thoughts beyond the body a desperate desire. The claustrophobia of internality. This matter is all I am. There is no other, no external. I am engulfed. And yet it is not me at all. An 'alien' body taken over by another, my awareness of it results from its strangeness. It is not the familiar body of thirty years or more, whose rhythms and routines I barely notice. Corporeal alterations have occurred of horrific proportions. Instead it has become an unfamiliar body which refuses the usual behaviours. The inverse of the 'clean and proper' body produced through rituals of cleanliness after years of training, this body has lost its form and its integrity, it has become abject. The breakdown of the system means the reversal of predictable directions: what belongs inside is violently pushed out; what should be expelled is stubbornly retained. I suffer it, but am absent. Who is the I of these bodily functions and misfunctions, the adult I who is recognised by others and reconises herself? Unwillingly returned to a preoccupation with bodily matter, the adult self is simultaneously drawn backwards into infancy and forwards towards death. The bodily turmoil has no definite results. It promises life and yet feels like the beginnings of death. It destroys in order to preserve. The body is poisoned with the hope of recovery.

THE MONSTROUS MATERNAL

[The abject] signals the precarious grasp the subject has over its identity and bodily boundaries, the ever-present possibility of sliding back into the corporeal abyss from which it was formed.

(Grosz, 1992:198)

The 'corporeal abyss from which it was formed', as Grosz puts it, returns us to the question of the maternal body, the body to which we were once connected. For some, our desire to escape abjection has its roots in a fear of the mother's body. But if we want to place the maternal body firmly in the realm of the cultural (rather than reiterate its biological and essentially asocial meaning), then we must insist on this connection as a construction marked by patriarchal culture (Butler, 1990:80–7); we must ask, as Laura Mulvey does: 'by what means of turning is the mother's interior associated with decay' (Mulvey, 1991:146)? Further, how and why has the maternal body been ascribed the 'powers of horror' and why is it 'the female body that has come, not exclusively but predominantly, to represent the shudder aroused by liquidity and decay' (Mulvey, 1991:146)?

For Kristeva, if 'the body must bear no debt to nature', if 'it must be clean and proper in order to be fully symbolic', then it must rid itself of all traces of its maternal connection (Kristeva, 1982:102). To enter the Symbolic Order, the subject must separate from the maternal body in order to achieve autonomy: 'a separation founded on feelings of disgust against the unclean and the undifferentiated' (Krauss, 1993:193). The maternal figure is thus constructed as abject and turned into a terrifying spectre who may protect the child from the burdens of responsibility, but also may prevent the proper individuation by clinging on greedily to her offspring. Seductively comforting, yet stiflingly claustrophobic, the maternal body continues to tempt and to repel in a patriarchal culture so bent on individuation and order. As Elisabeth Grosz asks:

> Can it be that in the West, in our time, the female body has been constructed not only as a lack or absence but with more complexity, as a leaking, uncontrollable, seeping liquid; as a formless flow; as a viscosity, entrapping, secreting; as lacking not so much or simply the phallus, but self-containment – not a cracked or porous vessel, like a leaking ship, but a formlessness that engulfs all form, a disorder that threatens all order?
>
> (Grosz, 1994:203)

The female body has been turned into a particular focus for suspicion in contemporary culture, argues Creed; 'deceptively treacherous', what appears 'pure and beautiful on the outside' may be 'rotten inside' (Creed, 1993:43). The ritual expulsion of the abject in patriarchal culture is manifested specifically in a dread of the interior of the female body and its generative power. Not being what it appears, hiding something inside, concealing its truth from the world, the body which can simultaneously be both one and more than one is repeatedly represented as a threat to the world of boundaries and individuation.

The taboo against desire between women in patriarchal culture also returns us to the maternal and to fears about its hold on us. To desire another commonly perceived as the same as the self is seen as a return to early maternal harmonies and to a lack of differentiation: a yearned for, but terrifying, memory. Reaching beyond the paternal law of difference and separation, and beyond the autonomy of 'the clean and proper body' produced by the order established by drawing a 'boundary between feminine and masculine' (Creed, 1993:25), lesbianism is seen to be a narcissistic romance with the self; its only 'other' is seen to be the imitative other of another feminine body (see Thynne, 1995). The difference which may produce lesbian desire remains unrecognised within homophobic discourse and instead same-sex desire is placed firmly on the side of similarity. The threat of maternal subsumption thus produces an anxiety about the perceived lack of difference between femininities. According to this logic, 'the desire to return to the original oneness of things, to return to the mother/womb, is primarily a desire for non-differentiation' (Creed, 1993:28).

Femininity and death are given symbolic connection through such analogies (Bronfen, 1992). The lesbian refusal of sexual association with life-saving masculinity is thus construed in patriarchal culture as suicidal narcissism. The desire for intimacy with another of the 'same sex' is thus represented as a symbolic death, an opting out of the pleasing processes of individuation. In the homophobic imagination the lesbian figure moves easily into a ghostly realm in which deathly femininity is doubly threatening.[27] As Creed argues, 'fear of losing oneself and one's boundaries is made more acute in a society which values boundaries over continuity and separateness over sameness' (Creed, 1993:29). The monstrousness of lesbian desire lies in its perceived devotion to sameness and continuity, which threaten to return the subject to a merging state with the maternal body.

The disgust lesbianism evokes may also be seen as a disgust with the maternal body in the perception of its most cloying manifestations and desires: do two femininities together produce a terror of unboundaried bodies? Perhaps the fear of lesbianism is not just a fear of a return to the maternal body and the threat of merging that such nostalgia evokes, but is also a fear of the generative potential of the maternal body in a mirrored bliss with itself. And what of reproduction? The cultural contempt for reproductionless sex (of the lesbian lovers) slides into the fear of its opposite: the parthenogenetic potential of femininity doubled. The feminine thus represents the possibility of excess, the possibility of being in excess of the self. Doubled, there is no guarantee of an ending, of separation or of stability. Too intense and too intimate. Fertility thus promises life, but also threatens to disrupt the boundaries of the body and of the self which are so central to a sense of order and systematicity. The generative power of the maternal has been constituted within the popular imagination as something awesome but terrifying. While the maternal is assumed to be connected to, and ultimately regulated by, paternal authority, it also has manifestations which suggest an autogenerative capacity.

The pregnant body especially defies these ideals of masculine individuation since it is more than one, but not yet two people.[28] Producing chaos and confusion in a culture of individuals, the pregnant woman has disturbed the conventional categories of subject and object, of self and other. What comes to represent the focus of this dread is the woman's 'monstrous womb' (Creed, 1992:43). Creed suggests that 'the womb represents the utmost in abjection for it contains a new life form which will pass from inside to outside bringing with it traces of its contamination – blood, afterbirth, faeces' (Creed, 1992:49). Thus, she argues:

87

[W]oman's womb is viewed as horrifying . . . because . . . it houses an alien life form, it causes alterations in the body, it leads to the act of birth . . . [The] womb . . . within patriarchal discourse . . . has been used to represent woman's body as marked, impure and a part of the natural/animal world.

(Creed, 1992:49)

The grotesqueness of the fertility of femininity lies in such disturbances:

the grotesque body . . . represents either the fertile depths or the convexities of procreation and conception. It swallows and generates, gives and takes. Such a body, composed of fertile depths and procreative convexities is never clearly differentiated from the world but is transferred, merged and fused with it.

(Bakhtin, 1984, in Dentith, 1995:244)

Pregnancy is frequently represented as a 'grotesque' state because of the perceived loss of boundaries which such a state represents in a culture so keen to secure them at the bodily level.[29] Indeed, the act of giving birth is seen as grotesque in so far as the body reveals its innermost depths. For Bakhtin, this grotesque body 'is ambivalent. It is pregnant death, a death that gives birth' (Bakhtin, 1984, quoted in Dentith, 1995:68). In his exploration of grotesque imagery Bakhtin stresses the connections between the body and other kinds of matter: 'the grotesque body . . . is a body in the act of becoming. It is never finished, never completed; it is continually built, created, and builds and creates another body. Moreover, the body swallows the world and is itself swallowed by the world' (Bakhtin, 1984, in Dentith, 1995:226). The grotesque body is a revolting, yet fascinating, counterpart to the twentieth-century Western body ideal with its clear and finished image. In a culture struggling towards bodily perfectability and control, the grotesque body reminds us of the internality we would rather forget and threatens to return us to a place we believed we had escaped.

Grotesque bodies are explored in the work of Cindy Sherman. Her 'performance' of the grotesque hybridity of the human/pig 'self-portrait' in 'Untitled no. 140' can be seen in Krauss (1993:144)[30]. Fascinated by the incongruity of this transformation, the spectator is troubled by the recombinant face, especially where human hand is raised to pig's mouth. To quote Bakhtin again:

Of all the features of the human face, nose and mouth play the most important part in the grotesque image of the body; the head, ears, and nose also acquire a grotesque character when they adopt the animal form or that of inanimate objects . . . Special attention is given to the shoots and branches, to all that prolongs the body and links it to other bodies or to the world outside.

(Bakhtin, 1984, in Dentith, 1995:226)

In 'Untitled no. 187' (see Figure 3.1) the monstrousness of pregnancy is suggested in the exaggerated plastic belly and breasts of the female form. A face threatens to emerge from the middle of the belly, pushing through the surface of the abdomen towards the outside, refusing the usual birth channels. The baby-like feet are positioned as if in the process of birth, but they could also be an extension of the grotesque 'mother'. The bodies are disturbing in their lack of individuality and their confusing relationships to procreation. The 'mother' figure looks down at the spectator (and the baby?) through the ridiculous mask of a clown with protruding nose, and her blonde hair and made-up eyes turn the masquerade of femininity into a grotesque performance.[31] Sherman's work shows less a Bakhtinian sense of playful celebration of the materiality of the body than a troubled, if parodic, exploration of the monstrousness of its mutability. Displaced and oversized body parts, uncontrolled organ growth and distorted recombinations both fascinate and repulse the viewer.

TALES OF MONSTROUS BIRTHS

Cancer and pregnancy have both been described as abject conditions by Kristeva (Kristeva, 1980:11). As such they are both 'borderline states in which there is confusion and lack of distinction between subject and object' (Grosz, 1992:198). Kristeva's account of changes to the female body in pregnancy is indistinguishable in this extract from a description of tumour growth:

> Cells fuse, split, and proliferate; volumes grow, tissues stretch, and the body fluids change rhythm, speeding up or slowing down. Within the body, growing as a graft, indomitable, there is another. And no one is present, within that simultaneously dual and alien space, to signify what is going on.
>
> (Kristeva, quoted in Grosz, 1990:95)

More than one, but less than two, the reassuring boundaries of self and other are lost in an unsettling haze. The malignant cells which belong to the self and yet are other to it, and indeed threaten its existence, disturb the subject's space. Pregnancy, too, shows the body hosting another that parasitically grows from the maternal body's apparently endless generative source. A borderline state which threatens the subject: 'live limb of a skeleton, monstrous graft of life on myself, a living dead. Life ... death ... undecidable ... My removed marrow, which nevertheless acts as a graft, which wounds but increases me' (Kristeva, quoted in Grosz, 1990:95). The foetus and the tumour are both constituted by cell growth. Normal and deviant divide their purpose, but cell division unites their mode of expansion. The analogy

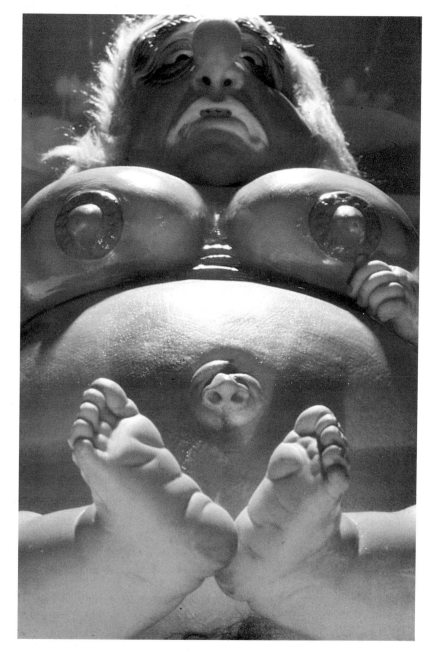

Figure 3.1 Cindy Sherman, 1989, 'Untitled no. 187'
Source: Krauss, 1993

becomes a mimetic image in the case of the teratoma, whose germ cell origins imitate pregnancy and release the same hormonal indicators. The teratoma tumour may even develop differentiated cells and show hair, teeth and nails on birth: a monstrous birth, delivered to the waiting medical gaze (Figures 3.2 and 3.3). With pregnancy and cancer, where is the certainty of separation? When is the cord really cut? The tumour promises separation after its surgical delivery into the world; yet the bond continues with the threat that some malignant cells remain in the warmth of the body to shelter from outside attack. The foetus is delivered but when is separation achieved? At what point are mother and infant independent of each other, and at what point is the cancer patient given the all-clear? Is there always an echo of attachment, is there always the possibility of return to that abject state of more-than-oneness with another?

Distinct in their respective associations with death and life, cancer and pregnancy represent opposite ends of the inevitable continuum which connect the two. Pregnancy might be understood as a state which is both romanticised and reviled in a culture in which the potential source of life also reminds us of the inevitability of its end. The loss of autonomy threatens a complete loss of self. In the case of cancer, regression is not just threatened by death itself, but by the infantalising processes of dependency. The loss of hair returns the body to a nascent state, fusing birth and death in the uncanny adult figure with the bald body. Collapsing the boundaries between the stages of maturity and compressing the temporal teleologies of the life cycle, cancer brings death into life, not just by its ultimate promise, but by the transformations it imposes on the adult body. In both states, the body is characterised by the threat of non-differentiation: where does the self end and the other begin?

Teratomas, being cancers of the germ cell (the egg or the sperm), mimic 'the beginning of life' with apparently authentic authority. The endodermal sinus tumour is characterised by 'aggregates of undifferentiated neoplastic cells ("embryonal cells")' (Fox and Langley, 1976:196). Egg cell division, after all, is the original story of 'life'. The Adam and Eve of contemporary biological discourse, the egg and the sperm are the specialized cells which need each other to be complete. Through a process called 'meiosis' the germ cells 'reduce their number of chromosomes by half' and become haploid cells, or gametes. When combining, the egg and the sperm are said to form a single cell 'with a complete and unique diploid set of chromosomes, half from each parent' (Varmus and Weinberg, 1993:5). But the teratoma goes it alone. Too impatient to wait for the correct pairing of opposites (the natural union of the two sexes), cell division in this case begins not the process of creation but that of potential destruction. The unfertilised egg

Figure 3.2 Mature cystic teratoma of the ovary. Note the prominent mamilla, large amount of hair and sebaceous material
Source: Jacobsen and Talerman, 1989:165

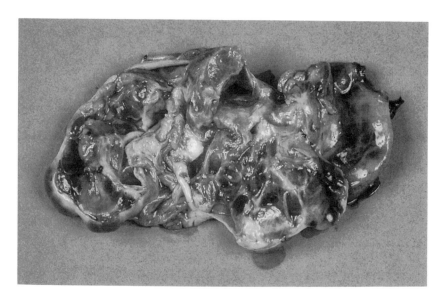

Figure 3.3 Struma ovarii. Note the numerous cysts of various sizes containing glistening colloid
Source: Jacobsen and Talerman, 1989:165

divides and tries to compensate for the lack of the masculine counter-part. But such parthenogenetic presumptions can only lead to trouble. This deviant foetus threatens the mother's body by destroying its internal 'social' order: 'the energies of these cells are directed exclusively toward their own proliferation, they no longer focus on helping to build a functional organ or tissue' (Varmus and Weinberg, 1993:38). Reproduction is replaced by narcissistic replication as function is outweighed by the reckless proliferation of aberrations. Not the healthy 'offspring' referred to in the textbooks, but the deviant daughters that spell destruction and social disintegration.

'Teratology' refers to the study of monsters. It is the study of abnormality and deviancy. Both marvels and freaks, monsters are the fascinating other against which the normal can be constituted (Grosz, 1991). Tracking the history of teratology, Rosi Braidotti argues that since the nineteenth century 'bodily malformations have been defined in terms of excess, lack or displacement of organs . . . following the classification system of monstrosity by Geoffroy Saint-Hilaire' (Braidotti, 1994:77–80). Braidotti's interest in the history of teratology arises from the fact that 'the constitution of teratology as a science offers a paradigmatic example of the ways in which scientific rationality dealt with differences of a bodily kind' (Braidotti, 1994:77–8). Significantly, teratology is the 'forerunner of modern embryology' (Braidotti, 1994:84). The associations of femininity and teratology have a long philosophical and scientific tradition. Going far beyond the generally problematic representation of 'woman' as the sign of 'otherness' or 'difference' in patriarchal culture, the role of the feminine in the development of the science of monsters also reveals a deeper connection. Drawing on the work of Foucault and Canguilhem, Braidotti highlights the centrality of questions of conception, origins and reproduction to the history of teratology: 'the *conception* of monsters is what really haunts the scientific imagination' (Braidotti, 1994:83, my emphasis). The mother is thus implicated in the reproduction of monsters; but more than this, her imagination is seen to play a part in its generation: 'the mother was said to have the actual power of producing a monstrous baby simply by (a) *thinking* about awful things during intercourse . . . (b) *dreaming* very intensely about something or somebody; or (c) *looking* at animals or evil-looking creatures' (Braidotti, 1994:86). Thus, not only is the generative function of woman in general perceived to be threatening, but also 'it is as if the mother, as a desiring agent, has the power to undo the legitimate procreation through the sheer force of her imagination' (Braidotti, 1994:86).

A 'teratogeny', or monstrous birth, questions the conventional wisdom of the beauty of creation. It turns the world upside down and the body inside out. Deviations and aberrations abound. The imagination runs riot. Margaret Atwood's short story 'Hairball' explores responses to one such monstrous birth. The fascination and repulsion that characterise the abject are vested in the two principal characters: Kat is intrigued and Ger is disgusted. The story begins thus:

> On the thirteenth of November, day of unluck, month of the dead, Kat went into the Toronto General Hospital for an operation. It was for an ovarian cyst, a large one.
>
> Many women had them, the doctor told her. Nobody knew why. There wasn't any way of finding out whether the thing was malignant, whether it contained, already, spores of death. Not before they went in. He spoke of 'going in' the way she'd heard old veterans in TV documentaries speak of assaults on enemy territory. There was the same tensing of the jaw, the same fierce gritting of the teeth, the same grim enjoyment. Except that what he would be going into was her body. Counting down, waiting for the anaesthetic, Kat too gritted her teeth fiercely. She was terrified, but also she was curious. Curiosity has got her through a lot.
>
> She'd made the doctor promise to save the thing for her, whatever it was, so she could have a look. She was intensely interested in her own body, in anything it might choose to do or produce; although when flaky Dania, who did layout at the magazine, told her this growth was a message to her from her body and she ought to sleep with an amethyst under her pillow to calm her vibrations, Kat told her to stuff it.
>
> The cyst turned out to be a benign tumour. Kat liked that use of *benign*, as if the thing had a soul and wished her well. It was big as a grapefruit, the doctor said. 'Big as a coconut,' said Kat. Other people had grapefruits. 'Coconut' was better. It conveyed the hardness of it and the hairiness, too.
>
> The hair on it was red – long strands of it wound round and round inside, like a ball of wet wool gone berserk or like the guck you pulled out of a clogged bathroom-sink drain. There were little bones in it too, or fragments of bone; bird bones, the bones of a sparrow crushed by a car. There was a scattering of nails, toe or finger. There were five perfectly formed teeth.
>
> 'Is this abnormal?' Kat asked the doctor, who smiled. Now that he had gone in and come out again, unscathed, he was less clenched.
>
> 'Abnormal? No,' he said carefully, as if breaking the news to a mother about a freakish accident to her newborn. 'Let's just say it is fairly common.' Kat was a little disappointed. She would have preferred uniqueness.

She asked for a bottle of formaldehyde, and put the cut open tumour into it. It was hers, it was benign, it did not deserve to be thrown away. She took it back to her apartment and stuck it on the mantelpiece. She named it Hairball. It isn't that different from having a stuffed bear's head or a preserved ex-pet or anything else with fur and teeth looming over your fireplace; or she pretends it isn't. Anyway, it certainly makes an impression.

Ger doesn't like it. Despite his supposed yen for the new and outré, he is a squeamish man. The first time he comes around (sneaks around, creeps around) after the operation, he tells Kat to throw Hairball out. He calls it 'disgusting'. Kat refuses point-blank, and says she'd rather have Hairball in a bottle on her mantelpiece than the soppy dead flowers he's bought her, which will anyway rot a lot sooner than Hairball will. As a mantelpiece ornament, Hairball is far superior.

(Atwood, 1991:41–3)

Cancer is dreaded as a disease of undifferentiated cells endlessly reproducing themselves, robbing the body of its internal recognition of subjects and objects. It is seen as a disease in which tumours threaten to break through the borders of the body and set its functions in reverse. Chemotherapy strips the body of its adult coverings and removes any sense of control over entry to, and exit from, its interior; the dread of the lack of differentiation; the return to the maternal state where the mergence of self and other threatens existence itself. The monstrousness of the figure of the lesbian reaches into unconscious depths to gain momentum. Both too feminine and too masculine in a homophobic culture, the lesbian disturbs the boundaries of sexual difference. Femininity doubled promises dreaded reabsorption, the suffocating maternal merging of like with like. Yet uncannily masculine in desiring women, the lesbian is also beyond the category 'woman'. Not dependent upon, but usurping, the masculine prerogative, lesbian desires echo the autonomy of masculinity, but remain only an imitative copy.[32]

Monsters involve some kind of doubling of the human form, a duplication of the body or some of its parts. The major terata recognised throughout history are largely monsters of excess, with two or more heads, bodies, or limbs; duplicated sexual organs . . . it is a horror at the possibility of our own imperfect duplication, a horror of submersion in an alien otherness, an incorporation in and by an other.

(Grosz, 1991:36)

The figurative speculations in this chapter have gestured towards the possible source of that bodily chill evoked by cancer, that physical shudder already so familiar to me: the L word had laid the emotional traces some years before. I thus found myself both strangely prepared for, and yet painfully shocked by, the horrors of the C word.

4

BODIES

The final pages are handwritten by quill pen. The ink is bright red blood. A sense of achievement fills the air. It is complete. The years of anguish are over. The release has a calming effect; it is done, I can let go. The end of the thesis. The flesh of the argument and of my body simultaneously knit together. The surgical binding closes the bisected abdominal wall as the conclusions of the project settle into place. The loose threads of the thesis and of the operation are tied up. The completed work of surgeon and academic harmonise: as the two walls touch, the wound begins to heal; as the finishing touches are applied, the ideas cohere on the page. Cells proliferate, tissues enmesh; concepts connect, resolution is achieved. A new beginning born out of a pleasing ending. Total satisfaction.

I awoke from the anaesthetic still in the throes of this dream. Amidst the postoperative nausea, I had the distinct feeling of completion. I could still see the red words on the page to prove it. I had done it. In the memory of this dream the processes of my mind and my body are fused. Under anaesthetic vivid imaginative narratives had played across the screen in which my body had provided the writing material – blood – which enabled the final words of an intellectual project to be written. The abdominal walls and the argument became analogous, providing interchangeable metaphors for processes of closure and completion. The work on the body and the work on the mind, instead of being in competition or conflict, were no longer distinguishable, but were operating together in harmony. The dream thus offered the classic Freudian wish-fulfilment on both counts: a completed PhD and successful surgery.

In addition to the lingering feelings entangled in the memory of this dream, another sensation pervaded. On waking from surgery I felt as if I had actually witnessed the operation; I had watched my body cut open and then stitched together. The clear sense of my internal body occupied my mind and, indeed, remained with me for several months. I felt sure I had seen inside myself and thus had an awareness of my body as 'flesh and blood' in a more literal way that was quite new. On leaving hospital, I began to see everyone through this physiological lens. This imagined iconography of the landscape of organs was incongruous with my sense of people's lives, including my own. It seemed impossible to reconcile the overwhelming feeling that we are just 'a bunch of cells and tissue' which might go wrong at any time, as mine had just done, with the knowledge of the 'personalities', what we think of as the uniqueness of the people themselves. I began to see everyone through these new X-ray eyes: the woman in front of me in the supermarket queue suddenly comprised skin, intestine, bladder, liver, lungs and kidneys.

WHAT IS REMEMBERED IN THE BODY IS REMEMBERED WELL

(Scarry, 1985:110)

When the body has been through trauma, our memory of it has a physical presence for weeks, months or even years after. Of course sometimes this is because of its lasting physical effects (for example, new limits to the body and its capacities). But there is something more than this: the somatic presence of the memory that reaches beyond the physical symptom. Like the kinaesthetic sense of which we are barely conscious and yet without which we struggle to function in the world, these 'bodily memories' are an invisible, yet tangible, presence (Scarry, 1985:110).[1] In such cases, remembrance may take a physical form in advance of any intellectual recognition of an association with the past.

Much writing on the subject of trauma and memory investigates the ways in which the shock of the trauma means that the experience of 'the events' can often not be fully held in the memory (see Caruth, 1995). As I discussed in Chapter 1, this produces both the desire repeatedly to retell the story, and the impossibility of ever achieving a satisfactory sense of having been witnessed. The traumatised person may find themselves rehearsing the impact of the shock through the reaction of another, yet needing to keep retelling new witnesses because their own shock continues to circulate within their emotional repertoire. There is often an ambivalent sense of both wanting to 'relive' and 'recapture' traumatic events, and yet there is psychic resistance to such a return. This is partly because the person wishes to forget and escape the trauma and partly because they may have absented themselves in some way from the traumatic event at the time as a way of coping with the physical and psychic pain. Hence, in the retrospective reconstruction of the narrative, the subject of the trauma may defer to another person who was present, if there was one, as a witness to the traumatic event at which they themselves were partially absent.[2]

My own memory of the the time I was ill is full of gaps, condensations and substitutions: not only do I get confused about the time-scale and sequence of events, but I have no memory whatsoever of some events which others have since related to me. This may be a result of the mechanisms of denial which protect the subject from the full emotional impact of extreme distress; or it may be part of the latency period of delayed shock (see Chapter 1). The memory loss one might expect about a period of physical trauma is compounded by the effect of some chemotherapy drugs. I now experience intermittent interference in my everyday memory function; like a faulty television, my memory sometimes goes blank for a minute or two, in relation to names, events and conversations.

What is just as striking as the loss of memory associated with trauma is the endurance and sensation of the consequent 'bodily memories'. There is a transformation of bodily perception that persists after the immediate trauma of the illness has passed. The desire to forget cannot overcome the stubborn presence of bodily memory. This is the physical dimension of what Cathy Caruth refers to as the 'return of the event against the will of the one it inhabits' (Caruth, 1995:5). Those suffering from 'post-traumatic stress syndrome' (PTS), suggests Caruth, are haunted by memories of particular events: 'to be traumatized is precisely to be possessed by an image or event' (Caruth, 1995:4–5). While people with cancer have not usually been considered within the PTS category, there are parallels in the structure of memory and the patterns of its insistent repetition. For at least eighteen months after the treatments I was aware of 'bodily memories' as a constant presence. The memory of the surgery and its aftermath made me acutely aware of the internality of my body, a sense that seemed to separate me from others and from my previous sense of embodied subjectivity. Although this imagined bodily interior has now receded, it can instantly be recalled several years later, through an associative image, smell, sound or dream.

But in what sense is this a *memory*, if it is to some extent based upon my absence from the events in question? How can I remember something I did not consciously experience? After all, during surgery I was anaesthetised. In fact my memory of this event is based on a phantasmatic witnessing. Unless we explain my feelings through the idea of an 'out of body' experience in the more spiritual sense, then my feeling of having seen myself 'cut open' during surgery is either a memory of a dream, or an imagined omnipotence, or both. As Annette Kuhn illustrates so eloquently in her own 'memory work' on a very different topic, 'remembering appears to make no insistence on the presence of the rememberer at the original scene of the recollected event. Remembering is clearly an activity that takes place *for*, as much as in, the present' (Kuhn, 1995:108). As Kuhn goes on to demonstrate, we may have memories of events which are historically located before we were born.[3] Thus, my memory of seeing my own bodily interior, and the consequent somatic sensitivities that informed my sense of presence in the world, are not entirely incongruous with my anaesthetised state at the 'event' in question.

Chemotherapy left traces of bodily memory in a rather different way. The sustained confrontation with the abject during chemotherapy discussed in Chapter 3 made an intense bodily impression. Long after I had adjusted to the 'side-effects' on a physical level, my body would 'remember' the traumas of the treatment. The trigger may have been an association of somatic sensation with place, taste or sound. Music listened to during chemotherapy became unbearable and favourite food from that time inedible. For several years after the chemotherapy, I would find myself suddenly (and for no apparent reason) overcome by nausea. It always took me some time to realise that the dates coincided with those of the chemotherapy. It was not that I looked at the date in my diary and then felt nauseous, but rather that the memory was always generated by bodily sensation, or, at least, that's how it felt.

These 'bodily memories' gradually fade but they never disappear entirely. They return unexpectedly, uninvited.[4] Such a transformation of the body in turn transforms self-perception. I have found it impossible ever fully to return to the more predictable and familiar (and external) relationship to bodily states that previously comforted my psyche, although I have become increasingly familiar with (though nevertheless always surprised by) the apparently inexplicable waves of nausea, or the sudden image of the abdomen's internal organs. These remembrances are the somatic forms of what Annette Kuhn has called 'the phantasmogoria of memory' (Kuhn, 1995:105). 'Phantasmogoria' here refers to 'a shifting series or succession of phantasms or imaginary figures, as seen in a dream or fevered condition, as called up by the imagination, or as created by literary description' (*Oxford English Dictionary*, quoted in Kuhn, 1995:105). Haunting icons of past trauma, they surface in the present repeatedly, if irregularly. But unlike the memories in Kuhn's account, the sense of place so crucial to memory formation is *internal* rather than external (Kuhn, 1995:114). It is the body's interior space that provides the substance and the staging of these memories: a 'bodily uncanny' that houses these strange sensations within the most familiar of places (see Donald, 1989; Chisholm, 1992).

For me these bodily memories are the lingering spectres of the trauma of having cancer, surgery and chemotherapy. The opposite of the nostalgic desire to regain the lost object of a better past, or the mournful desire to bring to life an absent love, these are the unwelcome memories which the subject would willingly exchange for oblivion. But the desire for forgetfulness is sabotaged by their menacing return. The intellectual will to forget is thwarted by the bodily presence of the past. Here, it is not the remembering that is the object of desire, but the forgetting. There is no term to connote the direct opposite of 'nostalgia': the desire to flee, rather than to return. Bodily memories linger long after their departure is required. Like the scars that become permanent reminders of the tissues below the skin, these bodily memories mediate against a complete forgetting.

But is there not a nostalgia at work here too, a nostalgia for the time when my body had a less obtrusive presence in my consciousness? Am I yearning for the familiar comfort of a separation between 'mind' and 'body', despite all the claims of its undesirability?[5] Is this not a desire to return to the golden age when my body was expected to look after itself, when the workings of its interior rarely came to mind? For the 'bodily presence' following cancer has brought with it not only the internal iconography of horror, but the terror of imminent death. This constant awareness of physicality is accompanied by the knowledge of its fragility. Thoughts of mortality send regular shock waves down the spine with a force that was previously kept at bay. A constant companion that I would willingly forego. This nostalgia is for the paradisical time I now imagine before the diagnosis when the intense physicality of bodily interiors was seldom contemplated and when death was less easily imaginable. In the narratives I tell myself (and that I relate here) I have constructed a mythic past for which I yearn: an age of innocence and immortality.

BODIES OF KNOWLEDGE

When I described the strange sensation of having seen my bodily interior to a friend she told me I had internalised the 'medical gaze'. Many Foucauldians would agree with her (see Chapter 2). The medical gaze refers to the construction of the body as an object of visual scrutiny within medical science which Foucault, and many others since, have documented.[6] According to these arguments, the development of modern science has meant that human bodies have become increasingly defined as the space in which 'organs and eyes meet', as Foucault describes it. The medical expert has defined his authority to diagnose and to treat through an ability to isolate symptoms, to attach them to organs and tissues and to see disease as an exclusively physical manifestation in one individual. In this context patients have come to be seen, and to see themselves, as *objects* of medical investigation. Foucault characterises this relationship between the doctor and the patient, 'this unique dialogue' (1973:xiv), as a 'simple, unconceptualized confrontation of a gaze and a face, or a glance and a silent body; a sort of contact . . . by which two living individuals are "trapped" in a common, but non-reciprocal situation' (Foucault, 1973:xv). Thus, one is not only aware of one's status as 'object', as the patient's bed becomes a field of 'scientific investigation' ((Foucault, 1973:xv), but, also, one is simultaneously the subject of this biomedical discourse, objectifying oneself.

Much as I may have yearned for a time when my ability to ignore the physicality of my bodily interior felt like a freedom, there are equally compelling arguments that designate this Cartesian construction of a separated mind and body as deeply problematic. Feminist scholars in

particular have objected to this distinction and its gendered associations and to the ways in which women have been ascribed the position
of 'body' within a hierarchical dualism. But perhaps my desire to escape
the constant awareness of the physicality of my body might be read as
a refusal of precisely the ascription of 'woman as body'. It is in the
context of this ongoing debate about the significance of bodily subjectivity to ideas about gender that this chapter addresses the competing
definitions of 'mind' and 'body' within biomedical and self-health
discourses.

What Foucault failed to point out, as in so many of his accounts of
the operations of power/knowledge relations in the contemporary
professions (medicine, psychiatry, the penal system), was that this '*non-
reciprocal*' exchange between doctor and patient takes place within the
context of other power imbalances, variously inscribed, if always contested, in cultural practices and processes: for example, inequalities of
race, class or gender.[7] The production of the basis for scientific
knowledge about the body, for example, took place in eighteenth-
century colonial Europe, and thus we might situate Foucault's account
of the invasion of the 'dark' mysteries of the body by science in the
context of an aggressive colonial desire to dominate and control not
only the unknown territory of the human body, but also that of non-
European cultures (Turner, 1984, 1987). The triumph of rational
discourse, with its expression of 'man's' desire to control the so-called
natural world, then, belongs to a larger Enlightenment project of White
supremacy, accompanying the imposition of Western medicine on non-
Western cultures (Picone, 1989). Similarly, the encoding and legitimation of certain professional practices, such as those of medicine, are
tied into the developments of industrial capitalism which enabled the
middle classes to consolidate their authority in the public sphere. The
specialization of certain kinds of knowledge and its concentration in
the hands of a small elite took place in the context of the establishment
of particular distinctions between different classes of people.[8] The
perpetuation of the exclusive ownership of these specialist knowledges
and practices by middle-class minorities might be seen, then, to be
integral to the development of biomedicine (Stacey, 1988).

Feminist readings of the history of biomedicine highlight the ways in
which the clinical gaze, described by Foucault, are so typically those of
the male professional whose object is the female body (Daly, 1979).
Accounts of this history have documented the ways in which the
development of some aspects of biomedicine meant a usurping of
conventional female forms of knowledge, such as midwifery, by masculine, and often alienating, practices, such as those of obstetrics.[9] These
critiques have focused on the forms of medical knowledge produced,
as well as the composition of the medical professions (Witz, 1992).

Thus, the masculinisation of medical knowledge refers to both the endowment of men with status and authority, but also the privileging of discourses of rationality, objectivity and progress within medicine. These have themselves been seen as central to the patriarchal project of controlling nature, and thus, according to its own construction, women. The Enlightenment project, at the heart of which has been the discourse of scientific discovery, progress and development, has been seen as a profoundly masculine, colonialist one. This overwhelming drive to see, to name and to know, which characterised the development of biomedicine, has been connected to a wider system of control and domination. Science and biomedicine have been criticised by feminists for the ways in which they legitimate masculine forms of knowledge about the female body through their claims to neutrality which ignore the power relations of medical pratice (Ehrenreich and English, 1974; Dreifus, 1977; Graham, 1984; Keller, 1985; Birke, 1986; Turner, 1987; Oakley, 1993; Doyal, 1994).

Since the 1970s women's health movements have sought to engender confidence in women to develop a knowledge of their own bodies. Books such as *Our Bodies, Ourselves* (Phillips and Rakusen, 1978) represented an intervention which aimed to demystify biomedical knowledge, and to supplement it, or even replace it, with information culled from women's health groups. Medical interventions and interpretations have increasingly been viewed with scepticism and women have tried to refuse the medical gaze, making decisions about how to treat their illnesses based on a number of sources of information, only one of which might be that of the biomedical experts. As well as the challenge to the macrostructures of biomedicine, and to the forms of knowledge it produces, feminism has also facilitated intervention at the micro-level. The often humiliating and degrading examination procedures carried out by the mainly male medical profession and the patronising attitudes to patients have also been criticised. In particular, the women's health movement has encouraged female patients to develop a sense of entitlement to accessible information about their bodies, and to reclaim a sense of control over decision-making about procedures. Rather than obediently following the instructions of doctors and consultants, many female patients have been encouraged to ask questions, to find out more before accepting the doctor's recommendation, or to pursue alternative courses of treatment in preference to biomedical ones. Thus, doctors' diagnoses, prescriptions and recommended treatments have been viewed by some female patients as only one amongst many sources of advice, rather than as the definitive authority. This relativising politics has enabled many women to resist the passivity and alienation of the patient role, and to combat their dependency on the masculine medical profession (Hepburn and Gutierrez, 1988; White, 1990; Hockey, 1993).

The impersonal and detached methods of communication employed within biomedicine have been criticised by feminists for the ways in which they reinforce the conventional notion of masculinity as 'rational' and femininity as 'emotional'. The procedures of communication are as much a part of the objectifying medical gaze as the forms of physical examination (Oakley, 1993; Gabe *et al.*, 1994).

THE DIAGNOSIS

After surgery for an ovarian cyst I keep vomiting for several days.

Why am I still being sick? Doesn't the anaesthetic usually wear off faster than this?

Eventually I am told they've taken a biopsy of the bowel.

As in all good narratives, each answer leads to a new question.

Why does a bowel biopsy produce continued vomiting?
The bowel is a very sensitive organ and stops working if it is interfered with. Vomiting is quite a common response.
And why have they taken a biopsy of the bowel?
To do some tests.
What tests, no one will say. I am baffled.
The director of the hospital pokes his head around the curtain which surrounds my bed on the surgical ward. Unannounced, he robs me of my fragile privacy. He is the one I most dread dealing with. I saw him on my first visit to the ward. Mobile phone in hand, exuding paternalistic pride and arrogance, he had sped through this ward full of women recovering from hysterectomies, calling out to them one by one at the top of his voice to ask if they had 'passed wind' yet (a crucial sign of recovery after such surgery, I was later informed).

I am throwing up as he enters. Ignoring this he announces casually:
You won't need further surgery but you may need further treatment. You've only got one child, haven't you? So we shall try and preserve your fertility in case you want another.
I don't have any children, I inform him.
Have one of mine, I've got too many.
And with this generous offer which amuses him enormously, he leaves.

I am puzzled. I am not aware that there is any possibility of needing further treatment. What could this piece of information mean? My head and my stomach spin. Waves of nausea are now accompanied by waves of panic and confusion.

Desperate to find out more, I ask for the doctor who performed the emergency surgery. Unlike her self-important boss, she sits down and at least pretends to have the time to talk to me. Though reluctant, she gradually lets slip a few more clues. I press her for an explanation. I may indeed need further treatment, she confirms.

What kind? I ask, genuinely – incredibly – ignorant.

She hesitates and resents being put on the spot.

Chemotherapy, she replies eventually.

There is a moment or so's pause while the name of the treatment connects to the disease in my mind. A sudden shudder passes through my body as the realisation hits me.

Do you mean I may have cancer?
We're testing to see if the cyst was benign or malignant. I'm sorry. We've had to take biopsies from various organs to check – bowel, the other ovary and so on. The cyst looked a bit nasty, but I can't tell you until the tests come back. You may need three months' chemotherapy. The test results will be back in a couple of days. She leaves.

I am left with the news. Alone, but surrounded by strangers. I don't think they planned it this way. I don't think they planned it at all. Perhaps that's the problem.

But the nurses are furious. They had plans. They had plans to keep it quiet until more definite news came. They are agitated. This unexpected revelation by a doctor has thrown them off course; they are left to deal with the fall-out. They mutter to one another under their breath.

I just make it down to the toilets, trailing the drip, hand on wound, surgical stockings on both legs. Away from those twenty or so strangers in front of whom I have just been given the worst news I could imagine. I look at myself in the mirror. Is this what a person with cancer looks like? Why do I expect a visible difference?

It's benign, it's malignant, it's benign. It must be benign. I am desperate to know more, but don't even know which questions to ask.

The next day I am still vomiting, so they decide to put a tube down my nose to suck up what is in my stomach. They push it down, I gag with each centimetre. I lie there waiting for them to bring it back up, but they tell me it will be left there for a few days. Surely not. My throat feels like I've swallowed a large chicken bone. Surely not. Not a few days! The temporary measure becomes a semi-permanent fixture.

I can't sleep because every time I swallow, I wake up. It's benign, it's malignant, it's benign. It must be benign.

The next day we all wait. And wait. At least I am not alone by this

105

time. I am prepared. Finally the doctor arrives. The results . . . won't be ready until tomorrow, she tells me. An endless deferral. The head of the hospital appears at the end of my bed and boasts of how many times he's had a tube like that inserted into his nose and stomach in demonstrations to medical students. We are all suitably impressed.

After two long days and nights of waiting, suddenly an entourage arrives unannounced. Where was the fanfare? They are all dressed up, dressed for a dinner party – bright colours, shiny materials, spruced hair-dos. There are about six or seven people round my bed all dressed in suits. At the back, the junior doctors; in front of them, the two (women) surgeons who had performed the operation; in front, the consultant. He is wearing a bright red silk tie. I have never met him before as he's been away on holiday. He steps forward slightly from his team; surely he isn't going to tell me the results in front of this audience?

I'm sure you have a thousand questions, but it's best for you to wait and ask Dr M, he announces nervously, avoiding my eye. A pause. The team observes how the patient is taking it.

Are you telling me I have cancer? (By chance I know that Dr. M is the cancer specialist.)
Oh yes, it's malignant.

Their faces all stare down at me. How am I going to react? Am I going to burst into tears and precipitate their flurried exit? If there are tears, nurses can take over. Their tension shows through their sympathetic looks. What is the purpose of this bizarre gathering? Is it some kind of medical ritual? Have they all been invited to witness a 'cancer diagnosis'?

Aren't I a bit young to have cancer? I ask. This is all I could think to say.
No, 32 is quite a typical age for a teratoma.

After the dinner-party group leave, nurses rush in and tell me to think positively. What on earth might that mean under such circumstances? What it means is don't cry, don't get upset. Perhaps a quiet tear or two, but no sobbing please, it'll upset the other patients. And be heroic, be brave (be a man?).

I have to wait for four days to see the oncologist. Friends bring in as much literature on cancer as they can find. I have to be better prepared for the next encounter than for the last. 'Aren't I bit young?' really isn't good enough. I read and read. I feel as if I am taking an exam. Dr M, I am told, is an exceptional consultant and treats people like intelligent human beings. Does such a consultant exist, I wonder?

MECHANISED BODIES

The story of my diagnosis is retold here to exemplify some of the limits of biomedicine. In particular, it highlights the insensitivity of bio-medical pratices to the needs of the patient, other than those of the physical body. In these exchanges my emotional response to the

diagnosis of cancer is so deeply feared, and anticipated as so inappropriate to the hospital context, that the consultant blocked out the
feelings of the patient in favour of his own emotional needs. These
chosen forms of communication demonstrate clearly that the patient is
viewed simply as a body with a disease. Why didn't one doctor sit down
and explain the situation to me? Why didn't the consultant come alone
to convey the bad news? Safety in numbers? Why had it been impossible
for any of the medical staff to utter the name of the disease I had? In
such a context, the patient often suffers because of the medical
profession's inability to process their own emotions; in the case of the
female patient and the male doctor, women are once again obliged to
facilitate, to cover for, men's emotional ineptitude:

> Biomedicine was founded on a Cartesian division of man into a
> soulless mortal machine capable of mechanistic explanation and
> manipulation, and a bodyless soul, immortal, immaterial, and
> properly subject to religious authority, but largely unnecessary to
> account for physical disease and healing.
>
> (Kirmayer, 1988:57)

In conventional medicine, illness is understood as an exclusively bodily
process and the body is typically contructed as 'a biochemical machine'
(Kirmayer, 1988:57). Following Descartes, this model separates not only
the body from the mind, but also the 'body from its environment'
(Stacey, 1988:163). As Andrew Ross argues:

> The professionals' bad attitude is often caricatured in the follow-
> ing way: biomedicine sees and treats the body as a functional
> machine that occasionally breaks down, and for whose dys-
> functions a physical cause and remedy can always be found by the
> repairman, the doctor.
>
> (Ross, 1991:50)

As has been argued in medical anthropology (Taussig, 1980; Scheper-
Hughes and Lock, 1986; DiGiacomo, 1992), the 'reification of illness
as organic disease' in biomedicine can be criticised for its dehuman-
ising effect on the patient (DiGiacomo, 1992:120). Doctors' metonymic
references to patients as their illnesses ('this is the teratoma I told you
about') reduces the patient's identity to a set of physical symptoms and
alienates them from the medical process. Such an approach to patients
exemplifies the extent of the biomedical belief in the autonomy of the
body: a 'singular premise guiding Western science and clinical medicine
... is its commitment to a fundamental opposition between spirit
and matter, mind and body, and (underlying this) real and unreal'

(Scheper-Hughes and Lock, 1987:8). Furthermore, this philosophy derives from an essentialist 'atomism' which extracts parts from the whole and, decontexualised, ascribes them meaning as things in themselves. Patients are left behind in this process in which their physical symptoms replace them and become the sum of their identities (Gordon, 1988:26) (see Figures 4.1 and 4.2). Processes of biomedical 'reification' read biological signs as having no cultural meaning, and furthermore, according to Taussig (1980), reinforce the ideological needs of the social order.

It is against these myopias of biomedicine that many alternative and self-health therapies have defined themselves. Above all, they have offered the patient the possibility of being regarded as more than just a set of bodily parts and symptoms. Indeed, when I visited the Bristol Cancer Help Clinic, it was with the most profound sense of relief that I responded to the doctor's request to tell her 'the whole story of the illness, including how [I] had felt at each stage'. In this and other such narrativisations, I found the possibility of bridging the gulf between body and emotion which had been established in the biomedical context. In general, alternative and self-health medicines have developed techniques and practices which attempt to rewrite the story of illnesses according to a different set of conventions from those employed within biomedicine. Most patients, like me, come to these alternative medicines having experienced the objectifying medical gaze and its alienating effects. Many of these approaches to health and healing claim to overcome the mind/body dualism which lies at the heart of Western medicine and, in their view, is one of the central causes of its limited effects. Biomedicine has yet to find a cure for cancer, it is claimed, precisely because it treats the body in isolation from other aspects of the self which are seen as equally important in the production of disease.

In this respect, these challenges coincide with feminist criticisms of the separation of the body from the emotions in Western biomedicine. The privileging of the concrete, the observable, the quantifiable is seen to be integral to a hierarchical value system in which the feminine has been defined as opposite, and inferior, to these qualities. Furthermore, these belief systems have been criticised for producing degrading and depersonalised doctor/patient exchanges, and medical practices in general. In this respect feminist interventions and alternative medicine share the common goal of redressing the imbalance created by patriarchal biomedicine. As Ross highlights:

> in recent years, the legitimacy of medical professionals has been
> further eroded, as popular consciousness absorbs the more general social critique of biomedicine's 'inhumanity' and lack of

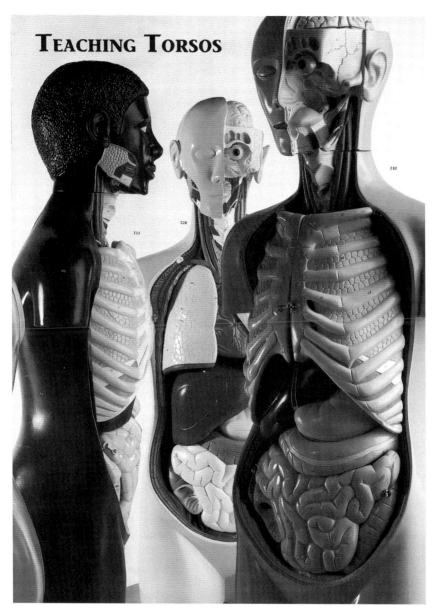

Figure 4.1 Sharing the Knowledge Medical Teaching Catalogue
Source: Denoyer Geppert International, 1995/6:9

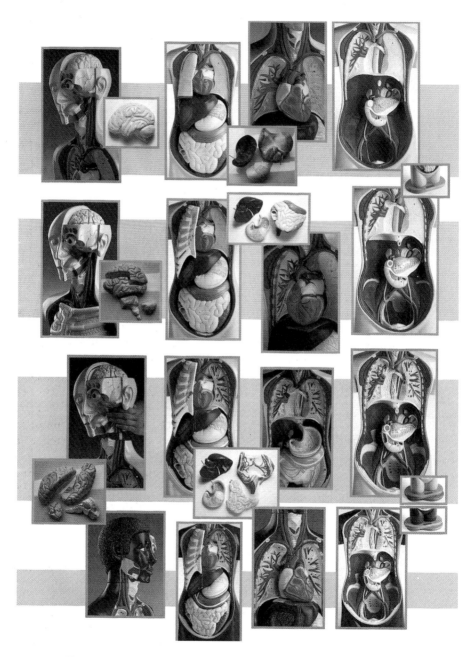

Figure 4.2 Sharing the Knowledge Medical Teaching Catalogue
Source: Denoyer Geppert International, 1995/6:11

caring for the patient. In a profession where the orthodox faith in the (large) technology fix has often led to consequences 'worse than the disease', the multitude of alternative health therapies (the women's alternative healthcare movement, for example) has made big inroads.

(Ross, 1991:50)

Many of the 'cure yourself of cancer' books depend heavily on certain aspects of alternative health philosophy. The self-health literature on cancer advocates a wider embrace, a more humanistic approach to cancer care, and an acknowledgement of 'the person inside the body'. But to what extent do these alternative and self-health practices overcome the mind/body dualism of biomedicine? And, furthermore, how compatible are they with the goals of feminism?

MINDFUL BODIES

As I emphasised in Chapter 1, there are numerous dimensions to alternative medicine, and enormous diversity and disagreements between the many different practices included in such a general category. These tend to get lost in blanket charges levelled against them, such as their individualism, essentialism or complicity with New Right discourses of personal responsibility (see Chapter 7, this volume; Coward, 1989; Wilkinson and Kitzinger, 1994). In what follows I am not suggesting that all forms of alternative therapy depend upon the same premises in their treatment of cancer; however, certain discourses about the mind/body relationship repeatedly recur in the self-health literature on cancer which do not overcome the dualisms of Western medicine in the way they claim to. For example, many alternative approaches to cancer evoke a rhetoric of 'Eastern' belief systems, such as traditional Chinese medicine; but they nevertheless continue to rely on the conventional mind/body dualism in their notions of causality (the mind causes bodily decline), whereas in the original Chinese conceptualisation, the body was understood quite differently from the mechanical Western model (see Elvin, 1989).

Many alternatives to biomedicine shift the emphasis away from medical technology as the solution to the disease and towards the internal self as the source of healing:

Natural/Alternative/Complementary Therapy covers an endless range of techniques, all of which help to remove the cause of 'dis/ease'. They affect the whole person, mind, body, spirit, stimulating a person's intrinsic ability to heal themselves.

(Editorial, *The Well Newsletter*, 1993:2)

111

Thus, rather than being the passive recipient of medical technologies, the patient is encouraged to participate in her/his own healing. Based on this 'amateurist principle' (Ross, 1991), these therapies supposedly demystify the powers of the professional and democratise the processes of healing. It is with the operations of these 'psychotechnologies' (Ross, 1991) in relation to cancer that I am particularly concerned. This term refers to the shift away from the conventional technologies of bio-medicine towards a view of the self (especially the psychological self) as a 'technology' of healing. My examples in the following section are drawn from an early, formative text on self-health (Simonton *et al.*, 1978). Although this is clearly not the most up-to-date example, I return to this work as it informs so many other more recent publications on cancer that I came across during my illness, and its models continue to inform many alternative and self-health practices which I encountered during that time (Brohn, 1987a, 1987b; Charles, 1990).[10]

> It is no longer possible to see the body as an object waiting for replacement parts from the factory. Instead we now view the mind and body as an integrated *system*.

> The real issue is no longer *whether* the mind and emotions affect the course of treatment; the question is rather *how* to direct them most effectively in support of it.
>
> (Simonton *et al.*, 1978:31–2, 89)

This example demonstrates a classic slippage in the discourses of self-health in so far as the mind refers to the emotions rather than to the intellect. What is emphasised throughout such accounts of cancer is that certain feelings, and, more important, certain (inappropriate) ways of dealing with feelings, can contribute to the onset of cancer. Bio-medicine is criticised for its privileging of the body at the expense of the mind. At the heart of the Simonton model, for example, is the inclusion of emotions in the health equation:

> It is our central premise that an illness is not purely a physical problem but rather a problem of the whole person, that it includes not only body but mind and emotions. We believe that emotional and mental states play a significant role both in *susceptibility* to disease, including cancer, and in *recovery* from all disease.
>
> (Simonton *et al.*, 1978:10)

What is referred to here as the 'mind' is actually the physiological processes through which emotions are processed in the body. In their model of cancer development, for example, feelings of despair, resulting from stress, are processed by 'the limbic system' (the visceral brain) which records stress and its effects. This is then passed on by 'the hypothalamus' (an area of the brain which receives messages from the limbic system and passes them on to the pituitary gland and endocrine system), which triggers a hormonal imbalance in the body and suppresses the immune system, leaving the body susceptible to the growth of abnormal cells. This chain reaction of the physical effects of emotional states is summed up in Figure 4.3:

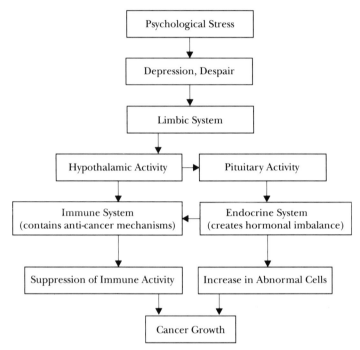

Figure 4.3 A mind/body model of cancer development
Source: Simonton *et al.*, 1978: 92

The Simontons rely heavily on previous medical studies of cancer (as well as on their own experience of treating patients at their clinic) to substantiate their claims. Hans Selye (1956), for example, is cited as a medical authority whose research proves the physical effects of stress on the body. He identified the damaging effects of the hormones produced by stress (often stimulated by our inability to follow what is called our fight-or-flee 'instinct' because of the 'unnatural' requirements of modern life). More importantly, according to the Simontons, he 'discovered that chronic stress suppresses the immune system which is responsible for engulfing and destroying cancerous cells or alien micro-organisms' (Simonton *et al.*, 1978:53). Bathrop (1977) is cited for his claims that bereavement weakens the effectiveness of the immune system (Simonton *et al.*, 1978:53). J. H. Humphrey and associates (1977), they argue, have demonstrated that the body's immunity to TB can be affected by hypnotic suggestion. Finally, George Solomon is drawn upon to prove the empirical connection between the 'hypothalamus' and the immune system (Solomon, 1969). (All cited in Simonton *et al.*, 1978: 53–4.)

The supposed causative connection between emotional states and the physical conditions under which cancer cells can begin to proliferate is extended to explain why cancer might occur in some people and not in others. It is the individual's ability, or rather lack of it, to cope with the stresses of modern life which determine whether or not they will develop cancer. Thus cancer, it is argued, is actually a symptom (indeed a metaphor; see Chapter 2) of the problems which exist elsewhere in the patient's life; furthermore, certain kinds of reactions to stress are likely to result in the growth of a malignant tumour and particular types of people are more likely to produce such reactions. The cancer patient, according to this model, probably had a series of stresses between six and eighteen months prior to their illness and responded to these problems with 'a deep sense of hopelessness' (Simonton *et al.*, 1978:10).

Drawing on various studies of cancer patients, they construct a psychological profile of a typical cancer patient. A suitable psychological environment is produced, they argue, which, rather than causing cancer, 'permits' it to 'develop' (Simonton *et al.*, 1978:75). Their five steps in a psychological process which frequently precedes the onset of cancer include:

> Experiences in childhood result in decisions to become a certain kind of person . . . the individual is rocked by a cluster of stressful life events . . . these stresses create a problem with which the individual does not know how to deal . . . the individual sees no way of changing the rules about how he or she must act and so feels trapped and helpless to resolve the problem . . . the individual puts distance between himself or herself and the problem, becoming static, unchanging, rigid.
>
> (Simonton *et al.*, 1978:72–5)

The resulting 'deep sense of hopelessness', 'triggers a set of physiological responses that suppress the body's natural defences' and make it susceptible to the production of abnormal cells (Simonton *et al.*, 1978:10). Thus, a causative relationship is suggested between emotions and the physical ability to fight disease.

This connection between psychological types and cancer, the Simontons claim, is something which has been observed for centuries. 'Writing nearly two thousand years ago in the second century A. D., the

114

physician Galen observed that cheerful women were less prone to cancer than were women of a depressed nature' (Simonton *et al.*, 1978:57). Similarly, A. H. Schmale and H. Iker observed a 'sense of hopeless frustration surrounding a conflict for which there was no resolution' in their female cancer patients which led them to develop a 'helplessness-prone personality type' with which they achieved a 73 per cent accuracy rate in their prediction of the development of cancer (Simonton *et al.*, 1978:65–6). This personality type can be traced back to a past history in which the patient(s) had 'experienced a lack of closeness with their parents, seldom demonstrated strong emotions and were generally low gear' (Simonton *et al.*, 1978:65). Traumas, such as bereavements, are also seen to spark off this emotional chain reaction, especially if the emotions of loss or guilt are not expressed. Elida Evans, a Jungian psychoanalyst, for example, is cited for her conclusions that many cancer patients had lost an important emotional relationship before the onset of cancer:

> [they] had invested their identity in one individual object or role (a person, a job, a home) rather than developing their own individuality. When the object or role was threatened or removed, such patients were thrown back on themselves, with few internal resources for coping.
>
> (Simonton *et al.*, 1978:62)

The model of the cancer personality type is to be found either implicitly or explicitly in much of the self-health literature on cancer. In particular, the arguments of Lawrence LeShan (1966, 1977) form the basis for many of the hypotheses. His work is not only central to the Simonton analysis, but also to many other studies, such as Rachel Charles's *Mind, Body and Immunity* (1990). LeShan argued that 76 per cent of cancer patients (as opposed to only 10 per cent of the non-cancer control group) displayed the same four components in their life histories: isolated youth; significant relationship in early adulthood became the centre of their life; loss of this relationship; resulting despair which was kept 'bottled up'. People who are 'dutiful, sweet-natured, obliging on the surface with a secret desperation underneath' and who have a 'total inability to express anger' are seen as those most prone to cancer (Charles, 1990:46). Charles offers a series of magazine-style personality tests and charts against which readers can measure themselves in her chapter, 'How healthy is your personality?' What the cancer patient needs to counteract these negative patterns, according to Charles, is a holistic approach to healing:

> this process involves you looking deep within yourself. It means considering your personality, your emotions, your values and your lifestyle, as well as the more practical aspects of diet and exercise.

It takes a great deal of courage to do this. There may be very good reasons why you need to be ill. If you become glowingly healthy, who will care for you then? It is a road towards self-acceptance, self-knowledge and yes, most especially self-love.

(Charles, 1990:5)

This prescription of love, laughter and self-realisation is again backed up with scientific evidence of the effect of emotional states on the immune system. Charles claims that 'laughter affects the immune system', using Norman Cousins (1981) as the example of the 'man who laughed his way back to health', and she offers the reader a chart to fill in to test their 'laughter quotient' (Charles, 1990:81–2). The healing quality of love is also appealed to. Even watching films about love is said to enhance the immune system; Charles also cites two Harvard psychologists, McClelland and Kirshuit, who discovered that people's immunoglobulin A could be raised in such a way (Charles, 1990:68). In addition to these external benefits, the patient also needs to develop through counselling in order to gain the confidence to become a person who is truer to themself and less concerned about the needs of others. According to Charles, the effects of counselling have also been shown to improve immunity (Charles, 1990:69). Another holistic advocate, Ian Pearce, recommends deep relaxation, visualisation and counselling as the path away from helplessness and hopelessness towards self-healing (Pearce, 1983:9).

The consensus within these 'psychotechnologies' is thus that the cancer patient's mental attitude is crucial to understanding the onset of their illness and to the possibility of their recovery. Indeed, the patient's beliefs about her/himself are seen to play a formative role in the development of the disease. However, I should stress that not all self-health approaches assume that everyone 'who gets cancer is covering up some inner pain and suffering'; according to Penny Brohn (co-founder of the Bristol Cancer Help Clinic, and ex-cancer patient), 'mental and emotional stress is not an automatic precursor to the development of cancer' (Brohn, 1987b:85–6). Rather, she argues that if someone believes that their psychological state *has* contributed to their illness, then a holistic approach facilitates their exploration of this connection, whereas biomedicine does not. She cites the case of a female patient at Bristol who believed that her guilt and anxiety concerning her anorexic daughter 'was the reason behind her cancer'. Anticipating the usual criticism, Brohn insists: 'I shall repeat many times that the issue in such a case is not whether this woman was right about any of this, but that she *believed* she was right' (Brohn, 1987b:85).

These, then, are some of the central discourses of the relationship between the mind and the body that continue to inform self-health cancer practices and literatures. Unlike biomedicine, these 'psycho-technologies' represent bodily modalities which incorporate feelings and emotional responses, both in terms of the cause and effect of the illness. According to several of these accounts, the fertile ground for the onset of cancer is provided by the destructive impact of stress, trauma and loss on the body of the patient. Similarly, the discharge of this distress, together with an exploration of its place in the patient's history and the impact of the illness on their life, are seen to aid recovery, as the new-found mental state impacts upon the damaged body. What is of particular concern is the effect of the build-up of unexpressed or unresolved emotions on the functioning of the immune system. In this 'hydrosomatic' representation of the body, the emotional pressure builds up and must be released to avoid bodily damage. Thus, cancer, and indeed illness in general, is seen as 'psychosomatic' in so far as the mind and the body are interconnecting systems, whose harmony depends upon the well-being of each.

The popularisation of certain psychoanalytic concepts, such as 'psychosomatic', is part of an emergent common-sense discourse about health and illness in contemporary culture. Many of these concepts can be traced through a history of psychoanalytic thought which investigated the relationship between psyche and soma from Freud and Breuer (1893–5) onwards. More specifically, some of these accounts take their cues, and indeed, their evidence, from psychoanalytic writings about the meaning of modern illness. Psychoanalysts, like Groddeck (1923) and Reich (1975), have sought to investigate the cultural meaning of cancer, rather than accepting its 'organic' presentation as a purely biological phenomenon. Indeed, Reich sought to explain Freud's own cancer of the jaw, for example, in terms of 'his unhappy personal life and his repression of emotion' (Turner, 1984:238); he believed that Freud smoked heavily because 'he wanted to say something that never came out of his lips' (Reich, quoted in Turner, 1984:238). Thus, Freud's bitten-back emotions found an outlet in the cancer through which he 'chose' to express them, Reich argued. Groddeck also saw cancer as a symbol of repressed emotions and desires (Turner, 1984:238). In this context, the body is read as the cultural map of the psyche. Bodily memories are seen to threaten the health of the person by holding trauma or tension within the body. Thus disease is the bodily expression of the distress that could not be fully forgotten.

SOMATISED PSYCHES

Psychoanalysis is clearly a key source of ideas about the mind/body relationship in alternative approaches to cancer, but how closely do the discourses of these contemporary psychotechnologies resemble those original *Studies in Hysteria* (1893–5), in which Freud and Breuer developed the basic theory of somatisation – the process whereby the psychic trauma manifests itself as a physical symptom? Although his work with Breuer is among some of Freud's earliest, and about which he changed his mind in later years, it nevertheless contains many of the central premises of psychoanalysis in their embryonic forms, later extended to explain other human neuroses. This work is particularly relevant here, since its concern centres upon the mental causes of some physical illnesses and returns us to the relationship between memory, trauma and disease with which I began the chapter.

Breuer and Freud claim that hysteria is prompted by external events.[11] While the symptoms are ostensibly spontaneous, their origin can be traced back to a precipitating trauma; while appearing idiopathic (primary, and not related to another disease), on closer examination, these symptoms prove to be connected to a previous, and unknown, event. They claim to have found a causal relation between psychic trauma and hysterical symptom, and they explain this through the mechanisms of repression and conversion. Repression is the process by which certain 'incompatible' or 'unacceptable' desires and wishes are forced out of the ego's consciousness and restricted to the unconscious region of the mind. In the case of hysteria the repressed memory of the trauma manifests itself in the physical symptom: 'the memory of the trauma . . . acts like a foreign body which long after its entry must continue to be regarded as an agent that is still at work' (Breuer and Freud, 1893–5:56–7). Hysteria is thus a method of defence through which 'excitation' is *converted* into 'a somatic innervation' (Breuer and Freud, 1893–5:187). Once the memory of the trauma is brought to consciousness and verbalised, through hypnosis or free association, the symptoms, it is claimed, disappear immediately (Breuer and Freud, 1893–5:57). Within the category of hysterical symptoms, they include neuralgias, anaesthesias, paralyses, epileptoid convulsions, chronic vomiting, anorexia, hallucinations, contractures and tics (Breuer and Freud, 1893–5:54). Thus, it could be argued that hysterics 'suffer mainly from reminiscences' (Breuer and Freud, 1893–5:58) as the affect of the trauma attaches to the memory and is repressed into the unconscious, thus remaining hidden from the patient. In particular, this mechanism is set into play when the immediate effect of the trauma is not expressed (for example, tears not shed, revenge not taken), which may be because of social convention and expectation, because the patient is not in a state where it is possible to react directly, because the loss is irreparable and simply unbearable, or a combination of these internal and external factors (Breuer and Freud, 1893–5:61). Thus, 'the ideas which have become pathological have persisted with such freshness and affective strength because they have been denied the normal wearing-away processes by means of abreaction and reproduction in states of uninhibited association' (Breuer and Freud, 1893–5:62).

Common to all hysterias, though in different forms, is the splitting of consciousness and the emergence of what Freud and Breuer call 'abnormal' (or hypnoid) 'states of consciousness' in which ideas 'are very intense but are cut off from associative communication with the rest of the content of consciousness' (Breuer and Freud, 1893–5:63). Depending on the form of hysteria the patient displays different processes and sequences of split consciousness. In the case of 'dispositional hysteria', these hypnoid states are already present before the onset of the illness, in which case 'they provide the soil in which the affect plants the pathogenic memory with its consequent somatic phenomena'; in those patients with 'psychically acquired hysteria', on the other hand, 'a splitting off of groups of ideas' results from the effects of a severe trauma or a 'laborious suppression' (Breuer and Freud, 1893–5:63). Thus, two psychic groups can be seen to be present in the same mind; after a hysterical attack the patient returns to normal life and the two states co-exist. Just as memories are aroused spontaneously, so the hysterical attack will occur in a patient; just as memories can be jogged in normal consciousness, so the hysteric can be provoked into an attack by associations. This can be aroused either 'by stimulation of the hysterogenic zone or by a new experience' which resembles the pathogenic one; 'in both a hyperaesthetic memory is touched on' (Breuer and Freud, 1893–5:68).

These general characteristics of hysteria seem at first to bear a strong resemblance to some of those said to contribute to the onset of cancer in the contemporary self-health literature. Cancer patients might be seen within these discourses as the modern hysterics whose repressed feelings have gathered over the years and manifested themselves in a tumour in a vulnerable (and highly symbolic) part of their bodies. Both sets of explanations share a belief in the damaging nature of unexpressed emotions; both assert the significance of early trauma on adult illness; and both ascribe pathogenic qualities to ideas and feelings. Finally, the possibility of recovery is asserted in each case with the correct work on the psyche with the help of a professional therapist (although in some alternative cancer literature you are invited to be your own therapist). In some senses, the hydraulic model of repressed feelings relentlessly seeking an outlet, which eventually manifests itself as physical disease, is common to both sets of practices. Even in the less mechanistic accounts where interpretative understanding replaces scientific explanation, they may seem to share a sort of hybrid 'bio-hermeneutics' (Gellner, 1985), in which a patient's distress is seen in terms of 'the inexorable press of biological drives or the need for psychic energy to find an outlet' (Kirmayer, 1988:74).

119

However, these early psychoanalytic writings present contextuality, multi-causality and specificity rarely found in the self-health discourses on cancer. In their case studies Freud and Breuer demonstrate the circuitous route of their explanations of different patients' hysterical symptoms, and Freud suggests that 'it is not possible to assign the same origin to all the somatic symptoms of these patients' (Breuer and Freud, 1893–5:150–1). Furthermore, they do not claim that all physiological symptoms have a psychic origin. Even in relation to patients of hysteria, upon whom they base many of their theories of the psychosomatic character of some disease, there are some physiological symptoms. In the case of Frau Emmy von N., for example, Freud distinguishes emphatically between the psychosomatic symptoms and 'others of the patient's somatic symptoms' which 'were not of a hysterical nature at all . . . but . . . an organic disorder' (Breuer and Freud, 1893–5:156). In addition to the diversity of the origins of hysterical symptoms, and to the variation between psychosomatic and organic ones, Freud also adds the causal contributory influence of heredity (Breuer and Freud, 1893–5:163).

While insisting on the possibility of the somatic effect of a pathogenic idea which has been expelled from consciousness, Freud also warns against any assumption that there might be a *single* traumatic memory or a *single* pathogenic idea as its nucleus (Breuer and Freud, 1893–5:73). There are at least three different structures in which hysteria may present psychical material: a nucleus containing the memories of the trauma surrounded by a profusion of 'mnemic material', 'groupings of similar memories' arranged in a linear sequence which share themes and are stratified concentrically around the nucleus, or an 'arrangement according to thought content, the linkage made by a logical thread which reaches as far as the nucleus and tends to take an irregular and twisting path, different in every case' (Freud, 1893–5:374–5).

Instead of the causal chain of relations between psyche and soma suggested in the model of Simonton *et al.* (1978), Charles (1990) and, more extremely, Hay (1988, 1989) (see Chapter 2), Freud's case studies demonstrate the impossibility of interpreting symptoms as direct tropes of the mind. It is the presence and function of the mechanisms of repression and conversion which precisely prevent such a crude, metaphorical reading. It is the centrality of the unconscious to psychoanalytic theory that distinguishes it from models of illness which see the body as expressing a direct representation of psychic distress. Thus, what might begin as an act of volition ('I do not want to think about that') might have quite a different outcome from that desired by the subject. Freud argues that incompatible ideas are not annihilated by repudiation, as might be intended, but rather are forced into the unconscious and isolated psychically from the ego.

Thus, in their respective conclusions, Breuer and Freud state quite clearly:

> [We do not believe] that they [hysterias] are all ideogenic, that is, determined by ideas. In this we differ from Moebius, who in 1888 proposed to define as hysterical all pathological phenomena that are caused by ideas.
>
> (Breuer, 1893–5:260)

> I should not like it to be wrongly thought that I do not wish to allow that hysteria is an independent neurotic affection, that I regard it merely as a psychical manifestation of anxiety neurosis and that I attribute to it 'ideogenic' symptoms only and am transferring the somatic symptoms (such as hysterogenic points and anaesthesias) to anxiety neurosis. Nothing of the sort.
>
> (Freud, 1893–5:343)

What this excursion into late nineteenth-century theories of hysteria demonstrates, whatever is made of the theories and methods of these two doctors, is that the relationship between the mind and the body in the history of psychoanalytic thought problematises a simple, causal reading of physical symptoms as signs of psychic distress.[12] While highlighting the connections between the soma and psyche in categorising some diseases as 'ideogenic' and some ideas as 'pathogenic', Breuer and Freud both insist on the indirect and layered constitution of such relationships. Furthermore, through their focus on the role of memory and of the unconscious, they demonstrate the limits of the subject's conscious control and volition, emphasising instead the apparently 'irrational' and 'illogical' course of many illnesses:

> In Freud, instincts had a goal and gave rise to much longer and more circumstantial accounts, as he pursued their migrations, their substitutions and the meshing of different aims or objects. It was now a complex circuit that had to be considered, and no longer a simple short shuttling between 'action' and 'reaction'.
>
> (Starobinski, 1989:368)

THE BODY'S OTHER

Freud and Breuer's work can be located in a broader set of ongoing discourses about the meaning of the body and its relationship to other aspects of 'human existence'. If recent histories, or even 'fragments for histories', of the human body reveal anything, it is the extent to which the body has been so widely understood to signify something other than its material self (see Feher *et al.*, 1989, Parts One, Two and Three). The body has been read by historians and cultural theorists as a text of

Concern

political, moral, sexual, religious and aesthetic values and meanings in a multitude of fashions which cross-cut science and art, public and private.[13] Histories of the body invariably represent histories of meaning systems in which the body is positioned through a shifting set of relationships, be it to the mind, the spirit, the soul, the personality, the psyche or the emotions. Thus, 'biohermeneutics' is not restricted to the psychoanalytic encounter, but rather permeates ancient, as well as contemporary, thought.

The discourses mapping the relationship of the psyche to the soma are preceded by those which produce a relationsip of the soma to the soul; these have been traced back, if rather unevenly, to classical cultures. Plato, for example, posited two models: both a 'soul of celestial origin imprisoned – or even entombed in the body' and 'a soul as the source of motion that dominates the body that it moves' (Alliez and Feher, 1989:48). In ancient thought between the first century BC and the second century AD, there was increasing concern about the 'soul's control over the body it inhabits' as the role of 'pathos' became more central: the superior soul, housed in the mortal body, was under threat from somatic afflictions against which 'every respectable individual spent his life struggling' (Alliez and Feher, 1989:54). Thus the desire to protect one's soul from the body resulted in 'the care of the self' explored by Foucault in his later work on the history of sexuality (Foucault, 1990). In other philosophical writings, the body is also seen as opposed to the soul: 'according to Socrates, body and soul are already irrevocably separated, just as are the visible and the invisible, that which is destined to lose its identity and that which keeps it forever, the dissoluble and the indissoluble, the mortal and the divine' (Loraux, 1989:15).

The belief that the soul is temporarily housed in the body is one which extends beyond classical antiquity. From early modern times the soul has been seen to be not simply *located* in the body, but to be *reflected* in its formation. The body was thus considered to be the mirror of the soul. According to Patrizia Magli, Western thought has been fascinated by the paradox that, on the one hand, as Lacan has pointed out, the face is the the most elusive of objects which defies permanent or stable fixing, and, on the other, the face is infinitely classified according to cultural codes of recognition. Magli argues that 'confronted with an ever-changing appearance, ancient physiognomists focused their investigations on an attempt to capture an immanent and univocal essence, and they did this by establishing norms through which to penetrate the secret behind the countenance' (Magli, 1989:87). 'Physiognomics' emerged as a 'pseudo-science', closely related to medicine, which constructed a typology of faces and features said to reveal truths about the soul, dating back in origin to around the fifth century

BC and sharing 'signs described by ancient physicians' (Magli, 1989:89). Derivative of *phusis* (nature) and *gnomon* (interpretation), physiognomics was said to enable knowledge of 'particular passions of the soul from the particular shape of the body' (della Porta, quoted in Magli, 1989:87). Based on beliefs about the meanings of certain codified equivalents, physiognomics established conventions of reading characteristics in the facial features such as 'hooked nose = greed, fleshy lips = sensuality' (Magli, 1989:89). These correlations are recognisable within contemporary discourses of racial stereotyping through which White culture has classified and subordinated its racial 'others'.[14]

What is significantly different in contemporary accounts that rely on the discourse of body types is that 'the soul' has been replaced by the notion of 'the personality'.[15] Indeed, as we saw in the psycho-technologies of cancer prevention, it is increasingly the cancer personality type which is to blame for the illness, not the person's soul. Although the soul has been reintroduced within holistic approaches to self-health (mind, body and spirit) this is very different from the classical idea of the 'soul', which is rarely located as the source of physical decline.

This connection between the psyche and the soul is not simply one of historical sequence in the history of bodily discourses. Their connection is also, of course, etymological. The term 'psyche' is now commonly used in its psychoanalytic rather than its spiritual sense. However, it continues to be defined as 'soul', 'mind', 'spirit', 'beyond or apparently beyond the physical' (*Chambers Dictionary*, 1972: 1085). In Greek mythology 'Psyche' was, in fact, the personification of the soul. Hence the *psychic life* of a person signifies two quite different things within religious and psychoanalytic discourse. This confusion may seem quite apposite given the widespread influence of Freudian thinking on Western thought. Psychoanalysis has been called *the* twentieth-century religion, not only because its followers have so venerated its founder, or because any objection to it can be incorporated into its own self-justification (conscious resistance *to* it only confirms one's need *for* it), but because the inexplicable or destructive elements in Western experience tend now to be located within the 'dark depths' of the unconscious mind instead of the evil soul and the wider forces which control it.[16] Thus, the relationship of the mind and body has been refigured in so far as the psyche has come to represent the twentieth-century soul in a Western 'godless' culture.

BODILY SENSATIONS

The gradual replacement of the concept of the soul with that of personality in medical discourse is evidenced in the history of the idea of 'cenaesthesia' (the internal perception of our own body).[17] Originally used in 1794, the term 'coenaesthesia' referred to the 'process by means of which the soul is informed of the state of its body, which occurs by means of the nerves generally distributed throughout the body' (Reil, quoted in Starobinski, 1989:355). Drawing on Descartes's tripartite categorisation of perception elaborated in *The Passions of the Soul*, Reil classifies three different organic apparatuses: the first is cenaesthesia, the second, 'sensation' ('excited by the senses and represents the world to the soul'), and the third, 'the activities which originate and are carried out integrally within the organ of the soul ... by means of these ... imagination and judgement are formed; the soul receives the representation of its powers, its ideas and its concepts, and is thus rendered conscious of itself' (Reil, quoted in Starobinski, 1989:355). This model formed the basis for a 'pathogenic classification' in which idiopathic, as well as general, disorders were seen to cause changes in cenaesthesia. In other words, the disruption of the senses within a person could affect their mental life. The brain might be sent misleading messages about the body, due to disturbances in the senses. Ailments characterised by problems in bodily representations included pica, bulimia, polydipsia, nymphomania and a host of other complaints previously classified within melancholia and hypochondria.

This 'sensualist' conception of mental life opened the way for a kind of 'imperialism of cenesthesia', according to Starobinski (1989:356–7). By the nineteenth century, however, any notion of the soul seems to have largely disappeared and instead the debate is continued within the discourses of the 'personality' in which cenaesthesia is seen as 'the source of all psychic life' (Starobinski, 1989:356–7). Ribot's immensely influential *Diseases of the Personality* (fifteen editions of which were published between 1883 and 1914) suggested that 'if mental life was determined by sensory activity, and if all sensory activity was made up of derivatives of the cenesthesia, then one could finish by asserting ... that our personality resided entirely in the messages, partially unconscious, that derived from bodily life' (Starobinski, 1989:357). The personality within this conceptualisation, then, is a 'kaleidoscope phenomenon' due to 'fluctuation in bodily states' (Starobinski, 1989:357). Thus, according to Ribot, states of the body produce sensations which in turn produce a 'physical personality' and 'the ego exists only on the condition of continually changing' (Ribot, quoted in Starobinski, 1989:357).

What is significant in this historical interrogation of the category of cenaesthesia is the indication it gives of broader transformations within medical discourse. It highlights the complexity of the interconnections between soma and psyche, which are so frequently superficially glossed as the mind/body dichotomy in the shorthand of debates about con-

temporary self-health cancer treatments. However, even more importantly for the purposes of my argument, Starobinski's scholarly investigation indexes the replacement of the soul with the psyche and now the
personality, and the concommitent emergence of the notion of the
responsible citizen who has a duty to be healthy (Starobinski, 1989:358,
and see Chapter 7, this volume). In this shift from soul to psyche we can
witness the *reversal of the directional causation* from feelings to bodies in
which emotions are attributed a pathogenic potential. Furthermore,
the emotional self now takes on a moral dimension as the psyche
becomes overdetermined as a signifier of morality and duty. Illness,
once again, though for different reasons, is constructed as a punishment (Picone, 1989:486). Individuals are thus increasingly under
threat, not from their bodies as such, but rather from their emotions,
especially from those designated negative which we store at our peril.
As one publication puts it in its title, *You Can't Afford the Luxury of a
Negative Thought* (Roger and McWilliams, 1991).

It is not that the somatic manifestations of emotional effects are
particularly new: connections between the body and emotions have
been theorised in many different ways in the past. Aristotle, for
example, interpreted wrath as a desire for vengeance or as a 'boiling
up of the blood around the heart' (Aristotle, quoted in Magli, 1989:88).
In Galenic medicine it was principally 'by way of the humours, and not
through the nervous information, that the body was capable of modi-
fying the activity of the soul, and in turn, being modified by the soul'
(Starobinski, 1989:354). Within this Galenic model 'the body was
understood to be composed of four humours or fluids (blood, phlegm,
black bile [or melancholia] and yellow bile [or choler]; the variant
mixture of these determined people's characters' (Graham *et al.*,
1989:26). The imbalance of the humours was seen to produce emotions,
such as too much yellow bile causing anger. Indeed, in *The Genesis of
Cancer* (1978), Rather details the history of changing beliefs about the
causes of cancer (humoral, tissue and cell theory) and offers examples
of seventeenth-century theorists who saw certain emotions as a causative
factor: 'Boerhaave [following Hoffman] includes among the precipitating causes of the cancerous change melancholy' (Rather, 1978:34).

However, in many of these previous accounts, the body affected the
emotions rather than the other way around. It was not until Freud that
this redirection of the causation became so pronounced; he hotly
contested the primacy of cenaesthesia and attempted to desomatise the
'causal system commonly accepted by his predecessors' (Starobinski,
1989:365). Freud's model may have been a far cry from the more
mechanistic and functional ones of self-health cancer literatures, but
he did introduce the notion of dreams and instincts as having a psychic,
not a somatic, origin. Before Freud the unconscious did exist as a term,

but it was conceptualised as the 'obscure murmurings of visceral functions – from which would emerge intermittently, conscious acts' (Starobinski, 1989:364).

Thus, although the mind and the body have been seen to affect each other since ancient Western thought, the typical direction of this influence before Freud was from the body to the mind. There is no doubt that although Freud and Breuer's path is a complex and circuitous one, it nevertheless reversed the direction of causality in this respect. To put it crudely, popular beliefs today are more likely to attribute physical symptoms to depression than they are melancholia to too much 'black bile'. Bodily sensations thus no longer threaten the soul's well-being and safety, but rather signify the individual's distress, or the somatised psyche. Replacing earlier moral concerns with the soul there has been an increasing preoccupation with the 'mind' in twentieth-century medical discourses. In the psychotechnologies of alternative and self-health cultures, what is meant by the mind in the notion of the somatic causes of illness such as cancer is not the intellect, but rather what has commonly been referred to as the psyche. Believing Western culture to have overvalued the intellect at the expense of the emotions, most alternative medical literature on cancer encourages patients to explore the possible causative factors in their emotional development. I have yet to find examples of beliefs about a lack of intellectual development causing disease. But are these beliefs about the pschye and the soma only to be found in the alternative accounts of cancer, or do they inform biomedicine, however indirectly? Has the increasing popularity of alternative and self-health therapies in cancer treatment had any significant impact on biomedical approaches?

BIOMEDICINE IN TRANSITION?

The more traditional rejections of alternative approaches to cancer continue to be widely represented in biomedical debates. Several studies of biomedical practioners' attitudes to these approaches in the 1980s reveal 'a certain degree of distrust, intolerance and misunder-standing' (Furnham and Bhagrath, 1993:238). The language of ration-ality and objectivity is used to question their validity and is rejected on the grounds of a lack of scientific evidence to prove their efficacy, as a quotation from a letter in the *British Medical Journal* exemplifies: 'Surely the economic limitations imposed on general practioners and their primary health care team require managers to prefer treatments that work rather than appeal to irrational sensibilities' (Egan, 1992:1096). Using words such as 'unorthodox', 'unproven' and 'questionable' to describe alternative therapies, biomedical literature makes its ostens-ibly neutral objections clear. Drawing on scientific studies which 'prove that there is no correlation between a number of psychosocial factors and the progression of cancer', one doctor writes, 'it is time to acknowledge that our belief in disease as a direct reflection of the mental state is largely folklore' (Angell, 1985:1571–2).

In medical textbooks on cancer, alternative approaches are rarely mentioned at all and where they are, they are, not surprisingly, evaluated according to biomedical criteria, rather than on their own terms. In *Cancer in Practice*, the authors present a summary of the available forms of treatment outside conventional oncology, but they nevertheless evaluate them within the discourses of biomedicine, focusing on the objectivity of the scientific method:

> Most of the progress that has been made in the fight against cancer has been as a result of critical scientific evaluation. The characteristic feature of the scientific method is the preparedness to expose favoured hypotheses or beliefs to the hazard of refutation . . . 'Alternative' treatments are treatments which, almost by definition, are outside conventional or orthodox medical practice, and which have not been exposed to or have not withstood the rigours of scientific evaluation . . . Not only are alternative treatments for cancer of unproven value, they are very rarely objectively assessed by their proponents.
>
> (Rees *et al.*, 1993:88)

Each of the therapies evaluated in their textbook are then presented within conventional evaluative criteria: 'special diets', for example, are referred to as having 'conceptual appeal' but readers are cautioned about the fact that 'there is no objective evidence that they can improve the long-term outlook for patients with cancer' (Rees *et al.*, 1993:89); a deficiency in beta-carotene is acknowledged to increase the risk of malignancy according to some epidemiological evidence, but again, no evidence is found that supplements 'improve the chance of a cure of cancer' (Rees *et al.*, 1993:90). Indeed, in the case of the controversial Laetrile, toxicity and a few incidences of death from overdose are reported.[18]

However, despite evidence of such hostilities in these respects, in evaluating the role of the patient's 'mind' in the progress of their disease, this biomedical account suggests that studies provide evidence which both confirms and contradicts the connection between loss, stress, personality, will to live and cancer prognosis. Many of the claims made about the impact of techniques of the mind (such as positive thinking, 'discharge' of emotional distress and a sense of hope) on the cause and cure of cancer are rejected as 'unproven' or 'unsubstantiated', but the authors nevertheless acknowledge the value of support groups for cancer patients and devote chapters of this other-

127

wise quite traditional textbook to subjects such as 'Quality of Life', 'Psychological Support' and 'Support for Patients with Cancer'.[19]

Much new research continues to confirm existing 'medical scepticism' about the use of alternative medical treatment. In the case of the study of the Bristol Cancer Help Centre, for example, the misleading claim that the Bristol Centre might harm cancer patients led to a general battle over the reputation of the Centre and resulted in headlines such as 'Death from Complementary Medicine' (Richards, 1990:510–11). Bagenal *et al.* (1990) published, and publicised, the results of their study of 334 women with breast cancer who attended Bristol and a control of 461 women with the same disease who did not. Their much criticised conclusions were that 'women with breast cancer attending the BCHC fare worse than those receiving conventional treatment only . . . For patients metastasis-free at entry, metastasis-free survival in the BCHC group was significantly poorer than in the controls . . . Survival in relapsed cases was significantly inferior to that in the control group' (Bagenal, 1990:609, 606). The many lines of defence against these allegations drew on both scientific discourses (the Bristol patients were younger and cancer grows faster in younger women, more conservative surgery tends to be carried out on younger women which might have affected their chances of survival, patients attending Bristol may have had more advanced malignancies before they went there) and those of alternative medicine (perhaps the Bristol women had lower hopes about the efficacy of conventional treatment and thus their survival, the Bristol patients may have had more cancer-prone personalities than those in the control group, failure to control for psychological factors invalidates the results of the research). Common-sense knowledge of health and illness was also appealed to: how could relaxation, counselling and an organic vegan diet be damaging to your health? (*The Lancet*, 1990:743–4).

Despite the attempt to defend the Centre's reputation and the numerous challenges to the research methodology and its conclusions by doctors, medical sociologists, Bristol patients and alternative practitioners, the work of the Centre has nevertheless suffered and services have been reduced. The counter-arguments successfully discredited the research on numerous grounds, but they did not have the scandal value of the findings, and received less media attention.[20]

However, while it is a negative example of medical evaluations of alternative practices, this research belongs to the beginning of a more general reevaluation of this relationship. Despite such attacks on alternative medicine, it could be argued that in the call for tighter regulations there is nevertheless an acknowledgement of the role of such practices in Britain's medical future (Smith, 1983:307). The British Medical Association produced a report which argues that complementary therapists should undergo some basic training in medical science and doctors should participate in such a programme. They also advocated a general register of members of each type of therapy, which only competent practioners could join (Kingman, 1993:1713). While this may seem like an inappropriate intervention for those who argue that the existing British Register of Complementary Practitioners already fulfils such a function, and that basic medical knowledge such as anatomy is already part of such practitioners' training, the BMA's engagement with alternative medicine is nevertheless significant: it set up a working party on the extent of usage of such therapies in Britain and Europe and subsequently published a report on its findings (Kingman, 1993:1713). In addition, the referral of patients to alternative practitioners is no longer considered 'unethical' (Pietroni, 1992a:565). Recent changes in doctors' responses to alternative medicine have been widely documented in the medical journals. The deputy editor of the *British Medical Journal* informs readers of the increasing interest in alternative medicine among doctors. He cites one survey of general practitioner trainees in Britain which showed that '70 of the 86 wanted training in techniques such as hypnosis, acupuncture, manipulation, homoeopathy, and herbalism. Twelve of the doctors had referred their patients for treatment to non-medical practioners – a step which a few years ago could have led to an appearance before the General Medical Council disciplinary committee' (Smith, 1983:307). Another study found 'a positive attitude towards complementary medicine in 86 out of 100 general practitioner trainees in 1982', and yet another that out of 200 general practitioners surveyed in the Avon district '38% had received some additional training in one form of complementary therapy' (Pietroni, 1992a:564–5).

The studies of Cassileth *et al.* (1984, 1985, 1991) and Cassileth (1989) clearly reject the claims that the patient's state of mind affects the development of cancer, but they demonstrate the perception of the need to examine claims of alternative and self-health claims about cancer. In a study of 359 patients with cancer, Cassileth *et al.* conclude: '[O]ur study of patients with advanced high-risk malignant disease suggests that the inherent biology of the disease alone determines the prognosis, overriding the potentially mitigating influence of psychosocial factors' (Cassileth *et al.*, 1985:1555). In another study of 'unproven' cancer therapy, the length of survival and quality of life in patients receiving 'unorthodox' in conjunction with conventional treatment is compared with patients just receiving the latter (Cassileth *et al.*, 1991:1180). This concluded that not only was there no difference in the survival rates of the two groups, but also that the quality of life in patients undergoing *conventional treatment only* scored higher. This obviously goes against the claims of many alternative cancer treatments

129

that they enhance quality, if not length, of life. However, it should also be noted that the 'quality of life' of patients of conventional treatment was also better at enrolment (Cassileth *et al.*, 1991:1184).

Despite their negative conclusions about alternative approaches to cancer care, both studies show an engagement with alternative beliefs and practices. To measure 'quality of life', for example, as well as survival rates, is to engage with a shift in medical discourse away from the purely mechanical model of the body, and to acknowledge the patients' need for emotional care. Futhermore, in their studies of cancer patients' use of alternative medicine, Cassileth *et al.* (1984) demonstrate its widespread popularity and impact upon cancer treatment. While defending the superiority of the scientific method of biomedicine against the appeal of these new unorthodox, unproven methods, Cassileth *et al.* nevertheless highlight the general dissatisfaction with conventional medical practice. They conclude: 'when patients turn toward alternative treatments, they are simultaneously moving away from perceived conventional care' (Cassileth *et al.*, 1984:112). This study also points to the increasing overlap between these two systems of biomedicine and alternative treatment in cancer care: 54 per cent of patients using conventional treatment, for example, were also using unorthodox therapies; and 60 per cent of the 138 unorthodox practitioners studied were also medically trained doctors (Cassileth *et al.*, 1984:105).

Indeed, as Cassileth (1989) goes on to argue, orthodox and unorthodox approaches to cancer may even share the influence of certain social and cultural changes. Contemporary beliefs in '"metabolic" therapies', he argues, 'emphasising diet, self care, vitamins, and internal cleansing, along with "immune-enhancing" regimens . . . reflect underlying social trends and values, such as the belief in assuming personal responsibility for one's health, the importance of self care and physical fitness, patients' rights movements, dietary emphases' (Cassileth, 1989:1247; see also Chapter 7, this volume). These changes, it is suggested, are in part a result of new emphases encouraged by *conventional* as well as alternative medicine:

> other features to which patients gravitate are available, *at least potentially*, within the conventional framework. These features include the opportunity for patients to participate actively in their own care; the inclusion of nutritional and dietary factors, which patients read about in their daily newspapers; and the opportunity for patients to develop a sustaining relationship with a primary physician whom they perceive to be caring and involved.
>
> (Cassileth *et al.*, 1984:112, my emphasis)

Cassileth *et al.* suggest that conventional medicine might learn from research on patients' disaffection with its alienating practices and begin to build some of the advantages of alternative medicine into their philosophy of treatment. Another study of the uses of alternative therapies by patients with terminal cancer in Australia advocates the need to understand this rising phenomenon within the conventional model of patient behaviour. Yates *et al.* argue that:

> people who are ill engage in a range of strategies, in efforts to have their disease cured . . . From this point of view it is surprising that more people with terminal cancer don't adopt alternative therapies, once they realise that conventional treatments are not going to save their lives.
>
> (Yates *et. al.*, 1993:214)

Further evidence of changes in biomedical practices can be seen in the ways in which some oncology departments in hospitals have begun to include some alternative practices within their hospital programmes. At The Royal Marsden Hospital in London, for example, cancer patients are offered counselling and psychotherapy, art therapy and therapeutic massage in addition to surgery, chemotherapy and radiation treatments. Following visits to the Bristol Cancer Help Centre, oncologists from Hammersmith Hospital in London have begun to offer some forms of 'complementary treatments' to their cancer patients. Forty-four per cent of their patients expressed an interest in trying some form of complementary medicine, and 22 per cent had used them previously for other illnesses (Sikora, 1989:1285). Again, drawing attention to the criticisms of the autocratic and patronising approach to the patient which has characterised hospital practice in Britain for so long, the combination of conventional and complementary medicine in cancer care is favoured as a more democratic alternative. The policy at Hammersmith, for example, diffuses the centrality of the patient/oncologist encounter, and provides emotional, social and informational support, in addition to the physical treatment (Burke and Sikora, 1992:62–6). This report in *Nursing Times* reaches an audience who may be more sympathetic to the aims of alternative medicine than many consultants. Indeed, it has been suggested that the refocusing of biomedical treatment through a holistic lens might be best suited to begin with nursing practice which has traditionally been more concerned with overall patient care (psychological, as well as physical) (Montbriand and Laing, 1991:325).

These calls for the integration of certain beliefs and practices which treat the patient as more than just a physical body extend beyond oncology into debates about general medical practice. Documenting the rapid growth in complementary medicines in Britain (approximately 50,000 practices of one sort or another in 1992 with a growth rate of 10 per cent a year) in the *British Medical Journal*, a senior lecturer in general practice at St Mary's Hospital, London, advocates their integration into an expanded primary health care system:

> My view is that although our roots may lie in medical schools and our current identity is that of general practice, out future lies as members and, at times, leaders, of an expanded primary health and community care team which, among others, must include selected complementary practitioners.
>
> (Pietroni, 1992a:566)

In the last ten years we have witnessed the beginning of what promises to be a fundamental shift in attitudes to alternative medicine. What is surprising, I think, is the amount of serious dialogue with alternative therapies to be found in contemporary biomedical journals. Even in the form of these critical exchanges, alternative medicine 'one of the few growth industries in contemporary Britain' (Smith, 1983:307)) is making an impact on biomedical beliefs and practices. As the above examples illustrate in a number of different ways, alternative medicines are not only being used by patients with cancer and other diseases, but are also increasingly recognised by medical doctors and nurses as a potential source of knowledge in patient care and support. In my own experience, having concealed my vitamins and mineral supplements from the medical staff at the hospital for fear of having them confiscated (as rumour had it they might be), I later discovered that most of the staff I encountered on the chemotherapy ward were interested in, if not sympathetic to, alternative approaches to cancer care. Once I had 'come out' as a patient who used such methods, several of the chemotherapy nurses wanted to talk to me about my experiences for their research projects in their own medical training. Indeed, my oncologist took his patients' use of alternative methods very seriously; during one pre-treatment examination he warned me against mocking them myself when I rather self-consciously drew humorous attention to the acupuncture studs in my ears which had been inserted to counter the nausea caused by chemotherapy.

This debate has brought with it an open recognition of the power imbalances between doctor and patient and the negative effects of what has too often been a brief and humiliating encounter; cancer patients, not surprisingly, have expressed dissatisfaction at the average time for an oncology consultation being 13.4 minutes, with 24 per cent of patients having less than 5 minutes (Burke and Sikora, 1992:62). Connected to this change is the acknowledgement that patients will no longer accept being treated as just physical bodies with symptoms. Increasingly, there is some attempt to debate the ways in which patient care might extend beyond 'the physical' to 'the emotional'. However, this gradual acceptance of the importance of what has been called 'the mind' in treating the *effects* of illness has not been extended to debates about its *cause*. Several advocates of the incorporation of alternative medicine into the conventional structures of cancer care continue to express caution about the dangers of the 'victim-blaming' condemnation of the patient as responsible for their own illness (and sometimes death) which characterise some of these 'psychotechnologies'. In tracing some of the changes in medical discourses of the mind/body relationship it is thus important to maintain a distinction between a more 'holistic' model which recognises the broader needs of the patient with cancer and one in which the patient's disease is merely considered to be the somatic manifestation of psychic 'dysfunction' (see Hay, 1988, 1989).

ALTERNATIVE SYSTEMS?

Having established the extent to which conventional medicine has been influenced by some of the 'mind/body' models of its alternative counterparts, this final section of the chapter takes a brief look at the question in reverse: in other words, it examines the question of how independent alternative and self-health approaches to cancer are from biomedical models of bodily knowledge. Some forms of alternative medicine are obviously based upon entirely different conceptual systems from Western medicine. Acupuncture, for example, is a practice of Chinese medicine which uses terms with no immediately recognisable Western counterpart. As Mark Elvin argues, the Chinese 'body' has quite a different meaning from Western understandings: *shen* might be translated as 'body person' and refers to ideas of 'person', 'self', 'life' or 'lifetime' (Elvin, 1989:275). It is thus difficult to 'translate' the philosophy of different Chinese acupuncture systems.[21] Put crudely, acupuncture uses needles to release blocks in the flow of *Chi* energy. Stephen Fulder sums up Seven Principles acupuncture thus:

> health is achieved through a balance between opposing forces represented by *yin* and *yang* . . . *Yin* is fire and *yang* is water: thus everything that is *yin* sinks like water and everything that is *yang* rises like fire. When either of these forces is out of balance, illness results.
>
> (Fulder, 1984:122)[22]

The other type of acupuncture, Five Elements, works through the belief that:

> all things, including man [*sic*], are composed of five fundamental forms of energy: wood, fire, earth, metal and water. The relationship between these five transformations is subject to certain

laws that govern the flow between them. Because the organs of the body are associated with the five elements, these cyclical laws can be applied to the workings of the body, enabling the practitioner to treat disorders.

(Fulder, 1984:122)

Little of the above description accords with Western beliefs about disease and its causes and there are numerous other examples of medical belief systems which work outside Western models. However, many forms of alternative medicine work within a framework that is much more familiar to the Western model of the body. Assessing the relationship of 'holistic' and 'psychosomatic medicine' to biomedicine, Kirmayer (1988) argues that the former two fail to overcome the Cartesian mind/body dualism of the latter because of the way in which they are 'so deeply entrenched in Western experience' (Kirmayer, 1988:58). Indeed, he argues that this dualism is reinforced by approaches which simply reverse the hierarchy, positing the mind as controller of the body:

> In the healing vision of psychosomatic medicine, mind and body are to be brought into harmony. Most often, however, this goal is described not as an equal marriage but as the reestablishment of the mind's dominance and control over the body and with it, of reason over emotion . . . invok[ing] the same values of rational control and distance from passion and bodily-felt meaning that are part of the mechanistic world view of biomedicine.
>
> (Kirmayer, 1988:58)

In the same vein, Helman's study (1988) revealed 'important agreements between lay and biomedical explanatory models of psychosomatic disorders', particularly with respect to chronic illnesses which conventional medicine could not explain or cure. Interviews with patients showed the extent to which they had internalised a view of themselves as 'too "obsessive", "perfectionist", and "anal", or "sensitive", or as people who "hold too much in"; their personalities, emotions, lifestyle, or physical weaknesses are blamed for their failure to conform to . . . [certain] ideal social values' (Helman, 1988:117).

This overlap between alternative and conventional medical belief systems can be seen in slightly different ways in the context of cancer care. The most common alternative therapies used by cancer patients in one study, for example, were, in descending order: 'metabolic therapy, diet treatments, megavitamins, mental imagery applied for antitumour effect, spiritual or faith healing, and "immune" therapy' (Cassileth, 1989:1248). What is involved in the most popular of these approaches, 'metabolic therapy', is summed up thus:

[It] rests on the notion that toxins and waste materials in the body interfere with metabolism and healing, and that cells lack the nutrients essential to health. Cancer and other chronic illnesses are viewed as the result of degeneration of the liver and pancreas, and of the immune and 'oxygenation' systems. Treatment is directed at cellular 'detoxification and restoration'.

(Cassileth, 1989:1248)

This 'alternative' approach to cancer differs from conventional medicine in some ways, but its vocabulary and conceptual system are clearly derived largely from scientific frameworks: the metabolism, the immune system, the cellular composition of the body.

Similarly, the language of the Simontons' model of disease, or Charles's explanation for her cancer, discussed earlier in this chapter, also employ highly Westernised, scientific language. Indeed, one might suggest that therein lies their credibility: perhaps their appeal is, in part, due to their common-sense use of relatively familiar models of the body, authorised through a scientific language. Simonton *et al.* (1978) utilise a combination of medical and psychological language (he has been a doctor, she a psychotherapist) to explain the development of malignant cells. Systems such as 'limbic', 'immune' and 'endocrine', and activities such as 'hypothalamic' and 'pituitary', form the basis for the connection between mind and body. Cancer growth is thus made possible because of the effects of emotions, such as depression and despair, on these physical systems and activities. According to Charles (1990), the 'immune system' responds directly to emotional stimulation, and thus again cancer might develop in a patient whose negative dispostion allows her/him to be vulnerable to the disease.

Scientific theories of the immune system form the basis for many alternative and self-health approaches to cancer. It might seem ironic to some that a mainstream scientific discourse like immunology, which has become increasingly influential on scientific understandings of disease and its cure, should authorise 'alternatives' to it. In the last twenty years its impact has transformed the language of medicine, and, with the HIV and AIDS epidemic, it will no doubt continue to play a central role in the biomedicine of the future. Its cultural purchase can be seen from the way in which its concepts and knowledge successfully translate across the alternative/conventional medical divide, demonstrating the interconnection between mind and body, on the one hand, and the organic character of physical disease on the other.

The exchanges and influences between biomedical and alternative models of the mind and body in the treatment of cancer can thus be seen to flow in both directions. Conventional medicine, in its own defence, has become more reflexive and self-critical about some of the problems with its rigidity about its previous exclusive concentration upon the physical body. In alternative and self-health medicines, while some have drawn upon non-Western practices, many have relied heavily on developments in the biological sciences and have combined these new systematic models of 'the body' with their own psychological models of 'the mind'. It is the cultural significance of these new forms of medical knowledge and, in particular, their effect on visualising health, which is the subject of Chapter 5.

5

VISIONS

There is an inevitable slippage from the visible to the mirage of absolute transparence, as if the light of reason could extend into the deepest murkiest depths of the human organism. As if truth consisted simply in making something visible.

(Braidotti, 1994:67)

SEEING THE SIGNS: BEFORE AND AFTER

In the first photograph [see Figure 5.1] I am watering the geraniums outside the kitchen door. The old stone house is built into the abbey wall of a small French village. Here at the back there is a daily watering ritual to perform as the hot sun begins to die down for the day. The setting is idyllic; the house is the envy of passers-by who have come to visit the abbey. Here I can be seen in holiday mode: casual, relaxed, contented, taking pleasure in 'playing house' away from home. I look healthy and fit. The shorts show off tanned legs that have been well-exercised. I smile, do not look up, aware that the photograph is being taken, but not willing to pose further. A picture of happiness; a picture of health.

In the second photograph [see Figure 5.2] I am sitting at a table writing a letter. The accoutrements of a holiday in the sun surround me: beach mat, airmail letters, sunglasses. The white walls behind belong to the patio of the rented studio flat in Crete. The patio provides some shade from the heat of the sun and also offers a sense of privacy. I do not look at the camera, but continue writing as if unaware of its presence. I am not wearing a hat or scarf. My head bent over the letter, you can see clearly the new growth of hair. Have I been ill or is this a radical fashion gesture or even a political statement? Chemotherapy may come to the minds of some who see me.

The first photograph was taken in July 1991. I found out I had cancer two months later. The tumour must already have been growing inside in July. Looked at with this knowledge, the first photograph offers a less innocent story. The paradise holiday preceded the nightmare diagnosis; the healthy, tanned body concealed a large and potentially lethal tumour. The story the photograph tells is now one of deception. I

Figure 5.1 Personal photograph (July 1991)

Figure 5.2 Personal photograph (April 1992)

look at this photograph with an endless sense of disbelief: am I missing something? Everyone said I looked so well that summer. Perhaps there *are* signs for all to see, a secret code, a hidden trace. Why can't I find it in this image?

The second photograph was taken in April 1992. The chemotherapy had finished a month before. With this knowledge in mind we can read this as a photograph of a 'cancer patient'. Chemotherapy had made me look ill, even though I was actually well again. But here, I was in that liminal space where there is no knowing. I study the image but the signs are ambiguous. Compared with Figure 5.1, I look ill; to others who know nothing of the circumstances, I look strange: my face is still puffy from the steroids and the dark rings under my eyes are more accentuated than usual; together with no hair, apart from the beginnings of a fine new growth, I am aware I am a sight. People clearly pondered the possibilities as they passed me by on the street: not the typical holiday-maker look. And yet retrospectively I know that the cancer had gone. The scarred and bloated body attracted sympathetic (and fearful, or just plain curious) gazes and yet it no longer housed a cancerous tumour. The convalescent look here suggests the presence of a disease that had in fact been banished.

Figures 5.1 and 5.2 are holiday snaps showing me involved in everyday activities. Like the 'before-and-after' genre that shows the miracles performed by make-up and a good haircut, these two photos contrast strikingly at first glance. The pairing technique is an especially popular form of representing femininity, drawing as it does on the cultivated competitive look between women. Before-and-after pairings typically show the transformation of the dowdy, plain face (and sometimes figure) into the strikingly glamorous one that would not be passed by unnoticed.[1] The combination shown here serves a rather different purpose. There is a disorientating effect in the comparison of these two photographs: in the first, I look healthy, but I have cancer; in the second, I look ill, but I do not have cancer. Neither shows me what I am looking for: the visible signs of the disease. For despite myself, I still want to equate seeing and knowing: the promise of certainty is sought in the visual evidence. The most striking announcement of cancer is the baldness of the chemotherapy patient. And yet this is an effect of the treatment and tells us nothing about the stage of the disease. Sometimes the baldness signifies recovery, sometimes imminent death. This 'before-and-after' combination has the purpose of rehearsing the sense of mismatch between surface appearance and deeper bodily knowledge, the discrepancy between outer contentment and inner turmoil. The shock is rehearsed in the question I pose to these photographs: is seeing really believing?

The body has tricked us all, it seems. We labour under the illusion that we can read its surface signs. The promise of eternal youth and immortality rests in the cultural preoccupation with the smooth appearance of the body's exterior.[2] In fact, outward impressions may not only deceive others, they may also deceive oneself. Some tumours grow undetected for years, surreptitiously reproducing millions of cells with none other than a deathly function. The secrets of the body repeatedly pass through the mind of the person with cancer. Not knowing, not seeing, not realising, the presence of the disease is replayed across the shock left by the diagnosis. Some might have had their suspicions, some might have seen the signs, some might have feared their genetic inheritance, but for many, as for me, the discovery comes out of the blue. The gaping discrepancy requires the mind to revisit the past. Memories of health and happiness conflict with the new arrival that belies their credibility. These versions of the past self are worked over and over until they are in dialogue with the present health crisis. But this uncanny mismatch requires a new story be written.

I search the photographs for a knowledge they refuse to display; I look to the images of the body to produce some guidance. I inspect them for the slightest hint of prediction. Yet why expect predictive visual evidence from a photograph? And why expect the body to offer straightforward indications? Perhaps the calm-before-the-storm narrative constructed around these contrasting images is simply a product of my retrospection, a way of symbolising the impact of the shock to myself and others. Perhaps all the problems of the summer of 1991 have been wiped out by the nostalgic desire to return to a time of innocence, a time that seems so much more idyllic only after its loss. Taking a step back from my search, I am reminded of the arguments. But they do not answer the desires and wishes that motivate my scrutiny of these images. On the one hand, I know that photographs are visual artefacts. Highly artificial constructions, they reveal nothing and tell us only about themselves. On the other hand, I find myself searching these 'frozen moments' for a sign that might shed some light on the bodily deceptions of that time. Photographs never lie: the old myths still catch us out. I continue to be seduced by the promise of visual truth despite my apparent critical distance.

Inspired by feminist work on photography and memory (Haug, 1987; Kuhn, 1995; Spence and Solomon, 1995), I use these two holiday snapshots both as 'memory prompts' and as a way of rehearsing the shock of the diagnosis (Kuhn, 1995:8). These two motivations are connected. My memory of the 'before' time, of the sense of bodily well-being of those summer months, is now suspended in a psychic space apart from my other perceptions of the past. It hangs there in punishing isolation and is accused of deception. Such a radical disjuncture is too much to absorb. '*Look at how well I looked*', I say to the reader/viewer, seeking recognition of the force of the unexpected diagnosis. I return repeatedly both to the photograph and to the memory of a healthy body that it prompts and still something resists the story that ensued: there is no sequence and no continuity. It is hard for the subject to accommodate such a radical disjuncture. It makes no sense. How could one look so healthy and be so ill? How is it possible that after the very first malignant cell division the body did not send out warnings? Does the body of the person with cancer have trouble recognising itself as diseased? How is it possible that a deathly disease remained hidden for so long? What visual signs are to be trusted in the future?

This chapter explores these questions, and the force of their stubborn persistence, through an investigation of changing images of the body's interior landscape. Feminist work on the history of the masculine medical gaze is drawn upon to analyse this powerful conjuncture of seeing, knowing and controlling. The chapter looks especially at how cancer is conceptualised as cellular dysfunction and immune system breakdown through a repertoire of proliferating visualising technologies. My general concern here is with the question of how the changing conceptualisations of the body's *visualisable* interior indicate new beliefs about health and illness in contemporary culture.

CELLULAR BODIES

According to contemporary oncology textbooks, cancer is a disease of the cells of the body. Cancer is characterised by 'uncontrolled growth, and the ability to infiltrate surrounding tissues and spread to distant sites . . . most cancers arise from a mutation in a single cell and therefore represent a monoclonal population, but some growths are polyclonal, indicating that they have developed following more than one mutation' (Rees *et al.*, 1993:3). Cells are usually reproduced with a purpose: they are hair cells, blood cells, liver cells, and so on. Different kinds of cells form different parts of the body: misodermal cells form organs, endodermal cells, bones, and ectodermal cells, skin. So-called normal cells are differentiated; each has a specific function. Malignant cancer cells are those which keep dividing and reproducing themselves without proper functional designation. They are (usually) less differentiated and eventually form a tumour which will metastasise (spread to another part of the body) through the lymphatic system, the bloodstream, the cerebrospinal fluid, the coelomic cavity or the soft tissue planes, unless treatment prevents their proliferation (Rees *et al.*, 1993:5–6). While there are enough different types of cancer (literally hundreds) to make the term almost meaningless, 'the unifying aspect of cancer is uncontrolled growth – the appearance of disorganized tissues that expand without limit, compromising the function of organs and threatening the life of the organism' (Varmus and Weinberg, 1993:25).

However, cancer has not always been conceptualised as a disease of cell development. As I discussed in Chapter 4, tumours were seen to be caused by abnormal accretion of 'humours' in Hippocratic medicine, and were, on the whole, thought best left untreated. In general, however, cancers were not really distinguished from other kinds of benign and inflammatory tumours, all of which were accounted for by a humoral theory of disease (Rather, 1978:10). This model of disease, modified by Galen, became canonical within medicine into the seventeenth century. Based on the ancient Greek model, this approach had four universal elements, 'fire, air, water and earth', which were brought into a relationship with four 'potencies or qualities, hot, cold, moist and dry'; these 'qualities' were seen to be assigned to the four humours of the body: 'blood, phlegm, yellow bile and black bile (melancholy) with varying degrees of precision' (Rather, 1978:11). Galen 'sought to differentiate more clearly cancer from inflammatory lesions and gangrene. Cancer was held to be caused by black bile; if the cancer ulcerated, the black bile was undiluted; if there was only a tumor, the pathogenic humor had been diluted' (Benedek and Kiple, 1994:102). The 'black bile' theory of cancer was superseded by a model of causation based on the lymphatic system that was 'discovered' in 1622. Cancer was seen as 'an inflammatory reaction to extravasated lymph, the type of lesion depending on its qualities' (Benedek and Kiple, 1994:102).

Cancer and its aetiology thus have a long history within competing scientific theories of disease (Rather, 1978). There may be alarmingly high rates of increase in occurrences of cancer today but it is not an exclusively modern disease.[3] According to one history of the disease, 'tumours have been found in Egyptian mummies dating from 2000 to 3000 B.C. and physicians . . . knew of and treated patients for cancer of several sites' (Benedek and Kiple, 1994:102). Indeed, it has been argued that cancer can be traced back to ancient Greece to designate diseases involving tumours. One historical study suggests that:

> Hippocrates himself is credited with having named the disease cancer from *karcinos*, the Greek word for crab, perhaps because some cancers of the breast have a crablike appearance or perhaps because the pain that cancer can produce resembles the pinching of a crab. Similarly, *neoplasm*, meaning 'new formation', and *oncology*, literally the 'study of masses', are derived from the Greek, as is the word *tumour*.
>
> (Benedek and Kiple 1994:102)

However, as this study states, 'despite its antiquity, the disease itself is viewed as largely a twentieth-century phenomenon', and despite the long history of scientific developments in cancer research it

142

is nevertheless 'usually viewed as a twentieth-century undertaking' (Benedek and Kiple, 1994:103).

The contemporary view of cancer as a problem of cells is now inextricably bound up with developments in cell biology and embryology. But it was not until the nineteenth century that theories of tumour development and embryo development became so closely aligned:

> In the eighteenth century the relation between embryology and pathology was distant, if it existed at all; in the nineteenth century the development of theories of tumor genesis and embryogenesis went hand in hand, with the same investigators, for example, Wilhelm His and Wilhelm Waldeyer, often contributing significantly to both fields of study.
>
> (Rather, 1978:4)

Medical textbooks today increasingly connect the aetiology of cancer with new genetic theory. Changes in the phenotype (composition) of cells 'which are associated with malignancy result from a genetic anomoly [involving] certain genes known as oncogenes ... these may be defined as genes whose changed expression or altered product is essential to the production or maintenance of the malignant state' (Rees *et al.*, 1993:3). What is as yet inexplicable is why, given that oncogenes are present in all human cell nuclei as 'proto-oncogenes', some are suddenly activated, while others remain dormant, or at least participate in only low-level activity in differentiation and growth control. Scientists speculate about the numerous factors which trigger the oncogene into excessive activity. The growth of interest in genetics within oncology has largely been a concern with understanding cell behaviour and mutation in an attempt to find out how cells are programmed and controlled (see Figures 5.3 and 5.4).

What interests me here in relation to these changing scientific models of cancer is the kind of cultural values embedded in this particular discourse of the *cellular body*. How might we understand cancer in the context of the increasing emphasis on the cell as a unit of information? And more generally, how are ways of seeing and imagining the body's cellular interior constitutive of new beliefs about health and illness? These questions are inextricable from the ways in which the body's interior is imaged through the new visual technologies of biomedicine, which in turn also influence alternative approaches to healing.

CELLS AND SELVES

Scientific knowledge presents itself to us through the guise of purely 'natural facts' (Martin, 1992:411). Yet, as we have already seen, its

143

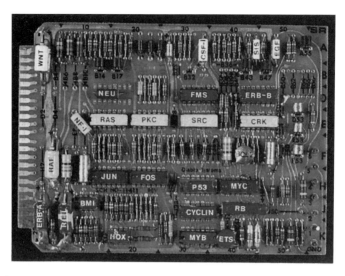

Figure 5.3 A fanciful model of the circuitry involved in cell signalling, with the extracellular factors on top and the transcription factors at the bottom
Source: Varmus and Weinberg, 1993:153

conceptualisations of the body not only change over time, and eventually contradict earlier ones, but also belong to a wider set of values, and metaphors, about the order of social and cultural, as well as biological, life. What disease is, where it comes from and what should be done about it are all questions whose answers depend upon historically and culturally specific knowledges about the body and its functions. So-called advances in scientific knowledge struggle to maintain their authority over previous understandings, and promise to lead us further along the road of medical progress. Each generation of scientists assures the public that *they* have discovered the truth about the body or that they will be the ones to find a cure for contemporary diseases, such as cancer. Scientific knowledge is not only reproduced through textbooks, but is represented to the public primarily through a wide and intertextual range of visual and print media. In Britain, BBC2 television and the 'serious' Sunday newspaper supplements repeatedly run features explaining new (and old) sciences to the public and debating the moral and ethical issues raised by the latest invention or discovery, be it *in vitro* fertilisation or genetic testing.[4] The placing of the cell centre stage in contemporary illnesses, such as cancer and HIV and AIDS, is part of its broader rise to prominence in the biological sciences. This is not to deny the importance, or indeed the existence, of cells, but rather to argue that their construction in popular and professional representations is always about more than a set of 'natural facts'.

Figure 5.4 A metaphor for cell signalling, with the milkman as an external
stimulating factor in the contol of internal events
Source: Varmus and Weinberg, 1993:120

Cells are endowed with more than just a physiological identity in scientific discourse. These supposedly biological units are, in fact, being increasingly 'endowed with personhood' (Martin, 1992:415). Nowhere are the cultural values of cell biology more visible than in the scientific and popular literature on reproduction.[5] As Emily Martin points out, the difference between the metaphorical depictions of the male and female reproductive systems in this material is instructive. Menstruation is depicted as the loss of something potentially productive which has gone to waste or died: the terms used to describe what happens to the uterine lining suggest 'failure and dissolution' (Martin, 1992:411). In contrast, the 'sheer magnitude' of spermatogenesis is marvelled at as a 'productive' miracle (and the 'wasteful wank' is never mentioned). Rather predictably, the activities of these 'masculine' and 'feminine' reproductive cells have been accorded typically gender stereotyped qualities: 'the egg is seen as large and passive. It does not *move* or *journey*, but passively "is transported", "is swept" . . . along the fallopian tube' (Guyton, 1984, and Mountcastle, 1980, quoted in Martin, 1992:412). Sperm, on the other hand, are described as moving with energy, velocity, purpose and power: 'together with the forces of ejaculation, they can "propel the semen into the deepest recesses of the vagina"' (Guyton, 1984, quoted in Martin, 1992:412). Once released, the sperm becomes the hero of the narrativised journey through dangerous and challenging territory on a mission to find the egg, who lies waiting in regal passivity, to be rescued (Martin, 1992:412). Quoting Jonathan Miller, co-author of *The Facts of Life* and producer of the BBC series *The Body in Question*, Martin demonstrates how widespread such gendered clichés have become: in Miller's account 'the sperm carries out a "perilous journey" into the "warm darkness", where some fall away "exhausted", but other "survivors" "assault" the egg, the successful candidates "surrounding the prize"' (Martin, 1992:413).

Recent research from laboratories investigating the sperm and the egg, Martin argues, has produced quite different information which would contradict this image of the heroic and powerful sperm: 'scientists have found that the forward propulsive force of the sperm's tail is extremely weak, so that rather than swimming forward with purpose, the sperm actually flail from side to side, swim in circles, mill around.' Instead of boldly entering the egg, 'the current picture is that adhesive molecules on the surface of the egg capture the sperm and hold it fast; otherwise, its sideways motions would lead it to escape and swim away' (Martin, 1992:413). However, as Martin goes on to argue, scientific textbooks and journals continue to write about the egg and the sperm within the gendered metaphors of conquest and submission; in language reminiscent of a medieval quest they combine romantic and adventure narratives and reinforce the cultural ascription of femininity as passively awaiting penetration.[6]

This analysis of the representations of the activities of the egg and sperm cell serves to demonstrate some of the ways in which *biological* knowledge is so clearly also *cultural*. This basic biological unit is bestowed with all kinds of human (and gendered) qualities that affect how we think of ourselves and our bodies. In particular, these new images of the cell may reconfigure the imaginative limits of self and other:

> endowing cells with personhood may play a part in the breaking down of boundaries between the self and the world, and a pushing back of the boundary of what constitutes the inviolable self. In other words, whereas at an earlier time, the skin might have been regarded as the border of the individual self, now these microscopic cells are seen as tiny individual selves ... It is possible that in the 1990s what was the patient (or person) has itself become *an environment* for a new core self, which exists at the cellular level.
>
> (Martin, 1992:415)[7]

This conceptualisation of the *cell as the microcosm of the self* has permeated all kinds of medical practice in recent years. There are numerous other studies which examine the relationship between the 'cell' and the 'self' in biological discourse.[8] Martin's research offers an especially vivid example of the implications of the personification of the cell for a feminist analysis of medical discourse. This personification of the cell is not only to be found in biomedicine, however. Alternative approaches to health and healing also rely on a metonymic model of the cell as a unit of the self, as the following example demonstrates.

At my local alternative health centre, leaflets advertising sessions with various practitioners abound. This particular one caught my eye because of the way in which cells and selves are conceptualised. It read as follows:

THE HEALING OF EMOTION

This is a magnificent time for all of us. We now have an opportunity to heal the conflicts within and awaken our fearless selves.

We can find that peaceful place within and accept all that we are without resistance.

We now have the capacity to clearly understand the purpose of our lives and what we have come here to give. It is time for each of us to recognise who we really are.

147

VISIONS

One to one sessions with xxx

In these sessions I will facilitate you in contacting your higher self.
Your higher self will open up the memory of this and past lifetimes.
Your higher self will show you the source of your emotional
blockages and limitations.

*These imprints of anger, hatred, jealousy, greed, fear, grief, despondency,
envy, worthlessness etc . . . are stored within the memory of the cells
in your body.*

Your higher self will help you unlock these memories, allowing you
to truly love yourself and let go of these powerful emotions. You will
feel lighter and more joyous; you will be able to experience a richer,
more ecstatic reality.

(My emphasis.)

This leaflet represents a model of the person imagined as a series of
intercommunicating entities: the life force, the body, the cell, are each
contained within the next, like Russian dolls. A greater life force,
suggested by the mention of 'the higher self' and 'past lives', frames the
present human life, whose embodiment contains millions of microcosms
of the self in the cells. The cells are personified: they have memories
which enable them to store past hurts. The body is thus endowed with
the capacities of the mind (memory) which registers and stores the
physical imprint of particular emotions on cellular formations. The
wrong emotional programming can damage the cellular composition of
your body. The higher force can mediate between the present and the
past self, retrieving information from the memories of the cells in the
body, and facilitating cell repair through expression. The key to our
problems might be 'right before our eyes', stored in the cells of our
bodies which contain information about our emotional histories and tell
us the truth about 'who we really are': the Urself. The prospective
patient, or client, is addressed with the direct second-person form of
'you', and as such is already offered an imaginary place within this
harmonious universe. Optimistic and confident in tone, the statement
promises, if not guarantees, predictable results. It encourages us to
assume that our experience of this therapy might produce the same
results as it has for many before us; thus we are connected to something
greater than ourselves, to a life force from which, with guidance, we can
benefit. With spirituality *and* science on our side, we cannot go wrong.

This formulation draws upon an informational model of the cell
based on genetic theory. It is used here to incorporate the human
capacity of memory within this micro-unit: past experience (especially

trauma) becomes 'information' that can be therapeutically processed. The two discourses of therapy and of science combine to offer a double legitimation: self-knowledge and cellular information produce a new model of healing. The omniscience that previously God exercised (to know all our thoughts as well as deeds) is translated here to a physical presence in the body: it is not God's knowledge of you that is now to be feared, but your own body's cellular memory of your past trauma. Your psychic history has become part of your cellular make-up: emotions translate into information. With the help of the therapist (and other forces) the information can be retrieved, re-experienced and the cells, and thus the body, repaired.

For the person with cancer, such a therapeutic promise cannot fail to engage the imagination. If cancer is the disease of wrongly programmed, or damaged, cells, then the appeal of a therapy which guarantees cell repair is obvious. The idea of the cell as a unit of the body which can be influenced by physical and mental 'input' is especially appealing because cancer is seen as a disease of cellular dysfunction. To control the cells is thus the route to controlling the whole system. If we could see the emotional imprints stored in our cells through the insight of our higher being, perhaps it might be possible to rid our bodies of these malignant cells which threaten to destroy us.

Albeit from very different perspectives, both the biomedical and alternative accounts seem to agree on this – that our own cellular miscomposition (whether biological or emotional) is a life-threatening business. Rather than being invaded by an external threat, the problem lies within: *we* may be a danger to *ourselves*. Both conventional and alternative accounts represent the cell as a metaphor of the self. In the scientific accounts of reproduction discussed above, cells are given individual identities: like us, they desire, they fear, they have intentions, they triumph, and they are satisfied. In this alternative account, the cell is a condensation of our identities and our emotional histories. These metonymic personifications are not entirely new. In the early nineteenth century, for example, medical textbooks wrote of the homunculus: 'a minute human form believed by the spermastic school of performationalists to be contained in the spermatazoon' (*Chambers Dictionary*, 1972:625). According to this school of thought the germ cell of the sperm contained a miniaturised prototype of the person into which it would eventually develop.

However, the personification of the cell in contemporary culture has a much wider and more pervasive significance. The category of the cell has become pivotal to today's representations of biology, of the body and of disease. In relation to HIV/AIDS and cancer, the cell and its (dys)functions are the main issues at stake in biomedical and alternative discourses alike. The cultural significance of new body metaphors stems from the increasing impact of these forms of scientific knowledge on perceptions of the self. As I shall go on to argue in Chapter 6, this is particularly important in a culture where the self is increasingly seen as an autonomous, self-regulating system of health or disease.

IMAGING THE BODY

The widespread conceptualisation of bodily interiors across these diverse health practices has been made possible by the emergence of certain discourses about the body more generally. In particular, the investment of the microscopic cell with the human qualities of the person in whose body it resides is a personification which depends upon the *visualisability of the body's interior*. Our sense of our own physical internality is embodied in commonplace metaphors which privilege particular 'ways of seeing'. Indeed, the contemporary personification of 'the cell' has been made possible through the establishment of certain discourses which have fundamentally reorganised the basic modes of visual perception in Western thought. As Rosi Braidotti puts it: 'we are moving beyond the idea of visibility, into a new culture of visualization' (Braidotti, 1994:68).

Following some archaeologists of medical knowledge (Foucault, 1973; Stafford, 1991) we might argue that the cell has only become thinkable as the inside of the body has become not only visible but visualisable.[9] In order to pursue this claim it is necessary to return to the question of the historical production of certain biomedical discourses. In her encylopaedic study of *Imaging the Unseen in Enlightenment Art and Medicine*, Barbara Maria Stafford offers a detailed historical analysis of the relationship between knowledge and perception in the eighteenth-, nineteenth- and twentieth-century arts and sciences. Modes of visual perception in the 'visual and medical arts', she argues, underwent a fundamental reconfiguration which continues to impact upon our twentieth-century understandings of ourselves and our world. Stafford describes her study as a 'metaphorology' of 'the radical shift under way since the eighteenth century from a text-based culture to a visually dependent culture . . . [T]here is [a] momentous historical shift toward visualization now taking place in all fields' (Stafford, 1991:xviii).

Stafford tacitly confirms Foucault's argument that medicine's major preoccupation in the eighteenth century was to make visible the invisible, to externalise the internal. Of central concern in this Enlightenment project, she argues, were 'the . . . relentless . . . attempts to break into the obscure secrets of the somatic', and this was not simply a scientific project, but also constituted a key area of overlap between aesthetics and biology, 'revealing, structuring and interpreting signs and symptoms that inherently could not be written' (Stafford, 1991:2). Thus, for Stafford:

analytical physiognomics, or the 'universal science' of the eighteenth century, was inseparable from the anatomizing project of Neo-classicism . . . For the age of encyclopedism, the human body represented the ultimate visual compendium, the comprehensive method of methods, the organizing structure of structures. As a visible natural whole, made up of invisible dissimilar parts, it was the organic paradigm or architectonic standard for all complex unions.

(Stafford, 1991:9,12)

The body's interior not only became the source of fascinated investigation, but also represented the way forward for making visible the interiors of other 'concealed territories'. The Enlightenment's 'body tropes' gave human physiology an optical manifestation and turned this previously mysterious space into a new spectacle. It is not that 'the representational problem of embodiment or personification' was something especially new: indeed, Stafford argues that this dated back to 'ancient rhetoric'. However, she continues, 'the activity of visibilizing, or incarnating, the invisible became endowed with a special urgency in early modern art and medical experimentation' (Stafford, 1991:17). The period's preoccupation with optical instruments such as 'microscopes, telescopes and amplifying glasses were believed to prove computable increments of insight into unseen and unknown terrain. Magnification, it had been hoped, would yield deep and precise information about deceptive superficial signs' (Stafford, 1991:469).

The relevance of the Enlightenment's multifaceted project, Stafford argues, lies in its centrality to many of our concerns today. This 'paradigm shift of Copernican proportions' (Stafford, 1991:477) anticipated our twentieth-century revolutions, such as in information technology in the 1980s and, more recently, the 'visionary computer developments' in the 1990s. These new medical imaging technologies open up the previously secret regions of the body to medical scrutiny by turning its 'invisible depths' into 'visible surfaces' (Stafford, 1991:1). According to Stafford, 'the Enlightenment paved the way for the advent of synthetic realism, disembodied information, animated automata, created environments and clairvoyant visualization devices' (Stafford, 1991:465). This formative influence can be extended to developments in medical technology and their implications for our beliefs about our bodies and ourselves. Stafford argues that:

Prophetically, the eighteenth-century viewer's struggle to pierce to the bottom of all blurred visual signals . . . seems to be fulfilled in twentieth-century transparent medical visualizations. Computer tomography x-ray imaging (CT), positron emission tomography (PET), magnetic resonance imaging (MRI), and ultrasound now probe noninvasively, but publicly, formerly private regions and occluded and secluded recesses.

(Stafford, 1991:26)

For the person with cancer today, it is standard treatment to have CT scans and MRIs, and for the tumour, or lack of one, to be registered on these new information screens. The details of cell growth are thus registered on a visual surface which supposedly allows consultants to see the smallest of tumours and intervene as early as possible. These new imaging technologies boast of practically military accuracy, and, like the technology in the Gulf War that will haunt our imaginations for years to come, have an aura of unquestionable precision which offers a fantasy of omnipotence, generating considerable excitement within medical innovation and popular representations of it. What is forgotten as these new technologies are embraced as the guarantors of the truth about our bodily interiors is that, like any other imaging technique, they may lead to confusion and disagreement. In my case, for example, when I was informed that a CT scan had shown a cyst on my other ovary and a 'bulky uterus' more than three years after my last treatment I did not doubt the information. I may have been in two minds about whether the cyst they indicated was visible was benign or malignant, but it never occurred to me that the scan reading might be mistaken. As it transpired, on further inspection with ultrasound, there proved to be nothing 'abnormal' at all: the radiologist had probably '*overread the image*'. This experience should come as no surprise to those sceptical about the reliability of visual evidence, and yet my own confusion and disbelief revealed an unexpected trust in scientific imaging technologies to tell me the truth about my body. Thus I found myself enaged in writing about the cultures of medicine and challenging the truth claims of its aspirations to objectivity and positivism, and yet when faced with evidence of its interpretative and contested practices, I responded with utter disbelief.

THE SPECTACLE OF THE WOMAN'S BODY

As many feminist critics have pointed out, these developments in medical imaging technologies have highly gendered histories. Many of these technologies have been used to investigate the 'private regions and occluded and secluded recesses' of the female body. In her study of the coincidence of the 'birth' of the cinema with the discovery of X-ray in 1895, for example, Lisa Cartwright explores the gendered ways of seeing that the cultural inscription of these new 'inventions' generated. She argues that:

although radiology was practiced almost exclusively by men in its first decades, women's bodies were often the test objects of early imaging research ... [T]he press's representation of the X ray as sexualised spectacle and as a new mode of illicit looking was not at all a misreading of the work of science but a foregrounding of the fact that visual pleasure, sexual desire, and the thrill of mortality were not just incidental to the male radiologist's conquest of the inner body.

(Cartwright, 1995:154)

The X-ray was seen as an exciting new technology which enabled deeper 'penetration' of the body and the 'display of previously imperceptible evidence of disease' and is thus a classic example of the extension of the 'surveillant gaze' into bodily interiors and the making of disease both 'visible and public' (Cartwright, 1995:147).

Cartwright takes the public campaign against TB earlier this century as a case study in 'medicine's public gaze'. Women, it seems, not only played a central role in these campaigns as the 'key agents of disease control' because of their responsiblity for 'family and community health', but the female body was also frequently represented in the public service films of this period as a 'key vector of TB contagion' (Cartwright, 1995:147). What was especially troubling about TB was the lack of visible signs of the disease and the feeling that the female body was unreadable in any reliable and public way: 'the woman's body symbolizes the threat of contagion, making quite literal the potential threat posed by the capacity of TB to be transmitted in the absence of any visible object or sign' (Cartwright, 1995:150).

As Cartwright argues, the placing of the female body as the central object of investigation, of visual fascination and of scientific exploration, links the history of medical technologies to the other twentieth-century technology of spectacle: the cinema. Giuliana Bruno (1992) details the connections between new modes of the visual perception of bodies in the anatomy lesson and the cinema. In both, a crowd gathers to watch the public revelation of another's body that is displayed through rituals of scrutiny and discovery: looking and learning go hand in hand. Referring to Walter Benjamin's theories of the 'masses' desire to bring things closer spatially', Bruno explores the ways in which the surgeon and the cameraman both endeavour to bring the body closer for visual scrutiny; but Bruno argues that 'Benjamin's conclusion that "the boldness of the cameraman is comparable to that of the surgeon"' ignores the missing link in this comparison: 'the dialectics of gender inscribed in such a gaze' (Bruno, 1992:243). For, as Bruno so eloquently argues: 'on the ashes of anatomy a female body is en*graved*. Cinema's analytic genealogy descends, in a way, from a distinct anatomic fascination for the woman's body' (Bruno, 1992:243). Thus, both developments in anatomy and in cinema rely heavily on the fetishistic spectacle of the female body for public consumption in such a way as to make the invisible visible (Bruno, 1992:245).

These overlaps between medical and cinematic technologies of culture highlight the importance of connections between visual pleasure, gender and technological innovation.[10] Recent developments in visual imaging in gynaecology, which has always presented endless examples of the scrutiny of the female body by a traditionally male profession, quite literally combine the cinematic and medical gaze. Ella Shohat, for example, offers a critical analysis of the uses of imaging technologies for women with endometriosis. In a laparoscopy a minute 'lighted periscope-like instrument' is inserted to enable the surgeon to 'inspect the organs in the abdomen'. 'In the case of video laparoscopy, the notion of scientific discovery is grafted onto a discourse of technological expansion into the "virgin land" of the female body, hitherto untouched by such a penetrating gaze', and the doctor becomes the filmmaker of the newly landscaped female body (Shohat, 1992:70,78). In contrast to the dissection of the anatomy lesson, where autopsies required the cutting open of the body to see inside, the video laparoscopy allows access to previously invisible interiors with the help of only a small incision. These new technological developments are heralded as triumphs in the battle against the unruly female reproductive system. According to Shohat, the institutionalised discourse of endometriosis tends to celebrate:

the 'revolution' of laser laparoscopy as a new weapon in science's video war against a self-destructive uterus. The laser, Prometheus-like, brings light into the body's dark corners. The once opaque womb is stripped of its mystery, and the light of scientific knowledge shines on the dark inner sanctum. Tropes of light and darkness, informed by Enlightenment ideas, are projected onto an out-of-control (female) nature.

(Shohat, 1992:79)

The visual technologies surrounding pregnancy also raise important questions about the gender politics of these new ways of imaging the interior of the female body. The possibility of 'seeing' the foetus during pregnancy through new imaging technologies has been integral to a radical reconceptualisation of the mother's body, and indeed of 'life itself'.[11] The 'biologization' of anti-abortion rhetoric (life begins at conception) can be seen in the replacement of religious definitions of 'life' with biological ones (Franklin, 1991:191). New medical technologies have been part of this redefinition of the foetus as detailed by Rosalind Petchesky: 'increasingly . . . the evidence marshalled by the anti-abortionists to affirm the personhood of the fetus is not its alleged possession of a soul, but its possession of a human body and genotype' (Petchesky, 1987, quoted in Franklin, 1991:191).

It is precisely the ways in which the foetus has been constructed 'as separate, as an individual in its own right, deserving of state protection and medical attention' (Franklin, 1991:191) that have led to the gradual subordination (or even disappearance) of the figure of the mother in debates about abortion.[12] In particular, the now widely circulated images of the foetus have been used in New Right battles to claim the 'rights' of the foetus against the 'rights' of the mother in recent anti-abortion campaigns. Indeed, the most widely circulated images of the foetus show it enclosed in the placenta, but as a separate entity from the mother's body. This 'visual representation of fetal autonomy' has performed ideological work in the transformation 'of the female body from a benevolent, maternal environment into an inhospitable waste land, at war with the "innocent person" within' (Stabile, 1992:179). As numerous feminists have argued, this construction of the foetus as an autonomous individual who is in need of 'protection' draws heavily on notions of the dangerous and threatening femininity of the mother (Hartouni, 1992; Stabile, 1992). The deployment of these foetal images by New Right groups has drawn heavily on a whole range of cultural fantasies and anxieties that stage a defenceless masculinity in need of protection from a powerful, selfish and destructive femininity (Phelan, 1993).

The dubious benefits for women of the increasingly invasive imaging technologies of biomedicine have thus been thoroughly debated by feminist cultural critics. This is not to say that all feminist work in this area is strictly 'anti-technology'; indeed, many of these theorists combine their critiques with discussion of the contradictory relationships between 'female patients' and the technology.[13] However, what these studies do show is that developments in the visual cultures of science are inextricable from masculine desires and fantasies and uses of the female body. It is in this light that some of the newer technologies of the visible might be regarded. Rosi Braidotti writes, for example, that through ultrasound techniques:

> the bioscientist is, quite literally, the great spectator in the spectacle of life; he can at long last represent the unrepresentable: the bottom of the ocean, outer space, but also the inside of the womb, the depths of the uterine chamber – that great mystery that has always held *men* in suspense.
>
> (Braidotti, 1994:68)

For Braidotti, new techniques in visual reproduction have intensified the compulsive search for truth through the power of vision.

Biosciences have extended medical intervention into 'the very structure of the living organism, right into the genetic program, thereby changing the bodily structure from within'; indeed, she argues, 'molecular biology has increased the biomedical gaze to infinite proportions, allowing for an unprecedented investigation of the most intimate and infinitesimal fibres of nature' (Braidotti, 1994:67).

As cancer is a term for hundreds of different diseases it is hard to generalise about the feminist politics of the use of imaging technologies in cancer treatment (though the arguments about the general problems of the 'masculine penetrative gaze' might still pertain). But there are a whole set of specific controversies around the use of scanning in breast cancer 'prevention'. With the odds of getting breast cancer having doubled in the United States since the 1940s, there is a now heated debate about the best forms of prevention of this disease that now affects one in eight women (Cartwright, 1995:161). Some feminists have challenged the public campaigns that present mammography as preventive. Alisa Solomon, for example, refers to a feminist activist on breast cancer, Judy Brady: 'there is a subtle message . . . that if you're a good girl and get your mammogram, you won't be punished with breast cancer. What's worse . . . is that mammography is presented as a *prevention* when, in fact, it's merely detection' (Solomon, 1992:161). Some have also argued strongly for wider campaigns on the lowest technology method of prevention: self-examination.

There is a complex history to the developments of X-ray and ultrasound mammography as prophylactic imaging (Cartwright, 1995). Medical discourses construct the breast as the physical manifestation of the enigma of femininity because of its unsuitability for X-ray techniques. As Lisa Cartwright details:

> the breast was characterized as too soft, too irregular in composition, and too changeable to image clearly . . . Rather than adapt the technology to its object (or to the dominant perception of its object), radiologists more often attempted to adapt the breast to the technique . . . [B]efore 1960, radiographers sliced, compressed, or halted physiological change in the breast in an attempt to bring it in line with the X ray.
>
> (Cartwright, 1995:159–60)

In this conceptualisation of the breast as a feminine organ that eluded the scrutiny of the medical gaze, women's bodies were constructed 'as inherently resistant to a technology that could save women's lives' (Cartwright, 1995:160). However, Cartwright is also wary of the feminist assumption that a 'surveillant gaze' is 'by necessity a totalizing mode of institutional domination and control of populations'; the demonisation of the 'optical tools of medical surveillance . . . or as militarized tools of social control' ignores the problems of exclusion of certain groups from these technologies (Cartwright, 1995:169). Arguing instead for a strategic intervention into breast cancer health politics that utilises both low- and high-tech methods, Cartwright suggests that women have too much to lose from the total rejection of these medical imaging techniques.

BODY SYSTEMS

The intensification of the *visualisability* of the body's interior is thus part of the long and complex history of the sexual politics of science and technology. Integral to this continuing debate is the question of how the body is currently being reconfigured by the new biomedical imaging technologies of 'postmodern' culture. These non-intrusive techno-logies turn 'the body inside out' through sound-waves, X-rays and ways of imaging: 'neither real nor imaginary, [these] ghostly simulations swim somewhere in between' (Stafford, 1991:48, 475). Thus, our contemporary postmodern culture, which some have characterised as the age of simulation, replication and the copy, in contrast to the previous markers of authenticity, reflection and the original (see Lury, 1993), was forecast by developments in the Enlightenment project, Stafford argues, in which visual dimensions of perception became an intensified cultural preoccupation. For Stafford:

> Our Postmodern times are preeminently visual times. Ours is now chiefly a postindustrial 'service' economy televising and videoing constructed, antisensual, and intangible somatic experiences rather than manufacturing actual tangible objects. Increasingly we contend with disembodied information. We communicate with images of people, with 'artificial persons', existing as bites, bytes and bits of optical and aural messages. Flesh and blood, or tactility, recede in the presence of mediated encounters.
>
> Speeding along this process of desubstantialization is the rapid development of hyperbolic systems. These are currently being perfected by the computer industry to produce 'virtual realities' or 'virtual environments'.
>
> (Stafford, 1991:26–7)

The inside of the body can be monitored and imaged through an ever-increasing number of technological options. The flesh-and-blood body is translated into a set of computer signals, a series of wavelengths, or a photographic reproduction. The significant knowledge about what is going on inside is captured as external image or code, mediated through technological processes which have invisible, though often damaging, effects. The previously significant substance of the body has been gradually turned into a flat surface of codes and images. The copy speaks more urgently and with more authority than the opaque and occluded 'original body'. This postmodern body can no longer be thought of as an organic machine in need of repair by the medical profession's expert knowledge. Rather, it has become a system, where inside and outside no longer signify separate spheres. These new forms of medical technology facilitate the imaging of the inside of the body in such a way that 'the venerable Cartesian dualism of mind and body, or of separate internal and external systems, has become outmoded. Nothing impedes us from beholding the "inside" and "outside" of things cast simultaneously on an artifical surface' (Stafford, 1991:475; see also Chapter 4, this volume).

The expansion of information technologies and communication systems, which have increasingly come to replace the manufacturing industries of Western countries, have laid the foundations for the formation and validation of different forms of knowledge and new ways of seeing the body and the self. The desire for greater and greater visibility of bodily interiors has continued in the context of a general shift from an industrial machine-age society to one in which new forms of technology have reorganised our thinking about our bodies and ourselves: 'today's information and communication machines do not merely convey representational contents, but also contribute to the fabrication of new *assemblages* of enunciation, individual and collective' (Guattari, 1992:18).

Donna Haraway characterises these general changes as 'a movement from an organic industrial society to a polymorphous, information system' (Haraway, 1989a:185). She goes on to argue that:

> In communications sciences, the translation of the world into a problem in coding can be illustrated by looking at cybernetic (feedback controlled) systems theories applied to telephone technology, computer design, weapons deployment, or data base construction and maintenance. In each case, solution to the key questions rests on a theory of language and control; the key operation is determining the rates, directions, and probabilities of flow of a quantity called information. The world is subdivided by boundaries differentially permeable to information. Information is just that kind of quantifiable element (unit, basis of unity) which allows universal translation, and so unhindered instrumental power (called effective communication).
>
> The biggest threat to such power is interruption of communication. Any system breakdown is a function of stress. The funda-

mentals of this technology can be condensed into the metaphor C^{3}I, command-control-communication-intelligence, the military's symbol for its operations theory.

(Haraway, 1989a:188)

In biological sciences these new theories have influenced thinking about the body and its functions and breakdowns. It has been argued that there has been a gradual, if uneven, shift in biological modalities from the body as a machine to the body as a system: 'In a sense, organisms have ceased to exist as objects of knowledge, giving way to biotic components, i.e., special kinds of information-processing devices' (Haraway, 1989a:188) (see also Crarey and Kwinter, 1992). In genetics, for example, the body is conceptualised through informational metaphors, broken down into microscopic units which can be reprogrammed. 'Gene therapy' offers a scientific promise of solutions to diseases such as Down's Syndrome and cystic fibrosis. We are tempted by the fantasy of the perfect body, and the perfect baby, which have become aestheticised ideals. The body is seen as a potentially correctly programmed system which, through scientific intervention, might be improved by the replacement of abnormal genes with normal ones. The physical body is thus translated into a model of 'codes', 'blueprints', 'sequences' and 'spelling errors' and its correct functioning likened to an information system (Stafford, 1991:26). These days, not only can limbs and organs be replaced, but so can these minute details of bodily programming. Indeed, the replicant is a better and more desirable body than the faulty original. Paul Rabinow predicts that:

> In the future, the new genetics will cease to be a biological metaphor for modern society and will become instead a circulation network of identity terms and restriction loci, around which and through which a truly new type of autoproduction will emerge, which I call 'biosociality'. If sociobiology is culture constructed on the basis of a metaphor of nature, then in biosociality, nature will be modeled on culture understood as practice. Nature will be known and remade through technique and will finally become artificial, just as culture becomes natural.
>
> (Rabinow, 1992:241–2)

AUTO-IMMUNITY: FROM BIOMEDICINE TO INFOMEDICINE?

Similarly, contemporary immunology constructs the body as a system, rather than a machine: 'immunobiology and associated medical practices are rich exemplars of the privilege of coding and recognition systems as objects of knowledge, as constructions of bodily reality for us' (Haraway, 1989a:188). Extending and transforming the project of mapping the body's inner space, outlined above, immune system discourse gives the cell and its relationship to the self a new significance (see Tauber, 1994). However, rather than the clinical gaze which sought to probe the organs and tissues of the body's interior in their spatial depth, the *informatic medical gaze* now exteriorises the textual system of the body and decodes it. The idea of the immune *system* is a relatively recent form of biomedical knowledge: according to Emily Martin this did not become well established until the 1960s (Martin, 1994). What is significant about this introduction of systems thinking into biology is the way in which it involves a reconceptualisation of boundaries of self and other: 'Systems thinking shows us that there is no outside; that you and the cause of your problems are part of a single system' (Senge, 1990, quoted in Martin, 1994:209). Thus, recent immunology produces a definition of health in which 'we seem invaded not just by the threatening "non-selves" that the immune system guards against, but more fundamentally by our own strange parts' (Haraway, 1992:321).

One model Haraway identifies within immunology is that of the body as a battlefield in which a corporate civil war is constantly in progress. This metaphor of the immune system as a battlefield pervades both popular and professional accounts of the body's functioning. In Nilsson's 'coffee-table art book', *The Body Victorious* (1987), for example, his 'photography of the alien inhabitants of inner space' include 'cancer cells . . . surrounded by the lethal mobil squads of killer T cells that throw chemical poisons into the self's malignant traitor cells' (Haraway, 1992:320). Recent immunology textbooks have similarly defined the human immune system through the themes of 'the self as defended stronghold, and extraterrestrialism in inner space' (Haraway, 1992:320). Under a diagram of the 'Evolution of Recognition Systems', one textbook explains: 'From the humble amoeba searching for food . . . to the mammal with its sophisticated humoural and cellular immune mechanisms . . . the process of "self versus non-self recognition" shows a steady development, keeping pace with the increasing need of animals to maintain their integrity in a hostile environment' (Playfair, 1984, quoted in Haraway, 1992:320). The challenge for the immune system, then, is to distinguish correctly between ally and enemy cells.

This model of the immune system as a bodily defence strategy is clearly informed by military culture (see Martin, 1994:49–62). Immune system imagery produces a rather 'chilling fantasy of the perfection of the fully defended "victorious" self' which is placed within the historical discourses of 'Star Wars-maintained individuality'; such an image of the self as an invincible unit is 'enabled by high-technology visualization technologies, which are also basic to conducting war and commerce, such as computer-aided graphics, artificial intelligence software, and specialized scanning systems' (Haraway, 1992:321). Furthermore, military doctrines draw on the new biological modalities of immune system discourse: one example cites the body's 'remarkably complex corps of internal bodyguards [which] . . . consist of reconnaissance specialists, killers, reconstitution specialists, and communicators that can seek out invaders, sound the alarm, reproduce rapidly, and swarm to the attack to repel the enemy' in order to describe the ideal composition of an 'elite special force' in the US army (Haraway, 1992:321).

As well as these militaristic versions of the human immune system, however, scientists have also produced understandings of how the body regulates itself which rely on other metaphors. The most common of these is the 'highly adaptable communication system with many interfaces' (Haraway, 1992:322). Within this model two cell lineages, the '*lymphocytes*' and the '*mononuclear phagocyte system*' combine with acellular products such as 'antibodies, lymphokines, and complement components' to 'maintain bodily coherence' (Haraway, 1992:322–3). The most familiar of these in popular discourse, and indeed in alternative medical books, are the different types of 'T cells (helper, suppressor, killer, and variations of these) and B cells (each type of which can produce only one sort of the vast array of potential circulating antibodies)' (Haraway, 1992:322). The acellular products have the important job of communicating between different parts of the immune system, and between it and the endocrine and nervous systems. Thus, Haraway argues, 'the hierarchical body of old has given way to a network-body of amazing complexity and specificity' (Haraway, 1992:323).

Some strands of immunology have been influenced by what has been called 'network theory' (Jerne, 1985, quoted in Haraway, 1992:323). Here, the body is not only conceptualised as a system, but also, importantly, as a self-regulatable system. Moving away from the notion of the immune system as a series of ally cells defending the body against alien intruders, this theory posits a model of the immune system as an infinite process of self-referentiality:

The concatenation of internal recognitions and responses would go on indefinitely, in a series of interior mirrorings of sites on immunoglobulin molecules, such that the immune system would always be in a state of dynamic internal responding. It would never be passive, 'at rest,' awaiting an activating stimulus from a hostile outside. In a sense, there could be no *exterior* antigenic structure, no 'invader,' that the immune system had not already 'seen' and mirrored internally. Replaced by subtle plays of partially mirrored readings and responses, self and other lose their rationalistic oppositional quality. A radical conception of *connection* emerges unexpectedly at the core of the defended self.

(Haraway, 1992:323)

The above configurations of ally/enemy, self/other and self/mirrored self map out different ways in which the immune system is thought to regulate the human body. What these different discourses all do is to present the body as a system of one kind or another which is in dialogue (or in conflict) with itself. The body is represented as more than a single unit, a concrete organism, a mechanical set of functions; instead it is a communication or information system, a network of cells which have relationships with, and responsibilities to, each other.

According to immune system discourse the body goes wrong when the system is overloaded and under pressure. Within immunobiology, for example, 'a stressed system goes awry; its communication processes break down; it fails to recognize the difference between self and other' (Haraway, 1989a:188). In the case of cancer, the failure of the immune system in this process of differentiation is crucial. Given that the normal and malignant cells are not only all part of the self, but have actually been produced by it, these processes of recognition and misrecognition are vital. Cancer is not a germ or a virus invading the body, but a disease of cellular malfunction. The body must therefore use its own mechanisms not to recognise an intruder in its inner space, but to recognise part of itself which has begun to reproduce itself on a microscopic level.

In immunology textbooks the cells of the immune system are also metaphorically represented. Haraway (1991) analyses Golub's standard undergraduate immunology textbook in which he traces Richard K. Gershon's (the 'discoverer' of the suppressor T cell) developing models of the organisation of the immune system. These models used the metaphor of a sort of divine orchestra to represent the patterns and flows of immune system activity. Beginning with a composition of cell 'co-operation', directed by the 'generator of diversity' (GOD) (1968 version), and moving through a series of different models to a composition of contestation (1982) in which helper and suppressor cells 'prompt' the orchestra, 'each urging its own interpretation', GOD has surrendered conductorship to the T cell, and is 'resigned to the conflicting calls of the angels and of help and suppression' (Golub, 1987, quoted in Haraway, 1991:205–6). These competing versions of the immune system are visually represented by Golub in diagrams of communicational and informational flows between figures with the human capacity to conduct, play instruments and participate in symmetrical spacial configurations. Thus, although only GOD and two other figures are actually personified with human faces, the other characters are ghostly forms who have human capacities, limbs and some facial features such as eyes and eyebrows (Haraway, 1989b).

In the case of germ cell cancer the basic reproductive unit, the egg, begins to replicate itself, and threatens the rest of the body. Thus, the cell which might potentially be the basis for the reproduction of another if fertilised, combines with a mirror image of itself, and in so doing becomes dangerous and destructive (see Chapter 2). The immune system must be able to recognise the presence of a benign other, such as a foetus, in which cells divide to form the organs and tissue of an other, and a malignant tumour, in which the cells of the self divide without purpose and without limit to form tumours. The self/non-self relationship is a highly confusing one in this case. The egg cell is part of the self, and yet its 'normal' function is either to combine with sperm and form a foetus, or to be expelled from the body each month; it is thus destined *not* to remain part of the self. Ironically, it is at its most dangerous, however, when it is most similar to its original form, the perfect, but lethal, copy. In remaining part of the body, and not being expelled by the immune system, the rapidly dividing cells of the germ cell tumour masquerade as the self, when they have already transformed themselves into the body's other.

BODYGUARDS

Immune system discourse has become central to cancer patients' understandings of their illness, whether they use conventional or alternative methods, or a combination of both. Whether imagined as a battlefield, a communication system, or a network of mirrored and distorted reflections, or a combination of these, the immune system is one of the most significant forms of scientific 'discovery' to have influenced popular perceptions of our bodies and our health in the last twenty years. Immune system imagery pervades numerous and diverse aspects of our contemporary culture:

> The immune system is a historically specific terrain, where global and local politics; Nobel Prize-winning research; heteroglossic cultural productions, from popular dietary practices, feminist science fiction, religious imagery, and children's games, to photographic techniques and military strategic theory; clinical medical practice; venture capital investment strategies; world-changing developments in business and technology; and the deepest personal and collective experiences of embodiment, vulnerability, power and mortality interact with an intensity matched perhaps only in the biopolitics of sex and reproduction.
>
> (Haraway, 1991:204–5)

Its introduction through the naming of Acquired Immune Deficiency Syndrome (AIDS) in the 1980s concretised the already prevalent usage of immune system discourse and increased the public and scientific interest in the field (Martin, 1994). The image of the body's immune system has even been incorporated into high-tech tourist and entertainment industries: for example, Haraway details the 'Met Life Pavillion' in the Epcot Centre of Walt Disney World, in which one ride 'called "Body Wars", promises that we will "experience the wonders of life" such as encountering "the attack of the platelets" ... the technology for this journey through the human body uses a motion-based simulator to produce three-dimensional images for a stationary observer' (Haraway, 1992:321–2).

Both biomedical and alternative approaches to cancer draw on and reinforce our existing ideas about our immune system and its cellular cast of characters. The most popular version which cancer patients are likely to encounter is some kind of common-sense account of the first and second models outlined by Haraway above. Biomedical treatment, such as radiotherapy or chemotherapy, aims to destroy the rapidly dividing cancer cells. Patients are told that (side-)effects occur because the treatments kill all fast-growing cells, both cancerous and otherwise. Thus, while treatment might be effective in dealing with the fast-growing cancer cells, it might also kill the fast-growing cells of the hair, nails, stomach lining, inside of the mouth, nerves and and skin pigment (or other cells, depending on drug combination). This 'scientific information' is given to patients to explain the reason for some of their physical pain and discomfort during treatment, such as (in my case) vomiting, digestive problems, mouth infections, hair loss, ringing in the ears, skin markings and numbness in the hands and feet. The treatment also destroys bone marrow cells and thus reduces the body's immunity. Patients on chemotherapy are given regular tests to see if their red and white blood cell and platelet count is high enough for the next treatment. When any of these counts is low, patients will experience infections, and may need intravenous antibiotics to assist the body's 'natural' defences which are weakened by the treatment. They are warned of fungal attacks, such as candida, which can take hold when 'the immune system is depressed' or when, to quote the usual euphemism, 'your resistance is a bit low'. The disease and the treatment are thus imaginable as a battle of cell life in the body's interior, in which the immune system struggles to maintain strength in the face of attack by anti-cancer treatments.

In alternative approaches to cancer, such as those presented in much of the self-health literature examined in this book, immune system discourse functions as a key source of authority. As I argued in Chapter 4, there is considerable overlap between conventional scientific and alternative models of the body in *some* aspects of cancer treatment, and immune system discourse is probably one instance which most heavily interconnects the two medical practices (see Ross, 1991; Martin, 1994).

In *An End to Cancer?*, for example, Leon Chaitow references Sir Macfarlane Burnet, Nobel Prize-winner for his work in immunology, who 'stated that there could be up to 100,000 cells in the body becoming cancerous each day'; however, 'the average person's immunization system (defence mechanism) is so effective that it efficiently destroys these cancer cells' (Chaitow, 1983:12). Similarly, Penny Brohn quotes Joseph Issels, from whom she received successful treatment for cancer, who argues that 'cancer can never occur in a healthy body' since 'a healthy body is a person who can recognise the cancer cells and reject them' (Issels, 1975, quoted in Brohn, 1987b:7). The difference within alternative approaches, however, is that patients are encouraged to see their immune system not as separate from their 'psychological system' but as combining with it to make up one integrated *system of the self*. The language of the immune system, which draws so heavily on models of communications between self and other, combines neatly with notions of the psychological self in which the construction of the self is theorised in relation to others (especially those within the 'kinship network'), and in relation to internalised others in the psyche.[14] Indeed, the final model of the immune network outlined above, in which 'subtle plays of partially mirrored readings and responses' reproduce an internal other which is merely a reflection of the self, might read to some psychoanalysts as a physical metaphor for the intrapsychic processes of the Lacanian subject locked into an indefinite mirror-stage.[15] This parallel highlights the imbrication of psychological models of the self and the biological models of immunity which self-health approaches to cancer draw upon.

The models of communicational and informational flows which have been influential in recent biomedical innovation are thus redeployed in some alternative therapies, which see them as a method of opening up the body's malfunctions to mental influence; mind and body are brought together within this model of good health as immune system control. In self-help cancer literature, contemporary beliefs about the psyche are filtered through scientific theories of the immune system to produce a systematised self which can be regulated and managed.

In *Mind, Body and Immunity* (1990), for example, Rachel Charles argues that 'emotional distress results in an imbalance of T-suppressor cells. In the case of cancer, an excessive production allows tumours to develop' (Charles, 1990:51). Retrospectively accounting for her own cancer, Charles writes that: 'Chronic anxiety over a long period had caused immuno-suppressant hormones to course through my bloodstream, leaving me vulnerable to disease. Eventually my body succumbed and the result was cancer' (Charles, 1990:4). According to Charles, we underestimate the intercommunication between the psyche and the body at our peril. For example, she cites 'psycho-neuroimmunology' as a source of information about personality types and health: type A personalities, 'competitive, ambitious and highly active', are more likely to get heart disease, according to this particular 'science', claims Charles (Charles, 1990:49). Conversely, the 'hardy personality' is less likely to fall ill, supported by a 'highly efficient immune system'. Echoing the language of immune system discourse analysed by Haraway above, Charles characterises these types in three words: 'commitment, control and challenge' (Charles, 1990:53). Although such a typology might suggest a rather fixed destiny in terms of who is likely to suffer ill-health and who will surface from the ups and downs of life unscathed, Charles presents a series of strategies which cancer, and other, patients might use to become an 'immune efficient person' (Charles, 1990:53). If readers are not sure which category they fit into, the author offers an irresistible women's-magazine-style quiz entitled 'Are You an Immune Efficient Person?' (Charles, 1990:53). If you score low, Charles suggests a combination of the peak immunity diet, counselling and changes in lifestyle:

> What we so often fail to appreciate is that the body has a staggeringly complex system for healing and regulating itself . . . Just as this delicately balanced system can be upset by poor diet, lack of exercise, long-term emotional problems and stress, so the opposite is also true: it can be positively encouraged to operate more effectively, so that the body is able to function efficiently and remain healthy.
>   If you are suffering from a serious disease, take heart in the knowledge that *you can actively assist in your own healing*.
>   (Charles, 1990:5, my emphasis)

Cancer patients who are really committed to challenging their condition are offered a vivid iconography of their bodily interiors as a system of diverse cells which are highly sensitive to their physical and emotional environment. Scientific definitions of the immune system offer a powerful and appealing set of images through which patients make sense of their illness and/or their recovery. Indeed, by participating in this informational system of self-health, patients can utilise the mind/body channel of communication and influence their own healing.

The visualisability of the healthy body as a system of information units that connect different aspects of the self (spiritual, emotional, physical) is an increasingly commonplace image in contemporary culture. Indeed, the immune system has become a popular trope for

166

conceptualising the internal body as a set of interlocking systems more generally in alternative medicines. Nature's Sunshine Products, for example, use just such an iconography in their 'Key Systems Product Range' (see Figures 5.5, 5.6 and 5.7). The body is represented as a series of interlocking systems: the digestive system, the immune system, the glandular system, the structural system, and so on. Herbal combinations have been designed to strengthen each specific system. But if there is a weak link in the chain (connecting these systems), we are told, the whole body will suffer. The weak link is represented here by a rather incongruous symbol of industrial modernity: the strong hands of the

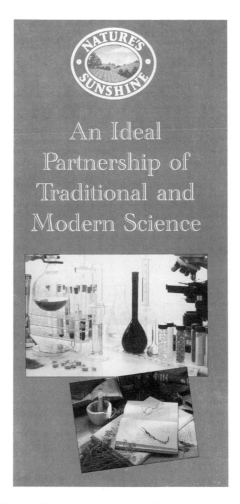

Figure 5.5 Nature's Sunshine Products leaflet

male worker placed either side of the broken link. It is our lifestyle that is most likely to result in such a broken link in our body systems:

> Weakness in a given body system may be the result of inherited weaknesses, injuries or environmental influences. The most common reason for 'weak links', however, is the stress caused by our own lifestyle choices. We work too hard, we rest too little and we neglect our bodies through poor nutrition . . . In short, we are starving our vital organ systems. . . The answer is simple. Find the weakest link and strengthen it! This is Nature's Sunshine Systems Approach to Natural Health.
> (Nature's Sunshine Products leaflet; see Figure 5.6)

Typical of many products on the market in the 1990s, Nature's Sunshine Products offer a combination of biomedicine and alternative medicine. The leaflet advertises its strength as just this combination: it is headed 'An Ideal Partnership of Traditional and Modern Science' and this accompanies the images of 'modern science' (brightly coloured,

W eakness in a given body system may be the result of inherited weaknesses, injuries or environmental influences.

The most common reason for "weak links", however, is the stress caused by our own lifestyle choices. We work too hard, we rest too little and we neglect our bodies through poor nutrition. Today's convenience foods have been so highly refined and processed that they have been robbed of many fundamental nutrients which are crucial to the health of individual body components. **In short, we are starving our vital organ systems.**

For most of us it is difficult to change the demands on our time and energy. Convenience foods allow us to spend less time preparing meals and more time doing the things we need to do. To change our eating habits is not always a practical option. So what is the answer?

T he practical and effective answer for many of us is nutritional support. We can take responsibility for our own health and ensure against deficiencies by supplementing our regular diet with vital nutrients - but which nutrients?

The answer is simple. Find the weakest link and strengthen it! This is Nature's Sunshine Systems Approach to Natural Health.

This brochure will acquaint you with the Key Product for each system. These Key System Products, along with herbal and vitamin formulations, are intended to enhance your level of health and have been historically and scientifically validated.

Your NSP Independent Distributor can help you discover the wonderful benefits of the Systems Approach to Natural Health.

Figure 5.6 Nature's Sunshine Products leaflet

synthetic chemicals and tablets, test-tubes and a microscope against a clinical white background, lit by artifical light) and 'traditional science' (muted-coloured herbs ready to be ground by hand, guided by the wisdom of ancient tomes, lit by 'natural' sunlight). But it is not just this cover that signifies this 'ideal partnership'; the images of body systems and their appropriate strengthening herbal remedies inside also represent a combination of the best of both worlds. This is an increasingly common use of visual images of scientific systems modelled within an alternative medical framework.

VISUALISING CANCER

In alternative approaches to cancer, the visual images of the cellular interior of the body and the immune system are invoked in the practice of visualisation. Here the visual imagery of the cells has been turned into a healing technology of the self. This practice, in which the disease and the immune system are given a vivid visual form, has been widely advocated for cancer patients. It is a practice which we might consider as more evidence of Barbara Stafford's claim that contemporary medical practices continue the Enlightenment project of making visible the body's previously 'occluded spaces', and in so doing bring them further under our control.

The Bristol Cancer Help Centre, following Simonton *et al.* (1978), have used visualisation as a core form of self-healing for many years (see Brohn, 1987b). Visualisation, it is argued, can be an effective technique for the transmission of healing messages to the body's immune system, particularly when it is in a state of deep relaxation. The aim is to use this technique to enhance the body's capacity for destroying the cancer cells. Visualisation is derived, in part, from motivational psychology and its uses of mental imagery to enable people to achieve their goals. So, for example, 'a golfer would visualize a beautiful golf swing with the ball going to the desired place. A business person would visualize a successful business meeting. A stage performer would visualize a smooth opening night. A person with a malignancy would picture the tumour shrinking and his [*sic*] body regaining health' (Simonton *et al.*, 1978:141). The process of imagining the illness allows us to communicate with our bodies through a 'visual and symbolic language' which is an effective method of channelling will-power (Simonton *et al.*, 1978:141). The Bristol Centre and many other alternative cancer care projects clai that this technique has produced results in terms of control of the disease. This technique was first used by Carl Simonton in 1971:

169

THE KEY SYSTEMS PRODUCT RANGE

ESSENTIAL PROTECTORS • Multiple Vitamins & Minerals • Antioxidant Arsenal

The "Essential Protectors Programme" consists of three state of the art products, that together fill in any nutritional gaps created by your diet, and provide basic nutritional insurance for the whole family.

SynerProTein

INTERNAL CLEANSING

Chinese TIAO HE Cleanse

The ten day nutritional programme based on a special herbal food combination.

Time tested Chinese herbal experience and respected western herbal nutrition combined to provide a 10 day programme

DIGESTIVE SYSTEM

Food Digestive Enzymes

Food Digestive Enzymes enhance the body's use of all foods - including proteins, fats and carbohydrates. These enzymes promote the body's ability to digest and absorb the nutrients it needs to function efficiently.

RESPIRATORY SYSTEM

ALJ

ALJ Formula is a herbal combination that assists the body's self-cleansing mechanisms. ALJ contains the following herbs that have historically been used to nutritionally support the respiratory system: Fenugreek seed, Fennel seed, Mullein leaf, Boneset herb & Horseradish root.

The major effects of the fenugreek and mullein are due to their high content of mucilage and mild saponins. Fennel has been noted by herbalists as a nutritional aid for helping digestion and for cleansing the urinary and respiratory systems.

INTESTINAL SYSTEM

Bowel Build

Bowel Build formula is food for the gastrointestinal tract itself, and contains nutrients essential for proper digestion and intestinal function.

This product is rich in vitamins and minerals such as beta-carotene, and selenium. It provides betaine HCl, pepsin, pancreatin and bile salts needed for the upper gastrointestinal tract. For the lower tract, each capsule of Bowel Build also contains 240 mg. of psyllium hulls, plus kelp plant and chlorophyll.

URINARY SYSTEM

URY

Often taken for granted, the kidneys are constantly serving to purify the blood, balance the body's fluid and maintain the correct ratio of sodium/potassium and glucose required for energy. Such a job description necessitates adequate rest, nutrition and added supplementation to help the body deal with the stress of our modern environment. Formula URY is designed to provide nutritional support for the many vital needs of the urinary system. It contains uva ursi leaves, hydrangea root, parsley herb, dandelion root and other herbs. These herbs are combined with vitamins and minerals essential to support healthy urinary tract tone and function.

GLANDULAR SYSTEM

Master Gland Formula

As a balanced food product for the endocrine system, Master Gland Formula is what its name implies - a master product for glandular health.

Master Gland combines natural herbal products with vitamins and minerals essential to glandular function and metabolism. Trace minerals are crucial to proper endocrine function. Overworked and depleted soils worldwide have exhausted the minerals in our food supply, making it practically impossible to ensure adequate mineral intake.

STRUCTURAL SYSTEM

SKL Formula

is a combination of the vitamins and minerals your skeletal system needs for optimal strength.

Target Endurance

developed to target the needs of the muscular system, is based on the concept that true health begins on a cellular level. Keeping the muscular system healthy helps us stay active and ensures proper function of muscles surrounding organs such as the heart, liver and lungs.

HSN-W

contains significant amounts of herbal silicon (27.9 mg per 100 gram). Silicon is important to the proper utilisation of calcium, another important mineral for the structural system.

Mega-Chel

Mega-Chel is nutrition for maximum circulation.

To supplement this life-saving function of the body, Mega-Chel includes multiple vitamins, minerals, glandular extracts, herbs and amino acids.

It is specifically designed to supply maximum nutrition to the circulatory system.

NERVOUS SYSTEM

Nutri-Calm

Nutri-Calm is a beneficial blend of vitamins and herbs that provides nutrition the body needs to better cope with a busy, modern world.

It contains the B-complex and C vitamins plus calcium in a nutritional base of herbs, bee pollen, and other nutrients. Calcium is included because it is used by the body to maintain the nerves in their normal, calm state. Vitamin C and herbs in the formulation work to balance and enhance a weakened nervous system.

IMMUNE SYSTEM

IMF

IMF (Immune Maintenance Formula) is a combination of vitamins, minerals and foodstuffs to help counter the effects of poor foods, pollution and other things harmful to people of modern societies.

It is rich in vitamins C, A, and E, as well as selenium and zinc.

The vitamins and minerals come in a base of cruciferous vegetables.

Figure 5.7 Nature's Sunshine Products leaflet

... with a patient whose cancer was considered medically in-
curable. The patient practiced three times a day visualizing his
cancer, his treatment coming in and destroying it, his white blood
cells attacking the cancer cells and flushing them out of his body,
and finally imagining himself regaining health. The results were
spectacular: the 'hopeless' patient overcame his disease and is still
alive and healthy.

(Simonton *et al.*, 1978:142)

The typical imagery used by cancer patients in their visualizations of
their treatments has been that of militaristic metaphors prevalent in the
first model of immune system discourse described by Haraway above.
Simonton *et al.* make the following recommendations to patients:

If you are receiving radiation treatment, picture it as a beam of
millions of bullets of energy hitting any cells in its path . . .
If you are receiving chemotherapy, picture that drug coming into
your body and entering the bloodstream. Picture the drug acting
like a poison. The normal cells are intelligent and strong and
don't take up the poison so readily. But the cancer cell is a weak
cell, so it takes very little to kill it. It absorbs the poison, dies, and
is flushed out of your body . . . Picture your body's own white
blood cells coming into the area where the cancer is, recognizing
the abnormal cells, and destroying them. There is a vast army of
white blood cells. They are very strong and aggressive. They are
also very smart. There is no contest between them and the cancer
cells: they will win the battle.

(Simonton *et al.*, 1978:144)

These mental images are of fighting and destruction: the cells of the
immune system and the cancer cells make up opposing armies which
will fight until death. According to the Simonton approach, the use of
some kinds of symbols of aggression, violence or force are necessary for
the visualization to be effective. Accounts are given of patients who
found these qualities hard to include in their images, and of how they
were helped to progress towards the inclusion of such symbols
(Simonton *et al.*, 1978:151–74).

However, more recently, many therapists at the Bristol Centre have
argued against the necessary inclusion of such aggressive 'masculine'
images, and have encouraged patients to use symbols which they find
effective. Examples such as '[cancer] cells dissolving like Alka Seltzers in
a beautiful blue healing liquid' and 'cell-bursting with a big darning
needle' are given (Brohn, 1987b:138–9). The crucial ingredient, Brohn
argues, is not one of battle, but of the cancer cells as weak and your
image of recovery as strong. Thus a powerful 'golden hoover' sucking

172

up dirt and rubbish or cancer cells as a 'plate full of ice cubes' melting in the midday sun are both acceptable alternatives to the more militaristic imagery (Brohn, 1987b:141–2).

Visualisation is one of the introductory sessions offered at the Bristol Centre (the others being nutrition, spiritual healing, relaxation and counselling). It has an immediate appeal to our contemporary understanding of the insides of our bodies as self-regulating systems in which we play a part in maintaining, the cells being the basic units which can be reprogrammed with new information if they begin to misbehave. Visualisation is imaging 'the desired outcome', it is a method for 'self-direction' (Simonton *et al.*, 1978:150). It is thus suggested that will-power might be able to have a direct effect on the body achieving some kind of cell control. The idea is that in states of deep relaxation, which patients can learn, the visualisation of images in the mind can communicate the wishes of the self to the body, and, ultimately, if practised regularly, can strengthen its capacity to expel unwanted cancer cells. Thus, rather like a form of self-hypnotherapy, mental messages might have a physical result if communicated to the body when it is in a receptive, relaxed state.

Many people with cancer at Bristol, and elsewhere, find visualisation a helpful technique to use during conventional treatments. It offers a focus for the mind which can help distract the patient from the needles and drips in chemotherapy, and from the intimidating technology of radiotherapy. One doctor at Bristol told me she had seen it used to protect the body from radiotherapy burns on the skin. To imagine a protective covering around areas of the body not being treated might also prevent further damaging effects of radiation, such as other kinds of cancer. Furthermore, it helps patients feel less negative about these painful and unpleasant treatments and less passive in the face of this impersonal treatment delivered by experts to the patient's waiting and supine body. To imagine chemotherapy as a beautifully coloured healing liquid might also make it easier to accept it being pumped into your body for four days. Some claim that if you feel positive about it, the treatment will work better. Finally, of course, some patients believe that the mind can, in fact, communicate messages to the body which help it fight the disease.

INSIGHTS?

Our contemporary beliefs about the meanings of illnesses such as cancer surface in a culture in which the body's interior has been afforded a new visual landscape through contemporary immune system discourse. This discourse has added another layer of cultural coding to this already overdetermined picture by synthesising, and conferring scientific validity on, the idea of the body as a self-regulating system: 'it is no longer possible to see the body as an object waiting for replacement parts from the factory. Instead we now view the mind and the body as an integrated *system*' (Simonton *et al.*, 1978:31–2). In particular, the immune system is seen as the interface between the emotional and the physical self: 'evidence that emotional loss can lead to a suppression of the immune system is an important clue to the causes of cancer' (Simonton *et al.*, 1978:53). Loss and stress are seen to interfere with the normal functioning of the body's natural defence system: 'chronic stress suppresses the immune system which is responsible for engulfing and destroying cancerous cells or alien microorganisms . . . The physical conditions . . . produced by stress are virtually identical to those under which an abnormal cell could reproduce and spread into a dangerous cancer' (Simonton *et al.*, 1978:53). This model of health and illness situates the causes and cures of disease in the individual's internal cell system, an autonomous interconnected set of information units which, under the correct conditions, should function through communication networks to maintain the body's well-being.

People's understanding of themselves and their health/illness is increasingly influenced by immune system discourse in which everything one does in life is seen as related to the functioning and health of the immune system (Martin, 1994). As Emily Martin's research shows, people's understanding of the immune system is based upon the image of a 'robust notion of an internal system of production that . . . exists to ward off continual threats', but within this framework 'people focus their attention on the well-being of the system rather than on creating an environment that is free from threat' (Martin, 1994:67). Martin cites one respondent:

> To me it's all systemic. You can't localize and say this pathology here doesn't affect there. To me it's all one. When you look at what is it [*sic*] that makes the immune system break down, well, there are so many co-factors now.
>
> (Rebecca Petrides, quoted in Martin, 1994:133)

Technological metaphors are widely used in the conceptualisation of the immune system as the body's defence:

> Basically, it's a real complicated series of things that ties everything together. And when something goes wrong in your body, signals go out, and cells go to attack it. I guess it's basically just a system of checks and balances, and most things the immune system in the body can deal with on its own . . . For the most part, it just sort of keeps everything in line with the metabolic

174

computer . . . Keep the good things running correctly and get rid of the bad things.

(Arthur Harrison, quoted in Martin, 1994:72)

The combination of three factors – the current beliefs about the aetiology of cancer, the popular mind/body metaphors of alternative medicine and the impact of immune system discourse – produces a configuration of cultural meanings in which the verdict of 'idiopathic' (a primary disease, not occasioned by another) seems the almost inescapable fate for the cancer 'patient'. The model of cancer as a disease 'occasioned' by the self (rather than an outside invader of the body by another) opens up the space for maximum interpretation and investigation of the self by the patient in order for them to heal themselves. Thus, seeing into the depths of a person's body is equivalent to seeing into the depths of the person's self. Through new forms of technological and imaginative visualisability, an intensified significance has been afforded to the emotional, psychic and psychological mean-ings of illnesses. If the body can be read as an informational text, then the 'imprints of emotions' on its cells (see pp. 147–8) can be translated (with the help of a native speaker). *Insight* into the body's secret places can offer *insight* into the personality. The script of the body's interior can produce clues as to the cause and cure of disease and it is seen as the individual's responsibility, if not moral duty, to monitor, process and act upon this information (see Hay, 1988).

Our sense of our bodily interiors is defined by a medical gaze which has not only seen inside the body through surgery and post-mortem pathology, but also through an endless proliferation of simulations and systems of information. Such changes have laid the foundations for an understanding of the body as a *visualisable system*, an understanding which pervades aspects of alternative/self-health and biomedicine. Within both approaches, cancer patients are encouraged to imagine cancer as an illness in which good and bad, or normal and deviant, cells battle to define the body's interior. Within immune system imagery, the cell is visualised with a renewed vividness. The personification and visualisation of reproductive cells has been widely accepted in popular and scientific representations of the body (Martin, 1992). With the 'discovery' of the immune system, the interior cell-life of the body is brought to life through a distinctive set of visual images (Martin, 1994). These images of the body as an interconnecting network of inter-dependent systems have become prevalent throughout contemporary health cultures. Their increasing pervasiveness might be attributed to the ways in which they condense and extend many of the changing discourses of the body and the self. Their popularity might result from their successful reconfiguration of some powerful images, fantasies and aspirations that have achieved a firm grip on our cultural imaginations in the 1990s. This model of a visualisable healthy body invokes a highly active and responsible self, a self that could be called upon to participate, to instigate change, to desire control through a repertoire of regimes of self-management.

6

SELVES

The multiplication of cells by mitosis occurs throughout the life of the individual. It occurs at a more rapid rate until growth is complete. Thereafter, new cells are formed to replace those which have died. Nerve cells are a notable exception. When they die they are not replaced.

In the secret places of her thymus gland Louise is making too much of herself. Her faithful biology depends on regulation but the white T-cells have turned bandit. They don't obey the rules. They are swarming into the bloodstream, overturning the quiet order of spleen and intestine. In the lymph nodes they are swelling with pride. It used to be their job to keep her body safe from enemies on the outside. They were her immunity, her certainty against infection. Now they are the enemies on the inside. The security forces have rebelled. Louise is the victim of a coup.

Will you let me crawl inside you, stand guard over you, trap them as they come at you? Why can't I dam their blind tide that filthies your blood? Why are there no lock gates on the portal vein? The inside of your body is innocent, nothing has taught it fear. Your artery canals trust their cargo, they don't check the shipments in the blood. You are full to overflowing but the keeper is asleep and there's murder going on inside. Who comes here? Let me hold up my lantern. It's only the blood; red cells carrying oxygen to the hear, thrombocytes making sure of proper clotting. The white cells, B and T types, just a few of them as always whistling as they go.

The faithful body has made a mistake. This is no time to stamp the passports and look at the sky. Coming up behind are hundreds of them. Hundreds too many, armed to the teeth for a job that doesn't need doing. Not needed? With all that weaponry?

Here they come, hurtling through the bloodstream trying to pick a fight. There's no-one to fight but you Louise. You're the foreign body now.

(Winterson, 1992:115–16)

To read cancer as a metaphor in contemporary culture is to see it as the disease in which the self has turned against itself – as a disease in which the cells of the body, the microcosms of the self, betray their host and

are led astray. These units of the self, whose job it is to keep reproducing themselves for the benefit of the whole organism, somehow get
the wrong end of the stick, the wrong information, the wrong instructions. The body's immune system, we are told, depends upon the
correct behaviour of certain types of cells; we think of cells as being
there to protect us from disease, not to be its source. Their mis-
guidance and confusion (or could it be malice?) slowly, but surely,
destroy the system, saturating it with masses of undifferentiated (or
insufficiently differentiated) cells (see Chapter 3). Eventually the
resulting tumours interfere with the functioning of key organs and the
body gives in, surrendering to the part of itself which has gone out of
control. The body is invaded from within; the cancer patient becomes
the foreign body.

The narrator's frustration in this passage is that of a thwarted reader
who has failed to read the signs of her lover's body correctly. It has
been read with desire rather than death or decay in mind. But inside,
the body has secretly been going haywire. For the helpless lover, the
knowledge of the presence of this hidden and insidious disease is
almost too much to bear. What does it mean to love a body with such
invisible evil auto-intent? The romantic fantasy of heroic intervention
on behalf of the defenceless lover displays a desire for her survival,
together with a sense of impotence at witnessing her self-destruction.
What more appropriate act for a romantic hero than the risk of self-
sacrifice on entering the lover's body to rescue her from herself?
Crossing the boundary between self and other, between outside and
inside, surely a devoted knight could intercept the enemy cells and
disperse their massed force and vanquish their threat? The force of
love must be stronger than that of death. After all, cancer cells are
simply misguided replicants, powerful only in their aimless multiplication. Originally, they were destined for production, not destruction; for life, not death.

The above extract is taken from Jeanette Winterson's novel, *Written
on the Body* (1992). The narrator's description of the cancer which
threatens to steal the lover away plays with the endless repertoire of
body metaphors in which cell types provide the cast of characters in this
imaginary interior physical landscape. As such, it brings together many
of the themes of the previous chapters in this book: heroic narratives;
metaphors of illness; the complex relationship of disease and desire;
the changing conceptualisations of the body and its visualisable interiors in contemporary medical beliefs and practices about cancer. This
chapter extends many of these debates in order to examine the ways in
which cancer cultures invite the patient to engage in particular regimes
of self-management and care. What forms of the self are at stake in such

practices which mark a symptomatic intersection between care, control, will-power and surveillence in the contemporary cultures of self-health?

MANAGING MYSELF

Fresh from the shock of the diagnosis, I devise a lifestyle for health. I am not sure if this is offensive or defensive, for I have no idea whether I still have cancer or not. Most of all it is a coping strategy, a way of reorganising time in a manner appropriate to the severity of the news. This is liminal time, filled with waiting and testing. I may be able to avoid chemotherapy, I am told. I find it impossible not to involve myself in the struggle for authorship of this particular trajectory; my desire to reshape this life story gone awry is overwhelming. To wait and to do nothing feels altogether too passive, and perhaps too frightening. So I seek a structure for my present time which offers the hopeful fantasy of influencing the events of future time. These tightly scheduled rituals of care secure the self firmly between their various demands. The narrative of the self is in crisis and a new structure is desperately needed to offer reassurance, if only temporarily.

I seek comfort in daily rituals of alternative healing. Visualisation is one amongst many. After meditating, I try to visualise myself healthy and my body as strong and capable of fighting the disease. This involves finding a suitable visual image of the disease. I find this almost impossible since I have no idea whether the cancer is still present in my body. There is a 50 per cent chance that the surgery got rid of it all. My superstitions warn against my imagining any cancer cells in my body; I might tempt fate. If the mind can affect the body, then I had better be careful. Nevertheless, I try. I even ask others to try on my behalf. There are plenty of images in the alternative medical literature: from the aggressive ones, hungry sharks eating a cauliflower, to the gentler ones, a block of ice melting in the sun.

Food and supplements offer endless scope for new regimes characterised by their preoccupying detail. The following text is taped on the wall as a prompt:

JACKIE'S REGIME

Breakfast: Organic muesli and soya milk and/or toast and peanut butter; 5ml liver herbs in 5ml water; 4 Combination K tablets; 1 vitamin B tablet

Mid-morning: 1 spoon vitamin C in water, followed 30 mins later by 1 large glass carrot juice

30 mins before lunch: 1 spoon vitamin C in water

With lunch: 5ml liver herbs in 5ml water; Combination K tablets; 2 primrose oil tablets; 1 vitamin E tablet; 1 zinc tablet; 1 selenium tablet

Mid-afternoon: 1 large glass carrot juice

30 mins before evening meal: 1 spoon vitamin C in water

With evening meal: 5ml liver herbs in 5ml water; 4 Combination K; 1 vitamin B

If no carrot juice available, take 3 beta carotene tablets at mealtimes

---

These are informed choices. I have done my research. Vitamin C in high doses 'helps to metabolize fats, carbohydrates and amino acids. Protects tissues, especially cell membranes, against oxidative damage by chemically "free radicals". Neutralizes sodium nitrate and sodium nitrite which are potent carcinogens' (Brohn, 1987b:64). My menu is 3mg a day and I am assured that I can't overdose on this vitamin as whatever doesn't get used, 'spills over into the urine . . . [as] it is water soluble' (Brohn, 1987b:65). Similarly vitamin A is seen 'to have a protective and therapeutic effect against certain cancers' (Brohn, 1987b:68). I dutifully drink 1–1½ pints of carrot juice a day, which is the best way to get this vitamin into your system. I gradually turn a very pale shade of orange which is at least empirical evidence that some effect is taking place. Certain supplements are recommended at Bristol in combination with each other. Selenium, for example, 'taken together with vitamins C and E . . . contributes to a powerful anti-oxidant cocktail that is believed to be very helpful in the control of cancer. It is also protective against atherosclerosis, and helps in the functioning of the immune system generally' (Brohn, 1987b:70).

In addition to the supplements my diet also changes dramatically. I embark on the strictest version of the 'Bristol Diet' I can find. The stricter the better: its harshness matches the emotional turmoil. The dedication and determination required to stick to the diet are quite sustaining in themselves: evidence of my will-power, an easy way to act out the struggle. I begin every meal with raw vegetables or fruit. I buy as much organic food as I can find and afford. I give up dairy food because of the hormones they use in the industry. I give up sugar and salt, which are seen to be carcinogenic, and I try to have as little fat as possible. I am already a vegetarian, so meat and fish are not an issue. I give up alcohol, except for the occasional glass of organic wine, and I limit my tea and coffee intake to one cup of low-caffeine tea a day, the rest of the time I drink herb teas. I drink organic carrot juice in between meals.

My days are structured around meditation and relaxation (and visualisation when possible), vitamin and mineral supplement intake, and three carefully planned organic meals. I have acupuncture to help my body recover from the surgery and the anaesthetic, and healing from some local spiritual healers. I also go to see Matthew Manning once a month. One of the most well-known healers in Britain, he offers hands-on healing for cancer patients, and has had some remarkable results, I am told. Finally, there are my visits to the hospital. Every week I attend my oncologist's clinic at the hospital where I had surgery. He gives me the results of the last blood test and takes some more blood for the next one. He also examines me for lumps in the neck and abdomen. 'In America', I am told, '[I] would be given three months' chemotherapy automatically.' I am grateful for the chance to try and avoid it.

In the first few weeks out of hospital my life story quickly becomes a series of clichés: it is a race against time; I feel I have to do everything possible; it's worth a try; I've nothing to lose. The narrative structure could not be more pronounced: a weekly countdown full of suspense. Each result is a form of closure, a step nearer safety. The AFP levels have a half-life of about a week, so the fall is satisfyingly dramatic: from

16000 to 8000, and then from 8000 to 4000. After a couple of good results we begin to plot a graph. Each week it is filled in with the latest triumph. The ritual visit to the hospital is followed by the ritual phone calls with news. The successes are a very public affair. Everyone is watching, listening, waiting. As the weeks go by the AFPs halve obediently: 4000, 2000, 1100, and so on, slowing down as they get near the normal level of below 10. My sense of victory increases as the levels decrease. Towards the end there is little doubt in my mind: my regimes of self-management are working. I tempt fate and arrange a party to celebrate. I ask my consultant when I can go back to work. I start to plan my teaching. I am down to 22: only one more week to go.

The following week the levels go up from 22 to 25. And by the week after, they have more than doubled. They rise as dramatically as they drop.

The graph on the wall at home is left unfinished, with the contours of success still promising triumph. The hero-narrative of the self in battle with the evil cells, and winning, suddenly looks very different. The illusion of control, of mind over matter, has disappeared. None of it, after all, has made any difference.

Nevertheless, I retain some of the 'cancer hero' mentality that has sustained my project so far [see Chapter 1]. I have two days to prepare for hospital for the first chemotherapy. A second trip to the Bristol Cancer Help Centre convinces me that continuing with my regimes might usefully help me deal with the treatment. In fact, a doctor there assures me that the drugs I am to have are manageable, and that a positive attitude makes all the difference. I will be fine, she confirms, she's seen it so many times; if you're determined to be all right, you will be. I have little time to mourn my fall from heroic status, as the chemotherapy starts almost immediately. I simply transfer the energy and determination from avoiding chemotherapy to surviving it.

I arrive at the hospital for the first dose. I am equipped with organic food, dozens of vitamins and minerals and I have a few visual images at the ready. My oncologist has warned me of hair loss and vomiting, so I take extra vitamin C against nausea and a homeopathic remedy against hair loss. I also have a diary to record what drugs I am given and what effects they have on me. I plan to get through the treatment by using these 'regimes of self-management' to structure my days in hospital as I have done my days at home.

The battle has been reconstituted. I am now required to embrace the treatment I have been struggling to avoid. Chemotherapy must be visualised as a positive intervention. Not poison, but pink champagne, they suggest in Bristol. The more I can think of it as an ally, the less it will harm me. The drugs are administered intravenously. They take three days. (Positive images for three days?) But I am prepared; I will 'sail through it', I am told. My mind and body brace themselves.

I write down the names of the drugs in the diary: Bleomycin, Etoposide, Cisplatinum. I take more vitamin C. The treatment begins.

Twenty-four hours into the treatment I am vomiting regularly, I have a high temperature, I am sweating and I ache everywhere with flu-like symptoms. None of the anti-emetic drugs work – instead they produce new unpleasant side-effects (one of them makes you feel as if you have an ants nest in your anus). Had someone offered me carrot juice or organic nut roast (both of which I have brought with me) I'd have certainly thrown it at them. Vitamins are out of the question. Regular vomiting renders such grand plans redundant. This goes on for three days. When I finally get home, I develop a burning, itchy rash all over my body. I scratch like crazy. I am readmitted for an antihistamine. The scratch marks remain all over my neck, arms, breasts, back and stomach. Traces of my desperation become permanent scars. Bleomycin can sometimes do this, I am told.

Back at home the itching has stopped but not the vomiting. We phone the hospital. Just hold on. It will stop eventually. No, there's no chance of dehydration, she's had plenty of fluids. But the sickness continues. The next day it's about every hour or so. And I am getting weaker and weaker. That evening, I collapse in the bathroom with my partner in attendance. My eyes roll, my teeth chatter and my throat croaks; my body goes cold and I pour with sweat. I am unconscious and my breathing is uneven. The hospital is phoned again. We should call the GP, we are told. Could the seizure be connected to the chemotherapy? Could one of the drugs cause a potassium deficiency as it says in our book? The doctor laughs at our amateur medical knowledge. I am just dehydrated, nothing to worry about.

When I return to hospital for a booster injection and tell the story it generates a medical panic. I have to have an ECG to test for brain damage and may even need a lumbar puncture to test the spinal fluid. This is probably caused by potassium deficiency from the drugs and I should have come straight into hospital, I am told. Tempers are rising, family appears on the scene and nurses are reprimanded. I should have stayed in hospital longer, I am told; next time, I am to stay in hospital until the vomiting stops.

Some days after the second treatment I awake with severe chest pains. Is this a heart attack? The cancer books are consulted again. Bleomycin can damage the lung tissue; perhaps this is it. The GP is called, my usual doctor arrives and is sympathetic. He is perplexed. Everything seems fine. On returning to the hospital I complain of the chest pain. An X-ray is taken, but all is clear. I insist that something is wrong. The chemotherapy is thus postponed until I have a lung function test at another hospital. This shows lung damage. One of the three drugs is therefore cut from the treatment, which lessens their overall effectiveness. And this may mean more treatments.

The vomiting continues after the third treatment, and after the fourth, I have a repeat performance of the first and the vomiting is relentless. In addition, I have now developed tinitus (a loud high-pitched ringing in my ears), neuropathy (numbness and tingling in my hands and feet), infections in my mouth, I have stopped menstruating, and I have intermittent chest pains. I am on steroids for a few months to try and help the lungs to repair themselves, and as a result my appetite for starch and sugar has increased tenfold. I put on about two stone in weight and my face is puffy from the steroids. My hair has all fallen out.

By the end of the fourth treatment my body has reached a limit. But I still have to have one more dose. I am vomiting, I have diarrhoea, my hands and feet are completely numb and my ears are ringing loudly all the time. My body has been transformed, colonised by the drugs and their side-effects. I can't walk properly in the mornings, as I have no feeling in my feet, which sends me off balance. My hearing is damaged and I find it hard to follow conversations if there is any competing background noise. All my body hair has fallen out and I am completely bald, except for a few stray eyebrow hairs. No eyelashes are left. My skin is marked with what look like whip marks. I am having hot flushes about once an hour because the other ovary has been affected and my periods have stopped. Am I beginning early menopause? No one can be sure. Urination becomes hard because the nerves in the bladder have also become numb.

My dreams focus on pollution and physical disgust: one night I dream I have to eat a huge pile of car tyres which are stacked up in front of me in a pyramid, and I keep protesting that I can't possibly eat them all. Why would one willingly poison oneself?, I keep thinking in the dream.

I write to my consultant and tell him of my fears. Receiving no reply, I go in for my fifth and final treatment. By this time I am without any pretence of self-control. Even the will-power I rely on to get me to the hospital is running out. To have to go for chemotherapy willingly is expecting a lot. When I arrive at the hospital something is odd: nurses smirk and no bed has my name on it. I perch on a spare one. My consultant appears on the ward. This is unprecedented. He thinks I've probably had enough. I can go home. It is over.

I look back on these changing strategies of self-health during chemotherapy. The drugs were very strong poisons whose effects completely took over my body, its organs and its functions. Against them, vitamins and organic food stood little chance, they even seemed laughable. There was one incident when a nurse spilled one of the bags of a chemotherapy drug and, with a barely disguised sense of urgency, several more nurses appeared in plastic gloves and aprons and cleared it up, taking great care not to get it anywhere near their skin. As I watched them mopping up so nervously, it was hard to believe that they could not even touch a drop of what was going by the bagful into my veins and around my body. If it took high quantities of these poisons to be pumped into my body with so many detrimental effects to get rid of the cancer cells, what chance did these mild, if dedicated, routines of self-management stand against such virulence?

I began the treatment full of conviction that my regimes might make the difference. Mental, physical and spiritual activities would get me through it unscathed, I was told (and a part of me had believed it, or at least had hoped). I came out of the experience completely physically devastated; the impact of the chemicals on my body had been so great that any notion of being 'in charge' of the whole process had been abandoned at an early stage. Indeed, with hindsight, such aspirations seem ridiculous. My comforting routines had been destroyed by the sheer force of the treatment, which I had entirely underestimated. I went into chemotherapy on a strict organic, low-fat, no sugar or salt, vegan diet, and I came out the other end eating lots of carbohydrates, sugar and fat. When the steroids stopped I gradually recovered my usual appetite. I could not bear to meditate (as I had planned to do twice a day) because anything which took me inside myself made me aware of the nausea and other physical discomforts. All I wanted was to be distracted: television, telephone, visits from friends. Anything to make me think and feel beyond my body. The internality of my body was unbearable.

How differently chemotherapy had turned out from my fantasy of it. How little effect I had had. If I was determined enough, I had been told, I wouldn't suffer any side-effects, or if I did, they would be minimal. The truly dedicated visualiser and meditator could control their body's responses through thought and will-power, and through nutrition and vitamins. The destruction of cancer cells through conventional methods could be assisted by the patient who committed themself to participating in the body's healing processes. But they did not obey my thoughts; they were not influenced by my visualisations; they were stronger than the force of my will-power.

This is the story of my failure to avoid chemotherapy which had become my main goal in life for these three months. It is a story in which my sense of self was chiefly determined by my will-power and the strength of my desire to control the course of the disease. In order to enter into 'the fight', I had had to produce heroic qualities. Each week the results had offered a renewed incentive. If the body is part of the whole system of the self, there is no room for doubt or hesitation – the campaign must be total; any weak connection and the whole network could crash. Had I not believed in it enough? Did my critical evaluations of the methods disturb the results? Should I have done more? Or should I not have done any of it? How would I have felt if I had had to have chemotherapy and I had not tried everything to avoid it?

Once the treatment started this became another story. The story of an onslaught. A physical devastation. A bodily transformation. A shock whose impact was much greater than that of the diagnosis. The news of having (had?) cancer was an unexpected trauma, but it was impossible to respond to, not only because of the shock, but because I had no idea what it meant. With no further treatment, it might have continued to feel unreal, even untrue. The trauma of the chemotherapy treatment was of a different order entirely. It was like paddling in shallow waters and being hit by a tidal wave.

The contrast between the self invented in my health strategy and the self that emerged from chemotherapy is rehearsed here through a sense of my own disbelief. The shock of the treatment and of my lack of impact in the light of its force leaves an absence to which I endlessly return in my memory (Caruth, 1995; see also Chapter 1, this volume). The failure of that promised triumph, the utter lack of control over the body. Mind over matter indeed; not this matter.

But why be so negative? With another turn, the story of failure could become the story of success. After all, I have survived thus far. I could tell the treatment story as a mark of my triumph. Perhaps you think I have. It was effective in the end, so why dwell on the failure? Mine too could be a triumph-over-tragedy narrative. I could be a survivor, a 'cancer hero'.[1]

THE LIMITS OF THE WILL

To participate in some of the alternatives to conventional medical treatments of cancer is to embark on a project of self-management. Conventional medicine often tends to treat the patient as the passive recipient of treatment done to them by others and over which they have little say, and about which they have no understanding (see Chapter 4). In contrast, these alternative processes of constant self-surveillance give the person with cancer a sense of active participation in their own health. Instead of putting one's body, and life, into the hands of experts, these forms of self-health enable the patient to feel they can do something. My own regime, detailed above, consisted of routines and timetables which structured my time on a daily and a weekly basis. The combination of the hospital 'countdown' of AFP levels, and my own ways of plotting my trajectory towards good health through graphs, lists and diaries (as well as endless verbal reporting to friends and family on the telephone) transformed my life at that time into a project of self-health.

While these regimes of self-management offer patients a sense of choice, autonomy and control at a time when they feel 'taken over' both by the disease and by the alienating and depersonalised medical establishment (see Chapter 4), they nevertheless leave those who do not truimph with a profound sense of failure (see Cassileth, 1989). There are very serious problems with a model of 'self-health' which offers the individual the aspiration of being completely in charge of their 'destiny' and the fantasy of total control over their bodies, mis-leadingly encouraging illusions of omnipotence and even immortality (see Chapter 1). Moreover, this model blames the 'patient' if the techniques do not work. Susan DiGiacomo launches a heartfelt critique of Bernie Siegel's highly popular *Love, Medicine and Miracles* (1986) which, she argues, reproduces just such victim-blaming mythology. 'One could scarcely imagine a harsher condemnation', she writes:

> those [patients] who experience the painful and dangerous 'side-effects' of radiotherapy and chemotherapy are said to be 'manipulating' their situation or 'resisting' the physician's efforts to help them get well. There are, Siegel concludes, 'no incurable diseases, only incurable people.'
>
> (Siegel, 1986, quoted in DiGiacomo, 1992:121)

Many alternative approaches to cancer imply that the person with cancer can determine the course of their illness through sheer will-power. They construct a model of health in which if you do all the right things for your body (feed it well, love it, encourage it, relax it, and so on) then it will be good to you and stay (or become) healthy. This model of the relationship between the body and the self is a highly rational and fair one, in which cause and effect are connected by an uninterrupted flow of information. The 'channelling' of energy (see Coward, 1989) in this project of self-healing requires the subject to exercise will-power and believe in the bodily effects of intentionality. Will-power is seen as a sign of health, and its display a necessary assurance of the patient's suitable psychological disposition and moral character (see Rabinbach, 1992). Indeed, according to Rosalind Coward, the body itself is attributed a certain 'will': 'In virtually all alternative therapies there is a strong and fundamental belief in the body's "natural" will towards health, in its inherent capacity to be well and return to health given the proper conditions' (Coward, 1989:23).

The mind-over-matter philosophy of much of the alternative literature on cancer thus 'reintroduces the value of rational self-control' (Kirmayer, 1988:75). This is particularly ironic, given how much these therapies seek to distinguish themselves from the rationalism of bio-medical traditions and indeed to critique the rationalism of modern Western culture. Throughout the alternative literature on cancer there are constant references to the importance of emotions and the limits of the medicine of modernity which has ignored this side of 'being human'. For example, Simonton *et al.* write:

> The human nervous system is the product of millions of years of evolution. For most of human existence the demands placed on the nervous system were very different from those placed on us by modern civilization. Survival in primitive societies required that humans be capable of immediately identifying a threat and making

a quick decision whether to fight or flee . . . But life in modern
society requires that we frequently inhibit our fight-or-flee responses.

(Simonton et al., 1978:51)

Indeed, this inhibition of our 'essential' need to behave according
to instinctive emotional mechanisms may lead to physical illness, we
are told:

> In a culture where feelings are given little importance and emo-
> tional needs vital to a person's well-being are frequently ignored,
> disease can fulfil an important purpose: it can provide a way to
> meet the needs that a person has not found conscious ways of
> meeting . . . Because cancer patients are often people who have
> put everyone else's needs first, they have obviously had difficulty
> permitting themselves these freedoms without the illness.

(Simonton et al., 1978:127)

None the less, accompanying these understandings of cancer as a
disease of modernity resulting from its inhibition of our 'natural'
emotional responses is an imperative to rational self-control which will
enable patients to regain their health.

The idea that physical disease can be affected by mental attitudes is,
however, not restricted to alternative medicine. According to Laurence
Kirmayer, aspects of biomedicine, such as psychosomatic medicine,
while including emotional life in diagnosis and treatment and thus
apparently breaking down the mind/body dualism traditionally associated with Western medicine, simultaneously reintroduce precisely this
binary through their ultimate goal of self-mastery: here the mind is
simply seen as more powerful than the body and ultimately able to
control it. Cecil Helman's pilot study of patients' own conceptualisations of their illnesses also shows that patients with chronic conditions, such as irritable bowel syndrome, colitis or asthma, had internalised concepts of a 'pathogenic' personality and saw their illnesses as,
in part anyway, resulting from their emotional dispositions (Helman,
1988:117).

Thus, there is an overlap between self-health and biomedical
accounts of the bodily effects of emotional patterns in some areas of
treatment. Even in traditional oncology there is some evidence of
doctors investing in patients' will-power, as well as relying on their
physiological methods of chemotherapy and radiotherapy. This is not
immediately apparent, but is embedded in the discourses through
which patient/doctor exchanges take place. In their account of discourses of hope in American oncology, for example, Del Vecchio et al.
argue that conventional medicine participates in propagating just such
beliefs:

187

The American discourse on hope incorporates popular and professional dimensions of our culture of biomedicine. Its emphasis
on 'will' – if one has enough hope, one may *will* a change in the
course of disease in the *body* – articulates fundamental American
notions about personhood, individual autonomy, and the power
of thought (good and bad) to shape life course and bodily
functioning.

(Del Vecchio *et al.*, 1990:61)

The psychologisation of the aetiology and course of cancer may be less
usual in Britain than in the United States; certainly in Britain there is
little work to suggest that the pervasiveness of such beliefs and the
gradual opening up of conventional medicine to some of its complementary alternatives has not immediately resulted in a rethinking of
its own physiological priorities and methods. However, these studies do
point to the pervasiveness of changing ideas about the power of the
'mind' and the importance of patients' psychological attitudes. Robert
Crawford's interviews with people about whether they consider themselves to be healthy suggests that the idea of health as 'self-control'
consistently informs contemporary perceptions: 'Health is discussed in
terms of self-control and a set of related concepts that include self-
discipline, self-denial and will power', Crawford argues, quoting one of
his respondents: 'To be healthy takes a little more discipline' (Crawford, 1985:66).

It is not only cancer that has produced theories of 'personality types'
leading to the implication that the person's psychological disposition
is responsible for their disease. Illnesses such as ME (myalgic encephalomyelitis) and post-viral syndrome have been surrounded by such mythologies. So too has rheumatoid arthritis. The 'rheumatoid personality'
has been characterised by 'rigidity, self-punishment and difficulty in
dealing with hostility' (Satterfield, 1992:221). As Ann Satterfield points
out in her artwork, these traits are likely to ensue from the experience
of living with the disease. What is also striking is the extent to which so
many of the personality-as-disease theories highlight the same characteristics for such different diseases – inability to express emotion,
difficulty in adapting to change, high levels of self-criticism. Against
these 'negative' (and noticeably 'feminine') personality traits, the
person with cancer, ME or rheumatoid arthritis is encouraged to be
positive, to exercise will-power and to control their thought patterns.

The appeal to fantasies of control through the power of individual
will, as found in alternative approaches to cancer, is part of broader
changes in contemporary cultural constructions of the self. In a culture
in which so many everyday practices have become pathologised as
potentially addictive behaviours, the exercise of our 'will-power' is

continually invoked. As Eve Sedgwick points out, in late twentieth-century Western cultures 'addiction can include ingestion *or* refusal *or* controlled intermittent ingestion of a given substance' (Sedgwick, 1992:583). Thus, there are groups for those who overeat, those who undereat (anorexics) and those who eat in irregular bursts (bulimics); similarly, there are classes for those who want to exercise in groups publicly (aerobics) and there are those who confess to their private obsession with body fitness. Once exercise (previously the symbol of 'freely choosing to be healthy') enters into the discourse of addiction, Sedgwick questions the meanings of rhetoric such as 'free will', 'choice' and 'healthy lifestyles'; for in this context of 'epidemics of the will', 'any substance, any behavior, even any affect may be pathologized as addictive' (Sedgwick, 1992:584).

Concepts such as 'workaholism', 'shopaholism', 'sexual compulsiveness' and 'relationship addiction' have become commonplace forms of description of our everyday behaviour. Indeed, Sedgwick reports that there have even been journalistic articles in the United States on 'addiction' to self-help groups and books which are themselves addressing the problem of addiction (Sedgwick, 1992:584). Our current 'conceptual landscape' is so marked by the proliferation of idioms which invoke individual will ('Just Do It' and 'Just Say No' being two of the hundreds of well-known examples from the world of advertising and political campaigning) that it is hard to imagine life without our daily negotiations of such commands. This imperative that free will be 'propagated', or multiplied, through work, play, relationships and the attendant forms of capitalist consumption has a profound significance in the context of health epidemics such as HIV/AIDS, and, indeed, the alarming rate of increase in cancers of many kinds as we approach the twenty-first century.[2]

If Rosalind Coward is right that 'health has taken over from sex as the main area of personal self determination' (Coward, 1989:13) at this time, then health practices, from diet and exercise to meditation and homeopathy, might be seen as part of a larger picture in which individuals produce themselves in an endless bid for self-control and effective exercise of will-power. The skill which is developed through such practices might be summed up as the 'micromanagement of absolutes' (Sedgwick, 1992:586), a phrase which rather accurately describes the project of self-health upon which I embarked when I had cancer.

AUTOPATHOGENY

As I suggested at the beginning of this chapter, cancer is a disease particularly vulnerable to autopathogenic interpretations (the idea that illness is self-generated), precisely because it is not caused by germs, viruses or infections, but by the cell division of one's own body. Scientific accounts of the aetiology of cancer trace the problem back to 'a mutation in a single cell' (Rees *et al.*, 1993:3). Typical accounts of cancer in the self-health literature also emphasise this: 'cancer results from changes within the normal body cells – it is not an invasion from outside, whatever irritants may induce the cells to change'; many go on to deduce that, because of this, 'the basic cause of all different types of cancer will be found within the body itself and not in the disease process or the tumour' (Chaitow, 1983:13). Thus it is concluded that since the original problem (uncontrolled cell division) can be located in the body, the cause of the illness *is* the body. It is claimed repeatedly in this literature that cancer cannot occur in healthy bodies.[3]

This interpretation is then compounded by the powerful metaphor of cancer as a bodily manifestation of the psyche of the patient (for example, cancer personality types; see Chapter 4). If the body articulates psychic distress, then cancer is not only caused by an unhealthy body but by an unhappy 'mind'. Audre Lorde writes of her fury at the implications of this view:

> Last week I read a letter from a doctor in a medical magazine which said that no truly happy person ever gets cancer. Despite my knowing better, and despite my having dealt with this blame-the-victim thinking for years, for a moment this letter hit my guilt button. Had I really been guilty of the crime of not being happy in this best of all possible of infernos?
>
> (Lorde, 1980:74)

As she goes on to write with her usual polemical force, the location of the problem within the self rather than in social, political or environmental spheres is easier and more convenient:

> Let us seek 'joy' rather than real food and clean air and a saner future on a liveable earth! As if happiness alone can protect us from the results of profit-madness.
>
> Was I wrong to be working so hard against the oppressions afflicting women and Black people? Was I in error to be speaking out against our silent passivity and the cynicism of a mechanized and inhuman civilisation that is destroying our earth and those who live upon it? Was I really fighting the spread of radiation, racism, woman-slaughter, chemical invasion of our food, pollution of our environment, the abuse and psychic destruction of our young, merely to avoid dealing with my first and greatest responsibility – to be happy?
>
> (Lorde, 1980:74–5)

As I suggested in Chapter 4, the autogenic view of disease characterises much of the alternative literature on cancer. Typical ideas about the cause/effect, mind/body relationship include: 'It used to be thought that cancer had a more profound influence on the patient's state of mind than the patient had on the development of the disease. It is now known that the personality and psychology of the patient has a profound effect on the course of the illness' (Chaitow, 1983:125). Similarly, it is argued that 'a positive attitude toward treatment was a better predictor of response to treatment than was the severity of the disease' (Simonton *et al.*, 1978:82). What the arguments in this and the previous chapter add to the picture of the mind/body relationship is the way in which the 'making visible' of the body's interior, and the tendency to personify the cell as a microcosm of the self, or as a register of the individual's will-power, has facilitated the extension of this auto-pathogenic view of cancer: according to this belief system, cancer is a *disease of the self*. For not only is cancer seen as the self at war with the self (the cell with the cell), but, through the model of the mind/body communication system, the disease is a physiological expression of the person's helplessness, hopelessness or lack of self-love.

These projects of self-management are increasingly extended to include prevention, as well as treatment, of illness. As both Crawford (1985) and Coward (1989) point out, health no longer means the absence of disease, but rather is a state which the individual produces and achieves through hard work and self-discipline. There is a new emphasis on prevention:

> Modern prevention is, above all, the tracking down of risks – not in the sense of the result of specific dangers posed by the immediate presence of a person or a group, but rather, the composition of impersonal 'factors' that make a risk probable. Prevention, then, is surveillance not of the individual but of likely occurrences of diseases, anomalies, deviant behaviour to be minimized and healthy behaviour to be maximized. We are partially moving away from the older face-to-face surveillance of individuals and groups known to be dangerous or ill (for disciplinary or therapeutic purposes), toward projecting risk factors that deconstruct and reconstruct the individual or group subject.
>
> (Rabinow, 1992:242–3)

Individuals are surrounded by information about themselves in relation to their chances of inherited disease (and indeed, passing disease on to their children), their food intake and their environment; they are thereby encouraged to map out the risk factors at stake in their particular situations.[4] These new forms of infomedicine invite an

191

obsession with genetic risk factors and a constant monitoring of one's own 'lifestyle'. The kinds of self-management practices detailed in this chapter, then, are intensified through the case of a life-threatening illness like cancer, but increasingly extend beyond the 'sick patient', to 'healthy people' interested in avoiding disease in the future. According to Rabinow, this shift in the focus and meaning of health will produce changes in the organisation of care and support services:

> It follows that other forms of pastoral care will become more prominent, in order to overcome the handicap and to prepare for the risks. These therapies for the normal will be diverse, ranging from behavior modifications, to stress management, to inter-actional therapies of all sorts . . . The nineties will be the decade of genetics, immunology and environmentalism – for, clearly, these are the leading vehicles for the infiltration of technoscience, capitalism and culture into what the moderns called 'nature'.
>
> (Rabinow, 1992:245)

This increasingly autopathogenic understanding of health as a problem of systems of the self arises at the cultural convergence of immune system discourse and self-help 'psychotechnologies' (see Ross, 1991; and Chapter 4, this volume). Each, though in very different ways, constructs our bodily identities as self-regulating systems in which the fault is internal rather than external.

The changes which have been discussed so far in this chapter all point towards an increasing concern with the 'self' in contemporary culture. 'Self-health' is one of many forms of self-production in which we are invited to engage. This is not merely another form of a culture of narcissism, but rather the emergence of a culture of 'instrumental deliberation' in which the artificiality of our self-assembly no longer undermines its authenticity. In fact, this DIY approach to finding 'the real self' (the Urself) is an example of what has been called 'inauthentic authenticity' (Grossberg, 1992). In a reversal of previous common-sense notions of authenticity, it is now increasingly the labours of self-nurturance and self-development that promise to reveal one's most authentic self to the world. In other words, the authentic self is the one that is in the process of transformation; we are required to be involved in actively 'working on ourselves'. Rather than avoiding the exchanges of the market to preserve the authentic self, contemporary health cultures encourage consumption (of healthy food, of alternative treat-ments, and so on) as a means of 'finding yourself'.

The self-conscious auto-production at stake in alternative healing therapies exemplifies the processes Giddens (1991) identifies through which 'self-identity and the body become "reflexively organized pro-jects" which have to be sculpted from the complex plurality of choices

192

offered by high modernity' (Shilling, 1993:181). In this detradi-tionalised 'high modernity', Giddens argues that individuals invest in particular lifestyles in order to give 'material form to a particular narrative of self-identity' in the absence of earlier moral authorities of modern or traditional societies (1991). The loss of a secure or stable self has forced people increasingly 'reflexively' to adopt lifestyles in order to sustain their self-identities (Shilling, 1993:181). Indeed, this project of auto-production requires a kind of 'hyperindividuation' through endless forms of consumption in order to achieve a sense of 'uniqueness' in a culture based upon copying and replication (Shilling, 1993:7).

GENDERED SELF-GENERATION

The ways in which alternative medical approaches to cancer construct the self are very much part of this broader cultural shift. The person with cancer is encouraged to see their recovery (and their identity) as a project in which the self is produced through various health (and consumer) practices. This model of the self is, in part, a product of the discourse of the *informational body* discussed in Chapter 5. For the informational body requires constant decoding; it expects to be read and to be ministered to accordingly. The monitoring becomes auto-matic: breast check in the shower in the morning; extra vitamin C for a sore throat; change of diet for constipation; new soap powder against skin allergies; cut out the dairy foods during hay fever season; no alcohol for candida; vitamin B before menstruation; lower fat intake for liver pain; regular exercise against bad circulation; stop exercising for a pulled muscle. We are thus encouraged to develop a relationship with ourselves in quite an unprecedented way. And this is not just a relationship with our bodies, though this is crucial, but also a rela-tionship with our emotional well-being: have I sorted out my childhood traumas? How is my sex life? Do I work effectively with my colleagues? Could I improve my relationship with my parents? Have I mourned my losses fully enough? Why has my daughter withdrawn herself from me? Why can't I get angry? What do my dreams tell me?

This *relational self* is a self that constantly reinvents itself through a process of taking stock and checking up on both a micro- and macro-scale. It is a sense of self that is produced through its relationship with itself, through an endless process of monitoring, of dialogue and of evaluation. According to this model different aspects of the self are in a 'relationship': an intrapsychic one in which the self and the other are internal to the whole system. Like any other relationship, our 'rela-tionship with ourselves' must be worked at and nurtured.

Feminist theorists from a variety of traditions have argued that patriarchal culture has designated the task of relationality to femininity.

From Klein to Chodorow to Irigaray, femininity has been theorised as the relational counterpart to the masculine autonomous self, that individuated state so long privileged as the desirable form of subjectivity.[5] However diverse feminist evaluations of 'relationality' might be, the relational subject of these discourses of self-health is unmistakeably an extension of existing feminine duties and obligations.[6] From this point of view, the discourses of self-health feminise the subject they constitute as relational and autogenic.

Furthermore, the care, love and nurturance of sick bodies (and troubled minds or broken hearts) call upon a repertoire of traditionally feminine skills, associated with motherhood and the kinds of work performed by a female labour force. This might, in part anyway, explain the appeal of alternative approaches to self-health to women. At one Cancer Care Centre in Britain, two-thirds of the patients taking up the available alternative therapies are women.[7] Given that women are typically 'responsible' for relationships in society generally, it may not be surprising to find that forms of health practice which involve developing *a relationship with oneself* are taken up by more women than men. But the question of gender extends further than this. It is not only of great significance that more women than men populate alternative health centres on both sides of the practitioner/patient divide, but it is also important to look at the gendering of the self generated by such discourses.

Much of the alternative literature on cancer addresses itself directly to women through discourses of emotional nurturance, bodily self-consciousness and moral responsibility which will already be familiar to those well-versed in the expectations of the feminine performance in this culture. Rachel Charles, for example, addresses women directly as dieters and consumers, reinforcing the desirability of thinness as a feminine ideal:

> One immediate advantage of the Peak Immunity Diet is that . . . you will lose weight! . . . A shopping spree definitely confirmed that I was back to size ten clothes. It's good to look so lean and fit . . . The immune system is put under a strain in a fat body and all sorts of miscellaneous problems can occur . . . Dr. Robert Good estimated that obese women are ten times more likely to develop a malignancy than their thin sisters.
>
> (Charles, 1990:203–4)

The inextricability of health and beauty for women is thus made quite explicit here. There are numerous other examples of this connection, such as the overlap between beauty parlours and alternative clinics in so many new businesses which advertise aromatherapy, ear piercing and sunbeds on the same site.

The representation of the cancer personality type is also noticeably gendered: the description of someone always caring for others, never putting themselves first and having problems expressing anger has strong connotations of feminine self-sacrifice, given women's typical roles as carers, or workers with the double burden of domestic labour. Indeed, the 'helplessness and hopelessness' characteristics which are attributed to cancer patients (Charles, 1990:48) could not better describe the situation of the many women in this society who have little control over their lives and futures. According to Charles:

> [W]omen are far more susceptible to auto-immune diseases than men . . . but no one understands why this should be so. Psycho-therapists have noticed that these patients tend to have great difficulty in expressing anger and store it up inside themselves. Mounting tension of this sort over a long period of time can certainly result in physical disorders.
>
> (Charles, 1990:31)

Charles does point to the problem of 'role conflict' as a possible cause of women's auto-immune vulnerability: 'Many apparently dedicated housewives feel underneath that they are "sacrificing" themselves for their families . . . As a result, hostility and resentment can build up over the years, and, if turned inwards . . . can cause physiological changes finally resulting in degenerative disease' (Charles, 1990:50). However, in the usual depoliticising move of much alternative medi-cine, the contexts (structures, institutions and belief systems) for such self-denial are ignored, and instead the individual is made all-powerful and held responsible for their own problems. The fact that women perform over 90 per cent of domestic labour in Britain in the 1990s despite the so-called sexual revolution is not recognised as a structural inequality. Instead, the forms of control exercised over women in the labour market and at home are attributed to the psychological problems of the individual women 'at fault'.[8]

Women may also be particularly vulnerable to the guilt and shame of being diagnosed with a disease like cancer. As I have argued, this general cultural taboo can be reinforced by some of the alternative approaches which 'blame the victim' for their disease. In their own defence, Simonton et al. acknowledge the problem of guilt and self-blame:

> Most of our patients who go through this process of self-examination see important links between their emotional states and the onset of their disease, as well as the ways they participated in these emotional states. But . . . some begin to feel guilty about their actions in the past . . . It is not our intent,

nor is it desirable, for you to feel guilty for having recognized that you've participated in your disease. There is a difference between being 'to blame' for something and having 'participated' in it.

(Simonton *et al.*, 1978:125)

Despite their protestations about their intentions, there is no doubt that many of these 'psychotechnologies' do indeed make patients feel guilty. Given the pervasiveness of feminine guilt and shame in general, especially in bodily matters, it may be that many female cancer patients are more susceptible to alternative discourses which attribute self-causation and which prescribe self-management. Furthermore, since self-scrutiny and self-surveillance are practically 'second nature' to femininity in this culture, to be on display for external approval being a requisite of daily life, the extension of these modalities of the self to health may seem like an automatic step for many women.

The textual addressee of many of the examples of self-health discussed above is a divided or fragmented self: a self driven by the mind at the expense of the needs of the body, or a self whose acquisitive desires have overtaken the more fundamental need for nurturance. In each case there is reference to the idea of a 'real self' underneath trying to resurface. Again and again these writers appeal to an innate sense of knowing what we really need, who we really are and what we really want. The diseased self which has cancer is seen to be out of touch with what we might call a kind of *Urself* (an original or 'primitive' self) which represents a deep or even ancient instinct about how to live in the world: 'I have long believed "Everything I need to know is revealed to me . . ." There is no new knowledge. All is ancient and infinite' (Hay, 1988:210). The notion of the Urself is both individual and collective: it is unique to each person in that we are the only ones who really know what we need; and yet it is also conceived of rather like some kind of collective unconscious, or as a collective memory of better ways of living. What has gone wrong with the person with cancer is that they have repressed, denied or ignored the wisdom of the Urself and have lived instead according to the judgements and decisions of the more superficial and uncaring parts of the self (often those associated with modernity and the excesses of late capitalism). The solution advocated in much of this literature is to reconnect with your Urself in order to be guided by its superior wisdom in the future.

In this sense we might see these approaches as forms of 'anamnesic medicine', anamnesis meaning 'a recalling to mind of innate knowledge'.[9] Anamnesic medicine requires the patient to reverse the process of forgetting and to excavate a previous consciousness which has become sedimented in the depths of the self. It is both nostalgic, in the sense of a longing for a lost object, and utopian, in the sense of its idealism for the future. This retrieval of lost or hidden knowledge about the self is seen as central to the healing process. It is not about becoming someone else, but rather *becoming who you are*.[10] The real you, who knows of a more caring and nurturing existence from the past, needs to return, take control and show the misguided parts of you the way forward. It is the loss of that Urself which is seen to have contributed to the onset of the disease. The reversal of amnesia is seen here as the responsibility of the self who *genuinely* wishes to recover.

If the self is divided or fragmented, as the above analysis suggests, into the Urself and the misguided, more surface, self, then it becomes possible to begin to develop the idea of 'having a relationship with oneself'. This *relational self* is central to the discourse of individual responsibility which is increasingly prevalent in self-health accounts of cancer. The only way such a conceptualisation of the self is possible is if the self is seen as split and thus seen to contain multiple subject and object relations. Within these models of health and illness, then, there is an assumption that one has a sense of oneself (or a part of oneself) as an object. The kind of splitting of the self described above in which you are encouraged to 'become who you already are', and indeed to 'become who you really are', constructs one part of the self as responsible for caring for the rest. The idea of having a relationship with one's self (as well as with others) thus invokes an *imperative to care*. This sense of obligation can be seen as an extension of the already well-established duties of femininity: the duty to care for the self, building on the feminine conscience to care for others (as wives, mothers, teachers, nurses, and so on). Building on the construction of femininity as responsible for the family, for the nation and for civilisation itself, the cancer patient is addressed through the further burden of being directly (and sometimes solely) responsible for their own health and illness (see Chapter 7).

However, while there are ways in which the discourses of self-health can be seen to reproduce and recreate the relational feminine subject, there are two significant ways in which this reading is problematic. First, this particular configuration of relationality is internal: in other words, the important relationship is with oneself and not, as is usually the case, with others. Indeed, patients are positively encouraged to 'put themselves first'. The healthy subject of the self-health discourses is not a self-sacrificing one who exists through meeting the needs of others, but rather, this relational subject prioritises the internal others of its self-regulating system. As such, feminists might welcome such an imperative to self-assertion.

The project of caring for oneself, advocated by alternative medicine in general, may thus be a welcome counter to many cultural prescriptions which urge women to care for everyone else. While reinforcing problematic assumptions about the individual nature of feminine self-denial, alternative practices nevertheless do encourage women to develop a sense of entitlement to time and care which they have so often lacked in the past, not because they are inadequate but because patriarchal culture has ascribed women the position of the other, the carer and the object. It could also be argued that by evoking continuous practices of self-production, alternative therapies are counteracting the patriarchal prescription of passivity, victimhood and matyrdom, which have conventionally been the fate of women. Instead of giving up control to (typically male) professionals, or accepting pain, disease or even death as further inevitable (and deserved) suffering, many women may be empowered through alternative medicines to put themselves first for once and to transfer their caring skills to themselves. Contradicting cultural expectations that femininity should be a display of endurance and selflessness, these practices encourage women to take up an active relationship to themselves and their lives which may facilitate their escape from previously constraining situations and habits.

Second, the subject of self-health is not straightforwardly feminised. If we begin to look at the kinds of narrative fantasies employed within these discourses, another story emerges. The successful achievement of the balanced system of the self is repeatedly represented through narratives of progress and conquest. The hero of such narratives has traditionally been masculine, whether in historical accounts, literary forms, or cinematic representations.[11] The patient's journey from sickness to health, from 'chaos to control', is represented as a heroic narrative which involves overcoming a series of obstacles in order to arrive at a place of safety. Obstacles such as bad habits, like smoking or poor diet, or negative thought patterns such as self-doubt, must be vanquished by the force of individual will-power. Like the masculine hero of the adventure narrative, the healthy subject emerges triumphant; having risked life itself, he is saved and has found a better world in the process. The triumph-over-tragedy structure of so many cancer stories (conventionally a feminine genre) thus combines with its masculine counterpart: melodrama and adventure narrative offer the perfect pairing.

The fantasies of self-health which pervade much of this alternative literature coincide with masculine ideals of mastery and invincibility. If the mind can control the body, masculinity can indeed vanquish the feminine threat and rationality can preside. In 'the fight against cancer' these forms of heroism accord with what Barbara Stafford has called 'a perverse denial of fallibility and a masculine delusion of divine potency' (Stafford, 1991:467). Indeed, the feminist critique can be further extended to question the motivations behind both these self-health fantasies and those operating within biomedicine more generally. Rosi Braidotti warns of the dangers of this fantasy of *self-generation* in the context of biomedicine: 'That biomedical technologies should en-courage the masculine fantasy of self-generation, reversing the Oedipal chain so as to feed the infantile fantasies of all-powerfulness through self-generation . . . [is] of great concern' (Braidotti, 1994:70).

The desire for such omnipotence raises fundamental questions about the ways in which the highly individualised 'self' of these self-health cultures relate to masculine values of science, such as objectivity, neutrality and a clear separation between subject and object. As Braidotti argues, 'the masculine element . . . consists precisely in the detachment, the perception of a clear and distinct determination of boundaries between self and world. Separation and autonomy are indeed the central features of the masculine standpoint' (Braidotti, 1994:72). The considerable overlap between alternative and biomedical approaches to cancer might thus be seen to share the powerful fantasy of the highly individuated and autonomous self that has characterised the masculine subject in patriarchal culture. At the symbolic level this has been described as a 'flight from the feminine' and indeed from the maternal body:

> In the feminist analysis, this detachment and objectivity are connected to the fantasy of self-generation, of being father/ mother of oneself, thus denying the specific debt to the maternal. Adrienne Rich and Luce Irigaray have also related the notion of scientific detachment and objectivity to the unwillingness or the downright denial of the fact that one is of woman born. It is a form of flight from the feminine.
>
> (Braidotti, 1994:72)

Another way to understand the appeal of these alternative approaches to cancer, however, is through their promise of self-determination which has typically remained a masculine privilege. Indeed, authority over their bodies is precisely what has escaped women for so long, and has been a central concern for second-wave feminist campaigns about sexuality, male violence and reproduction.[12] A sense of agency in this respect might be seen to sit comfortably with feminist demands for bodily autonomy.

The gendered meanings of these new forms of self-production, such as those at stake in the management of one's health, have become especially slippery in a culture so saturated with the proliferation and diversification of self-identities. In some ways, the idea of the self as a project, even a way of life, has been integral to definitions of femininity in patriarchal culture. For women to be required to engage con-tinuously in multiple practices of monitoring themselves and their social relations is not especially novel. In this sense the supposedly new 'deliberative self' of postmodern culture (Lyotard, 1984, in Shilling, 1993:181), the different paths/voices of 'self-reference developing a processual subjectivity' (Guattari, 1992), or the 'reflexivity of self-identity' which is said to characterise late modernity (Giddens, 1991), might be seen as extensions of what is very much part of current demands already made of femininity.

However, there has been an extension of even the most deliberative of feminine selves to new horizons of self-monitoring, surveillance and scrutiny. The systematisation of the self and of the body affords new meanings to the reflexive self and requires our reassessment of such forms of subjectivity. While these new forms of self-knowledge also reproduce masculine notions of autonomy, mastery and self-determination and, to some extent, reinforce their privileged place in patriarchal culture, their centrality to alternative practices might also open up the rewards of such masculine preserves to female patients, enabling women to overcome some of the limitations of restrictive forms of femininity. Furthermore, instead of deferring to the masculine authorities of science and medicine for our salvation, women themselves are offered the fantasy of authorship of their own destinies. For some, such changes may offer liberatory potential: the shift away from mechanical modernity might mean leaving behind some of its masculine hierarchies and authoritative meta-narratives; however, power brings with it responsibility, and responsibility for one's own health (as well as for everyone else's) might justifiably be seen as yet another burden to add to women's already impossible remit in this culture. Furthermore, the interiorisation of illness has a particular resonance in a culture characterised by the increasing privatisation of health services, the dissolution of professional authority and the destruction of welfare provision. In this changing cultural landscape, 'the individual' is endowed with unprecedented responsibility for their own well-being.

7

RESPONSIBILITIES

I

After the fourth chemotherapy treatment my psyche joins my body in its state of rebellion. I cannot do it again. I thought it would get easier as the body adjusted to the onslaught, but this last treatment was utterly unbearable. As I begin to recover enough to take stock, I list the symptoms to myself: the vomiting has gone on longer than usual; diarrhoea now accompanies it; the fingers and toes have lost almost all feeling; the few stray eyebrow hairs have fallen; the tinnitus is becoming deafening as I lie awake at night. The accumulation of side-effects suggests a body that has reached its limit, a frame stretched to breaking point. This body is in serious revolt; its functions have gone haywire; its surfaces are no longer familiar. Just as my bodily flows have gone into reverse, so my will-power has finally changed direction. Without my noticing, I have become unable to imagine subjecting myself to the final treatment. I know I am supposed to repeat the performance just one more time, but something in me resists the inevitability of the prescribed course of five doses. Previously I had felt confident in my endless supply of stamina for physical endurance, but I now find myself drained of it. Even anger fails to energise.

Should I convey all, or any, of this to my consultant? If the cancer did come back again, I would have to start from scratch: another four or five doses of chemotherapy. And there would be no negotiation at that stage. So, should I really convey my doubts to him now, with so much at stake? If I leave the power to decide with them, they are also answerable. Or rather, if I don't intervene, then I am not. Why would I want to encroach on such professional prerogatives which may protect my future conscience? Do I really want to be subject to guilt and blame? 'The patient protested and refused to finish the recommended treatment.' Or even, 'the patient informed us of her acute symptoms and so we omitted the last dose; sadly, it might have made the difference.' I fear I may come to berate myself for interfering. And yet my deepest inclination is to stop the treatment now. I have had enough. In all senses.

As I write the letter, detailing my symptoms and voicing my misgivings about further chemotherapy to the consultant, I am haunted by voices, the ones that call softly 'you'll be sorry' as if to test my resolve. My consultant has emphasised that the first

201

course of treatment is the crucial one: 'it's important to get it right now, we may not have another chance.' His words fill my imagination and play on all my anxieties. As I post the letter, I am aware that taking responsibility is also taking a risk. I have no idea of the outcome. Shall I have the fifth dose? If not, will four have been enough?

II

I walk into the quiet room. It has pale-washed walls; a couple of well-cared-for pot plants stand on the table. The counsellor is seated across from an empty chair. I sit down. He is a middle-aged bearded man whose confident air is slightly undercut by a nerviness. We go through the usual preliminaries. How am I feeling? When did I find out? I must be in shock.

We only have an hour and he is trying to make his mark. He wishes to be the agent of revelation; I sense he has been rather successful in this role in the past. Do I know why I have cancer? My reply frustrates him. He takes a risk, he breaks a rule, he fulfils a desire: he talks about himself. He knows why he had had cancer, he tells me. His brutal upbringing had scarred him, emotionally and then physically. But not for life. He is a different person now. I too have the chance to change, to learn and grow, as he did.

What had my childhood been like, he asks? Any particular traumas? Any losses? Did I know why I had cancer? He knew why he had had 'his cancer'. His parents had been unable to really love him. His school had been barbaric. The distress had accumulated. 'His cancer' had revealed all this to the world and indeed to himself. What did I think 'mine' was trying to tell me?

He tries another tack. Was I afraid of self-exploration? Sometimes you have to go right into the depths of despair before you can surface anew (be reborn?). I could do things differently now and stay healthy. It is my choice. Do I really have no idea why I had cancer? Am I willing to take the risk, to seize the opportunity, to receive the gift? It's not a question of blame, but a question of cause and effect, of responsibility.

Responsible: correspondent or answering to something ... capable of being answered ... answerable, accountable (*to* another *for* something), liable to be called to account ... morally accountable for one's actions ... capable of rational conduct ... answerable to a charge ... capable of fulfilling an obligation or trust.

Responsibility: A charge, a trust or duty for which one is responsible.

(*Oxford English Dictionary*, 1989:1571)

A sense of responsibility promises a willingness to be called to account. It suggests a number of guarantees: trust, liability and morality. It relies on a cause-and-effect logic: the responsible decision is the one taken by the rational subject who has evaluated all the information and is willing to exercise judgement; the responsible citizen is the one who does this in full knowledge of the situation *and its consequences*, the one who has the confidence of conviction to take the risk and accept the repercussions.

There are of course competing definitions of responsibility in contemporary culture but, whatever the formulation, it is underpinned by a rhetoric that assumes a shared moral code. Responsibility operates discursively within the framework of an unspoken contract between parties that obligations will be met, judgements upheld and consequences faced. Within this context, risks are taken on the understanding that blame may be attributed and even that punishment might follow. Most important, the notion of responsibility presumes *an investment in a future* in which the terms will remain constant. To take responsibility is to accept the significance of a past promise. It thus implies a teleology, a particular form of linear narrative in which there is continuity over time and in which the outcomes of actions and decisions can be judged; praise and criticism are appropriately awarded on the basis of agreed criteria. The past, present and future are connected by a moral thread that assumes a cause-and-effect linearity. There is no ultimate closure to this trajectory, but rather a temporal structure that guarantees accountability and endlessly reproduces itself as new futures are mapped out on the basis of this implicit (or sometimes explicit) contract.

Responsibility for health is especially suited to such teleological formulations. Perceptions of health operate within a temporal structure that trace and attribute causes in the past and predict outcomes in the future. Given the ways in which both alternative and biomedicine rely heavily on a belief in cause and effect for their respective explanations of health and illness, the notion of taking responsible measures in order to avoid, or produce, specified consequences has a particular credence. Low-fat diets reduce cholesterol, regular exercise improves circulation, meditation lowers effects of stress, vitamin B eases PMT, a positive outlook generates good health; all such formulations construct a cause-and-effect linearity that promises a better future. Invest in your health today, and reap the benefits tomorrow.

The question of accountability has been a crucial one within health matters throughout the emergence of medicine as a profession.[1] Health professionals must take responsibility and be accountable for their decisions: when to operate, when to switch off the machine, when to increase and decrease the dosage. The medical profession has its own codes of conduct that rely on certain notions of responsible behaviour and operate within a particular set of historical conventions, offering its own forms of self-protection.[2] However, what is significant in the 1990s is the high levels of *individual responsibility* for health that are being increasingly demanded of people, both in terms of prevention and cure. In the contemporary health cultures of biomedicine and even more so in its self-health counterparts, it is the 'patient', as well as the 'medical expert', who is constituted as the agent of physical well-being within the discourse of responsibility.

Open any Sunday supplement or 'lifestyle' magazine, watch any of the popular television programmes on health, fitness (or, indeeed, cookery) and you are faced with recommendations, advice and schedules for a new and healthier future. In addition to the longstanding penny-in-the-slot weighing machines in the local chemist, you are now invited to check your cholesterol levels, your lung capacity and your fat/muscle proportions in a variety of locales: the supermarket, the fitness room, the community centre and entertainment arcade, as well as the more traditional chemist. You are constantly exorted to monitor an excess of sugar, salt, alcohol, TFAs (transfatty acids), hydrogenated vegetable oils, caffeine and nicotine, as well as the required intake of fibre, vitamins, minerals, mono-unsaturated fat and complex carbohydrates. Recently the press has been full of stories about doctors refusing to treat patients who had not taken care of themselves prior to contact with the health system: the man who dies before receiving heart surgery because his smoking habits made him a low priority, the children whose sweet-eating habits were used to justify denial of dental treatment.[3] Wherever you look, the message in 1990s Britain is loud and clear: take reponsibility for your own health.

But what exactly does taking responsibility for our health mean and how has the remit of such an imperative shifted over the last twenty years, given the changing political and cultural contexts of health care in Britain? What are the different notions of responsibility that operate within, for example, feminist debates, self-health literatures and health promotion projects? And how might we understand these competing definitions in relation to the New Right politics of the 1980s and 1990s that relocated responsibility firmly with the individual? In Britain these have taken the form of a Thatcherite and post-Thatcherite rhetoric of individual responsibility concomitant with the promotion of private health care and the marketisation of the National Health Service. Following my discussion of the growing significance of particular notions of the self in the construction of health and illness in Chapter 6, this chapter examines the shifts in the discourse of responsibility in health care and situates these developments within cultural changes in the 1980s and 1990s more generally. Although I focus on the British context, many of the general trends I shall identify can be traced across a number of other Western countries in which state funding and public spending is being withdrawn and the discourses of individualism are among the most prevalent in debates about the health of nations.

PATIENT POWER

Figure 7.1 shows the patient's perspective. The view from the hospital bed that invites the spectator to pause and wonder not only what the story might be but also whose point of view will be represented. The absent subject in the bed is the absent subject in the discourse. Patients have traditionally been constructed as passive, compliant and obedient within biomedicine.[4] The expert authority of the medical professional depends upon its exclusivity and its specialisation (Stacey, 1988). What would it be like to challenge this authority and make the experts the objects of scrutiny?

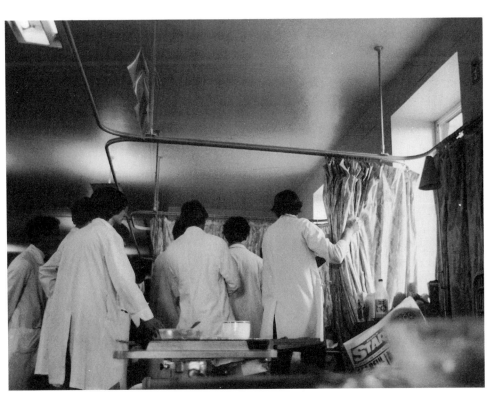

Figure 7.1 'The patient's perspective', Jo Spence, 1982
Source: Spence, 1995:107

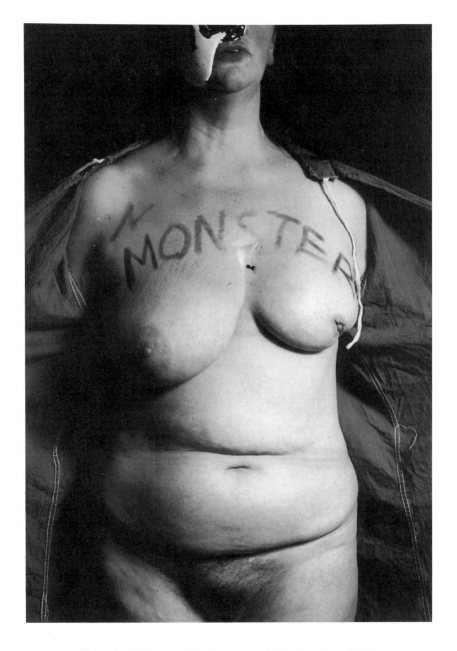

Figure 7.2 'Monster', Jo Spence and Dr Tim Sheard, 1989
Source: Spence, 1995:207

Figure 7.2 shows a woman reckoning with loss. The exposure challenges the taboos around mastectomy and the imperative to reveal only the conventionally aestheticised female form. This image explores the ways in which discourses are literally inscribed on the body. What secret monstrosities are hidden beneath the surface of the image? How can a woman with cancer gain any sense of agency in the face of medical objectification? Can she ever become the speaking subject? Is it futile to try and take charge?

Jo Spence's work has brought issues of medical power and authority to the fore. With a commitment to the democratisation of access to technology, she uses photography to draw attention to the power relations embedded both in image-making and knowledge production more generally. Her work asks questions about the relationships between identity, power and cultural reproduction. How have working-class people become the objects of middle-class expertise? How have women's bodies been produced as objects of glamour? What taboos operate to keep pain and loss out of sight? Can we ever escape the limits of our own (inherited) psychic landscapes?

By investigating such issues Jo Spence 'put herself in the picture' (Spence, 1987). Using herself as the subject of much of her photography, she interrogated the cultural politics of health in the 1980s and 1990s. She challenged the received wisdoms of conventional medicine and experimented with the benefits of alternative healing systems (see Figure 7.3). Her refusal to accept some of the practices of biomedicine and her insistence upon her own right to agency in the face of a breast cancer diagnosis are emblematic of a radical intervention into the health practices during the last twenty years. This work puts the patient's perspective centre stage. It is this perspective that is missing from most medical accounts. Medical expertise (like expertise in general) has relied on exclusivity, on the privileged knowledge of the few over the general ignorance of the majority (McNeil, 1987; Stacey, 1988). Keeping patients 'ignorant' about their illnesses and treatments has long legitimated the wisdom of the medical profession. The power imbalance in biomedical encounters between doctors and patients has traditionally been especially acute.[5] Add to this professional imbalance those of further social inequalities, such as race, class, gender or sexuality, that give some a sense of entitlement over others, and the position of some patients can become more vulnerable still.

'Empowering the patient' has been a theme within feminist health politics for nearly thirty years. Jo Spence's photography belongs to a much wider movement for change. At its heart lies an insistence on patients' rights, the demand for equal access to health and a profound challenge to the imbalance of power invested in traditional biomedicial expertise that leads encounters with doctors to be humiliating ones for

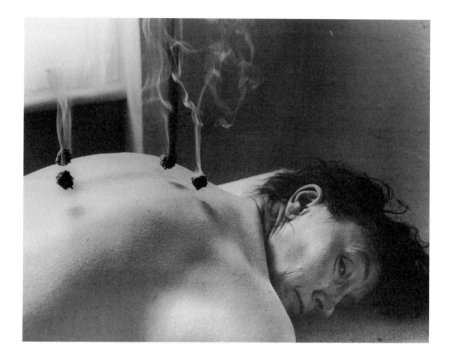

Figure 7.3 'Acupuncture treatment', Maggie Murray, 1984
Source: Spence, 1995:117

so many women. One strategy within this context has been for women to inform themselves about their health and to develop confidence in understanding their own bodies (see Chapter 4).[6] Central to this move has been the idea that the individual negative experiences of women at the hands of the medical profession are not isolated instances but are part of a more general structural institutionalisation of class, race and gender inequalities. To be pressured to have a hysterectomy, to be prescribed the Pill beyond its use-by date, to be given Depoprovera without warning of its side-effects, to be shamed and patronised by doctors, have all been seen as the problems not of individual women in so-called First and Third World countries, but rather as part of the exercise of Western patriarchal and colonial medical expertise. As I have detailed throughout this book, feminists have challenged the authority of scientific knowledge and its widespread ascription as heroic liberator in the process of development and modernisation. The desire to take back some control over health has occurred in reaction to the history of the patriarchal medical science that has constructed the female body as enigma, problem and object of study (Keller, 1985). In such a context 'seizing our bodies' (Dreifus, 1977) has been part of an attempt to reframe the story of health and illness in such a way as to give patients some power and some sense of agency and control (Lupton, 1994).

Taking responsibility for one's health in this context has meant, first, finding out information usually reserved for the medical specialists; second, avoiding unnecessary medical intervention; and third, finding alternative and less harmful treatments (often herbal or homœopathic). The politics of health here are firmly located within a challenge to the institutional histories of medical expertise and to the disempowering effects of its practices. Responsibility for health is at stake in so far as women have attempted to establish alternative ways of seeing and knowing their bodies and alternative strategies for the dissemination of such knowledges. While the aim of such strategies has been individual empowerment, this has generally been part of a broader, collective politics (albeit a highly contested collectivity).[7] A feminist politics of health has attempted to connect personal and political, individual and social, even as those categories have been the subject of heated debates. Responsibility within these diverse contexts has been mobilised as a way of articulating oppositional aspirations and experimental practices: taking responsibility for health has thus been articulated as a challenge to patriarchal authority. The inscription of the patient as more than an object of medical expertise has thus been part of a shift in the power relations of biomedical practice. Whereas previously medical experts typically took almost exclusive responsibility for health, challenges from the 1970s onwards have attempted to loosen the prerogative to such expertise. Patients have demanded to be better informed, to be included in decision-making processes, to be treated as more than just physical 'bodies' and to have their own knowledge about their health valued (Lupton, 1994).

What is difficult from the perspective of the 1990s is to hold on to the specificity of these political interventions. Uniting these highly diverse strategies has been a commitment to a critical evaluation of biomedicine and the power/knowledge relations of its practices, and a licence to explore alternative forms of healing. Empowerment of individual women has thus been part of a broader instititutional and structural intervention. Biomedicine has not been rejected in its entirety, but rather its discursive practices at all levels have been opened up to rigorous critical investigation and reformulation.[8] It has, however, become almost impossible to maintain this definition of responsibility within its more collective or oppositional forms in the face of competing discursive moves, namely the impact of the New Right on ways of thinking about health. The feminist challenge to medical authority has taken on quite another significance in the light of subsequent (and concomitant) changes in the health cultures of the 1980s and 1990s in

Britain in which patients are now individual consumers with charters, doctors are operating within a (much reduced) competitive market of services, and professional expertise of all kinds has been the subject of political attack from the New Right. The specific forms of New Right thinking shaped in the British context by Thatcherism are offered below as an indicative synthesis and will, no doubt, echo many similar discursive changes in other national contexts.

THE RIGHT VALUES

On Thursday, 3 May, we won a great victory. Yes, it was a victory for realism and responsibility.

(Margaret Thatcher, 1979, in Cooke, 1989:96)

Prosperity comes not from grand conferences of economists, but from countless acts of personal self-confidence and self-reliance.

(Margaret Thatcher, 1980, in Cooke, 1989:111)

Because we give people the chance to better themselves, they accuse us of encouraging selfishness and greed. What nonsense. Does someone's natural desire to do well for himself, to build a better life for his family and provide opportunities for his children, does all this make him a materialist? Of course it doesn't. It makes him a human being, committed to his family and his community *and* prepared to take responsibility on his shoulders.

The truth is that what we are actually encouraging is the best in human nature. The prosperity brought about by our policies offers a wider choice to more people than ever before . . .

We can only build a responsible, independent community with responsible, independent people. That's why Conservative policies have given more and more of them the chance to buy their own homes, to build up capital, to acquire shares in their companies . . .

Greater responsibility gives more dignity to the individual and more strength to the community. That's the belief at the heart of Conservatism. And we must make it live.

(Margaret Thatcher, 1988, in Cooke, 1989:269–71)

Thatcherism and its aftermath depend heavily on the notion of individual responsibility that continues to mark contemporary culture in Britain.[9] As the above examples show, 'taking responsibility' for oneself and for one's family are represented as a sign of good citizenship; more than this, they are seen to be an inevitable aspect of human nature. Capitalist market forces are represented here as the necessary outcome of the selfish drives of human beings. Concepts such as 'self-reliance' and 'self-confidence' situate responsibility firmly within the realm of the individual. Constructed in opposition to the social welfarism of the traditional Left (labelled the 'Nanny State' by its critics in Britain) by a prime minister who denied the significance of her gender until she was finally ousted by the 'men in grey suits', Thatcherism places the highest value on the power of the individual and on his capacity to fend for himself and for his family. Within this New Right rhetoric the individual is the source of social values, the origin of beliefs, the cause of change; the idea of social/communal responsibility is only seen as significant in so far as it is generated by individuals. Responsibility to/for others, so crucial within the radical health politics of the previous two decades, is confined within Thatcherism to a narrowly defined 'family', or is seen to be the positive, but not required, by-product of individuals taking responsibility for themselves.[10] The belief in collective responsibility represented by the welfare state has thus increasingly been replaced by the notion of the personal responsibility of the individual.

These changes have all relied on the promotion of a *hyperindividualism*: the individual as the supreme authority; the individual as the agent of his fate; the individual as culpable in the face of failure. The responsible subject protects his family, finds work for himself and conquers adversity. Where this highly individuated self *is* connected to others, it is as provider and protector: a sense of self achieved through a duty to defend and serve the family (read women and children). This form of what has been called 'patriarchal individualism' ties the subject into a story of self-realisation through material acquisition, paid work and capital investment.[11] The context for such individual improvement, according to Thatcher's account above, is a market that is presented as liberating, empowering and harmonious with the needs of individuals and families. Social inequalities, such as class, race and gender, disappear along with 'society', which has been blamed for too long for the problems of Britain; all we are left with is the individual, the family and the nation. The only legitimate notions of oppression are attached to the 'new oppressed' who suffer from the legacy of the evil 1970s: fathers, White unemployed people, or even the heterosexual nuclear family.[12]

Furthermore, responsibility is defined here not just in terms of moral reliability or rational judgement but in terms of resources. The responsible individual is thus the one who is willing to rely on his own resources to cope with life's problems and challenges. Such rhetoric has become part of the everyday justifications of the cutbacks in welfare provision and of the gradual undermining of the National Health Service in Britain.[13] The patient's responsibility for 'his' own health is an ever-increasing duty. In this sense, the forms of patriarchal individualism that operate within such a discourse need to be viewed in conjunction with the sexual division of caring practices in contemporary culture. There is no doubt that the withdrawal of state support for health care in Britain has produced an increased burden of informal and unpaid care by women. The discourse of responsibility that Thacherism institutionalised in British culture relies on a masculine subject in so far as it appeals to a fantasy of self-reliance, but it also relies on a sense of duty to care historically ascribed to femininity. It appeals to an already over-developed sense of responsibility *for others* that has characterised women's roles as nurturers and informal carers throughout the twentieth century.[14] The discourse of individual responsibility has also been integral to the redefinition of the internal funding systems of the National Health Service in Britain (Robinson and Le Grand, 1994). The market-based model for running the National Health Service has drawn heavily on the notion of individual accountability: of doctors, hospital departments, of supporting services, and of the newly formed, self-governing trusts that run many hospitals in Britain today. Responsibility for public health has been redefined here in terms of financial responsibility and accountability (Jones, 1994:165).

These changes occurred simultaneously with the promotion of private health care in Britain throughout the 1980s and 1990s. The increase in prescription charges, the introduction of commercial management practices and the contracting out of laundry, domestic and catering services in the National Health Service were accompanied by a rapid expansion in private hospitals and private health care insurance for the wealthier and more privileged sectors of society (see Jones, 1994:165–8). During the 1980s the number of people using private health care through insurance grew and those paying for it directly declined; private health insurance through companies, trade unions and the civil service became more widespread for those people in society who typically belong to its healthiest groups (White, middle-class and wealthy) (Jones, 1994:166). Throughout the 1980s a number of 'professions' came under government scrutiny and often attack. Perhaps more protected than some more traditionally 'left-wing' professions such as social work and teaching, the professional expertise and autonomy of biomedicine has nevertheless also been challenged. In the reorganisation of the health system in Britain, hospitals have come to be run by managers without medical training and have lost some control over spending and resource-led decisions. These changes have been accompanied by a more general 'loss of faith' in medical professionals which I discuss later in this chapter.[15]

Changes in the National Health Service occurred within a more general culture of privatisation and marketisation of public services and state benefits in the 1980s and 1990s (the buses and railways, catering and cleaning staff in schools, refuse collection, pensions, and so on). The decade of enterprise culture, the 1980s saw a dramatic withdrawal of public health provision and an aggressive attack on trade unions and on 'the caring professions' (medicine, education, social work, and so on). Clearly intending radically to reduce the remit of the welfare state, to privatise services such as health and to discredit those professionals associated with what the Conservatives named 'dependency culture' or the 'loony Left', Thatcherism symbolised the end of society and the beginning of can-do self-development, entrepreneurialism and choice-based free markets. In this consumerised culture all kinds of activities have been subsumed within the language of the market; patients (like students and public transport passengers) have become customers: consumers of products, rather than users of services.[16]

The rhetoric of Thatcherism has attempted to depoliticise social issues by blaming individuals for their 'problems', such as homelessness, unemployment, discrimination and poor health. There is now a widespread willingness to blame any 'victims' of these policies for their own situations: obvious examples might be the claims that unemployed people do not *really* want to work, or that single mothers are socially irresponsible, or that black people should leave Britain if they don't like the racism. For critics such as Robert Crawford, these New Right philosophies coincide with an emergent belief in 'lifestyle medicine'. Both shift emphasis away from poverty, poor housing, urban decay, unemployment and radiation and pollution levels, and blame individuals for their health problems. This 'victim-blaming ideology' has diverted attention away from the social programmes of 1960s health promotion towards a new philosophy which might be summed up as, 'living a long life is essentially a do-it-yourself proposition' (Crawford, 1977:665). The subjects of discourses of responsibility for health and illness thus find themselves in the vortex of controversies about the nature of disease, its aetiologies and its significance.

THE ALTERNATIVE TURN

Accompanying the sedimentation of the power of the individual in New Right discourses has been the rapid expansion of alternative medicines which themselves tend to place great emphasis on individual responsibility for health. The last twenty years have seen a veritable explosion of alternative medical practices. There are now more and more different types on offer: in the early 1980s homeopathy and acupuncture became relatively widely available, along with techniques more closely associated with mechanical manipulation, such as osteopathy and chiropractice; now in the mid-1990s there are many more different techniques to choose from.[17] In fact even for the enthusiast it is hard to keep up with all the new practices and techniques: cranio-sacral therapy; Bach flower remedy; aromatherapy; iridology; Alexander technique; reflexology; chi kung. The list seems endless (see Fulder, 1984; Sharma, 1992; British Medical Association, 1993). There are choices not just between practices, but within practices: two quite differently principled acupunctures, numerous kinds of yoga, and so on. There are also practitioners who offer a whole range of treatments: one healing therapist might offer counselling, herbalism and 'touch for health', for example. Hybridities are also evolving: techniques from various practices might be translated and recombined to suit the needs of the individual patient or the interests of individual practitioners.

Most of these alternative medicines are not state-funded in Britain but have to be paid for privately. There are exceptions: there is an NHS hospital of homœopathy in London; some hospitals offer alternative treatments as back-ups, such as the Royal Marsden providing art therapy and massage for chemotherapy patients. More recently there have been attempts to have doctors refer patients to local health centres for acupuncture or chiropratice. Indeed, there are more and more stories now of partnerships between alternative and biomedical initiatives. At present, though, most alternative medicine is still private, despite the desire on the part of many patients and practitioners for it to be widely and freely available. Patients are customers and, in paying for this service, expect quite different treatment from practitioners than from the usual medical staff such as GPs and hospital doctors. Indeed, practitioners are dependent on clients for their income and so have a high investment in treating patients in such a way that they will wish to keep attending. Thus, there are financial, as well as moral or medical, motivations for treating patients with respect in this mutually beneficial exchange. The patient, or rather the patient who can afford it, has undergone a change of status: no longer the dependent and powerless recipient of medical directives from doctors, the patient, or client, in the alternative context makes decisions about who to see and what treatments to seek. Alternative practitioners are thus both powerful and vulnerable in ways that conventional doctors are not.

The 'consumerisation of the patient' could be seen as part of the gradual 'deprofessionalisation of the medical profession' that confirms the erosion of its 'cultural authority' (Saks, 1994:84), although Saks argues that while 'the authority of the British medical profession has certainly been thrown into question to some degree by the growing public demand for the alternatives to medicine ... [nevertheless] the legitimacy of medical authority remains broadly intact' (Saks, 1994:98). But part of the appeal of these new forms of alternative medicine is undoubtedly their contrast to conventional medical practice: whether in terms of disillusionment with medical knowledge or in terms of the dissatisfaction with doctors' professional behaviour, patients are opting for alternative medicine in search of more supportive, caring treatments which offer help with problems traditionally untouched by biomedicine.

Patients dissatisfied with medical doctors' briskness, disrespect and even dictatorial directives seek out the contrast offered by alternative approaches.[18] Alternative medical practices generally constitute a very different kind of patient: an adult with responsibilities and choices, as opposed to a child with neither. The agent of health here is not the medical expert but the patient, who is typically encouraged to participate actively in their recovery. The establishment of a positive, informal and mutually respectful dialogue is clearly an important aim of many alternative practices (although, as my own stories indicate, these are not always realised) (Budd and Sharma, 1994). Ursula Sharma contends that it is precisely the relocation of responsibility with the patient which appeals to patients of alternative medicine (Sharma, 1992:2). Studies in doctor/patient interaction demonstrate that in fact modes of communication in this context are changing, but have a long way to go before being satisfactory to patients. The majority of patients of alternative medicine in Sharma's study had tried conventional treatments for their medical problems and had developed a number of reasons for their dissatisfaction: 'orthodox medicine has too little time for the patient, is invasive, relies overmuch on drugs and technology, addresses symptoms rather than causes' (Sharma, 1992:41). Patients primarily make pragmatic choices about treatments which worked and in many chronic cases found that biomedicine had little to offer (Sharma, 1992:100).

As well as seeking 'better treatments', patients also seek an alternative to the traditional doctor/patient relationship of biomedicine. The kinds of things which people value in alternative therapies are more time with the practitioner, a more caring approach to healing, a sense of understanding the treatment process and a feeling of being involved in the healing. One patient is reported as saying that their herbalist 'does explain what she is doing and I feel more active in the treatment' (Sharma, 1992:41). In another study doctors are criticised for their 'formal and arrogant behaviour' and alternative practitioners are welcomed as people with whom patients can develop trusting relationships (Sharma, 1992:75). This sense of participating in the treatment can also affect patients' confidence and self-esteem more generally: one interviewee reported to Sharma that 'I make up my own mind about these things. Before, I just accepted it [the discomfort of chronic rhinitis]. Now I feel that I am in control of my life' (Sharma, 1992:51).

While all patients of alternative medicine may be drawn to a more 'democratic' and 'caring' model of treatment, it is no coincidence that it is women who make up the highest proportion of patients and, indeed, its practitioners.[19] For many female patients, being addressed as a social agent may be a welcome contrast to their previous biomedical experiences. Moreover, the cultures of alternative health are based upon philosophies more traditionally associated with the cultural competences of femininity: communication, caring, gentleness, natural remedies. The apparent lack of hierarchies (compared with bio-medicine at least), and the emphasis on emotions and feelings as well as physical symptoms, also contribute to the impression that alternative medicine is less conventionally masculine than its bio-medical counterpart. All these factors contribute to the culture of alternative health centres being perceived as welcoming to women. In particular, their appeal lies in the way in which the alternative medical discourses construct female patients as subjects rather than objects of health; in so doing they contradict the cultural tendencies towards female passivity, lack of agency and low self-confidence (Bakx, 1991, quoted in Saks, 1994).

But there are nevertheless problems presented by some of these beliefs and practices. What are the consequences of these new forms of inclusion and involvement of the patient in health which so many alternative approaches advocate, for example? And how desirable is this new-found responsibility for one's own health, and therefore one's illness? While fully acknowledging the benefits in the expansion of alternative medicines, and recognising the sexual politics of their challenge to traditional biomedicine, I nevertheless want to suggest that this emergent 'participatory and responsible' patient theory brings with it some troubling and onerous duties. My encounter with this discourse of the responsible patient has been in the context of the cancer cultures in 1990s Britain and while I do not take these to represent *all* alternative medicines, they are symptomatic of a certain trend among some of them. I found individual responsibility for health to be one of the most pervasive discourses running through the self-health literatures on cancer and it is to a detailed, and critical, analysis of this material that I now wish to turn.

TRAJECTORIES OF RESPONSIBILITY

We are each 100% responsible for all our experiences. Every thought we think is creating our future. The point of power is in the present moment. When we really love ourselves, everything in our life works. We create every so-called 'illness' in our body. We must release the past and forgive everyone.

(Hay, 1988:back cover)

Self-health approaches to cancer rely on the discourses of individual responsibility for their explanatory purchase. But what kind of individuals are being constructed and what kinds of responsibilities are being attributed to them? First, there are numerous examples of the aetiology of the disease being located within the individual. As discussions in previous chapters have revealed, this often takes the form of representing the disease as an expression of that person's lifestyle:

> We cannot cheat nature's response. If we do those things that are bound to lead to disease then we must expect to become diseased. It is no good expecting a miraculous reprieve from the consequences of our actions. Cancer is the end result of all that we do to ourselves and all that we eat. We are the cause of our own disease, we can also be the cause of our own good health.
>
> (Chaitow, 1983:101)

Chaitow's account differs from the biomedical discourses which construct cancer as a malfunction of the 'natural' regulation of the cell system; for Chaitow, cancer is simply the logical conclusion of our abuse of ourselves. Far from being an instance of excessive and unregulatable 'nature' (as in the medical accounts), the location of the aetiology of the disease within the individual's choice of diet and lifestyle produces instead a model of the natural body as a rational system responding to our choices. Both accounts agree that cancer is a disease characterised by its interiority; drawing on biomedical accounts of the body and its cell systems, Chaitow states: 'Cancer results from changes within the normal body cells – it is not an invasion from outside, whatever irritants may induce the cells to change' (Chaitow, 1983:13). However, where these accounts part company to some extent is in their understanding of what causes the body's interior systems to 'malfunction'. For Chaitow, the cell system breaks down not because of its internal faults, but because the whole body is protesting: 'the basic cause of all the different types of cancer will be found to be within the body itself and not in the disease process or tumour' (Chaitow, 1983:13). The cause of cancer is thus firmly situated within individual actions and choices.

As I discussed in Chapter 4, in many self-health explanations to cancer, the disease is seen to be a physical manifestation of psychic distress. Rachel Charles, for example, saw her cancer as a form of protest against herself: 'The fact was that my body was beginning to complain furiously at the intolerable strain that I had imposed on it. How could I have treated myself with such lack of consideration?' (Charles, 1990:3). Her solution is to seek out a new life in the peace and quiet of a rural idyll:

217

I had an overwhelming longing for the countryside, to feel the rain and wind beat against me, to be close to nature and its elemental forces. I felt poisoned by my city environment, by the fume-laden air and the relentless noise. I felt dazzled by the constant glare of advertisements, oppressed by the crowds and threatened by the honking aggression of the uncaring traffic.

(Charles, 1990:3)

In this account the aetiology of the disease is once again placed firmly within the realm of individual responsibility ('How could I have treated myself with such a lack of consideration?'). However, in this example, the individual blame is also connected to the evils of modernity (traffic, consumerism, pollution, and so on) which the person with cancer had tolerated unnecessarily. Charles's account urges cancer patients to opt out of the pressures of uncaring modernity and seek a healthier lifestyle in the countryside.

According to Simonton *et al.*, the cancer patient can decide to recover if s/he wants to: 'it's up to you to decide to get well again'; 'Everyone participates in his or her health or illness at all times. This book will show people with cancer or other serious illnesses how they can participate in getting well again . . . We use the word *participate* to indicate the vital role you play in creating your own level of health' (Simonton *et al.*, 1978:3). Similarly, Charles argues:

What we so often fail to appreciate is that the body has a staggeringly complex system for healing and regulating itself . . . Just as this delicately balanced system can be upset by poor diet, lack of exercise, long-term emotional problems and stress, so the opposite is true: it can be positively encouraged to operate more effectively, so that the body is able to function efficiently and remain healthy.

If you are suffering from a serious disease, take heart in the knowledge that you *can actively assist* in your own healing.

(Charles, 1990:5, my emphasis)

In several accounts it is not enough simply to change the physical conditions of one's life (such as diet and living or working environment) unless we also change our *attitudes and beliefs*. For example, Simonton *et al.* suggest that: 'We all participate in our own health through our beliefs, our feelings and attitudes towards life' (Simonton *et al.*, 1978:3); indeed, according to their argument each of us has a responsibility to change our negative thought patterns because of the way they can directly affect our bodily health: 'Each person can assume responsibility for examining, even altering, beliefs and feelings that do not support the treatment, that do not move in the direction of

218

affirming life and health' (Simonton *et al.*, 1978:32). The power to recover is thus placed in the hands of the individual and it becomes our choice, indeed our challenge. If you follow the imperative to take responsibility for your disease and recognise that 'you are the one in charge . . . [then] you will feel empowered' (Charles, 1990:7).

Integral to the process of accepting responsibility for one's disease within these accounts is a full participation in the treatments offered. Indeed, many of these writers suggest that recovery depends upon the patient's attitude to treatments. Simonton *et al.* claim that 'a positive attitude toward treatment was a better predictor of response to treatment than was the severity of the disease' (Simonton *et al.*, 1978:82). Indeed, they argue that by taking responsibility for one's own recovery by having a positive attitude towards treatment, people can abandon their victim mentality which may have made them ill in the first place and which will ensure better health in the future:

> patients who have actively participated in a recovery from cancer
> . . . have a psychological strength, a positive self-concept, a sense
> of control over their lives that clearly represent an improved level
> of psychological development . . . [They] have a positively altered
> stance toward life. They expect that things will go well, and they
> are victims no longer.
>
> (Simonton *et al.*, 1978:77–8)

In this transformation from victim to hero, the person with cancer is encouraged to see their disease as a metaphor of their previous mental state and their recovery as a physical sign of their new mental energy and confidence. Thus, the cause, the effects of the treatment and the ultimate recovery and future prevention of cancer are all placed within the power of the individual whose responsibility it is to heal themself by exercising their will-power and making the correct choices in life.

Like many of these self-health approaches to cancer, Louise Hay's polemic relies heavily on a subjectivist philosophy. She suggests that: 'no person, no place, and no thing has any power over us . . . We create our experiences, our reality and everyone in it' (Hay, 1988:7). Hay expresses this view of health and illness as the unqualified truth of existence. Any rejection of such claims is typically seen as more evidence of its validity: 'poverty is only a belief in your consciousness . . . How do you react to this statement? Do you believe it? Are you angry? . . . GOOD! I have touched something deep inside you, that very point of resistance to truth' (Hay, 1988:119–20). According to such an approach the environment, the social order, institutional constraints and poverty have little or no role in people's health or illness at all.

Some of these texts address what they see as specifically women's responsibilities quite directly. Charles, for example, writes of women's tendency to be both victims and martyrs (Charles, 1990:70). Indeed, avoiding taking responsibility is seen as a strategy for excusing one's victim mentality:

> Martyrs may consciously restrict themselves from real achievement . . . Many housewives find themselves in this role. Being out there in the big wide world is a scary prospect and martyrdom is a useful way of protecting themselves. They may say, 'I gave up a successful career for you' and hold a lot of inner resentment, blaming their lack of achievement on their spouse . . . Long-held bitterness of this kind can lead to disease.
>
> (Charles, 1990:73)

Here women are chastised for using their responsibilities to others as a way of avoiding taking responsibility for themselves. If women lose confidence while being housewives, according to this account, they only have themselves to blame. Indeed, their resentment towards their spouse, which may seem quite understandable given inequitable divisions of status and labour, is not only turned against them here but also blamed for the onset of their disease.

Indeed, responsibility for future generations (traditionally also seen as a requirement of femininity) is also played upon in these accounts of self-health:

> For those planning families it should be important to ensure that the next generation starts with a better chance of survival than the last. Noxious substances present in the mother can be passed to the infant in the mother's milk. Surely it is the expectant mother's responsibility to ensure that she feeds her offspring healthy milk.
>
> (Chaitow, 1983:101)

Women are thus called upon not only to be responsible for their own health and well-being, but to be responsible for the next generation's vulnerabilities to cancer. Like the recently constructed 'foetal alcohol syndrome' in which the mother is culpable, this discourse represents the 'carcinogenic mother' as endangering other lives through her imperfect body fluids: the height of abject femininity is evoked here through the chilling image of the soured milk of the bad mother.[20]

Several critics have objected to this cultural logic whereby the responsible patient is blamed for their illness: the patient is individually at fault for becoming ill and likewise culpable if s/he fails to recover. What might at first appeal as a validating and empowering discourse in which the patient is treated as a person with some agency in an otherwise alienating situation can quickly become a nightmare of blame and retribution. In offering the patient a sense of agency (a welcome contrast to conventional medical practice in which patients are favoured for their compliance, perhaps), these self-health discourses (like their Thatcherite counterparts) lose sight of any social, economic or environmental forces which affect health and offer instead an entirely individualistic world view which posits the patient and her/his will-power at the centre of a manipulable universe.

Some practitioners are aware of this criticism and deny that blame is an inevitable by-product of the discourse of the responsible patient. But, as Rosalind Coward argues, 'the implications of this personal responsibility are unavoidable' despite the fact that:

> Most practitioners would insist that they are not creating 'guilt' for illness. In other words, they argue that personal responsibility for getting well and a predisposition towards illness does not amount to a moral condemnation of an individual for falling ill. Many proponents of alternative therapies insist that these ideas of disease, of the imbalance of the body and the predisposition towards illness have no critical implications for the state of the individual who falls ill.
>
> (Coward, 1989:77)

The kinds of disclaimers put forward by alternative practitioners (both Simonton *et al.* and Brohn insist they do not seek to make patients feel guilty) do little to counter the more powerful suggestions of these discourses of personal responsibility which interiorise social problems, attribute an almost omnipotent power to the individual, and privilege psychological causes over all others in explaining disease. In particular, Coward argues, 'stress' is seen as the key cause of physical problems, and whether or not we cope adequately with stress depends upon our personality, not upon the external factors producing stress. As one alternative practitioner put it, 'people . . . are not being stressed by external events beyond their control but are stressing themselves' (Harrison, 1984, quoted in Coward, 1989:84). There is a general consensus in alternative medicine, Coward argues, that 'disease is "self-created and self-cured"' (Coward, 1989:84).

This model of self-induced disease is central to the construction of the cancer 'personality type' discussed in Chapters 2 and 4.[21] The type of personality likely to develop cancer is described thus: 'There is often an overtone of passive subservience. They are not the types to become aggressive or anti-social. They want to be liked' (Gawler, 1986, quoted in Coward, 1989:85). Like many other such typologies, this description echoes stereotypes of appropriate 'feminine' behaviour: passive, subservient, relational and approval-seeking. Not only does this description not add up to the personality most highly valued in late twentieth-century Britain (Sontag, 1977), it also corresponds to those unenviable attributes of stereotypical femininity. This emergent discourse of responsibility thus produces a very specific notion of the patient of which we need to be wary for a number of important reasons. First, as well as offering the promise of agency, it also constitutes the patient through moral notions of duty. Far from contradicting conventional definitions of femininity, the category of the responsible patient with a duty to be healthy may further reinforce the endless burdens of femininity. Second, the disappointment if the treatment does not work may be especially acute for the patient who has been encouraged to believe they can intervene in the course of any disease. Finally, given the patterns of guilt and shame which operate through the cultural construction of gender, the tendency to 'blame the victim' within these alternative therapies may have an especially profound resonance for many women.

The model of 'psycho-incubation', in which the physical disease develops because of a psychological state of mind, furthermore produces a new moralism in contemporary health cultures: 'if health is wholesome, it is clear that the well body expresses a morality, an attitude' (Coward, 1989:88). In the case of cancer there are quite clear moral judgements at stake:

> a sick body, a neglected body, is a sign of something mentally or spiritually wrong. This is not a simple world of evil and good where those with cancer are tainted with Satan's mark. But it is a world where individual intentions, strength of will and commitment to a life style which is right and harmonious have their rewards in visible good health. And it is a world where wrong attitudes – neglect of self-expression and needs – have their punishments. It is a world of heroes and victims.
>
> (Coward, 1989:88)

The kind of moral high ground claimed by some alternative approaches to cancer has strong religious connotations. Although some types of alternative medicine have been committed to a kind of 'pantheistic spiritualism' or a mysticism associated with 'oriental religions', alternative medicine's implicit moralism has been seen to reproduce elements of 'Christian puritanism': 'much of the entangling of health and morality and the implication of personal responsibility for well-being, is more than tainted with puritanism' (Coward, 1989:89). The salvation of the soul promised by religious conversion (with its requisite abandonment of previous sins and adoption of new values) is seen to be replicated here by the new 'healthy lifestyles' that cancer patients are urged to adopt. Indeed, Coward argues that where people in the past turned to religion to pursue the fantasy of an inner truth, an essential self or sense of wholeness, so now people turn to the alternative health movement for such a purpose:

> It is extremely hard to avoid reading an article on health these days that does not stress that we have responsibility for our own health, and that we can choose to be well or sick. Indeed, we can even choose whether we live or die. It is as if disease has itself become a kind of morality, demonstrating the level of the individual's personal control over their life.
>
> (Coward, 1989:92).

Similarly, Robert Crawford argues that health has become the new symbolic place of salvation in a secular and 'detraditionalised', society: 'In disenchanted, secular, and materialist cultures, health acquires a greater symbolic importance. Health substitutes for salvation and becomes a salvation of its own'. (Crawford, 1985:62–3)

What emerges from Crawford's and Coward's analyses is that this discourse of individual responsibility is not restricted to alternative health practices, but has become part of everyday common-sense discourse about health and illness. Even in the mid-1970s, and this tendency has certainly intensified since then, public debate involved the construction of the individual and her/his lifestyle as the main cause of the nation's health problems and health bills. Quoting examples from the *New York Times*, such as claims that 'health is a *duty*' and the suggestion that health insurance might introduce 'a reward punishment system based on individual choices', Crawford criticises this move as a 'politics of retrenchment'. This 'blame-the-victim mentality' thus not only relocates responsibility for health with the individual, but might be institutionalised through economic sanctions in which individuals might literally have to pay for their unwise 'lifestyle' choices. Not surprisingly, those blamed for their bad habits tend to be groups which are already disapproved of in society. Class and race inequality are further reinforced, for once again those with the least resources are policed by those with the most: 'During the period of rapid health sector expansion, higher morbidity and mortality rates for the poor and minorities were explained by emphasizing life-style habits, especially their health and utilization behaviour' (Crawford, 1977:670). Furthermore, accompanying this general shift towards a discourse of health and away from a discourse of medicine has been a parallel move towards an assumption of duty rather than rights. For Crawford, this notion that 'you are dangerous to your health' signals a profound depoliticisation of medicine and an avoidance of state responsibility for its citizens. This has been replaced by the notion of health as a form of individual citizenship.

HEALTHY CITIZENS

It is not only in these self-health literatures that patients are constituted through a moral duty to take responsibility for their own health. In public health practices there is also a strong reliance on the idea of individual responsibility. What accompanies this discourse of individual responsibility is a form of moral citizenship that produces a new 'imperative of health' (Lupton, 1994). For some critics, the resurfacing of certain kinds of health promotion is part of the remoralisation of health in the late twentieth century. According to Muriel Gillick (1984), for example, recent changes in discourses of health can be seen to echo the high moralism around health of past centuries. Documenting the American traditions of individual responsibility for health through 'physical hygienism' which date back at least to John Wesley, 'whose *Primitive Physick*, published in 1764, regarded sickness as punishment for earthly sins', Gillick identifies continuities with today's attribution of responsibility for health to the patient. Famous late nineteenth-century American capitalists (for example, Sylvester Graham and John Kellogg) were associated with a form of physical hygienism which stressed 'temperance, vegetarianism, and exercise – as well as cleanliness, loose clothes, sexual moderation and fresh air . . . as prerequisites to good health' (Gillick, 1984:369). Within such traditions, 'physiological rectitude' was the basis for social and personal redemption, curing social problems such as crime and poverty, as well as disease (Gillick, 1984:370). The trajectory here concerned progress and personal improvement for the general good of society and, indeed, nation. Gillick argues that such individual responsibility for healthy body and healthy nation was undermined by the emergence of the germ theory of disease, which, with the accompanying developments in immunisation, sanitation and public health care, meant that the new medical professionals increasingly adopted sole responsibility for health. However, she argues, since the 1960s 'there has been a resurgence of interest in the role of personal habits in producing sickness' (Gillick, 1984:369).

As an example of this resurgence, Gillick analyses the changing cultural significance of 'jogging' in America; previously identified with militarism and competitive sport, this activity is now seen as a sign not only of health and fitness, but also of moral superiority and 'a means to personal and social renewal' (Gillick, 1984:371). Participation in regular exercise of this kind has come to constitute a form of national, indeed even global citizenship, shifting the emphasis of 'responsibility for environmental change from society to the individual, and . . . redefining "being ill" as "being guilty"' (Gillick, 1984:384). Certain voices in the running movement make this moral stake quite explicit. One popular philosopher of the movement writes: 'The cause of man's [*sic*] infirmity is to be found in man himself. Germs and microbes [are] not the problem. No virus has produced these miseries ... It [is] a loss of the body's integrity, its balance, its ability to remain in equilibrium with its environment, its capacity to cope' (Sheehan, 1977, quoted in Gillick, 1984:381). For Gillick, the increasing cultural significance of this kind of individualisation of illness threatens to undermine our liberation from the discourse of sin and sickness which was achieved by the triumph of medical science over religious 'superstition' in the past.

Making a much broader critique of the exercise of medical authority on working-class communities through health promotion strategies, Martha Balshem's study of a community cancer prevention project also highlights the prevalence of the attribution to individuals of responsibility for illness and death. Initially sent into an urban working-class community in Philadelphia to encourage residents in this 'cancer hot spot' to stop smoking, change their diet and go for regular scans, Balshem found herself increasingly critical of the politics of such an intervention. The recipients of this health promotion programme, 'Project CAN-DO', the residents of Tannerstown:

> resisted the message that these high cancer rates were associated with their personal habits. They pointed a finger instead at air pollution from the large chemical plants next to the community and at occupational exposure, air pollution from heavy street traffic, and chemical adulteration of food and water.
>
> (Balshem, 1993:3)

Despite popular medical directives to the contrary, these residents were twice as likely to attribute the cause of cancer to 'environmental factors' as to 'lifestyle' ones (Balshem, 1993:70). After some time spent working as part of this health promotion team, Balshem felt that such preventive initiatives directed the responsibility for cancer towards individuals and away from social factors: 'It is a central tenet of modern preventive medicine that people bear responsibility for their sickness, through control over their lifestyles' (Balshem, 1993:5). This approach, Balshem argues, led to the blaming of working-class people for their health problems and thus the denial of responsibility of any other organisations for the high rates of cancer in that area.

Several residents in this study, however, rejected this attribution of personalised responsibility for cancer and expressed a scepticism, even a fundamental mistrust, of scientific expertise and professional knowledges in general. One respondent is quoted as saying: 'Over the last two decades everything has been this causes cancer and that – and people are to the point now where they think everything you eat causes cancer and nobody really knows what causes cancer' (Balshem, 1993:76). The limits of medical knowledge about the causes of cancer produce anger and resentment towards the arrogance of medical authority, which is ridiculed for many of its directives:

> Every time you turn, like, no matter what you listen to – TV, radio, what have you, all right – this causes cancer, that causes cancer – you know what I mean? So, like, you know, like, all right, I opened my eyes this morning, I just breathed in twenty-nine gallons of cancer. You know what I mean? So, like, just opening your eyes, you're saying 'hello, cancer'.
>
> (Balshem, 1993:75)

There was a shared sense that given the changing and even contradictory pieces of information, there was little point in trying to take control of one's medical fate in the way advised by the health promotion unit; God, fate and the sheer enormity of the nuclear threat and of environmental pollution made a change of diet seem superfluous. Unlike heart disease, which is seen as a mechanical problem, cancer is seen as a mysterious disease whose aetiology relies upon a complex cosmology of religion and luck. Refusing the blame attributed to their lifestyles by medical professionals, this community instead made science into the object of criticism, ridiculing its arrogance and exposing its limits and contradictions.

In one case study presented in Balshem's book, the patient is blamed (if implicitly) for his cancer and consequently the medical confusions around diagnosis are circumvented. Told retrospectively by his wife, the story reveals how the inclusion of details of the patient's 'heavy drinking' and 'years of smoking' in his medical records implied that his terminal cancer was his responsibility, indeed, his fault. The doctor's misguided assumptions that his cancer originated in the lung led to misdiagnosis and mistreatment which was reluctantly confirmed by the doctors after an autopsy. Although never said directly, the presence of comments on his lifestyle in his records not only laid the blame with his personal habits, but, furthermore, led to mistaken assumptions about the kind of cancer he was suffering from (Balshem, 1993:91–124).

The stories represented in Balshem's study put questions of responsibility, causation and blame at the centre of contemporary debates about cancer. Caught between medical science and community work, health promotion's preventive drive often leads to attributions of blame to patients. In focusing on individual lifestyle rather than industrial or environmental causes, it can deflect attention away from political issues and shift responsibility solely onto the patient. What these examples share is the reconstitution of health and illness through the notion of *the responsible patient* and the accompanying intensification of the duties of healthy citizenship.[22] It is in this that the common ground with self-health can be found.

A further context for the cultural resonance of discourses of individualised responsibility for health is the contemporary perception of risk. Kept in a state of heightened awareness about the rapidly proliferating number of local and global risks and dangers to the healthy body, we are easily seduced by fantasies of individual agency, autonomy and self-generation. Environmental pollution, chemicals in food, the ozone layer depletion and the negative effects of stress are all repeatedly monitored and recycled as a source of cultural anxiety in our everyday lives. As Kelleher, drawing on Giddens (1991) and Beck (1992) argues: 'the contemporary western world is a risk-oriented world in which people are continuously warned about the dangers of overeating, drinking polluted tap water and breathing air from a polluted environment' (Kelleher, 1994:113). These have taken on a particularly overwhelming dimension with respect to cancer: for example, in the United States, 'the fear of cancer is becoming more widespread. A recent Gallup Poll found that cancer is by far the disease most feared by Americans, almost three times its nearest competitor' (Crawford, 1977:676–7). In such a context, Crawford suggests that medical science cannot deliver its grand promises of progress towards a disease-free future.[23] The contradiction between people's heightened awareness of the threat of certain diseases (such as cancer, HIV and AIDS, heart disease) on the one hand, and their expectation that science would provide solutions and medicine would provide cures on the other, has resulted in a trend towards an individualism which at least offers people some explanation for the diseases around them. Crawford argues that 'in the face of these trends, it is fascinating and revealing that we are witnessing the proliferation of messages about our own personal responsibility for health and an attack on individual life-styles and at-risk behaviours' (Crawford, 1977:668).[24]

FROM A RIGHT TO HEALTH TO A DUTY TO BE HEALTHY

The belief in the duty to be healthy belongs to a widespread shift in Western culture during the second half of the twentieth century. There has been a profound change in perceptions of responsibility for health since the 1960s. To offer one final example, Herzlich and Pierret (1987) found that interviewees in their study in France started taking much more responsibility for their own health. In contrast to the 1960s, when patients believed that their role was a passive one in deference to medical expertise, in the 1980s they felt a more individualised sense of responsibility. Generalising from their interviews, Herzlich and Pierret claim that:

> In the 1960s [the right to health] implied the development of a medical infrastructure and the reduction of inequalities in access to the health-care system; in the 1980s it is a matter of making all individuals responsible for their health and motivating them to modify their behaviour and habits. Medicine is playing an instrumental role in this movement, which tends to make health into a supervalue, an end in itself . . . health is becoming life itself. It therefore becomes necessary, as medicine recommends, to do everything to avoid becoming ill. This demands eating a proper diet by following the recommendations of nutritionists, abstaining from certain substances that are labelled unnecessary and . . . dangerous, such as tobacco, leading a healthy and hygienic life by exercising and adopting a balanced rhythm of life . . . the 'right to be sick and to receive adequate treatment' has been replaced by the 'duty to be healthy'.
>
> (Herzlich and Pierret, 1987:52–3)

According to Herzlich and Pierret, changes in medical treatment, made possible through scientific innovation, have produced a transformation in the dominant discourses through which people make sense of their health. Science continues to provide the frameworks through which people understand their health and illness and has made possible an interiorisation of illness. They refer to this as the 'turn to the infracorporeal', and suggest that the interior of the body has increasingly become the significant text to be read: 'Illness has today become an individual phenomenon . . . In order to decode our illnesses we no longer rely on the global vision of our bodies or even the perceptible reality of our symptoms, but turn to the infracorporeal messages furnished by medical science'. They argue that 'certain new etiological models have individualised illness even further by stressing the involvement of genetic mechanisms or complex immunological processes' (Herzlich and Pierret, 1987:97,49). The disappearence of so many infectious diseases has also meant that different illnesses are now feared (though the HIV/AIDS epidemic has surely reversed this to some extent):

> In the 1960s, then, there was a twofold discourse about illness and medicine . . . that of an anguished threat but also of a possible victory. This was indeed a turning point; our informants easily slipped from one category into the other. At times they said that infectious disease, the kind that can be cured, is 'real illness' and saw the other kind, cancer, as but a fortuitous accident that

medical progress would soon bring under control. But very quickly, the other register emerged: was cancer, perhaps, the only 'real' disease, the only one worth talking about? Now in the 1980s, the second theme has won out. The very success of the struggle against infectious disease has made us forget the fight. Despite the development of therapeutics, there is a certain disenchantment, and more and more critical voices are being raised. Henceforth, the collective consciousness is haunted by a fear of cancer.

(Herzlich and Pierret, 1987:47–8)

Cancer has been particularly prone to this individualising discourse:

cancer is the protoype illness of our time – *cancer is the illness of individuals in their relations with society.* It is indeed the illness of the individual but this individual can only be conceived of in relation with society as a whole. At the same time cancer is also an illness produced by society, but one that manifests the flaws of the present-day individual.

(Herzlich and Pierret, 1987:62)

Drawing on Foucault, Herzlich and Pierret argue that science replaced religion as the central discourse through which health and illness were represented. A new mechanistic model of the body and its functions enabled the professional to develop his expertise about the body and its interiors and to treat illness as a kind of machine breakdown which specific knowledges could be relied upon to facilitate repair. For Herzlich and Pierret, the eighteenth and nineteenth centuries saw a radical shift away from the discourse of illness as divine retribution towards the discourse of the body as a machine whose smooth functioning could be maintained through professional medical intervention. But this argument needs to be brought up to date and extended to include more recent models of illness, such as the informational one discussed in Chapter 5. This new model of the body as an information system, whose delicate balance must be regularly monitored by the individuals themselves, is one which no longer deals solely with questions of physical input and output, but rather with the fine tuning of a multi-layered, highly sensitive system of mind/body (and sometimes spirit). The individuals charged with this onerous responsibility must learn to read their bodily texts through modes of self-knowledge and exploration. The patient is required to develop a sophisticated therapeutic literacy to decode her/his well-being accurately. These shifts in conceptions of illness – from divine retribution, through mechanical breakdown to mind/body system dysfunction – have very different implications for the question of responsibility. To put it crudely, the divine punishment model places the responsibility with 'mankind' and possibly the community; the machine model places the responsibility with the medical profession; and the systems model places the responsibility with the individual patient.

But does this new construction of the responsible patient indicate the demise of medical science in beliefs about health? Has a continued reliance on science for new models of health and illness nevertheless been accompanied by a gradual questioning of the legitimacy of its authority? In what ways might the uses of biomedical imagination to visualise the flows of the bodily interior occur simultaneously with the general demise of medical science as the saviour of the modern age? In other words, have the heroic fantasies that science once fulfilled for modernity been fundamentally disturbed or dislocated?

A LOSS OF FAITH?

Such questions are posed with a sense of urgency within the cancer cultures of the 1990s. Many people having chemotherapy and radiotherapy weigh up the benefits of these treatments against their negative long- and short-term effects. This scepticism is part of the general reevaluation of many biomedical methods and drugs which are increasingly thought to have iatrogenic effects on the patient's health.[25] While modern scientific innovations may be seen to have provided cures for illnesses such as cancer, people are nevertheless more and more aware of the ways in which they have also produced many of the health problems of the late twentieth century. Cancer is widely reported as being on the increase because of radiation levels, exposure to electromagnetic fields and food additives; melanomas (skin cancers) are seen to be increasing because of ozone depletion. The irony of technological developments themselves producing the cancer and then curing it with some of the same inventions (as in the case of radiation) does not escape the attention of many cancer patients.

Scientific and technological 'progress' and medical developments are thus implicated in many of our current and future health problems and it has been claimed that science in general is suffering a 'crisis of legitimation'.[26] Of particular significance to the question of whether biomedicine is losing its authority is the debate about the status of scientific knowledge in contemporary Western culture more generally. Lyotard's *Report on knowledge* in the mid-1980s charts the changes in the status of knowledge which has occurred across the most 'developed' countries in the West. His argument maps the collapse of the legitimating meta-narratives of science which he considers to be at the heart of the 'postmodern condition', a condition within which knowledge has been relativised, moral certainties contextualised, and diversity and plurality have become the flagships of the future.

Central to this shift, according to Lyotard, is a transformation in the role of the professional and the expert.[27] No longer necessary for the transmission of the kinds of knowledge which increasingly characterise the late twentieth century, professional ownership of expertise has become more and more questionable. The emergence of informational cultures in the West have further contributed to existing forms of intellectual commodification (Lury, 1993). The increasing dominance of computer culture has meant that all knowledge must be translatable into 'units of information'; thus, knowledge is increasingly produced as an 'informational commodity' and the previous indivisibilty of expert from expertise is replaced by an exteriorization of knowledge and a relativisation of the knower (Lyotard, 1984:4). In biomedicine such a separation threatens the fundamental authority of doctors over their patients, for if medical knowledge is available for all to judge, then it no longer holds the status of professional expertise. Ownership of such specialist knowledges is no longer the automatic prerogative of the professional, but can be contested in the market by the amateur. In the past, scientific knowledge relied on the acceptance of certain very specific assumptions for its legitimacy. Science, according to Lyotard, has distinguished itself from other forms of knowledge by claiming to be a set of denotative statements which refer to objects available to others for observation, to be judged by experts (Lyotard, 1984:19). What Lyotard names the language game of *denotation* must be privileged in science to the exclusion of all others in order for the truth value of its claims to be legitimate. In other words, what makes knowledge *scientific* is its reference to something external to itself described in a language which can be scrutinised by others with similar training and qualifications.

Lyotard's central argument which is of relevance to my concerns here about the shift in responsibility for health is that in postindustrial and postmodern culture, science is no longer able to gain legitimation from the progress narratives of modernity which had previously justified its authority. Modern science has relied heavily on cultural narrativisations as sources of legitimation for its truth claims. As many cultural critics have pointed out, narration is not limited to story-telling and myth-making in the fictional sense of purely imaginative creations, but is also a cultural form which organises other kinds of knowledge (see Chapter 1). In the case of science, narrative arranges information as the epic stories of the struggle against the limits of nature, the successes and failures of heroes and victims, and the forward movement in time towards potential resolutions. Rather than appealing to some kind of transcendental authority, modern science recognised that the rules of proof are an integral part of the game of science and thus can only function through the consensus of the experts in that field (Lyotard,

1984:29). In this context, 'narrative knowledge makes a resurgence in the West as a way of solving the problem of legitimating new authorities' (Lyotard, 1984:30), and the people are called upon to consent through what he calls 'a mode of deliberation'. Science thus casts itself as serving humanity and its expertise relies on consensual validation.

Lyotard identifies two narratives which serve to legitimate modern science: the political and the philosophical. The first, the political, legitimates science through the narrative of the liberation of humanity. The hero here is liberty. The second, the philosophical, is the narrative of the pursuit of knowledge. Here the hero is the meta-subject of speculation. The first (science for the people) legitimates the scientific project through an appeal to the belief that people have the 'right to science'; the second (science for its own sake) does so through an appeal to the idea that knowledge is, in and of itself, a worthwhile goal (Lyotard, 1984:31). In contemporary postmodern culture, however, Lyotard argues, these two narratives no longer function as satisfactory legitimation of the scientific project. Their foundational claims and legitimising authority have been undermined by changes in the relationship between knowledge, power and technology. Although uneven and incomplete, this dissolution of modernist legitimations has had a profound effect on the status of scientific knowledge in contemporary culture: 'the grand narrative has lost its credibility, regardless of what mode of unification it uses, regardless of whether it is a speculative narrative or a narrative of emancipation' (Lyotard, 1984:37).

Although reluctant to answer questions of straightforward determinism and causation, Lyotard does offer some possible factors which have combined to produce such a breakdown in these 'grand narratives of speculation and emancipation'. New techniques and technologies, the redeployment of advanced liberal capitalism, new forms of individualism and a new emphasis on the means rather than the ends have all contributed to the 'decline of the unifying and legitimating power' of these narratives. However, it would be wrong to see this analysis of the 'postmodern condition' as suggestive of a rigid periodisation, or even a radical departure from previous cultural 'conditions', such as modernity. Rather, Lyotard insists, 'the seeds of delegitimation and nihilism' were already present in the nineteenth century and, since then, there have been signs of this 'crisis' of scientific knowledge (Lyotard, 1984:38). Indeed, the collapse of their legitimating power was written into these modernist narratives and thus their erosion is seen here to have been almost inevitable. The merging of technological innovation and scientific knowledge, and the welding of money and science with the first industrial revolution, established a kind of functionalism to science which has culminated in the instrumentalist approach characteristic of the late twentieth century. The new legitimacy that emerged

was thus of perfomativity: 'technology became important to contemporary knowledge only through the mediation of a generalised
spirit of perfomativity' (Lyotard, 1984:45). Lyotard thus argues that the
grand narratives of modern science contained the seeds of their own
destruction (Lyotard, 1984:39).

The power of the modernist meta-narratives lay, in part, in their
universalist claims. However, within the postmodern condition the
forms of knowledge which circulate refuse such unification and demand instead increasing specification and particularisation. The multiplication of new forms of language, such as the 'genetic code' and
'graphs of phonological structures', defy the bounds of a universal
metalanguage which 'speaks to them all', and thus speculative and
humanistic philosophy has been forced to 'relinquish its legitimation
duties' (Lyotard, 1984:41). According to Lyotard, changes within scientific practice itself have required new forms of legitimation. Both the
increase in the number of methods of argumentation and the rise in
the complexity of ways of establishing proof have meant that the
'principle of a plurality of formal and axiomatic systems capable of
arguing the truth of denotative statements' has replaced that of a
universal metalanguage (Lyotard, 1984:43). Thus, it is not the end of
knowledge which Lyotard proclaims, but its proliferation: 'data banks
are the encyclopedia of tomorrow ... they are "nature" for postmodern man [sic]' (Lyotard, 1984:51). The instrumentality of knowledge production might be indicated by the shift from the central
question of: is it true? to that of: is it of use? (followed by: is it saleable,
is it efficient?) (Lyotard, 1984:51). Lyotard thus sums up this transformation:

> the relation of knowledge is not articulated in terms of the
> realization of the life of the spirit or the emancipation of human-
> ity, but in terms of the users of a complex conceptual and material
> machinery and those who benefit from its performance cap-
> abilities. They have at their disposal no metalanguage or meta-
> narrative in which to formulate the final goal and correct use of
> that machinery. But they do have brainstorming to improve its
> performance.
>
> (Lyotard, 1984:52)

In characterising postmodern science, Lyotard argues that it is
developing in relation to quite different modes of legitimation. Typical
of postmodern culture more generally, postmodern science is now
'theorizing its own evolution as discontinuous, catastrophic, non-
rectifiable, and paradoxical. It is changing the meaning of the word
knowledge while expressing how such a change can take place' (Lyotard,
1984:60). In this reflexive mode, science is no longer able to appeal to

233

external truths and universal proofs to secure its reputation, but rather, is forced to rely upon a more locally determined set of legitimating criteria. Indeed, according to Lyotard, in contrast to previous narratives about objectivity, universal truth and verifiable proof, postmodern science now draws attention to the ways in which 'even discussions of denotative statements need to have rules' (Lyotard, 1984:65). It is the awareness of the negotiability of these rules (metaprescriptive utterances) and of the processes of involving 'players' in that negotiation that has had a destabilising effect on existing forms of legitimation. What form this negotiation might take has been widely debated in contemporary social theory. In contrast to other critics such as Habermas and Luhman, Lyotard rejects any hope of reassuring systematisations in the midst of such localised and negotiated value, and he thus sees *consensus* amongst the scientific community as a receding possibility in this respect; indeed, he argues firmly that the principle of consensus is rapidly being replaced by that of dissension. Instead, the 'language games' of postmodern science are 'heteromorphous' and 'subject to heterogenous sets of pragmatic rules', paralogy being the sole force of legitimation (Lyotard, 1984:65).

Thus, it is not that there are no methods for legitimating knowledge in postmodern culture, but rather that any belief in the rules, and any faith in the players, is always *provisional* and *temporary*. Along with other spheres of life (for example, sexual, national and familial), professional activities have come to be dominated by temporary contracts rather than permanent institutions. Change, and perhaps eventual cancellation, have become almost inevitable dimensions of professional work in a culture where the rules of legitimacy are constantly contested and indeed ultimately recognised as merely rules.

THE RELOCATION OF THE GRAND NARRATIVES

So what impact has this general shift in forms of legitimation of scientific knowledge had on the status of medical expertise and how has this growing sense of provisionality affected perceptions of responsibility for health? How might we evaluate the increasing pressure on patients to take responsibility for their own health in the light of Lyotard's claims? If Lyotard is right, and science is no longer unproblematically hailed as the liberator of 'mankind' in the steady march towards progress and development, then should we assume that this fundamental crisis of legitimation extends to all aspects of Western culture? What I think we see instead is the displacement and relocation of the legitimation function to other aspects of contemporary society. In the case of health, what has accompanied this emergent (though uneven) scepticism about biomedicine, its drugs and its experts is the search for alternative certainties and new progress narratives. Today's cancer cultures are in fact saturated with the desire for truth, certainty and progress. While there is definitely a shift in location away from biomedicine as the sole guarantor of such absolutes, these desires are nevertheless still powerful cultural imperatives.

I want to suggest that the crisis in legitimation of biomedical knowledge suggested by Lyotard has been accompanied by the *neolegitimation* or the *professionalisation* of the patient through the powerful discourse of individual responsibility for health. The demise of one kind of expertise has been accompanied by the emergence of another in the form of self-knowledge that lies within the individual (see Turner, 1990:10). This is evidenced in the rise in popularity of self-health strategies during the last fifteen years and in particular in the emergence of the notion of patients as the new experts of their own well-being within such philosophies.[28]

In the self-health literature on cancer quoted earlier in this chapter, the loss of faith in medical expertise is coincidental with a new attribution of responsibility to the patient for her/his health. This involves the individualisation of illness which has increasingly come to define the health cultures of late twentieth-century Western societies. The cultures of self-health surrounding cancer invite patients to take charge of their lives and to become the authors and agents of their own health trajectories. Rather than looking to scientific solutions alone (if at all), cancer patients are urged to look within themselves. Self-knowledge, not medical knowledge, offers the key to good health. This knowledge is waiting to be discovered; it is already formed but we have failed to recognise it for the truth value it might offer us: 'inside each of us there is a source of wisdom that we can call upon. Part of our unconscious mind knows absolutely everything about us, who we are, where we have been and where we are going' (Charles, 1990:74). The path to healing involves a voyage of self-discovery that leads towards a liberation from negative ways of thinking and living. It is in our power, we are told, to begin to take charge of ourselves, our lives and our health:

> this process involves looking deep within yourself. It means considering your personality, your emotions, your values and your lifestyle, as well as the more practical aspects of diet and exercise. It takes a great deal of courage to do this. There may be very good reasons why you need to be ill. If you become glowingly healthy, who will care for you then? The holistic road to health involves asking yourself difficult, personal questions. It is a road towards self-acceptance, self-knowledge and, yes, most especially, self-love.
> (Charles, 1990:5)

I believe we create every so-called 'illness' in our body. The body, like everything else in life, is a mirror of our inner thoughts and beliefs . . . Every cell within your body responds to every single thought you think and every word you speak. Continuous modes of thinking and speaking produce body behaviours and postures and eases or dis-eases.

(Hay, 1988:127)

These accounts of the self-generation of disease map out clear traject-ories: rediscover your 'true' self and find the path towards liberation. You can be the hero of your own story, the author of your own salvation, the agent of your own triumph-over-tragedy narrative. Through self-knowledge you will progress along the path of self-healing: 'By being true to themselves . . . several cancer patients have gone into complete remission' (Charles, 1990:86). No one else can do this for you, since it is only knowledge that comes from within that truly heals. These are narratives in which all the players reside within the arena of the self: the problem and the solution are conceptualised as internal to the subject. The obstacle to be overcome is a misguided or corrupt self that has taken over from an authentic self whose resurrection promises recovery from illness (see Chapter 6).

These examples are chosen here for the ways in which they crystallise aspects of the discourse of individual responsibility especially clearly. But my argument applies much more widely; the beliefs about know-ledge, progress and salvation embedded within these accounts pervade the discourse of responsibility more generally. The discourse of respons-ibility generates a linear narrative by assuming a shared moral code of predictable and enduring continuity. As I suggested at the beginning of this chapter, the notion of responsibility is premised on the assump-tion that someone can be called to account for decisions taken by a rational and informed subject who sees the risks and accepts the repercussions. Responsible decisions provide an investment in the future through a linear teleology based on stable categories, generalis-able judgements and demonstrable failings. Indeed, we might say that the discourse of responsibility sustains precisely those values under threat in the 'postmodern condition'; it restores lost certainties, it promises continuities and it appeals to universal criteria.

The constructions of self-development through progress narratives are deployed not only within self-health books aimed at cancer patients, but also, as we have seen, within many practices in public health and biomedicine. More than this, they suffuse numerous areas of con-temporary social life, from the rhetoric of enterprise culture so widely disseminated since Thatcherism to the language of therapy and coun-selling which is becoming increasingly part of everyday discourse.

Despite variations across these fields, there is nevertheless a strikingly common invocation of the progress narrative of self-realisation and actualisation. It is on this basis that the imperative for individuals to take responsibility for their own well-being has been widely advocated.

Whether it is doctors or patients who are responsibile for health, the cultural narratives remain much the same. The increasing attribution of responsibility for health to patients is clearly part of a change in the status of biomedical science and its modern forms of expertise. But what is bypassed in Lyotard's account of the postmodern condition is the extent to which modernity's meta-narratives have been relocated within the individual. Both the narrative of liberation and the narrative of the pursuit of knowledge operate in a compressed form in contemporary constructions of self-health: the former, the hero of the narrative of liberation, is central to these accounts, but is no longer the hero of the liberation of humanity but of the self, usually from the limits of the past; the latter, the hero of the pursuit of knowledge, is also invoked, but again not as the hero of scientific knowledge but as the hero of self-knowledge for its own sake. The meta-narratives of modernity, which used to legitimate medical science, have thus been condensed into heroic narratives of the individual's progress towards self-health. The health cultures of the 1990s continue to reproduce the meta-narratives of progress and liberation, but they are increasingly transformed into microcosmic forms of individual salvation and self-knowledge.

8

ENDINGS

MYSTERY AND MASTERY

What unites modern science with the self-health cultures of the 1990s is the desire for mastery. It is the desire to see, to know and to control. It is the desire to fix meaning and to make outcomes predictable. It is the desire to prove that one has power over disease, the body and the emotions. In short, it is what has been identified as the masculine 'urge to fathom the secrets of nature' (Keller, 1990:177).

In reaching for the limits of knowledge, rewards are also sought, since the pursuit of truth is a moral activity. In moving the world further along the narrative of progress, recognition is expected, citizenship is achieved. For who would question such motives, who would caution against such self-evidently legitimate desires? There is little room in either the world of science or of self-health for reflexivity, self-criticism or contingency (Phillips, 1994).[1]

What is intolerable to both modern science and to self-health philosophies is mystery. The unexpected recovery must be explained by doctors, the rapid deterioration of the patient psychologised by the self-health therapist. The only narrative space for mystery is as an object to be known. The 'secrets of nature' function to 'articulate a boundary: an interior not visible to outsiders' (Keller, 1990:178). These secrets have traditionally been associated with femininity and with the possibility of procreation; it is thus 'a short step from the secrets of women to the secrets of nature' (Keller, 1990:178). The secrets of each have proved both 'threatening and alluring' and have produced 'a definitive response ... the scientific method – a *method* for undoing nature's secrets: for the rendering of what was previously invisible, visible' (Keller, 1990:178). The depths of the self also hide secrets that must be uncovered. For secrets cause cancer, we are told (Hay, 1989:22). Guilty secrets, forgotten traumas, past hurts, unforgiving resentments – these lurk beneath the smooth surface of the body and fester. Self-health urges us to seek out the hidden secrets that the body has buried, to explore the murkiest or most troubled areas and to release ourselves from self-destruction, from dis-ease.

Scientific enlightenment has been described as 'a drama between visibility and invisibility, between light and dark, and also between female procreativity and male productivity – a drama in need of constant reenactment at ever-receding recesses of nature's secrets' (Keller, 1990:178–9). Self-health enlightenment is a drama between past and present, between tradition and modernity and between nature and artifice. Both aim to reveal the truth, to solve mysteries and to discover secrets. The same quest for the secret of life is pursued in these apparently very different worlds. While the definitive, masculine world of science may seem opposed to the deliberative, feminine world of self-health, both offer the same fantasies of invincibility. Unlike science, self-health explores the emotions, is concerned with care and nurturance and attracts a majority of women as practitioners and patients; and yet its models of self-fulfilment combine these traditionally feminine qualities with firmly masculine goals. The subject of these discourses of self-health is one which brings together the mystery of femininity with the unifying heroism of masculine achievement. Indeed, the health quest reinvents classic fantasies of masculine heroism (see Chapter 1). These are the fantasies of adventure and of conquest, the fantasies of progress and of success. In crossing into the dangerous territories of the feminine (the unknown, the interior, the mysterious), the subject risks all and surfaces stronger, wiser and more confident of the knowability of such other territory. The curiosity is satisfied and the threat is vanquished. The boundaries of the subject are reaffirmed and autonomy and individuation rehearsed once more. As such, this treacherous and uncharted journey to truth might be seen as a conquering of femininity:

> the enigma that Woman has posed for men is an enigma only because the male subject has construed itself as the subject par excellence. The way (he fantasizes) that Woman differs from him makes her containable within his imagination (reduced to his size) but also produces *her as a mystery for him to master* and decipher within safe or unthreatening borders.
>
> (Grosz, 1994:191, my emphasis)

If femininity is imagined as the dangerous, yet intriguing, space of otherness and of permeability, then the masculine hero can re-emerge from his discoveries as the definitive subject. The secrets of life and of femininity are thus grasped in the course of the masculine journey to invincibility.

And what of the secrets of death? Knowledge promises to elevate us above nature and to protect us from her ultimate demand. The closures that can be controlled by the will defer thoughts of absolute closure, of death. For death is the most unthinkable and unknowable aspect of nature. We are offered the promise that 'in fathoming the secrets of nature, we will fathom the ultimate secrets (and hence gain control) of our own mortality' (Keller, 1990:177). These are the fantasies of transcendence and ultimately of immortality that lie behind the notion that by knowing enough we will never have to face the terror of death. For death can never be known. In being the only certainty, it robs us of any illusion of certainty.

In conquering nature's secrets, do we imagine we can establish an immutable boundary around ourselves that will protect us from death? The threat of collapse of the boundaries between inside and outside, between self and other, 'affront a subject's aspiration toward autonomy and self-identity' (Grosz, 1994:193–4). These fantasies of invincibility are a disavowal of mortality as well as of the threat of the feminine. It is here that femininity and death have been most closely associated with one another in Western discourse, for both serve as tropes for what is 'superlatively enigmatic' (Bronfen, 1992:xiii). As Bronfen argues:

[T]he fear of death translates into the fear of Woman, who, for man, is death. She is constructed as the place of mystery, of not knowing, Freud's 'dark continent', as the site of silence but also of the horrifying void that 'castrates' the living man's sense of wholeness and stability.

(Bronfen, 1992:205)

Both death and femininity are used to represent that which is inexpressible, inscrutable, unmanageable and horrible in Western culture, and, as such, both 'are ascribed the position of alterity' (Bronfen, 1992:xiii). Bronfen suggests that '[a]s Other, Woman serves to define the self, and the lack or excess that is located in the Other functions as an exteriorisation of the self, in respect to both gender and death' (Bronfen, 1992:181).

The desire for order and control, for permanence and immutability, produces a masculine drive to mark out the boundaries of a separate territory: 'femininity and death cause a disorder to stability, mark moments of ambivalence, disruption or duplicity and their eradication produces a recuperation of order, a return to stability' (Bronfen, 1992:xii) The figure of the dead female body in literature and art, Bronfen argues, serves a particular purpose: 'Over her dead body, cultural norms are reconfirmed or secured, whether because the sacrifice of the virtuous, innocent woman serves a social critique and transformation or because a sacrifice of the dangerous woman reestablishes an order that was momentarily suspended due to her presence' (Bronfen, 1992:181). However, this eradication is never fully satisfying and hence has to be rehearsed with obsessive repetition, since:

> the regained order encompasses a shift; that is to say it is never again/no longer entirely devoid of traces of difference. The recuperation is imperfect, the regained stability not safe, the urge for order inhabited by a fascination with disruption and split, and certainty emerging over and out of uncertainty.
>
> (Bronfen, 1992:xii)

The boundary between life and death in contemporary Western culture is thus the source of endless fascination, but only in so far as death might be placed firmly at a distance from the subject once again. Taboos are imposed on death, dying and the dead in order to maintain a clear distinction between life and death, and yet these prohibitions are always partially marked by failure. Cultural practices around death have aimed at policing the prohibition of death that seeks to guarantee an absolute separation between life and death and expels any signs of ambivalence.[2] The horror of diseases such as cancer and HIV and AIDS is precisely that they bring death into life where it finds no legitimate place in this culture (see Chapter 4).

For caught in the circularity of contemporary discourses of health is the endless repetition of a promise, a promise that guarantees certainty. Somewhere, be it in the blood test or the CT scan, be it deep in the Urself of the patient or in the visualisation of healthy cells, somewhere there is a solution. Be it doctors or patients who are legitimised as experts, their burden is to be the guarantor of truth. The shift from one to the other has simply relocated the source of the solution, but not its terms or conditions. For there must be closure. The narrative demands that we rehearse the reassurance of closure, the calming effects of knowing.

WRITING AS A 'SYMPTOM OF NOT DYING'

Metaphors proliferate endlessly around the act of writing: writing as therapy, as healing, as salvation, as redemption, as transcendence, as mourning, as deferral, as reparation.[3] Writing is the most tropic of activities. In telling a story such as this, my motives, as well as my arguments, are bound to be scrutinised. This book might be seen as a symptom, not of disease, but of recovery and return. Inspired by Claire Pajaczkowska's article entitled 'Art as a Symptom of Not Dying', I have come to think of the production of this book through the metaphor of writing as a 'symptom of not dying' (Pajaczkowska, 1995:74). In assessing the value of a book such as this one, it is impossible not to confront the relationship between writing and death. Is my investment in this project a defence against my own mortality: a reassuring fantasy of permanence in textual reproduction? Do I hesitate to finish this book for fear of what might follow? Has it protected me from death? As long as I keep writing I might indulge in a fantasy of control, of authorship of the narrative trajectory of my health, a fantasy that contradicts my knowledge of my own mortality. Or does this piece of writing display a lingering fear of death's imminence: having said my bit, must I prepare to die? When I have imagined symptoms, or when they have been found on medical scans, I have found myself doing a deal with an unnameable being: just let me finish the book, then I'll go peacefully. Or is the writing itself a sign of life: I must still be alive, I am producing – 'I write therefore I am'?

Perhaps I am writing to remember: anamnesic writing. **Anamnesis**: 'a patient's remembrance of the early stages of his [sic] illness' (Chambers Twentieth Century Dictionary, 1974:44). The stories of the illness and the treatments, and the thoughts that surround them, might be better remembered if committed to print. The shock-effects of the traumas require a public recognition to ease their impact. Narrative offers a path out of the pain and a guarantee that it will not be forgotten. This may be the kind of remembering that heals. Restorative writing. But perhaps I am also writing to forget. Narrative places experience firmly in the past. In the telling it is over. With others knowing, am I finally allowed to forget?[4] The stories become more familiar and less personal in their continual reiteration. They no longer 'belong to me' but become part of a repertoire of collective narratives of cancer. Narrative might be characterised as 'a way of *consuming* the past, a way of forgetting' (Jameson, 1984:xii). In the sedimentation of narrative form, 'time ceases to be a support for memory' and the past might be 'consigned to oblivion' (Lyotard, quoted in Jameson, 1984:xii). Or perhaps I am writing to defend myself against the impossibility of remembering. The psyche protects us from the full or lasting knowledge of trauma. But the lost knowledge of trauma is accompanied by other, less welcome, losses: the loss of youth, of predictable temporalities and of ignorance of mortality. Here there is a sense of the impossibility of a return to an easier consciousness, a nostalgic yearning for the time before the illness, a time now romanticised as blissful innocence, the time of the pre-mortal self.

The restaging of temporalities sends shock waves through the conventional patterns of bodily predictability (Hagestad, 1996). The trajectories of 'woman's life cycle' have traditionally been mapped out across her reproductive 'functions'. In the case of endometriosis, Ella Shohat has suggested that hormonal treatments:

produce pseudomenopause, forcing a young woman to proleptic-
ally experience a kind of flash-forward: in her early 20s she is
turned into a simulacrum of youth with the physiology of a woman
in her 40s or 50s trapped inside her . . . Pseudomenopause,
then, is a painful preview of aging and mortality.

(Shohat, 1992:70)

This hybrid figure occupies the space of 'pre/postmenapausal woman'
who is obliged to rethink the meaning of her 'life cycle'. Through the
effects of cancer treatments my body now also tells another story: a
premature ageing, a set of unexpected limits. The body's contours have
been transformed, its surfaces transfigured, its organs reorganised, its
modes of perception realigned. There are losses to be reckoned with.
Perhaps writing offers the pleasure of linearity, a pleasure that no
longer exists in my corporeal narrative; perhaps it compensates for the
loss that prolepsis confers.

Writing may also facilitate mourning. The mourning process is said
to involve 'an identification between living mourners and the newly
deceased in that both are located between the world of the living and
the world of the dead' and this process is only successfully completed
'when the wound death inflicted on a lover's narcissism is healed
because the mourner feels secure in his possession of an internal
"good" image of the lost beloved' (Bronfen, 1992:326–7). The other
has to become part of the self before another love object can be
adopted: 'Successful mourning is repetition as forgetting a lost object
sufficiently to reinvest one's love in another' (Bronfen, 1992:327).
According to this (psychoanalytic) account, writing might be seen as a
form of repetition that facilitates a forgetting. If mourning involves the
incorporation of the lost object, how are we to mourn the lost objects
of health, youth, the belief in immortality; how are we to incorporate
the old self within the new? Temporality is permanently refigured in
cases where the body has been 'unmade' (see Scarry, 1985). Having
prematurely visited the boundary of finitude we wish to reserve for the
future, am I writing to defer the full impact of such knowledge?

Death confers authority upon the narrative and the narrator. Death
seems to promise a 'moment of truth'. One's life flashes past as a series
of images, so we are told. The words from the deathbed take on an
'unforgettable or eternal quality', as the remembered events come
to duplicate the person's life. For Benjamin, the power of such deathbed story-telling implies something about narrating more generally.
Bronfen sums up his argument thus:

All s/he has to tell is imbued with authority and it is this
'authority', arising from the aporia of speaking or writing in the

shadow of death and against it, that lies at the origin of all narratives. Death is the sanction for all that a storyteller might relate. *She or he borrows authority from death.*

(Bronfen, 1992:80, my emphasis)

Such an authority is conferred on cancer narratives by virtue of their subjects. Death has been reckoned with and the stories that emerge bear the weightiness of a promised enlightenment. In this sense many cancer narratives are bound up in the view of death that Foucault identified as emerging in the late eighteenth century, in which individuality and uniqueness are expressed through death. Here, death is seen to afford 'the absolute point of view over life and opening on its truth' (Foucault, 1973, quoted in Bronfen, 1992:76). According to Foucault, whereas the baroque perception of death was as a kind of 'irrevocable and egalitarian gesture', the 'modern' perception began to see death as 'constitutive of singularity' and as the moment in a person's life where 'individuality and absolute rarity could finally be attained' (Bronfen, 1992:77). Narrative authored by 'cancer survivors' offers readers a mode of witnessing the person's uniqueness and special qualities; in nearing death these brave individuals have revealed their best qualities to the world. This culture of exceptionalism echoes Foucault's characterisation of the modern view of death: 'Witnessing death affirms a sense of personal individuality in the survivors, while society resorts to rituals that imply the refusal to accept mortality' (Bronfen, 1992:77). Thus, in this vision of death as the source of knowledge and yet ultimately unthinkable, romance and refusal go hand in hand.

This combination lies at the heart of the appeal of many contemporary cancer narratives. We read them in our search for the truth about life as we simultaneously find ourselves refusing the inevitability of death. In the face of cancer there is a compulsive desire to identify the 'net gain'. Having had cancer, I must be wiser, as well as older, now. This is the romance around death and dying that confers obligations on those who have visited its borders to return with a new understanding, a knowledge that will make life bearable for everyone in the face of much-feared finality. Cancer narratives frequently offer such reassurances. They belong to the 'net-gain' narratives which we like to tell ourselves in the light of misfortunes. The gains somehow soothe the wounds caused by unexpected trauma. This leads to the familiar cliché, 'cancer was the best thing that ever happened to me'. According to this version we become wiser as we approach death. Progress through wisdom. The person who has had cancer is presented as a sagacious messenger whose purpose is to remind everyone of the preciousness and the precariousness of life. The so-called 'survivors' of cancer are seen to possess knowledge of the secrets of life, as well as the secrets of death. They are heroised for their confrontation with death, which is presumed to have enlightened them about how to live life. They are the bearers of knowledge. They have lived to tell the tale.

NOTES

1 HEROES

1 The most useful of these is Reynolds (1988).
2 There are hundreds of books on alternative approaches to cancer. These include: Simonton *et al.* (1978); Chaitow (1983); Kushi (1984); Brohn (1987a, 1987b); Hay (1988, 1989); Charles (1990). Although some of these books are by no means recent publications, they nevertheless continue to inform alternative approaches to cancer treatment in 1990s Britain. They are referred to throughout this book as indicative of the broader trends they continue to represent (see note 6 below for a commentary on the different trends in the United States).

I use the term 'alternative' – rather than 'complementary' or 'holistic' – medicine throughout. I am aware of the debate about these terms and of the arguments about 'complementary' suggesting a more positive tone of collaboration with conventional medicine, but 'alternative' medicine is still widely used to refer to practices such as acupuncture, homeopathy and chiropractice that are by and large still kept relatively separate from biomedical institutions and operate within an 'alternative' (and sometimes oppositional) belief system about health and healing. For a more detailed discussion of these terms, see Sharma (1992).
3 See, for example, Hay (1988, 1989); Siegel (1993). Although there is considerable overlap between this work and the kinds of books mentioned above in note 2, Hay and Siegel in particular tend to be more evangelical and spiritual in tone.
4 For examples of this genre, see in particular Brohn (1987a) and Charles (1990).
5 Medical misdiagnosis is an integral part of the narrative in Butler and Rosenblum (1991). Speculation about the causative effects of radiation are part of the mother's story of her son's death from leukaemia in Renouf (1993). These types of narrative tend to be much less concerned with heroising the person with cancer and offer fuller explorations of the despair and futility of the suffering involved.
6 For an explicit example of the use of the cancer hero narrative, see Chapter 1, 'From victims to heroes by force of circumstance', in Kfir and Slevin (1991). The heroisation of the cancer patient and the progress narrative that informs such a construction continues to pervade the cancer subcultures of 1990s Britain. This version of living with cancer is not only repeated in influential books on the subject from both the United States and Britain (see notes 2, 3 and 4 above) but also informs many alternative approaches

246

to cancer, including some of those practiced at the Bristol Cancer Help Clinic and at numerous alternative health centres throughout Britain. Thus, I base my generalisations in this chapter on a *cultural narrative* that I encountered over and over again, not only in print, but also in practice. As a cancer patient in 1990s Britain, it was the most prevalent way of fighting the illness that I came across. Moreover, it continues to be a conceptualisation that informs everyday exchanges and media reports about cancer and its 'survivors'. However, I am grateful to Arthur Frank for his thoughtful suggestions about the national and historical specificity of this particular cancer narrative. According to Frank, more recent publications in the United States are indicative of a move away from these earlier forms of heroisation; his counter-examples to my general claims include: Wilber (1991); Lerner (1994); Dossey (1996); Sharp (1996). I do not believe such publications have had a major impact on the heroic cancer cultures of Britain yet, but, if Frank is right, and they are signs of a significant shift in the United States towards a different and less monolithic kind of story-telling, then perhaps similar changes may follow in the British context in due course. For a detailed sociological analysis of different forms of cancer narrative in the United States, see Frank (1995).

7 For further details on changes in the National Health System in Britain, see Robinson and Le Grand (1994).

8 The burden of caring in the home has traditionally fallen to women; see Finch and Groves (1983). The cutbacks in spending on the public health service in Britain and elsewhere have doubtless increased the demands on women as informal carers.

9 There is a vast critical literature on narrative in English literature, film and cultural studies. For an introduction to theories of narrative, see Rimmon-Kenan (1989).

   After writing this chapter I discovered a study of collective illness narratives which is highly pertinent to my argument here: see Frank (1995). See also Frank (1991).

10 For a discussion of the ways in which this basic narrative formula operates across popular film genres, see Neale (1980).

11 For a discussion of the place of narrative in the way we understand 'self-identity' in late modernity see Giddens (1991), especially Chapter 3.

12 The distinction between the public and the private in representations of the self is discussed in Derek Duncan's forthcoming study of autobiographical writing by gay men diagnosed as HIV positive. Duncan examines the autobiographies of Monette and Jarman, suggesting that 'like auto-biography, AIDS insists on the public significance of private behaviour', and that 'bringing the private act of recollection into the public domain transforms a potentially solipsistic practice into an empowering political and collective challenge'. See Duncan (1998, forthcoming).

13 This refers to the subheading of Duncan (1998, forthcoming); see note 12 above.

14 This argument is made by Duncan who draws on José Arroyo's chapter 'Death, Desire and Identity: The Political Unconscious of "New Queer Cinema"' (Arroyo, 1993). In particular, Duncan develops Arroyo's suggestion that a queer cinematic aesthetic might be characterised by 'a deep structural anxiety regarding narrative temporality, an anxiety . . . that results from the knowledge of AIDS and of its effects on the body' (Duncan, 1998, forthcoming). Here, Duncan is making a specific argument about the

connections between sexual identity and health which do not parallel cancer; however, his analysis is suggestive of the ways in which illness more generally disrupts narrative coherence in relation to the projection of identities.

15 Gunhild Hagestad has written persuasively about temporal changes connected with experiences of cancer. She writes: 'Critical illness not only presents you with the issue of finitude, but more importantly, it threatens the very foundations of time structuring by removing you from life's comforting rhythms. It becomes a struggle not to *fall out of time*' (Hagestad, 1996:205).

16 See Pete Boss's examination of how the interior of the body has become the site of horror in contemporary cinema, in Boss (1986). See also Brophy (1986) and Tudor (1989).

17 Boss cites films such as *The Manitou* (1977) which deal with fears about the loss of control of the human body (1986:22).

18 Sigourney Weaver stands out as a notable exception in her heroic performance in the *Alien* films. For a discussion of the gendering of cinematic heroics, see Tasker (1993). The relationship between the heroine and the monster in the *Alien* films is discussed in Creed (1993); for a discussion of this connection, see Chapter 3.

19 See Kfir and Slevin (1991).

20 There are numerous success stories about 'conquering cancer', including Brohn (1987a), Hay (1988), and Charles (1990).

21 Oncogenes have been a source of great fascination in recent media presentations of cancer. BRCA1 (the breast cancer gene) in particular has received widespread media coverage; see, for example, 'Genetic Key To Mastectomy Risk' in *The Guardian*, Tuesday 7 December 1993, p.17. Oncogenes are considered to be the genetic switches responsible for changes in cellular reproduction associated with the onset of cancer. Research into oncogenes now comprises a rapidly expanding field of genetic research.

22 To quote this claim more fully: 'the cancer establishment ... tells you over and over again that "resistance is futile". The first radiologist I saw, a woman, called me a non-cooperator when I asked questions about the treatments and warned that bad things would happen to me if I remained militant' (Martindale, 1994:9).

23 For a discussion of the 'defended self' in immune system discourse, see Chapter 10, in Haraway (1991).

24 Critical analysis of 'enterprise culture' in Britain can be found in Franklin *et al.* (1991) and in Keat and Abercrombie (1991).

25 There are important exceptions to the more dominant linear progress narratives which heroise the patient. One personal account of the experience of having cancer that does confront disillusionment and despair is by Angie Wilkie, who writes about the difficulties she had with friends and family in terms of their response to her illness (Wilkie, 1993). Sandra Butler and Barbara Rosenblum's 'dialogue diaries' also counter the cancer patient as hero model (Butler and Rosenblum, 1991). On a more philosophical level, Gillian Rose writes about living with cancer in her extraordinary memoir which begins with the epitaph: 'Keep your mind in hell and despair not' (Rose, 1995). Arthur Frank begins his autobiographical account of having cancer, *At the Will of the Body*, by resisting the typical hero narrative; he states: 'What I have to tell relates no cures I have discovered or medical

miracles. I got sick, went through the prescribed treatments, engaged in my share of obnoxious behavior, managed to cope, and lived to tell the tale' (1991:4–5). I am grateful to Arthur Frank for bringing to my attention recent publications in the United States which move away from the survivor as hero model, such as Grealy (1994); see also note 6 above. For an analysis of what he calls the 'chaos narratives' of contemporary experiences of illness, see Frank (1995).

26 I am referring here to the work in Caruth (1995). In her excellent introduction to this collection, Cathy Caruth suggests that in cases of post-traumatic stress disorder, 'the pathology consists . . . solely in the *structure of its experience* or reception: the event is not assimilated or experienced fully at the time, but only belatedly, in its repeated *possession* of the one who experiences it. To be traumatized is precisely to be possessed by an image or event' (Caruth, 1995:4–5).

27 Caruth argues that 'trauma is not experienced as a mere repression or defense, but as a temporal delay that carries the individual beyond the shock of the first moment. The trauma is a repeated suffering of the event, but also a continual leaving of its site' (Caruth, 1995:10). This suggests that the re-experiencing of the event might carry with it what Laub calls a 'collapse of witnessing' with regard to the Holocaust: 'history was taking place with no witness: it was also the very circumstance of *being inside the event* that made unthinkable the very notion that a witness could exist . . . The historical imperative to bear witness could essentially *not be met during the actual occurrence*' (Laub, 1995:66,68).

28 For Caruth, this 'impossibility of knowing that first constituted' the event results in a necessity of a 'new kind of listening, the witnessing, precisely, *of impossibility*' (Caruth, 1995:10).

29 For a discussion of the public/private distinction mobilised in relation to definitions of trauma, see Laura Brown's article on sexual abuse, 'Not Outside the Range: One Feminist Perspective on Psychic Trauma'. Brown challenges the way in which post-traumatic stress disorder is readily accepted in instances of public trauma such as 'war and genocide . . . natural disasters, vehicle crashes, boats sinking in the freezing ocean' in which their 'victims are rarely blamed for these events' (Brown, 1995:101–2), and yet in cases of sexual abuse the category is contested. The example she cites at the beginning of the chapter is of a woman suing her step-father for repetitive and continuous abuse. In court there was doubt about whether the woman could have PTS since the abuse had not been 'outside the range of human experience' (given how widespread it is), a phrase which is used as a defining criterion (Brown, 1995:100).

30 Cancer support groups can be found in most towns and cities in the United Kingdom. These can be contacted through the Bristol Cancer Help Centre (Tel. 01179 809505) and Back-Up (freephone 0800 181199).

31 AFP stands for alpha fetoprotein, a substance that teratomas release into the blood. AFP levels thus produce a relatively reliable way of monitoring tumour activity and even cell division at a microscopic level.

32 Alternative practitioner friends have offered numerous accounts of different kinds of conservatism within their alternative medical organisations; in particular the raising of feminist and lesbian and gay issues has often met with a great deal of resistance.

33 For a discussion of this relationship, see Duncan's analysis of the auto-biographical writing of Monette and Jarman: 'Monette writes to repair and

offset his loss [the death of his lover], and the resulting text is structured round this memorialising, redemptive energy, to produce an elegant elegy and epitaph. As he concedes: "writing about AIDS was a small measure of power over the nightmare"'; this is contrasted somewhat with Jarman's approach which is 'more defiant and more inclusive of others: "before I finish I intend to celebrate our corner of Paradise, the part of the garden the Lord forgot to mention"' (Duncan, 1998, forthcoming).

34 Duncan looks at both Monette's and Jarman's writing in relation to Leo Bersani's critique of the 'culture of redemption' (Bersani, 1990, quoted in Duncan, 1998, forthcoming). For Duncan, both writers seem 'to share the same redemptive aesthetic and belief in the restorative powers of writing. Bersani attacks the belief in the restorative or moral function of art, on the grounds that it devalues not only art but also the historical experience thought to motivate it. He writes: "Claims for the high morality of art may conceal a deep horror of life. And yet nothing perhaps is more frivolous than that horror, since it carries within it the conviction that, because of the achievements of culture, the disasters of history somehow do not matter. Everything can be made up, can be made over again"' (Bersani, 1990 quoted in Duncan, 1998, forthcoming).

35 Gillian Rose has proposed that writing might be reconsidered through the religious trope of sacrament (Rose, personal correspondence).

36 The function of the category of 'experience' and its relationship to personal and theoretical writing has been widely investigated within feminism. See in particular: de Lauretis (1984, 1987, 1988); Fuss (1989); Miller (1991); Stanley (1991); Probyn (1993); Braidotti (1991, 1994).

37 For a recent discussion of the difficulties of writing about the 'self' in feminist work, see Probyn (1993). Attempting to explore the relationships between ways of thinking and ways of being a gendered subject, Probyn writes: 'As one way of placing the self, I argue that it should be seen as a mode of holding together the epistemological and the ontological. I want to emphasize the importance of ontological moments of recognition – moments when I realize my gendered being' (Probyn, 1993:4).

38 The relationships between the categories of 'experience', 'the self' and 'knowledge' are explored throughout Probyn (1993).

39 For an analysis of the role of confession in autobiographical writing, see Felski (1989) and Wilson (1989). See also Foucault (1979:59–62) on the ways in which confession is a central aspect of the construction of the speaking subject in contemporary culture.

40 The distinction between 'testimony' and 'confession' is explored by Gregg Bordowitz's chapter 'Dense Moments' (1994). For Bordowitz, the term 'testimony' is more appropriate than 'confession' for his autobiographical account of living with HIV/AIDS because: 'The testimony is the story of a survivor. The confession is the story of a sinner.' He also claims that 'through testimony one bears witness to one's own experiences to one's self. Through confession one relinquishes responsibility for bearing witness to and for oneself' (1994:25). Arthur Frank offers a detailed discussion of the 'ethics of testimony' in his account of illness narratives in Frank (1995).

41 I am indebted to Adrian Heathfield for suggesting these connections between writing and immortality to me in relation to this project. See Adrian Heathfield, 'Facing the Other: Performance, Encounter and Death' in 'Identity and Representation in Contemporary Performance' (unpublished PhD thesis forthcoming, University of Bristol); see also Phelan (1996).

2 METAPHORS

1 For further details, see Gershenson and Rutledge (1987).

2 The power relations between alternative health practitioners and their patients are discussed in Sharma (1992) and Budd and Sharma (1994).

3 Homophobia refers to a fear of same-sex desire that leads to discrimination against lesbians and gay men. For critical discussion of homophobia see Weeks (1977) and Kitzinger (no date). For contemporary debates on lesbian and gay cultures, see Abelove *et al.* (1993) and Bristow and Wilson (1993).

4 Wilkinson and Kitzinger (1994) are similarly critical of Hay and other self-help advocates in their work on breast cancer. For a personal critique of these kind of approaches to cancer, see Arthur Frank's chapter, 'Comforters and Accusers' in Frank, 1991:108–14.

5 One writer explores these connections in his book of the title *Worried Sick: Our Troubled Quest for Wellness* (Barsky, 1988).

6 See Richardson (1987); Watney (1987); and Patton (1990).

7 Some gay critics have argued that Sontag's rhetoric itself blames gay men for contracting HIV/AIDS; see Miller (1993).

8 Biology and medicine have been identified as a form of cultural knowledge by a number of feminists including Birke (1986); Martin (1987, 1994); Haraway (1989b, 1991); Franklin and McNeil (1991); Braidotti (1994); and Lupton (1994).

9 Miller (1993) claims that militaristic metaphors are crucial sources of empowerment to gay men fighting homophobia and campaigning for better health care for HIV/AIDS patients.

10 This subheading is a quotation taken from Foucault (1973:xi).

11 Foucault extends his elaboration of this fusion of vision, language and objects in *The Order of Things* (1970). Here, he restricts his analysis to medical knowledge, but what he finds is the basis for a positivism that informs beliefs in scientific rationality and objectivity which continue to inform much social as well as medical thought in contemporary culture. The publication dates are misleading in so far as *The Order of Things* was originally written in French after *The Birth of the Clinic.*

12 For a discussion of the 'objectivity debates' in science, see Harding (1986).

13 The taken-for-grantedness of biomedical perspectives has been thoroughly challenged by feminists; see, for example, Keller (1985); Oakley (1993) and Lupton (1994).

14 The mode of perception that characterises the biomedical gaze has been situated within the growing preoccupation with visuality in twentieth-century Western culture; see Jordanova (1989), Bruno (1992); *camera obscura* 28, 29 (1992); Braidotti (1994); and Cartwright (1995).

15 For an analysis of 'body horror' films, see Boss (1986) and Brophy (1986). See also Creed (1993) for a discussion of the place of femininity in horror films. This argument is explored more fully in Chapter 3.

16 For a sociological consideration of stigmatisation as the management of 'spoiled identities', see Goffman (1964).

17 Debates continue to proliferate in contemporary critical theory about the exact mechanisms of the numerous formations of metaphor and their function. For a more detailed discussion of the work of Lyotard and Lacan in this context, see Quick (1995). I am grateful to Andrew Quick for drawing my attention to recent work in the area, in particular to Phelan (1993).

3 MONSTERS

1 Research into how taboos operate around same-sex relationships has shown the high use of euphemism as ways of discussing these relationships: see, for example, Harvey (1997).

2 Recent research has shown that some women who might generally be considered to be in a 'lesbian' relationship still find it difficult to say the word 'lesbian'; see, for example, Angela Green, doctoral research in progress, Cheltenham and Gloucester College of Higher Education.

3 The term a 'friend of Dorothy's' refers to gay men because of their subcultural attachment to Judy Garland who played Dorothy in the film *The Wizard of Oz*; see Dyer (1986) for a discussion of this form of subcultural fandom. DDP is shorthand for 'definite dyke potential'.

4 For a sociological analysis of the concept of 'stigma', see Goffman (1964).

5 For a historical analysis of homosexual politics and questions of 'visibility', see Weeks (1977).

6 For a discussion of lesbian and gay theories of identity categories, see Butler (1990); Fuss (1991); McIntosh (1993).

7 There are numerous studies comparing risks and prevention strategies in different national contexts; see, for example, Vessey and Gray (1985).

8 Performativity refers to the ways in which some kinds of speech are also acts, such as 'I thee wed', or 'I forgive'; see Austin (1962). This idea of 'speech acts' has been extended as a way to think about how gender and sexuality categories might be considered within a performative frame; see Butler (1990, 1993) and Sedgwick (1990).

9 This argument (as does Sedgwick's in the previous paragraph) draws upon Foucault's challenge to the 'repressive hypothesis'. In his work on the history of sexuality, Foucault draws attention to the ways in which modes of regulation are productive of the categories they seek to control. Thus, for Foucault, prohibition and production go hand in hand. See Foucault (1979).

10 One challenge, for example, has come from a sociological position that disputes generalised claims such as 'death is the one great taboo of our age', since this proclamation is so prevalent as to undermine its taboo status (Walter, 1992:33). Another study shows that far from being invisible, hidden, or restricted solely to the private, death is widely represented by the media, for example, who 'are generating a very public discourse of death' (Walter *et al.*, 1995:593). Similarly, it has been argued that 'far from living in a "death denying" society, open awareness and acknowledgement of dying is a script particularly suited to the conditions of late modernity, where the project of self-awareness is a central preoccupation' (Seale, 1995:610–11). All these writers criticise the use of the concept of taboo to describe our contemporary attitude to death because of evidence that proves its presence rather than its absence. But I use the term here in its more pyschoanalytic and contradictory sense, to refer not just to the prohibition, repression, denial and silencing that takes place around these categories, but precisely because I understand it to also refer to the generative dynamics of such cultural processes.

11 A second challenge to the use of the term taboo has appeared from an entirely different theoretical location. This critique is made on the grounds of a poststructuralist suspicion of the psychoanalytic theory of repression that informs the idea of taboo. Butler, for example, cautions us against

a model of a repressive or prohibitive culture that may ignore its productive and constitutive dimensions (Butler, 1990:91).

12 I am grateful to Sarah Franklin for pointing out the cultural and historical specificity of this 'popular imagination' in relation to beliefs about sexuality and disease. What I explore here are the fears generated in contemporary British culture with a very specific set of 'post-Darwinian' ideas about 'nature', 'biology', 'reproduction' and 'life'; see Haraway (1991); Strathern (1992) and Duden (1993).

13 In what follows I thus write from within the many homophobic discourses I have encountered in this culture. What is produced is a condensation of common-sense views of lesbianism which express fear, dread, disgust and contempt with which I am especially familiar from a British context. These may seem less familiar to readers outside this very specific location. In entering such forms of rhetoric I am aware that some might feel there is a danger of reinforcing these homophobic beliefs; instead, I hope that my exploration challenges their legitimacy and hatred while also acknow- ledging the power of their grip in this culture.

14 For a discussion of 'AIDS narratives', see Duncan (1998, forthcoming); for a discussion of the homophobia surrounding representations of AIDS in the 1980s, see Watney (1987).

15 Images of lesbians in mainstream cinema have been characterised by an emphasis on their predatory role and lascivious sexual appetites; see Dyer, (1977, 1990); Weiss (1992); Wilton (1995).

16 See Franklin (1995) for an analysis of the narrativity of the reproductive telos and its relationship to heterosexual romance.

17 This quotation is from the film *Desert Hearts* (Deitch, 1985), and is Cay's response to Vivian's question: 'Does everything have to unravel so quickly?'

18 For a discussion of the construction of homosexuals as 'the enemy within' see Stacey (1991) and Smith (1995).

19 For a detailed consideration of the problems with Kristeva's location of the sources of the abject within the maternal body, see Butler (1990:79–92).

20 I use Kristeva's work here to explore homophobia, aware of the ironies of so doing, given the criticisms that have been made of her writing on homosexuality, which has been widely challenged by those seeking to expose the heterosexual presumptions of psychoanalytic theory (Traub, 1991). In particular, Kristeva's theories of sexual difference have been criticised for the ways in which she places female homosexuality on the side of the semiotic, the maternal and psychosis: 'The key to Kristeva's view of the psychotic nature of homosexuality is to be understood . . . in her acceptance of the structuralist assumption that heterosexuality is coextensive with the founding of the Symbolic' (Butler, 1990:84).

21 For a discussion of genetic theories of 'proto-oncogenes', see Varmus and Weinberg (1993:67–100).

22 This phrase was coined by Jerry Falwell, the moral majority advocate in the United States.

23 See Franklin *et al.* (1998, forthcoming) for a discussion of the increasing cultural significance of the concept of 'life itself'.

24 This term is relative, however, and contested, and scientists disagree about whether any cell is ever 'undifferentiated'. I am grateful to Aylish Wood for her patience in explaining many of the theories to me. See also Varmus and Weinberg (1993).

25 Adrienne Rich's notion of 'compulsory heterosexuality' was first used in her 1980 article and has had a major impact on feminist theory since then (Rich,

1980). Judith Butler draws on this and on Monique Wittig's concept of the 'heterosexual contract' to develop her arguments around the 'heterosexual matrix' (Butler, 1990).

26 Kristeva sees the skin as a particularly significant part of the body in its role as interface between inside and outside; she writes of the skin that it is 'the essential if not the initial boundary of biological and psychic individuation' (Kristeva, 1982:101).

27 The theme of the ghostly or apparitional positioning of the lesbian figure in this culture has been explored in White (1991) and Castle (1993).

28 The idea of pregnant women being more than one person and less than two in such a way that troubles the logic of patriarchal law and science has been discussed in Franklin (1991).

29 See Chapter 2, this volume, Braidotti (1994); and Grosz (1994). For a discussion of 'the female grotesque', see Russo (1994). For a range of essays on 'deviant bodies' more generally, see Terry and Urla (1995). Debates about grotesque and deviant bodies clearly raise issues of 'disability'; there is a vast literature on the politics of disability within sociology and social policy. For a discussion of the feminist politics around disability see Begum (1992).

30 See Phelan's discussion of Sherman's work (Phelan, 1993:60–70).

31 Judith Williamson has written on the explorations of femininity in Sherman's work (Williamson, 1986). I also draw here on her public lecture accompanying Sherman's exhibition, 'Possession', at Manchester City Art Gallery, on 15 October 1995.

32 To say that lesbianism is only a poor copy of heterosexuality might imply that heterosexuality has the status of an original; but as Butler argues, heterosexuality is itself simply an imitative copy that endlessly reinvents itself (1991).

4 BODIES

1 Oliver Sacks discusses this phenomenon in his case studies in *The Man Who Mistook His Wife for a Hat* (1986); kinaesthesia is also a concept central to the body philosophy of the Alexander Technique; see Gelb (1987).

2 Childbirth narratives are another example of stories that are told by subjects who may have absented themselves from the event due to the pain and trauma. Discussions with women about their experience of childbirth often involves a witnessing or recounting by the partner who was present at the event. For a discussion of childbirth narrative, see Cosslett (1991).

3 The primal scene fantasy refers to the Freudian theory that the child imagines itself to have been present at its own conception; see Freud (1908, 1925).

4 Kuhn uses the term 'memory flashes' for such moments in her work on memory and photography (1995).

5 In a typically dualistic (Cartesian) model of the mind/body, it is generally the mind which has been associated with the functions of memory and not the body. Scarry (1985) offers an account of how the body might be conceived as 'remembering'.

6 For further discussion, see Chapter 5, Cartwright (1995); and *camera obscura* nos 28, 29 (1992).

7 For feminist critiques and appraisals of Foucault's work, see Diamond and Quinby (1988); McNay (1992); Ramazanoglu (1993).

8 For a detailed historical account of the rise of the medical professions, see

Stacey (1988) and, with specific reference to nursing, see Witz (1992). The loss of faith in medical professional expertise is discussed in Chapter 7.

9 See Stacey's discussion of the history of midwifery (Stacey, 1988:90–1).

10 As I discussed in Chapter 1 (see note 2), I use the work of Simonton *et al.* (1978) as examples of these models of mind and body, despite their being rather dated within some areas of alternative cancer care because I argue that they continue to inform many contemporary practices I encountered during my treatment in Britain in the early 1990s. I am grateful to Arthur Frank for discussions on this point, and while I recognise that there are more recent reworkings of some of these ideas, especially in the United States, many of the books I came across and practices I encountered were clearly still using the Simonton model; this was certainly true of my visits to Bristol Cancer Help Clinic, many conversations with alternative practitioners, such as the Reiki healer (see Chapter 2) and can be found in Brohn (1987a, 1987b); Charles (1990); and much work influenced by Hay (1988, 1989).

11 Hysteria is etymologically derived from the Greek word meaning womb; hence 'women being much more liable than men to this disorder, it was originally thought to be due to a disturbance of the uterus and its functions' (*Oxford English Dictionary*, 1993:807).

12 Freud's work has of course been extensively criticised by feminist theorists. For examples of the 'feminism and psychoanalysis' debates, see Mitchell (1974); Gallop (1982); Sayers (1986); Rose (1986); Steedman (1986); Brennan (1989); Wright (1992); de Lauretis (1994); McClintock (1995).

13 The changing models of the body are analysed in Scheper-Hughes and Lock (1987); Braidotti (1994); and Grosz (1994).

14 For a discussion of the racialisation of the body and the construction of otherness through representations of the body, see Gilman (1992).

15 Facial types have been linked to personality types; for example, in the discourses of female stardom in Hollywood cinema, see Levin (1970).

16 The Channel 4 series *Without Walls* devoted a whole programme to challenging the ways in which Freudian psychoanalytic theory has influenced twentieth-century thinking and has become the religion of a godless society (1995).

17 Cenaesthesis refers to a general sense of existence arising from the sum of the bodily impressions (as distinct from the definite sensations of special senses); kinaesthesis is more associated with movement and the bodily perception of the sensations that accompany voluntary motion.

18 There are heated debates in cancer research about the use of 'Laetrile'; see, for example, Chaitow (1983:129–46).

19 Alternative medical treatments are increasingly discussed in biomedical journals such as *The Lancet*, the *British Medical Journal* and *The New England Journal of Medicine*.

20 See, for example Lorch *et al.* (1990/1).

21 There are two main types of acupuncture practised in Britain, each of which has its own traditions, philosophy and training programmes: Five Elements and Seven Principles; see Fulder (1984) for details.

22 For a critique of the model of the healthy body as one with balanced energy, see Coward (1989:64).

5 VISIONS

1 A recent public example of the before-and-after photo-technique can be found in the feature on Chelsea Clinton that shows a previously plump,

gawky, camera-shy girl, with mousy hair and an Alice-band, transformed into 'The Spice Girl in the White House . . . the toast of New York', a process described as the 'babe-ification of Chelsea Clinton'. See 'Real Life', *The Independent on Sunday*, 9 March 1997.

2 The disavowal of death in contemporary Western cultures means that it is both denied and yet ever-present. See Chapters 1 and 8, this volume; see also Bronfen (1992); Baudrillard (1993); Heathfield (PhD thesis forthcoming).

3 The high rates of increase in cancer have been widely documented. For example, 'It is estimated that a U.S. woman's odds of getting breast cancer now stand at one in eight, double the odds of 1940' (Cartwright, 1995:160); for comparable national statistics, see Vessey and Gray (1985).

4 Science is presented for public consumption through media representations, both fictional and documentary in form. There are a number of 'serious' regular British television programmes dedicated to representing science and technology, such as *Horizon*, and *Tomorrow's World*, as well as series on particular topics, such as *Cracking the Code* (on genetics) and *The Body in Question* presented by the media/medical figure, Jonathan Miller. Hollywood cinema also has a long history of fictional constructions of science and scientists (see Tudor, 1989). Notable recent examples include *Jurassic Park* (Spielberg, 1992) and *Species* (Donaldson, 1995), both of which include explanatory sections on scientific 'facts' within the narrative (see Franklin, 1997 forthcoming).

5 Feminist analyses of popular representations of reproduction include Martin (1987, 1992); Petchesky (1987); Franklin (1990); Newman (1990); Duden (1993).

6 For an analysis of the gendering of hero narratives in contemporary scientific discourse, see Franklin (1995).

7 This is not to suggest that people universally absorb all these values without question; indeed, Martin herself offers an ethnographic study of how the ideas are taken up by a group of young people actively engaging with, and challenging, the assumptions of Lennart Nilsson's *The Miracle of Life*, a video replete with many of the egg-and-sperm metaphors outlined above. However, the numerous and critical interactions with popular texts representing scientific knowledge do not undermine the fact that this shift in scientific discourse has occurred and is significant to the forms of cultural knowledge it produces (Martin, 1992).

8 A number of other studies have examined metaphorical constructions of the cell in connection with notions of the self (see, for example, Spanier, 1991) and of society more generally (see, for example, Weindling, 1981).

9 For a detailed discussion of Foucault's work on visibility as a guiding principle in biomedical knowledges about the human body, see Chapter 2.

10 Feminist work on gendered perceptions in visual culture include Petchesky (1987); Jordanova (1989); Mulvey (1989); Franklin (1991); Cartwright (1995). See also two special issues of *camera obscura* (28 and 29).

11 See Franklin, in Franklin *et al.* (1998, forthcoming).

12 The debate about the concept of 'foetal personhood' is one particularly well-developed case study where feminists working on science and technology have investigated the impact of visual images on public debates about women's rights. See, for example, Petchesky (1987); Franklin (1991); Hartouni (1992); Stabile (1992); Duden (1993); and Franklin and McNeil (1993). See also McNeil and Litt (1992) for a critical discussion of 'foetal alcohol syndrome'.

13 Both Cartwright and Shohat, for example, argue that in offering critical

studies of the visual medical technologies (of breast radiography and video laparoscopy respectively) they are not necessarily anti-technology (Cartwright, 1995:169), and Shohat (1992:84).

14 These models of the self and the other are reminiscent of object relations theory in which the individual psyche contains internalised versions of a number of 'others'; see Mitchell (1986) and Benjamin (1990).

15 See Lacan (1977). For discussions of the mirror stage in relation to cultural representation, see Williamson (1978); Coward (1984); and Wright (1992).

6 SELVES

1 See Chapter 1 for a discussion of heroism and cancer narratives. Many popular books on cancer address the person with cancer through the discourse of heroism; see for example, Kfir and Slevin (1991). See also note 6 from Chapter 1, this volume, for a discussion of non-heroic cancer narratives.

2 References to the increase in rates of cancer are detailed in note 3 in Chapter 5.

3 This idea that cancer cannot develop in a healthy body is widely promoted in self-health literatures on the subject; see, for example, Siegel (1986, 1993); Hay (1988, 1989); and Charles (1990).

4 The imperative to make decisions in relation to the calculated risks of getting different types of cancer is proliferating. While screening for some cancers may pick up early signs of the disease in some cases, the results are often ambiguous and produce a number of difficult 'choices' about treatments and preventions. Some women are increasingly opting for mastectomies as a preventive measure against breast cancer.

5 Psychoanalytic theories of gendered subjectivity have typically argued that *individuation* is represented as masculine and *relationality* as feminine; despite variations in the explanations for this, a number of feminists have used these arguments to explore the patriarchal value ascribed to the former over the latter: see Chodorow (1978); Irigaray (1985a, 1985b); and Benjamin (1990).

6 Feminine relationality is not just a psychic formation, but is also integral to patriarchal social divisions of labour. The duties and obligations that women have traditionally performed in caring for others (mainly men, children and elderly relatives) are a central part of the sexual division of labour. Feminists have criticised the forms of naturalisation and legitimation of women's unpaid and unrecognised work, otherwise known as the 'labours of love'. For details of the feminist challenges to such inequalities, see Walby (1990).

7 Cancer Care in Lancaster (UK) is not unusual in this. In most alternative health centres women make up by far the highest proportion of practitioners. For further details, see Sharma (1992).

8 There are numerous studies which show that women continue to perform a very high percentage of domestic labour (paid and unpaid); for details, see Walby (1990).

9 For a discussion of this term 'anamnesic' in relation to cultural change more generally, see Appignanesi (1989:13).

10 Celia Lury has referred to this process in a rather different context; see Lury (1997).

11 The heroic narratives of popular culture have been widely debated by

feminist critics. For a discussion of classic narrative trajectories of Hollywood cinema, see Cook (1985) and Chapter 1, this volume.

12 For clear and accessible introductions to the feminist debates about sexuality, violence and reproduction, see chapters on these subjects in Richardson and Robinson (1993).

7 RESPONSIBILITIES

1 For a critical analysis of the historical emergence of the medical profession see Turner (1987) and Stacey (1988) and for specific reference to the ambiguous status of the nursing 'profession', see Witz (1992). For details of the ways in which women have continued to be excluded from power in the hierarchies of the medical profession see also Doyal (1994).

2 Stacey (1988) discusses the forms of self-protection that have been built into the structures and ethics of the medical profession.

3 During 1995 there were a number of controversies reported in the British media concerning the refusal of treatment to patients with lung disease over a certain age who had smoked for a given number of years.

4 Studies have shown that patients who refuse 'to conform to the clinical regime' or to 'accept the dependency that sickness implies' are generally labelled as problems by nursing staff (Kelly and May, 1982:148–9). Rigid classification of appropriate patient behaviour tends to discourage the expression of emotions such as fear, distress or anger and to produce a depersonalised patient ideal (Lorber, 1975). Isobel Menzies's study uses Kleinian psychoanalytic theory to explain nurses' need to depersonalise patients and to deny the significance of the individual. Patients are often referred to by bed number or by type of illness in order to protect nurses from the high levels of anxiety that might follow from personal attachments to patients (Menzies, 1988).

5 There are numerous instances of patronising exchanges between male doctors and female patients; in one example cited in Oakley, a doctor's response to a patient's dissatisfaction with her diagnosis was as follows: 'I will tell you what's wrong with you, I will tell you what your symptoms are, and I will tell you what to do. I am the doctor and you will kindly not forget that fact' (quoted in Oakley, 1993:32). Women's complaints about these alienating experiences at the hands of male medical professionals have been documented in feminist research in this area; see, for example, Miles (1991).

6 The feminist strategy of demystifying medical expertise about women's bodies by collective information sharing is exemplified by publications such as *Our Bodies, Ourselves* (Boston Women's Health Collective, 1976); I am grateful to Maureen McNeil for pointing out to me that this group originally called itself 'The Doctors Group', drawing attention to its intention of highlighting the politics of medical knowledge. The title of the book *Seizing Our Bodies* (Dreifus, 1977) similarly typifies the early feminist strategies of challenging the authority of expertise about women's bodies. The designation of menstruation, pregnancy, childbirth and the menopause as medical concerns has meant that women have considerably more contact with the medical profession than men. In particular, feminist work has challenged the medicalisation of women's bodies and questioned the division of labour and of knowledge that such expertise has re-

produced; see Ehrenreich and English (1974, 1979); Miles (1991); Roberts (1992); Oakley (1993); Doyal (1994).

7 The collectivity of the politics around 'women's health' has been contested from its inception and issues of difference, specificity and context have been increasingly widely debated within this area, as in all areas, of feminism (see Hockey, 1993). Gender inequalities are cross-cut and refigured through their intersection with class, race, sexuality and national and international divisions; see Doyal (1979, 1994); White (1990); Ahmad (1993); Graham (1993); Wilkinson and Kitzinger (1994).

8 Unlike many of the individualistic self-health strategies criticised in Chapter 5, feminists have attempted to connect individual empowerment with challenges to structural inequality; the individual woman is thus generally understood to be located within broader cultural and social practices and institutions.

9 It should, however, be noted that in one speech, Tony Blair, the leader of Labour Party, also relied heavily on the discourse of individal responsibility to define a set of policies which he called 'new Labour': 'At the heart of all these policies is our basic belief that with rights come responsibilities. That we have duties to each other as well as to ourselves. In the past we were too concerned about the rights to worry about the responsibilities' (*Sunday Express*, 7 January 1996, p.22).

10 For critical debates about 'Thatcherism' see Hall (1988); Jessop and Bonnett (1988); and Franklin *et al.* (1991). For an account of the place of Thatcherite discourses within the cultures of alternative medicine, see Coward (1989).

11 The term 'patriarchal individualism' is used in the feminist analysis of Thatcherism in Franklin *et al.* (1991:201–3).

12 The 'new oppressed' is a term coined by Maureen McNeil in her chapter, 'Making and Not Making the Difference: The Gender Politics of Thatcherism' in Franklin *et al.* (1991:221–40).

13 For details of the changes in state support for the National Health Service in Britain, see Jones (1994) and Robinson and LeGrand (1994).

14 For an account of women's informal, unpaid caring work, see Finch and Groves (1983) and Walby (1990).

15 Although there are numerous reasons for such a loss of faith, it must be noted that changes in perceptions of medical authority in Britain coincided with the increase in numbers of Black people working in the health service. The image of the doctor as saviour or the nurse as angel came up against racist responses to black people entering the health service during the postwar period. These fantasies of doctors and nurses as the heroes and heroines of health combined fantasies of science as the salvation of humanity with the notion of white culture as the benevolent patron of the developing world. Both rely heavily on the belief that Western science and technology represented progress and would benefit global development and modernisation.

16 This broader cultural change might be summed up by what has been called the emergence of 'entitlement cultures of the 1990s' in which consumerisation has brought with it a sense of entitlement to services (and servicers) as products. The issuing of various 'charters' in conjunction with public services in Britain supposedly set out what customers could expect from these services. The Patient's Charter details what can be expected and demanded of the National Health Service and yet its individual address belongs to a broader location of responsibility for health with individuals and families. Critical debates about the entitlement cultures operating in

educational settings have focused upon the ways in which the staff/student relationships in higher education have been commodified; see Franklin (1993) and Skeggs (1995).

17 There has been a striking proliferation of alternative therapies in Britain during the last ten years. In one article on the availability of such treatments in London a total of twenty-five different techniques are listed, from the Alexander Technique, Chi-kung and Iridology to Polarity therapy, Reflexology and Vedic Tantric astrology (*Evening Standard Magazine*, October 1993, pp.71–6).

18 For a detailed discussion of the alternative health practitioner/patient relationship see Budd and Sharma (1994).

19 Women make up the highest proportion of alternative health practitioners; see Sharma (1992). This is doubtless because of alternative medicine's associations with the more traditionally 'feminine' values of caring and nurturance, its more holisitic approach which pays attention to emotions as well as physical illnesses and the relative ease with which women are able to enter these healing professions in contrast to their biomedical counterpart.

20 For a feminist analysis of the highly contentious 'foetal alcohol syndrome' debates, see McNeil and Litt (1992).

21 The phenomenon of the 'personality type' being attached to certain illnesses is particularly in evidence in discourses surrounding 'female' health problems and is closely connected to the patriarchal notion of women as generators of their own diseases. Shohat, for example, writing of endometriosis, claims that:

> Despite the differences between changing historical moments, most endo theories share a structural positioning of women as the generators of their own diseases. Writing from their specific sexual, class, racial and national context, scientists have systematically closed their eyes to the startling fact that the disease has been diagnosed in girls in their early teens as well as in women who have given birth to over ten children – a contradiction of the hegemonic endo theory that 'prolonged cyclic menstruation not interrupted by pregnancy constitutes a major risk factor for the disease'. Science's rush to search for the origins of endo in the fertile area of female deviation recalls AIDS discourses in relation to gay men: the victims are blamed for bringing the disease upon themselves. Relegated to the realm of the metaphysical, endometriosis is seen as the inevitable conclusion to the hubris of 'going against nature'. Just as AIDS is deemed God's revenge on 'unnatural' homosexual conduct, endometriosis is deemed God's revenge on the unnatural conduct of preternaturally ambitious professional women.
>
> (Shohat, 1992:65)

22 See Young (1980); Kirmayer (1988); and Lock and Gordon (1988).

23 For discussions of risk perception and understandings of science and technology see Wynne (1987) and Beck (1992).

24 See Mary Douglas's recent collection of cultural criticism on the subject of risk and blame (Douglas, 1992).

25 For examples of patients' criticisms of the medical profession, see Miles (1991) and Oakley (1993). For a discussion of biomedicine as 'iatrogenic' see Stacey (1988:173).

26 This challenge to the authority of medical professionals needs to be seen

in the context of widespread questioning of the authority of other professionals in Britain in the last fifteen years, including social workers (see Beatrix Campbell's account of the 'Cleveland Case', in Campbell, 1988) and legal professionals whose 'misjudgements' were exposed with regard to the wrongful imprisonment in Britain of the Guildford Four and the Birmingham Six.

27 For analyses of the gendering of expertise and the history of science, see McNeil (1987).

28 Ursula Sharma warns against the assumption that the turn to alternative medicines is necessarily a sign of disillusionment with biomedicine. Instead, she suggests that while this may be the motivation of some patients, there are others for whom the use of both alternative and conventional medicine does not present a contradiction (see Sharma, 1992).

8 ENDINGS

1 For a fuller discussion of the problems we have in contemporary culture accepting the place of 'contingency' in our lives, see Phillips (1994:3–21).

2 For critical analyses of the implementation (and yet the failures) of prohibitions around death in Western culture see Bronfen (1992); Baudrillard (1993); and Heathfield (PhD thesis forthcoming). For discussions of the appropriateness of the use of the concept of taboo in relation to anxieties around death in contemporary society, see Walter (1992); Seale (1995); and Walter et al. (1995).

3 The place of writing in culture has been widely metaphorised; see Duncan (1998, forthcoming) and Chapter 1, this volume.

4 On the complex relationship between remembering and forgetting, see Adam Phillips's detailed, but accessible, discussion of Freud's psychoanalytic theory of these processes (Phillips, 1994:22–38).

BIBLIOGRAPHY

Abelove, Henry and Halperin, David (eds) (1993) *The Lesbian and Gay Studies Reader*, London: Routledge.

Abercrombie, Nicholas and Keat, Russell (eds) (1991) *Enterprise Culture*, London: Routledge.

Abiodun, O. A. (1991) 'The Need for a Holistic Approach to Patient-Care', *East African Medical Journal* 68(1):25–8.

Abrams, M. H. (1988) *A Glossary of Literary Terms* (5th edn), New York: Holt, Rinehart & Winston Inc.

Ahmad, W. I. U. (ed.) (1993) *Race and Health in Contemporary Britain*, Buckingham: Open University Press.

Alliez, Eric and Feher, Michel (1989) 'Reflections of a Soul' in Michel Feher, Ramona Naddaff and Nadia Tazi (eds) *Fragments for a History of the Human Body*, Part Two, Boston: Zone Books/MIT Press, pp. 46–85.

Angell, M. (1985) 'Disease as a Reflection of the Psyche', *New England Journal of Medicine* 312(24): 1570–2, and correspondence in 313(24): 1354–59.

Appignanesi, Lisa (ed.) (1989) *Postmodernism*, ICA Documents 4, London: Free Association Books.

Armstrong, D. (1983) *Political Anatomy of the Body: Medical Knowledge in Britain in the Twentieth Century*, Cambridge: Cambridge University Press.

Arroyo, José (1993) 'Death, Desire and Identity: The Political Unconscious of "New Queer Cinema"' in Joseph Bristow and Angelia R. Wilson (eds) *Activating Theory: Lesbian, Gay and Bisexual Politics*, London: Lawrence and Wishart, pp.70–96.

Atwood, Margaret (1991) 'Hairball' in *Wilderness Tips*, London: Bloomsbury, pp. 39–56.

Austin, J. L. (1962) *How to Do Things with Words*, Oxford: Clarendon Press.

Ayala, Francisco J. and Kiger, John A. jun. (1984) *Modern Genetics* (2nd edn), California and Massachusetts: The Benjamin/Cummings Publishing Company.

Bagenal, F. S., Easton, D. F., Harris, E., Chilvers, C. E. D. and McElwain, T. J. (1990) 'Survival of Patients with Breast Cancer Attending Bristol Cancer Help Centre', *The Lancet* 336 (8715): 606–10.

Bakhtin, Mikhail, M. (1984) 'The Grotesque Image of the Body and its Sources' in *Rabelais and His World* (trans. Helene Iswolsky), Bloomington: Indiana University Press.

Balshem, Martha (1993) *Cancer in the Community: Class and Medical Authority*, Washington and London: Smithsonian Institution Press.

Barsky, Arthur J. (1988) *Worried Sick: Our Troubled Quest for Wellness*, New York: Little, Brown & Co.

Bataille, Georges (1962) *Death and Sensuality: A Study of Eroticism and the Taboo*, New York: Walker.

Bathrop, R. W. (1977) 'Depressed Lymphocyte Function after Bereavement', *The Lancet* 1 (16 April): 834–6.

Batsleer, Janet, Davies, Tony, O'Rourke, Rebecca and Weedon, Chris (1985) *Rewriting English: The Cultural Politics of Gender and Class*, London: Methuen.

Baudrillard, Jean (1993) *Symbolic Exchange and Death*, London: Sage.

Baum, M. (1993) 'Breast Cancer 2,000 BC to 2,000 AD – Time for a Paradigm Shift?', *Acta Oncol* 32(1): 3–8.

Beatie, Alan (1993) *Health and Wellbeing: A Reader*, Basingstoke: Macmillan, in association with Open University Press.

Beck, Ulrich (1992) *Risk Society: Towards a New Modernity* (trans. Mark Ritter), London: Sage.

Beck-Gernsheim, Elizabeth (1995) 'Health and Responsibility in the Age of Genetic Technology' in Paul Heelas, Scott Lash and Paul Morris (eds) *Detraditionalisation*, Oxford: Blackwell, pp. 23–48.

Begum, Nasa (1992) 'Disabled Women and the Feminist Agenda' in Hilary Hinds, Ann Phoenix and Jackie Stacey (eds) *Working Out: New Directions for Women's Studies*, London: Falmer Press, pp. 61–73.

Belsey, Catherine (1980) *Critical Practice*, London: Methuen.

Benedek, Thomas and Kiple, Kenneth F. (1994) 'Concepts of Cancer' in Kenneth F. Kiple (ed.) *The Cambridge World History of Human Disease*, Cambridge: Cambridge University Press, pp. 102–10.

Benjamin, Andrew (ed.) (1989) *The Lyotard Reader*, Oxford: Blackwell.

Benjamin, D. (1993) 'The Efficacy of Surgical Treatment of Cancer', *Medical Hypotheses* 40(2): 129–38.

Benjamin, Jessica (1990) *The Bonds of Love: Psychoanalysis, Feminism and the Problem of Domination*, London: Virago.

Beral, V. (1987) 'The Epidemiology of Ovarian Cancer' in E. Sharp and W. P. Soutter (eds) *Ovarian Cancer: The Way Ahead*, Chichester: John Wiley & Sons, pp. 21–31.

Bersani, Leo (1990) *The Culture of Redemption*, Cambridge, Massachusetts and London: Harvard University Press.

Bertalanfly, L. von (1971) *General Systems Theory*, London: Penguin/Allan Lane.

Birke, Linda (1986) *Women, Feminism and Biology*, New York: Methuen.

Black, M. (1962) *Models and Metaphors*, Ithaca, New York: Cornell University Press.

Bleehen, Norman M. (ed.) (1984) *Ovarian Cancer*, New York: Springer Verlag.

Boffin, Tessa and Gupta, Sunil (1990) *Ecstatic Antibodies: Resisting the AIDS Mythology*, London: Rivers Oram Press.

Bordowitz, Gregg (1994) 'Dense Moments' in Rodney Sappington and Tyler Stallings (eds) *Uncontrollable Bodies: Testimonies of Identity and Culture*, Seattle: Bay Press, pp. 25–44.

Boss, Pete (1986) 'Vile Bodies and Bad Medicine', *Screen* 27(1): 14–24.

Boston Women's Health Collective (1976) *Our Bodies, Ourselves* (2nd edn), New York: Simon & Schuster.

Bourke, I. and Goodane, H. (1992) 'Cancer Positive' (letter), *British Medical Journal* 304 (6839): 1445.

Bourne, I. H. J. (1992) 'Another Look at Holistic Medicine' (letter), *Journal of the Royal Society of Medicine* 85(5): 307.

Boyd, R. (1979) 'Metaphor and Theory Change: What is "Metaphor" a

Metaphor For?' in Andrew Ortony (ed.) *Metaphor and Thought*, Cambridge: Cambridge University Press, pp. 356–408.

Braidotti, Rosi (1991) *Patterns of Dissonance: A Study of Women in Contemporary Philosophy*, Cambridge: Polity Press.

—— (1994) *Nomadic Subjects: Embodiment and Sexual Difference in Contemporary Feminist Thought*, New York: Columbia University Press.

Brennan, Teresa (ed.) (1989) *Between Feminism and Psychoanalysis*, London: Routledge.

Breuer, Joseph and Freud, Sigmund (1893) 'On the Psychical Mechanism of Hysterical Phenomena: Preliminary Communication' in Freud and Breuer *Studies on Hysteria* (1893–1895).

Bristol Cancer Help Centre (1990) (letter; comment) *The Lancet* 336 (8716): 683, and 336 (8717): 743–4.

Bristow, Joseph and Wilson, Angelia R. (eds) (1993) *Activating Theory: Lesbian, Gay and Bisexual Politics*, London: Lawrence & Wishart.

British Medical Association (1993) *Complementary Medicine: New Approaches to Good Practice*, Oxford: Oxford University Press.

Brohn, Penny (1987a) *Gentle Giants: The Powerful Story of One Women's Struggle against Breast Cancer*, London: Century Hutchinson.

—— (1987b) *The Bristol Programme: An Introduction to Holistic Therapies Practised by the Bristol Cancer Help Centre*, London: Century Hutchinson.

Bronfen, Elisabeth (1992) *Over Her Dead Body: Death, Femininity and the Aesthetic*, Manchester: Manchester University Press.

Brophy, Philip (1986) 'Horrality – the Textuality of Contemporary Horror Film', *Screen* 27(1): 2–13.

Brown, Laura (1995) 'Not Outside the Range: One Feminist Perspective on Psychic Trauma' in Cathy Caruth (ed.) *Trauma: Explorations in Memory*, London and Baltimore: The Johns Hopkins University Press, pp. 100–12.

Brownsworth, Victoria (1993) 'The Other Epidemic: Lesbians and Breast Cancer', *Out* (March): 61–3.

Bruno, Giuliana (1992) 'Spectatorial Embodiments: Anatomies of the Visible and the Female Bodyscape', *camera obscura* 28: 239–62.

Buckman, R. (1990) 'Catfish Man of the Woods: Alternative Medicine, Appalachian Style', *Canadian Medical Association Journal* 142(11): 1298.

Budd, Susan and Sharma, Ursula (eds) (1994) *The Healing Bond: The Patient–Practitioner Relationship and Therapeutic Responsibility*, London: Routledge.

Bullough, William S. (1967) *The Evolution of Differentiation*, London and New York: Academic Press.

Burke, C. and Sikora, K. (1992) 'Cancer – The Dual Approach', *Nursing Times* 88(38): 62–6.

Butler, Judith (1990) *Gender Trouble: Feminism and the Subversion of Identity*, London: Routledge.

—— (1991) 'Imitation and Gender Insubordination' in Diana Fuss (ed.) *Inside Out: Lesbian Theories, Gay Theories*, London: Routledge, pp. 13–31.

—— (1993) *Bodies That Matter: On the Discursive Limits of 'Sex'*, London: Routledge.

Butler, Sandra and Rosenblum, Barbara (1991) *Cancer in Two Voices*, San Francisco: Spinster Book Co.

Cairns, John (1978) *Cancer: Science and Society*, San Francisco: W. H. Freeman and Co.

Campbell, Beatrix (1988) *Unofficial Secrets: Child Sexual Abuse – the Cleveland Case*, London: Virago.

camera obscura (1992) Special issues on 'Imaging Technologies, Inscribing Science', Nos 28, 29.

Carter, Erica and Watney, Simon (eds) (1989) *Taking Liberties: AIDS and Cultural Politics*, London: Serpent's Tail.

Cartwright, Lisa (1995) *Screening the Body: Tracing Medicine's Visual Culture*, Minneapolis and London: University of Minnesota Press.

Caruth, Cathy (ed.) (1995) *Trauma: Explorations in Memory*, London and Baltimore: The Johns Hopkins University Press.

—— (1995) 'Trauma and Experience' in Cathy Caruth (ed.) *Trauma: Explorations in Memory*, London and Baltimore: The Johns Hopkins University Press, pp. 3–12.

Cassileth, B. R. (1989) 'The Social Implications of Questionable Cancer Therapies', *Cancer* 63: 1247–50.

Cassileth, B. R., Luske, E. J., Strause, T. B. and Bodenheimer, B. J. (1984) 'Contemporary Unorthodox Treatments in Cancer Medicine: A Study of Patients, Treatments and Practitioners', *Annals of Internal Medicine* 101: 105–12.

Cassileth, B. R., Luske, E. J., Edward, J., Miller, D., Brown, L. J. and Miller, C. (1985) 'Psychosocial Correlates of Survival in Advanced Malignant Disease?', *New England Journal of Medicine* 312 (24): 1551–5.

Cassileth, B. R., Luske, E. J., DuPont, G., Blake, A. D., Walsh, W. P., Kascius, L. and Schulte, D. (1991) 'Survival and Quality of Life among Patients Receiving Unproven as Compared with Conventional Cancer Therapy', *New England Journal of Medicine* 324 (17): 1180–5.

Castle, Terry (1993) *The Apparitional Lesbian: Female Homosexuality and Modern Culture*, New York: Columbia University Press.

Chaitow, Leon (1983) *An End to Cancer? The Nutritional Approach to its Prevention and Control*, Wellingborough, Northamptonshire: Thorsons.

Charles, Rachel (1990) *Mind, Body and Immunity: How to Enhance Your Body's Natural Defences*, London: Methuen.

Charlton, B. G. (1992) 'Philosophy of Medicine: Alternative or Scientific?', *Journal of the Royal Society of Medicine* 85(8): 436–8.

Chisholm, Diane (1992) 'The Uncanny' in Elizabeth Wright (ed.) *Feminism and Psychoanalysis: A Critical Dictionary*, Oxford: Blackwell, pp. 436–40.

Chodorow, Nancy (1978) *The Reproduction of Mothering: Psychoanalysis and the Sociology of Gender*, Berkeley, California: University of California Press.

—— (1989) *Feminism and Psychoanalytic Theory*, New Haven: Yale University Press.

Christie, V. M. (1991) 'A Dialogue between Practitioners of Alternative (Traditional) Medicine and Modern (Western) Medicine in Norway', *Social Science and Medicine* 32(5): 549–52.

Clarke, A. E. (1990) 'Caring and Responsibility: The Crossroads of Holistic Practice and Traditional Medicine', *Contemporary Sociology: An International Journal of Reviews* 19(5): 742–3.

Cohen, M. (1992) 'Eastern and Western Medicine – Complementary in Practice, Equal in Status', *American Journal of Acupuncture* 20(2): 137–42.

Connor, J. F. H. (1991) 'Alternative Medicine and American Religious Life', *Social History of Medicine* 4(1): 164–5.

Conrad, P. (1991) 'Holistic Health and Biomedical Medicine: A Countersystem Analysis', *Contemporary Sociology: An International Journal of Reviews* 20(4): 621.

Cook, Pam (ed.) (1985) *The Cinema Book*, London: British Film Institute.

Cooke, Alistair B. (1989) *Margaret Thatcher: The Revival of Britain: Speeches on Home and European Affairs 1975–1988*, London: Aurum Press.

Cosslett, Tess (1991) 'Questioning the Definition of "Literature": Fictional and

Non-Fictional Accounts of Childbirth' in Jane Aaron and Sylvia Walby (eds) *Out of the Margins: Women's Studies in the Nineties*, London: Falmer, pp. 220–31.

Cousins, Norman (1981) *Anatomy of an Illness as Perceived by the Patient: Reflections on Healing and Regulation*, London: Bantam Books.

Coward, Rosalind (1984) *Female Desire: Women's Sexuality Today*, London: Paladin.

—— (1989) *The Whole Truth: The Myth of Alternative Health*, London: Faber and Faber.

Crary, Jonathan and Kwinter, Sandford (eds) (1992) *Incorporations*, Boston, Massachusetts: Zone Books/MIT Press.

Crawford, Robert (1977) 'You are Dangerous to your Health: The Ideology and Politics of Victim Blaming', *International Journal of Health Services* 7(4): 663–80.

—— (1985) 'A Cultural Account of "Health": Control, Release and the Social Body' in J. McKinlay (ed.) *Issues in the Political Economy of Health Care*, London: Tavistock.

—— (1987) 'Cultural Influences on Prevention and the Emergence of a New Health Consciousness' in N. Weinstein (ed.) *Taking Care: Understanding and Encouraging Self Protective Behaviour*, Cambridge: Cambridge University Press.

Creed, Barbara (1993) *The Monstrous Feminine: Film, Feminism and Psychoanalysis*, London: Routledge.

Currie, Graham and Currie, Angela (1982) *Cancer: The Biology of Malignant Disease*, London: Edward Arnold.

Daly, Mary (1979) *Gyn/Ecology: The Metaethics of Radical Feminism*, London: The Women's Press.

Davis, Adele (1979) *Let's Get Well*, London: Unwin Paperbacks.

de Lauretis, Teresa (1984) *Alice Doesn't: Feminism, Semiotics, Cinema*, London: Macmillan.

—— (1987) *Technologies of Gender: Essays in Theory, Film and Fiction*, Bloomington, Indianna: Indiana University Press.

—— (1988) 'The Essence of the Triangle: or, Taking the Risk of Essentialism Seriously', *differences* 1(2): 3–37.

—— (1994) *The Practice of Love: Lesbian Sexuality and Perverse Desire*, Bloomington, Indianna: Indiana University Press.

Del Vecchio, Mary Jo, Good, Bryan J., Schaffer, Cynthia and Lind, Stuart E. (1990) 'American Oncology and the Discourse on Hope', *Culture, Medicine and Psychiatry* 14: 59–79.

Dentith, Simon (1995) *Bakhtinian Thought: An Introductory Reader*, London: Routledge.

Denzin, Norman, K. (1991) *Images of Postmodern Society: Social Theory and Contemporary Cinema*, London: Sage.

DiGiacomo, Susan M. (1987) 'Biomedicine as a Cultural System: An Anthropologist in the Kingdom of the Sick' in H. Baer (ed.) *Encounters with Biomedicine*, New York: Gordon & Breach, pp. 315–46.

—— (1992) 'Metaphor as Illness: Postmodern Dilemmas in the Representation of the Body, Mind and Disorder', *Medical Anthropology* 14: 109–37.

Diamond, I. and Quinby, L. (eds) (1988) *Feminism and Foucault: Reflections on Resistance*, Boston, Massachusetts: Northeastern University Press.

Dickman, S. (1991) 'New Cancer Center in Germany Combines Clinical Research with Alternative Medicine', *Annals of Oncology* 2(10): 699–700.

Docherty, Thomas (ed.) (1993) *Postmodernism: A Reader*, Hemel Hempstead, Hertfordshire: Harvester Wheatsheaf.

Donald, James (ed.) (1989) *Fantasy and the Cinema*, London: British Film Institute.

—— (ed.) (1991) *Psychoanalysis and Cultural Theory*, London: Macmillan/ICA.

Dorr, R. and Fritz, W. (1980) *Cancer Chemotherapy Handbook*, London: Kimpton.

Dossey, Larry (1996) *Prayer is Good Medicine*, San Francisco: Harper.

Douglas, Mary (1966) *Purity and Danger: An Analysis of the Concepts of Pollution and Taboo*, London: Routledge & Kegan Paul.

—— (1992) *Risk and Blame: Essays in Cultural Theory*, London: Routledge.

Doyal, Lesley (1994) 'Changing Medicine? Gender and the Politics of Health Care' in Jonathan Gabe, David Kelleher and Gareth Williams (eds) *Challenging Medicine*, London: Routledge.

Doyal, Lesley with Pennell, I. (1979) *The Political Economy of Health*, London: Pluto.

Doyal, Lesley, Naidoo, Jennie and Wilton, Tamsin (1994) *AIDS: Setting a Feminist Agenda*, London: Taylor & Francis.

Dreifus, Claudia (ed.) (1977) *Seizing Our Bodies: The Politics of Women's Health*, New York: Vintage Books.

Duden, Barbara (1991) *The Woman Beneath the Skin: A Doctor's Patients in Eighteenth Century Germany* (trans. Thomas Dunlop 1987), Cambridge, Massachusetts: Harvard University Press.

—— (1993) *Disembodying Women: Perspectives on Pregnancy and the Unborn* (trans. Lee Hoinacki), Cambridge, Massachusetts: Harvard University Press.

Duncan, Derek (1998, forthcoming) 'Solemn Geographies: AIDS and the Contours of Autobiography' in Kate Chedgzoy and Murray Pratt (eds) *Queer Bodies*, London: Cassell.

Dunham, W. R. (1990) 'Holistic Medicine' (letter), *Journal of the Royal Society of Medicine* 83(12): 812.

Dyer, Richard (ed.) (1977) *Gays and Film*, London: British Film Institute.

—— (1986) *Heavenly Bodies: Film Stars and Society*, London: British Film Institute and Macmillan.

—— (1990) *Now You See It: Studies on Lesbian and Gay Film*, London: Routledge.

Eagle, R. (1978) *Alternative Medicine*, London: Futura.

Easthope, Gary (1986) *Healers and Alternative Medicine: A Sociological Examination*, Aldershot: Gower.

Egan, V. (1992) 'Complementary Medicine Needs Critical Evaluation' (letter), *British Medical Journal* 305(6861): 1096.

Ehrenreich, Barbara and English, Deirdre (1974) *Complaints and Disorders: The Sexual Politics of Sickness*, London: Compendium.

—— (1979) *For Her Own Good: 150 Years of the Expert's Advice to Women*, London: Pluto Press.

Elvin, Mark (1989) 'Tales of *Shen* and *Xin*: Body–Person and Heart–Mind in China during the last 150 years' in Michel Feher, Ramona Naddaff and Nadia Tazi (eds) *Fragments for a History of the Human Body*, Part Two, Boston: Zone Books/MIT Press, pp. 266–349.

Ernst, E. (1993) 'Complementary Medicine – Scrutinising the Alternatives', *The Lancet* 341(8861): 1626.

Evans, Elida (1926) *A Psychological Study of Cancer*, New York: Dodd Mead & Co.

Featherstone, Mike (ed.) (1990) *Global Culture: Nationalism, Globalization and Modernity*, London: Sage.

Featherstone, Mike (1991) *Consumer Culture and Postmodernism*, London: Sage.

Featherstone, Mike, Hepworth, Mike and Turner, Brian S. (eds) (1991) *The Body: Social Process and Cultural Theory*, London: Sage.

Feher, Michel, Naddaff, Ramona and Tazi, Nadia (eds) (1989) *Fragments for a History of the Human Body*, Parts One, Two and Three, Boston: Zone Books/MIT Press.

Felski, Rita (1989) *Beyond Feminist Aesthetics: Feminist Literature and Social Change*, Cambridge, Massachusetts: Harvard University Press.

Fernandez, James (1986) *Persuasions and Performances: The Play of Tropes in Culture*, Bloomington: Indiana University Press.

Finch, Janet and Groves, Dulcie (eds) (1983) *A Labour of Love: Women, Work and Caring*, London: Routledge & Kegan Paul.

Fletcher, John and Benjamin, Andrew (eds) (1990) *Abjection, Melancholia and Love: The Work of Julia Kristeva*, London: Routledge.

Foss, L. and Rothenberg, K. (1988) *The Second Medical Revolution: From Biomedicine to Infomedicine*, Boston: Shambala.

Foucault, Michel (1970) *The Order of Things: An Archaeology of the Human Sciences* (published in French 1966), London: Tavistock.

—— (1973) *The Birth of the Clinic: An Archaeology of Medical Perception* (trans. A. M. Sheridan Smith), London: Tavistock.

—— (1979) *The History of Sexuality Vol. 1: An Introduction* (trans. Robert Hurley), Harmondsworth, Middlesex: Penguin.

—— (1990) *The History of Sexuality Vol. 3: The Care of the Self* (trans. Robert Hurley), Harmondsworth, Middlesex: Penguin.

—— (1991) *Discipline and Punish: The Birth of the Prison* (trans. Alan Sheridan), Harmondsworth, Middlesex: Penguin.

Fox, H. and Langley, F. (1976) *Tumours of the Ovary*, London: Heinemann Medical.

Frank, Arthur (1991) *At the Will of the Body: Reflections on Illness* Boston: Houghton Mifflin.

—— (1995) *The Wounded Story Teller: Body, Illness and Ethics*, Chicago and London: University of Chicago Press.

Franklin, Sarah (1990) 'Deconstructing "Desperateness": The Social Construction of Infertility in Popular Representations of New Reproductive Technologies' in Maureen McNeil, Ian Varco and Steven Yearley (eds) *The New Reproductive Technologies*, London: Macmillan, pp. 200–29.

—— (1991) 'Fetal Fascinations: New Dimensions to the Medical Scientific Construction of Fetal Personhood' in Sarah Franklin, Celia Lury and Jackie Stacey (eds) *Off-Centre: Feminism and Cultural Studies*, London: HarperCollins/Routledge.

—— (1993) 'The Gender Agenda in the Context of the Restructuring of Higher Education', paper delivered at the Agenda for Gender Conference 18 March 1993 at Birkbeck College.

—— (1995) 'Romancing the Helix: Nature and Scientific Discovery' in Lynne Pearce and Jackie Stacey (eds) *Romance Revisited*, London: Lawrence & Wishart, pp. 63–77.

—— (1998, forthcoming) 'Life Itself' in Sarah Franklin, Celia Lury and Jackie Stacey *Second Nature*.

Franklin, Sarah and McNeil, Maureen (1991) 'Science and Technology: Questions for Cultural Studies and Feminism' in Sarah Franklin, Celia Lury and Jackie Stacey (eds) *Off Centre: Feminism and Cultural Studies*, London: HarperCollins/Routledge, pp. 129–46.

—— (1993) 'Procreation Stories', *Science as Culture* 3(4): 477–83.

Franklin, Sarah, Lury, Celia and Stacey, Jackie (eds) (1991) *Off-Centre: Feminism and Cultural Studies*, London: HarperCollins/Routledge.

Freud, Peter (1990) 'The Expressive Body: A Common Ground for the Sociology of Emotions and Health and Illness', *Sociology of Health and Illness* 12(4): 452–77.

Freud, Sigmund (1908) 'On the Sexual Theories of Children' in *On Sexuality* (trans. James Strachey) (Penguin Freud Library Vol. 7, 1977), Harmondsworth, Middlesex: Penguin.

—— (1913–14) 'Totem and Taboo' in *Origins of Religion* (Penguin Freud Library Vol. 13, 1990), Harmondsworth, Middlesex: Penguin.

—— (1914) *The Psychopathology of Everyday Life* (Penguin Freud Library Vol. 5, 1975), Harmondsworth, Middlesex: Penguin.

—— (1925) 'Some Psychical Consequences of the Anatomical Distinction Between the Sexes' in *On Sexuality* (trans. James Strachey) (Penguin Freud Library Vol. 7, 1977), Harmondsworth, Middlesex: Penguin.

Freud, Sigmund and Breuer, Joseph (1893–5) *Studies on Hysteria* (trans James and Alex Strachey) (Penguin Freud Library Vol. 3, 1974), Harmondsworth, Middlesex: Penguin.

Fulder, Stephen (1984) *The Handbook of Complementary Medicine*, Sevenoaks, Kent/London: Hodder & Stoughton/Coronet Books.

Fulder, S. and Munro, R. (1981) *The Status of Complementary Medicine in the U.K.* London: Threshold Foundation.

Furnham, Adrian and Bhagrath, Ravi (1993) 'A Comparison of Health Beliefs and Behaviours of Clients of Orthodox and Complementary Medicine', *British Journal of Clinical Psychology* 32: 237–46.

Fuss, Diana (1989) *Essentially Speaking: Feminism, Nature and Difference*, London: Routledge.

—— (ed.) (1991) *Inside Out: Lesbian Theories, Gay Theories*, London: Routledge.

Gabe, Jonathan, Kelleher, David and Williams, Gareth (eds) (1994) *Challenging Medicine*, London: Routledge.

Gallop, Jane (1982) *Feminism and Psychoanalysis: The Daughter's Seduction*, London: Macmillan.

Garfield, E. (1990) 'On the Dangers of Alternative Medicine', *Current Comments* 21(May): 3–8.

Gelb, Michael (1987) *Body Learning: An Introduction to the Alexander Technique*, London: Aurum Press.

Gellner, Ernst (1985) *The Psychoanalytic Movement*, London: Paladin Books.

Gershenson, D. M. and Rutledge, F. N. (1987) 'Endodermal Sinus Tumor and Embryonal Carcinoma of the Ovary' in M. Piver and M. Steven (eds) *Ovarian Malignancies: Diagnostic and Therapeutic Advances*, London: Churchill Livingstone/Longman.

Giddens, Anthony (1991) *Modernity and Self Identity: Self and Society in the Late Modern Age*, Cambridge: Polity.

Gillick, Muriel R. (1984) 'Health Promotion, Jogging and the Pursuit of the Moral Life', *Journal of Health Politics, Policy and Law* 9: 369–87.

Gilman, Sander L. (1988) *Disease and Representation: Images of Illness from Madness to AIDS*, Ithaca and London: Cornell University Press.

—— (1992) 'Black Bodies, White Bodies: Toward an Iconography of Female Sexuality in Late Nineteenth-Century Art, Medicine and Literature' in James Donald and Ali Rattansi (eds) *'Race', Culture and Difference*, London: Sage/ Open University Press.

Glasser, R. (1976) *The Body is the Hero*, New York: Random House.

Glassner, B. (1989) 'Fitness and the Postmodern Self', *Journal of Health and Social Behaviour* 30: 180–91.

Glushkov, Viktor N. (1966) *Introduction to Cybernetics* (trans. Scripta Technica Inc), New York and London: Academic Press.

Goffman, Erving (1964) *Stigma: Notes on the Management of the Spoiled Identity*, Englewood Cliffs, New Jersey: Prentice-Hall.

Golub, Edward S. (1987) *Immunology: A Synthesis*, Sunderland, Maine: Sinauer.

Goodman, N. W. (1993) 'The Alternative to Magic Medicine' (editorial), *British Journal of Hospital Medicine* 50(1): 71.

Gordon, Deborah R. (1988) 'Tenacious Assumptions in Western Medicine' in Margaret Lock and Deborah Gordon (eds) *Biomedicine Examined*, Dordrecht, The Netherlands: Kluwer Academic Publishers, pp. 19–56.

Graham, Elspeth, Hinds, Hilary, Hobby, Elaine and Wilcox, Helen (eds) (1989) *Her Own Life: Autobiographical Writings by Seventeenth-Century Englishwomen*, London: Routledge.

Graham, Helen (1990) *Time, Energy and Healing*, London: Jessica Kingsley.

Graham, Hilary (1984) *Women, Health and the Family*, Brighton: Harvester.

—— (1993) *Hardship and Health in Women's Lives*, Hemel Hempstead, Hertfordshire: Harvester Wheatsheaf.

—— (1994) 'Surviving by Smoking' in Sue Wilkinson and Celia Kitzinger (eds) *Women and Health: Feminist Perspectives*, London: Taylor & Francis, pp. 102–23.

Gray, C. (1990) 'British MDs Face Growing Pressure from Alternative Medicine' *Canadian Medical Association Journal* 143(2): 132–3.

Grealy, Lucy (1994) *Autobiography of a Face*, Boston: Houghton Mifflin.

Griggs, Barbara (1986) *The Food Factor: An Account of the Nutrition Revolution*, Harmondsworth, Middlesex: Penguin.

Groddeck, Georg Walther (1923) *The Book of the It*, New York: New American Library.

Grossberg, Lawrence, Nelson, Carey and Treichler, Paula A. (eds) (1992) *Cultural Studies*, London: Routledge.

Grosz, Elizabeth (1990) 'The Body of Signification' in John Fletcher and Andrew Benjamin (eds) *Abjection, Melancholia and Love: The Work of Julia Kristeva*, London: Routledge pp. 80–104.

—— (1991) 'Freaks', *Social Semiotics* 1(2): 22–38.

—— (1992) 'Julia Kristeva' in Elizabeth Wright (ed.) *Feminism and Psychoanalysis: A Critical Dictionary* , Oxford: Blackwell, pp. 194–200.

—— (1994) *Volatile Bodies: Towards a Corporeal Feminism*, Bloomington: Indiana University Press.

Guattari, Felix (1992) 'Regimes, Pathways, Subjects' in Jonathan Crary and Sandford Kwinter (eds) *Incorporations*, Boston, Massachusetts: Zone Books/MIT Press, pp. 16–35.

Guyton, Arthur, C. (1984) *Physiology of the Human Body*, Philadelphia, Pennsylvania: Saunders College Publishing.

Guzley, G. J. (1992) 'Alternative Cancer Treatments: Impact of Unorthodox Therapy on the Patient with Cancer', *Southern Medical Journal* 85(5): 519–23.

Hagestad, Gunhild O. (1996) 'On-time, Off-time, Out of Time? Reflections on Continuity and Discontinuity from an Illness Process' in V. L. Bengtson (ed.) *Adulthood and Aging: Research on Continuities and Discontinuities*, New York: Springer, pp. 204–22.

Hall, Stuart (1988) *The Hard Road to Renewal: Thatcherism and the Crisis of the Left*, London: Verso.

Hamaoka, T. *et al.* (1989) *Immune System and Cancer: Proceedings of the International Symposium of the Princess Takamatsu Cancer Research Fund* 19.

Haraway, Donna (1989a) 'A Manifesto for Cyborgs: Science, Technology and Socialist Feminism in the 1980s' in Elizabeth Weed (ed.) *Coming to Terms: Feminism, Theory, Politics*, London: Routledge, pp. 173–204.

—— (1989b) 'The Biopolitics of Postmodern Bodies: Determinations of Self in Immune System Discourse', *differences: A Journal of Feminist Cultural Studies* 1(1): 3–45.

—— (1991) *Simians, Cyborgs and Women: The Reinvention of Nature*, London: Free Association Books.

—— (1992) 'The Promises of Monsters: A Regenerative Politics for Inappropriate/d Others' in Lawrence Grossberg, Carey Nelson and Paula A. Treichler (eds) *Cultural Studies*, London: Routledge, pp. 295–337.

Harding, Sandra (1986) *The Science Question in Feminism*, Milton Keynes, Buckinghamshire: Open University Press.

Harding, Susan (1987) 'Convicted by the Holy Spirit: The Rhetoric of Fundamentalist Baptist Conversion?', *American Ethnologist* 14: 167–81.

Harris, R. (1976) *Cancer: The Nature of the Problem*, Harmondsworth, Middlesex: Penguin.

Harrison, Shirley (1987) *New Approaches to Cancer*, London: Century Hutchinson.

Hartouni, Valerie (1992) 'Fetal Exposures: Abortion Politics and the Optics of Allusion', *camera obscura* 29: 131–50.

Harvey, David (1990) *The Condition of Postmodernity*, Oxford: Blackwell.

Harvey, Keith (1997) 'Everybody Loves a Lover: Gay Men, Straight Men and a Problem of Lexical Choice' in Keith Harvey and Celia Shalom (eds) *Language and Desire: Encoding Sex, Romance and Intimacy*, London: Routledge.

Haug, Frigga (ed.) (1987) *Female Sexualization*, London: Verso.

Hawkes, Terence (1972) *Metaphor: The Critical Idiom*, London: Methuen.

Hay, Louise (1988) *You Can Heal Your Life*, London: Eden Grove.

—— (1989) *Heal Your Body: The Mental Causes for Physical Illness and the Metaphysical Way to Overcome Them*, London: Eden Grove.

Heathfield, Adrian (forthcoming) 'Identity and Representation in Contemporary Performance', University of Bristol: Unpublished PhD thesis.

Heller, T., Bailey, L. and Patterson, S. (eds) (1992) *Preventing Cancers*, Milton Keynes, Buckinghamshire: Open University Press.

Helman, Cecil G. (1988) 'Psyche, Soma, and Society: The Social Construction of Psychosomatic Disorders' in Margaret Lock and Deborah R. Gordon (eds) *Biomedicine Examined*, Dorrdrecht, The Netherlands: Kluewer Academic Publishers.

Hellman, S. (1993) 'Dogma and Inquisition in Medicine: Breast Cancer as a Case Study', *Cancer* 71(7): 2430–3.

Hepburn, Cuca with Gutierrez, Bonnie (1988) *Alive and Well: A Lesbian Health Guide*, New York: The Crossing Press.

Herzlich, Claudine and Douglas, Graham (1973) *Health and Illness: A Social Psychological Analysis*, London: Academic Press.

Herzlich, Claudine and Pierret, Janine (1987) *Illness and Self in Society* (trans. Elborg Forster), Baltimore, Maryland and London: The Johns Hopkins University Press.

Hockey, Jenny (1993) 'Women and Health' in Diane Richardson and Victoria Robinson (eds) *Introducing Women's Studies*, London: Macmillan, pp. 250–71.

Holmes, Susan (1992) 'Have Alternative Methods Got a Place in the Treatment of Cancer?', *Journal of the Royal Society of Health* (February): 15–19.

Huebscher, R. (1992) 'Spontaneous Remission of Cancer: An Example of Health Promotion', *Nurse Practitioner Forum* 3(4): 228–35.

Hutschnecher, Arnold (1953) *The Will to Live*, New York: Thomas Y. Crowell Co.

Illich, I. (1975) *Medical Nemesis*, London: Calder & Boyars.

Irigaray, Luce (1985a) *This Sex Which Is Not One* (trans. Catherine Porter with Carolyn Burke), Ithaca, New York: Cornell University Press.

—— (1985b) *Speculum of the Other Woman* (trans. Gillian Gill), Ithaca, New York: Cornell University Press.

271

Jacobsen, G. Krag and Talerman, A. (1989) *Atlas of Germ Cell Tumours*, Copenhagen: Monksgaard.

Jameson, Frederic (1984) 'Foreword' in Jean-François Lyotard *The Postmodern Condition: A Report on Knowledge*, Manchester: Manchester University Press, pp. vii–xxv.

Jarman, Derek (1993) *Blue: Text of a Film by Derek Jarman*, West Sussex: Little Hampton Printers.

Jerne, N. (1985) 'The Generative Grammar of the Immune System', *Science* 229: 1057–9.

Jessop, B. and Bonnett, K. (1988) *Thatcherism*, Cambridge: Polity Press.

Jones, Ann Rosalind (1984) 'Julia Kristeva on Femininity: The Limits of a Semiotic Politics', *Feminist Review* 18: 56–73.

Jones, Helen (1994) *Health and Society in Twentieth-Century Britain*, London: Longman.

Jordanova, Ludmilla (1989) *Sexual Visions: Images of Gender in Science and Medicine between the Eighteenth and Twentieth Centuries*, Hemel Hempstead, Hertfordshire: Harvester Wheatsheaf.

Keat, Russell and Abercrombie, Nicholas (eds) (1991) *Enterprise Culture*, London: Routledge.

Keat, Russell, Whiteley, Nigel and Abercrombie, Nicholas (eds) (1993) *The Authority of the Consumer*, London: Routledge.

Kelleher, David (1994) 'Self Help Groups and their Relationship to Medicine' in Jonathan Gabe, David Kelleher and Gareth Williams (eds) *Challenging Medicine*, London: Routledge, pp. 104–17.

Keller, Evelyn Fox (1985) *Reflections on Gender and Science*, New Haven and London: Yale University Press.

—— (1990) 'From Secrets of Life to Secrets of Death' in Mary Jacobus, Evelyn Fox-Keller and Sally Shuttleworth (eds) *Body/Politics: Women and the Discourse of Science*, London: Routledge, pp. 177–91.

Kelly, Michael P. and May, David (1982) 'Good and Bad Patients: A Review of the Literature and a Theoretical Critique', *Journal of Advanced Nursing* 7: 147–56.

Kfir, Nira and Slevin, Maurice (1991) *Challenging Cancer: From Chaos to Control*, London: Routledge.

Kingman, S. (1993) 'Complementary Medicine: Controls Needed Says BMA' (editorial), *British Medical Journal* 306(6894): 1713.

Kirmayer, Lawrence J. (1988) 'Mind and Body as Metaphors: Hidden Values in Biomedicine' in Margaret Lock and Deborah. R. Gordon (eds) *Biomedicine Examined*, Dorrdrecht, The Netherlands: Kluewer Academic Publishers, pp. 57–93.

Kitzinger, Celia (no date) 'Heteropatriarchal Language: The Case Against "Homophobia"', *Gossip* 5.

Kleinman, Arthur (1984) 'Indigenous Systems of Healing: Questions for Professional, Popular and Folk Care' in J. Warren Salmon (ed.) *Alternative Medicines: Popular and Policy Perspectives*, London: Tavistock.

Kottow, M. H. (1992) 'Classical Medicine vs Alternative Medical Practices', *Journal of Medical Ethics* 18(1): 18–22.

Krauss, Rosalind (1993) *Cindy Sherman 1975–1993*, New York: Rizzoli.

Kristeva, Julia (1980) *Desire in Language* (trans. Leon Raudiez), New York: Columbia University Press.

—— (1982) *Powers of Horror. An Essay on Abjection* (trans. Leon Raudiez), New York: Columbia University Press.

Kuhn, Annette (1995) *Family Secrets: Acts of Memory and Imagination*, London: Verso.

Kuhn, Thomas S. (1979) 'Metaphor in Science' in Andrew Ortony (ed.) *Metaphor and Thought*, Cambridge: Cambridge University Press, pp. 356–408.

Kulick, Don and Wilson, Margaret (eds) (1995) *Taboo: Sex, Identity and Erotic Subjectivity in Anthropological Fieldwork*, London: Routledge.

Kushi, Michio (1984) *The Cancer Prevention Diet: The Nutritional Blueprint for the Relief and Prevention of Disease*, Wellingborough, Northamptonshire: Thorsons.

Kushi, Michio and Jack, Alex (1986) *The Book of Macro-Biotics: The Universal Way of Health, Happiness and Peace*, Tokyo and New York: Japan Publications Inc.

Lacan, Jacques (1977) 'The Mirror Stage as Formative of the I as Revealed in Psychoanalytic Experience' in *Ecrits* (trans. Alan Sheridan), London: Tavistock.

Lakoff, Georg and Johnson, Mark (1980) *Metapors We Live By*, Chicago: Chicago University Press.

Lancet, The (1989) (Editorial) 'Psychosocial Intervention and the Natural History of Cancer', 2–14 October (8668): 901.

—— (1990) Letter pages (8717): 743–4.

Lash, S. and Friedman, J. (eds) *Modernity and Identity*, Oxford: Blackwell.

Laub, Dori (1995) 'Truth and Testimony: The Process and the Struggle' in Cathy Caruth (ed.) *Trauma: Explorations in Memory*, London and Baltimore: Johns Hopkins University Press, pp. 61–75.

Lerner, Michael (1994) *Choices in Healing*, Boston: MIT Press.

Le Shan, Lawrence (1966) 'An Emotional Life History Pattern Associated with Neo-Plastic Disease', *The Annals of the New York Academy of Sciences* 125: 780–93.

—— (1977) *You can Fight for Your Life: Emotional Factors in Causation of Cancer*, New York: M. Evans & Co.

—— (1984) *Holistic Health: How to Understand and Use the Revolution in Medicine*, Wellingborough, Northamptonshire: Turnstone Press.

Levin, Martin (ed.) (1970) *Hollywood and the Great Fan Magazine*, New York: Arbor House.

Levine, Stephen (1987) *Healing into Life and Death*, Bath: Gateway Books.

Levy, S. M. and Wise, B. D. (1989) 'Psychosocial Risk Factors, Natural Immunity and Cancer Progression: Implications for Intervention' in M. Johnston and T. Marteau (eds) *Applications in Health Psychology*, New Brunswick, New Jersey: Transaction Publications.

Lister, J. (1983) 'Current Controversy on Alternative Medicine', *New England Journal of Medicine* 309(24): 1524–7.

Lock, Margaret and Gordon, Deborah R. (1988) (eds) *Biomedicine Examined*, Dorrdrecht, The Netherlands: Kluewer Academic Publishers.

Loraux, Nicole (1989) 'Therefore, Socrates is Immortal' in Michel Feher, Ramona Naddaff and Nadia Tazi (eds) (1989) *Fragments for a History of the Human Body*, Part 2, Boston: Zone Books/MIT Press, pp. 12–45.

Lorber, Judith (1975) 'Good Patients and Problem Patients: Conformity and Deviance in a General Hospital', *Journal of Health and Social Behaviour* 16(2): 213–25.

Lorch, Jennifer, MacWhinnie, Ian, Smith, Heather and Stacey, Meg (1990/1) 'The Bristol Cancer Help Centre Research Study', *Caduceus* 12(Autumn/Winter): 4–10.

Lorde, Audre (1980) *The Cancer Journals*, San Francisco: Spinster's Ink.

Lupton, Deborah (1994) *Medicine as Culture: Illness, Disease and the Body in Western Societies*, London: Sage.

—— (1995) *The Imperative of Health: Public Health and the Regulated Body*, London: Sage.

Lury, Celia (1993) *Cultural Rights: Technology, Legality and Personality*, London: Routledge.
—— (1997) *Prosthetic Culture*, London: Routledge.
Lyotard, Jean François (1984) (published in French in 1979) *The Postmodern Condition: A Report on Knowledge* (trans Geoff Bennington and Brian Massumi), Manchester: Manchester University Press.
McClintock, Anne (1995) *Imperial Leather: Race, Gender and Sexuality in the Colonial Contest*, London: Routledge.
MacCormack, Carol P. and Strathern, Marilyn (eds) (1982) *Nature, Culture and Gender*, Cambridge and London: Cambridge University Press.
McIntosh, Mary (1993) 'Queer Theory and the War of the Sexes' in Joseph Bristow and Angelia R. Wilson (eds) *Activating Theory: Lesbian, Gay and Bisexual Politics*, London: Lawrence & Wishart, pp. 30–52.
McMullin, M. (1992) 'Holistic Care of Patients with Cervical Cancer', *Nursing Clinics of North America* 27(4): 847–58.
McNay, Lois (1992) *Foucault and Feminism*, Cambridge: Polity.
McNeil, Maureen (ed.) (1987) *Gender and Expertise*, London: Free Association Books.
McNeil, Maureen and Franklin, Sarah (1991) 'Science and Technology: Questions for Cultural Studies and Feminism' in Sarah Franklin, Celia Lury and Jackie Stacey (eds) *Off-Centre: Feminism and Cultural Studies*, London: HarperCollins/Routledge, pp. 129–46.
McNeil, Maureen and Litt, Jacquelyn (1992) 'More Medicalising of Mothers: Foetal Alcohol Syndrome in the USA and Related Developments' in Stephen Platt, Sue Scott, Hilary Thomas and Gareth Williams (eds) *Private Risks and Public Dangers*, Aldershot: Avebury Press, pp. 112–32.
Magli, Patrizia (1989) 'The Face and the Soul' in Michel Feher, Ramona Naddaff and Nadia Tazi (eds) *Fragments for a History of the Human Body*, Part 2, Boston, Massachusetts: Zone Books/MIT Press, pp. 86–127.
Marsh, P. (1990) 'Alternative Medicines Battle', *British Medical Journal* 300(6739): 1543–4.
Martin, Emily (1987) *The Woman in the Body: A Cultural Analysis of Reproduction*, Boston, Massachusetts: Beacon Press.
—— (1992) 'Body Narratives: Body Boundaries' in Lawrence Grossberg, Carey Nielson and Paula A. Treichler (eds) *Cultural Studies*, London and New York: Routledge, pp. 409–19.
—— (1994) *Flexible Bodies: Tracking Immunity in American Culture From the Days of Polio to the Age of AIDS*, Boston, Massachusetts: Beacon Press.
Martindale, Kathleen (1994) 'Can I Get a Witness?, *Fireweed* 42: 9–15.
Menzies, Isobel (1988) *Containing Anxiety in Institutions: Selected Essays by Isobel Menzies*, London: Free Association Books.
Miles, Agnes (1991) *Women, Health and Medicine*, Milton Keynes, Buckinghamshire: Open University Press.
Miller, D. A. (1993) 'Sontag's Urbanity' in Henry Abelove, Michèle Aina Barale and David M. Halperin (eds) *The Lesbian and Gay Studies Reader*, London: Routledge.
Miller, Nancy (1991) *Getting Personal: Feminist Occasions and Other Autobiographical Acts*, London: Routledge.
Mitchell, Juliet (1974) *Psychoanalysis and Feminism*, Harmondsworth, Middlesex: Penguin.
—— (1986) *The Selected Works of Melanie Klein*, London: Penguin.
Money, Stirling and Greer, Steven (1989) *Psychological Therapy for Patients with Cancer*, Oxford: Heinemann Medical Books.

Montbriand, M. J. and Laing, G. P. (1991) 'Alternative Health Care as a Control Strategy', *Journal of Advanced Nursing* 16(3): 325–32.

Mountcastle, Vernon B. (1980) *Medical Physiology* Vol. 2 (14th edn), London: The C.V. Mosby Co.

Moynihan, C. (1993) 'A History of Counselling', *Journal of the Royal Society of Medicine* 86(7): 421–3.

Mulvey, Laura (1989) *Visual and Other Pleasures*, London: Macmillan.

—— (1991) 'A Phantasmagoria of the Female Body: The Work of Cindy Sherman', *New Left Review* 188 (July/August): 136–51.

Murray, V. S. G. (1992) 'Investigating Alternative Medicines', *British Medical Journal* 304(6818): 11.

Neale, Stephen (1980) *Genre*, London: British Film Institute.

Nelson, Cary, Treichler, Paula A. and Grossberg, Larry (1992) 'Cultural Studies: An Introduction' in Larry Grossberg *et al.*, *Cultural Studies*, pp. 1–22.

Newlands, E. S., Begent, R. H. J., Rustin, G. J. S., Holden, L. and Bagshawe, K. D. (1984) 'Chemotherapy for Malignant Ovarian Germ Cell Tumours' in Norman Bleehen (ed.) *Ovarian Cancer*.

Newman, Janet (1990) 'Sex Education and Social Change: Perspectives on the 1960s', The Open University: Unpublished PhD thesis.

Nicholson, Linda J. (ed.) (1990) *Feminism/Postmodernism*, London: Routledge.

Nilsson, Lennart (1987) *The Body Victorious: The Illustrated Story of Our Immune System and Other Defences of the Human Body*, New York: Delacorte.

Oakley, Ann (1993) *Essays on Women, Medicine and Health*, Edinburgh: Edinburgh University Press.

Ortony, Andrew (ed.) (1979) *Metaphor and Thought*, Cambridge: Cambridge University Press.

Pajaczkowska, Claire (1995) 'Art as a Symptom of Not Dying', *New Formations* 26(Autumn): 74–88.

Park, Katherine and Dalston, Lorraine (1981) 'Unnatural Conceptions: The Study of Monsters in Sixteenth- and Seventeenth-Century France and England', *Past and Present: A Journal of Historical Studies* 92(August): 21–54.

Paterson, J. R. (1992) 'Another Look at Holistic Medicine', *Journal of the Royal Society of Medicine* 85(11): 713.

Patton, Cindy (1990) *Inventing AIDS*, New York: Routledge.

Pearce, Ian C. B. (1983) *The Holistic Approach to Cancer*, Saffron Waldon: C. W. David and Co. Ltd.

Pearce, Lynne and Stacey, Jackie (eds) (1995) *Romance Revisited*, London: Lawrence & Wishart.

Pellitier, Kenneth (1977) *The Mind as Healer, The Mind as Slayer*, New York: Delta.

Personal Narratives Group, The (ed.) (1989) *Interpreting Women's Lives: Feminist Theory and Personal Narratives*, Bloomington and Indianapolis: Indiana University Press.

Petchesky, Rosalind (1987) 'Foetal Images: The Power of Visual Culture in the Politics of Reproduction' in Michele Stanworth (ed.) *Reproductive Technologies: Gender, Motherhood and Medicine*, Cambridge: Polity, pp. 57–80.

Phelan, Peggy (1993) *Unmarked: The Politics of Performance*, London: Routledge.

—— (1996) *Mourning Sex*, London: Routledge.

Phillips, Adam (1994) *On Flirtation*, London: Faber and Faber.

Phillips, Angela and Rakusen, Jill (1978) *Our Bodies, Ourselves*, London: Penguin.

Pickering, Andrew (ed.) (1992) *Science as Practice and Culture*, Chicago and London: University of Chicago Press.

Picone, Mary (1989) 'The Ghost in the Machine: Religious Healing and Representations of the Body in Japan' in Michel Feher, Romana Naddaff and Nadia Tazi (eds) *Fragments for a History of the Human Body*, Part Two, Boston, Massachusetts: Zone Books/MIT Press, pp. 466–89.

Pietroni, Patrick C. (1991) *The Greening of Medicine*, London: Victor Gollancz.

—— (1992a) 'Partners in Practice: Relationship between General Practice and Complementary Medicine', *British Medical Journal* 305(6853): 564–6.

—— (1992b) 'Alternative Medicine', *Journal of Medical Ethics* 18(1): 23–5.

Piver, Steven M. (ed.) (1987) *Ovarian Malignancies: Diagnostic Therapeutic Advances*, London: Churchill Livingstone/Longman.

Playfair, J. (1984) *Immunology at a Glance* (3rd edn), Oxford: Blackwell.

Probyn, Elspeth (1993) *Sexing the Self: Gendered Positions in Cultural Studies*, London: Routledge.

Quick, Andrew (1995) 'Meaning and Language in New Performance', University of Bristol: unpublished PhD thesis.

Quin, C. E. (1990) 'Another Look at Holistic Medicine' (Editorial), *Journal of the Royal Society of Medicine* 83(6): 343–4.

Rabinbach, Anson (1992) 'Neurasthenia and Modernity' in J. Crary and S. Kwinter (eds) *Incorporations*, Boston, Massachusetts: Zone Books/MIT Press pp. 178–89.

Rabinow, Paul (1992) 'Artificiality and Enlightenment: From Sociobiology to Biosociality' in J. Crary and S. Kwinter (eds) *Incorporations*, Boston, Massachusetts: Zone Books/MIT Press, pp. 234–52.

Ramazanoglu, Caroline (ed.) (1993) *Up Against Foucault: Explorations of Some Tensions between Foucault and Feminism*, London: Routledge.

Rather, L. J. (1978) *The Genesis of Cancer: A Study in the History of Ideas*, Baltimore and London: The Johns Hopkins University Press.

Raven, Ronald, Hanham, Iain and Mould, Richard F. (1986) *Cancer Care: An International Survey*, Bristol and Boston: Adam Hilger Ltd.

Readings, Bill (1991) *Introducing Lyotard: Art and Politics*, London and New York: Routledge.

Rees, Gareth, Goodman, Sally and Bullimore, Jill (1993) *Cancer in Practice*, Oxford: Butterworth-Heinemann/Reed International Books.

Reich, Wilhelm (1973) *The Cancer Biopathy* (trans A White *et al.*), New York: Farrar, Strauss & Giroux.

—— (1975) *Reich Speaks of Freud*, Harmondsworth, Middlesex: Penguin.

Renouf, Jane (1993) *Jimmy: No Time to Die*, London: Fontana/HarperCollins.

Reynolds, Trish (1988) *Your Cancer, Your Life*, London: MacDonald/Optima Paperbacks.

Rich, Adrienne (1980) 'Compulsory Heterosexuality and Lesbian Existence', *Signs* 5(4): 631–60.

Richards, T. (1990) 'Death from Complementary Medicine' (Editorial), *British Medical Journal* 301(6751): 510–11.

Richardson, Diane (1987) *Women and the AIDS Crisis*, London: Pandora.

Richardson, Diane and Robinson, Victoria (eds) (1993) *Introducing Women's Studies*, London: Macmillan.

Richmond, C. (1990) 'Report on UK Cancer Survival Rates Raises Questions about Alternative Medicine', *Canadian Medical Association Journal* 143(9): 922–3.

Ricoeur, Paul (1986) *The Rule of Metaphor: Multi-disciplinary Studies in the Creation of Meaning*, London: Routledge & Kegan Paul.

Rimmon-Kenan, Shlomith (1989) *Narrative Fiction and Contemporary Poetics*, London: Routledge.

Roberts, Helen (ed.) (1992) *Women's Health Matters*, London: Routledge.

Robinson, Ray and Le Grand, Julian (eds) (1994) *Evaluating NHS Reforms*, Newbury, Berkshire: Kings Fund Institute/Policy Journals.

Roger, John and McWilliams, Peter (1991) *You Can't Afford the Luxury of a Negative Thought*, London: Thorsons/HarperCollins.

Rose, Gillian (1995) *Love's Work*, London: Chatto & Windus.

Rose, Jacqueline (1986) *Sexuality in the Field of Vision*, London: Verso.

Ross, Andrew (1991) *Strange Weather: Culture, Science and Technology in the Age of Limits*, London: Verso.

Roth, Lawrence and Czernobilsky, B. (eds) (1985) *Tumors and Tumorlike Conditions of the Ovary*, London: Churchill Livingstone/Longman.

Russo, Mary (1994) *The Female Grotesque: Risk, Excess, Modernity*, London: Routledge.

Sacks, Oliver (1986) *The Man who Mistook his Wife for a Hat*, London: Picador/Pan Books.

Said, Edward (1993) *Culture and Imperialism*, London: Vintage Books.

Saks, Mike (1992a) 'Alternative Medicine in Britain', *Social Policy and Administration* 26(3): 265.

—— (1992b) *Alternative Medicine in Modern Britain*, Oxford: Clarendon Press.

—— (1994) 'The Alternatives to Medicine' in Jonathan Gabe, David Kelleher and Gareth Williams (eds) *Challenging Medicine*, London: Routledge, pp. 84–103.

Salmon, J. W. (ed) (1985) *Alternative Medicine: Popular and Policy Perspectives*, London: Tavistock.

Sarup, Madan (1988) *An Introductory Guide to Poststructuralism and Postmodernism*, Hemel Hempstead, Hertforshire: Harvester Wheatsheaf/Simon & Schuster.

Satterfield, Ann (1992) 'Pages from *Treament*', *camera obscura* 29: 215–25.

Sayers, Janet (1986) *Sexual Contradictions*, London: Methuen.

Scarry, Elaine (1985) *The Body in Pain: The Making and Unmaking of the World*, Oxford: Oxford University Press.

Scheper-Hughes, Nancy and Lock, Margaret M. (1986) 'Speaking "Truth" to Illness: Metaphors, Reification and a Pedagogy for Patients', *Medical Anthropology Quarterly* 17(5): 137–45.

—— (1987) 'The Mindful Body: A Prolegomenon to Future Work in Medical Anthropology', *Medical Anthropology Quarterly* 1(1): 6–41.

Schjeide, Ole A. and de Vellis, Jean (1970) *Cell Differentiation*, New York: Van Nostrand Reinhold Co.

Seale, Clive (1995) 'Heroic Death', *Sociology* 29(4): 597–614.

Sedgwick, Eve Kosofsky (1990) *Epistemology of the Closet*, Berkeley, California: University of California Press.

—— (1992) 'Epidemics of the Will' in J. Crary and S. Kwinter (eds) *Incorporations*, Boston, Massachusetts: Zone Books/MIT Press, pp. 582–95.

—— (1994) *Tendencies*, London: Routledge.

Selye, Hans (1956) *The Stress of Life*, New York: McGraw-Hill.

Sharma, Ursula (1991) 'Holistic Health and Biomedical Medicine: A Countersystem Analysis', *Sociology of Health and Illness* 13(2): 286–8.

—— (1992) *Complementary Medicine Today: Practitioners and Patients*, London: Tavistock/Routledge.

—— (1993) 'Contextualising Alternative Medicine', *Anthropology Today* 9(4): 15–18.

Sharp, F. and Soutter, W. P. (1987) *Ovarian Cancer: The Way Ahead*, Chichester: John Wiley & Sons.

Sharp, F., Mason, W. P. and Leeke, R. E. (eds) (1990) *Ovarian Cancer: Biological and Therapeutic Challenges*, London: Chapman & Hall.

Sheard, T. A. B. (1990) 'Bristol Cancer Help Centre' (Letter), *The Lancet* 336(8716): 683.

Sheehan, G. (1977) *Dr. Sheehan on Running*, New York: Random House.

Shilling, Chris (1993) *The Body and Social Theory*, London: Sage.

Shohat, Ella (1992) '"Laser for Ladies": Endo Discourse and the Inscription of Science', *camera obscura* 29: 57–90.

Shweder, Richard A. (ed.) (1984) *Culture Theory: Essays on Mind, Self and Emotion*, Cambridge: Cambridge University Press.

Siegel, Bernie (1986) *Love, Medicine and Miracles*, New York: Harper & Row.

—— (1993) *Living, Loving and Healing: A Guide to a Fuller Life, More Love and Greater Health*, London: Aquarian Press/HarperCollins.

Sikora, K. (1989) 'Complementary Medicine and Cancer Treatment', *Practitioner* 233(1476): 1285–6.

Simonton, O. Carl, Matthews-Simonton, Stephanie and Creighton, James L. (1978) *Getting Well Again*, London: Bantam Books.

Sinfield, Alan (1989) *Literature, Politics and Culture in Postwar Britain*, Oxford: Basil Blackwell.

Singer, Merrill (1990) 'Postmodernism and Medical Anthropology: Words of Caution', *Medical Anthropology* 12: 289–304.

Singer, M., Baer, H. A. and Lazarus, E. (1990) 'Introduction: Critical Medical Anthropology in Question', *Social Science and Medicine* 30(2): v–viii.

Skeggs, Beverley (1995) 'Women's Studies in Britain in the 1990s: Entitlement Cultures and Institutional Constraints', *Women's Studies International Forum* 18(4): 475–85.

Smith, Ann Marie (1995) *Cultural Margins*, Cambridge: Cambridge University Press.

Smith, Meg (1992) 'The Burzynski Controversy in the US and in Canada: A Comparative Case-Study in the Sociology of Alternative Medicine', *Canadian Journal of Sociology* 17(2): 133–60.

Smith, T. (1983) 'Alternative Medicine', (Editorial), *British Medical Journal* 287 (6388): 307.

Soloman, A. F. (1969) 'Stress, The Central Nervous System and Immunity', *Annals of the New York Academy of Science* 164: 335–43.

Solomon, Alisa (1992) The Politics of Breast Cancer', *camera obscura* 28: 157–78.

Sontag, Susan (1977, this edn 1991) *Illness as Metaphor*, London: Penguin.

—— (1988, this edn 1991) *Aids and its Metaphors*, London: Penguin.

Spanier, Bonnie B. (1991) '"Lessons" from "Nature": Gender Ideology and Sexual Ambiguity in Biology' in Julia Epstein and Kristina Straub (eds) *Body Guards: The Cultural Politics of Gender Ambiguity*, London: Routledge, pp. 329–50.

Spence, Jo (1987) *Putting Myself in the Picture*, London: Camden.

—— (1995) *Cultural Sniping: The Art of Transgression*, London: Routledge.

Spence, Jo and Solomon, Joan (eds) (1995) *What Can a Woman Do With a Camera?*, London: Scarlet Press.

Stabile, Carol (1992) 'Shooting the Mother: Fetal Photography and the Politics of Disappearance', *camera obscura* 28: 179–206.

Stacey, Jackie (1987) 'Desperately Seeking Difference', *Screen* 28(1): 19–28.

—— (1991) 'Promoting Normality: Section 28 and the Regulation of Sexuality' in Sarah Franklin, Celia Lury and Jackie Stacey (eds) *Off-Centre: Feminism and Cultural Studies*, London: HarperCollins/Routledge, pp. 284–304.

Stacey, Margaret (1988) *The Sociology of Health and Healing*, London: Unwin Hyman.

—— (1991) 'Nature, Wholeness and Healing', *Caduceus* 14: 40–3.

Stafford, Barbara (1991) *Body Criticism: Imaging the Unseen in Enlightenment Art and Medicine*, Boston, Massachusetts: MIT Press/Zone Books.

Stainton-Rogers, Wendy (1991) *Explaining Health and Illness: An Exploration of Diversity*, London: Harvester Wheatsheaf.

Stanley, Liz (1991) *Feminist Praxis: Research, Theory and Epistemology in Feminist Sociology*, London: Routledge.

Starobinski, Jean (1989) 'The Natural and Literary History of Bodily Sensation' in Michel Feher, Ramona Naddaff and Nadia Tazi (eds) *Fragments for a History of the Human Body*, Part Two, Boston, Massachusetts: Zone Books/MIT Press, pp. 350–93.

Steedman, Carolyn (1986) *Landscape for a Good Women: A Story of Two Lives*, London: Virago.

Strathern, Marilyn (1992) *After Nature: English Kinship in the Twentieth Century*, Cambridge: Cambridge University Press.

Sturrock, John (ed.) (1979) *Structuralism and Since: From Lèvi-Strauss to Derrida*, Oxford: Oxford University Press.

Synott, Anthony (1993) *The Body Social: Symbolism, Self and Society*, London: Routledge.

Talerman, Aleksander (1985) 'Germ Cell Tumors and Mixed Germ Cell-Sex Cord-Stromal Tumors of the Ovary' in Lawrence Roth and B. Czernobilsky (eds) *Tumors and Tumorlike Conditions of the Ovary*, London: Churchill Livingstone/Longman, pp. 75–95.

Tasker, Yvonne (1993) *Spectacular Bodies: Gender, Genre and the Action Cinema*, London: Routledge.

Tauber, Alfred I. (1994) *The Immune Self: Theory or Metaphor?*, Cambridge: Cambridge University Press.

Taussig, M. T. (1980) 'Reification and the Consciousness of the Patient', *Social Science and Medicine* 14B: 3–13.

Terry, Jennifer and Urla, Jacqueline (eds) (1995) *Deviant Bodies*, Bloomington: Indiana University Press.

Thomas, Keith (1983) *Man and the Natural World: Changing Attitudes in England 1500–1800*, Harmondsworth, Middlesex: Penguin.

Thynne, Lizzie (1995) 'The Space Between: Daughters and Lovers in *Anne Trister*' in Lynne Pearce and Jackie Stacey (eds) *Romance Revisited*, London: Lawrence & Wishart, pp. 103–16.

Traub, Valerie (1991) 'The Ambiguities of "Lesbian" Viewing Pleasure: The (Dis)articulations of *Black Widow*' in Julia Epstein and Kristina Straub (eds) *Body Guards: The Cultural Politics of Gender Ambiguity*, London: Routledge, pp. 305–28.

Treichler, Paula A. and Cartwright, Lisa (eds) (1992) *camera obscura* 28 and 29 (Special Issues on 'Imaging Technologies, Inscribing Science'), Bloomington: Indiana University Press.

Tudor, Andrew (1989) *Monsters and Mad Scientists: A Cultural History of the Horror Movie*, Oxford: Basil Blackwell.

Turner, Bryan (1984) *The Body and Society: Explorations in Social Theory*, Oxford: Basil Blackwell.

—— (1987) *Medical Power and Social Knowledge*, London: Sage.

—— (1990) 'The Interdisciplinary Curriculum: From Social Medicine to Postmodernism', *Sociology of Health and Illness* 12(1): 1–22.

Turner, Victor (1967) *The Forest of Symbols: Aspects of Ndembu Ritual*, Ithaca, New York: Cornell University Press.

Vachon, D. (1993) 'Using the Power of Belief in Acupuncture and Holistic Medicine – Case Studies', *American Journal of Acupuncture* 21(1): 33–40.

Vanessa Press (ed.) (1986) *Bits of Ourselves: Women's Experiences With Cancer*, Fairbanks, Alaska: Vanessa Press.

Varmus, Harold and Weinberg, Robert A. (1993) *Genes and the Biology of Cancer*, New York: The Scientific American Library.

Vessey, M. P. and Gray, Muir (eds) (1985) *Cancer Risks and Prevention*, Oxford: Oxford University Press.

Vile, Richard G. (ed.) (1992) *Introduction to the Molecular Genetics of Cancer*, Chichester, Sussex: John Wiley & Sons.

Wade, Dorothy (1982) 'A Quiet Revolution', *New Statesman and Society* 2(55): 37.

Walby, Sylvia (1990) *Theorising Patriarchy*, Oxford: Basil Blackwell.

Walter, Tony (1992) 'Modern Death: Taboo or Not Taboo?', *Sociology* 25(2): 293–310.

Walter, Tony, Littlewood, Jane and Pickering, Michael (1995) 'Death in the News: The Public Invigilation of Private Emotion', *Sociology* 29(4): 579–96.

Warner, J. H. (1990) 'Alternative Medicine and American Religious Life', *American Historical Review* 95(5): 1644–5.

Watney, Simon (1987) *Policing Desire: Pornography, AIDS, and the Media*, Minneapolis: University of Minnesota Press.

Watt, James and Wood, Clive (eds) (1988) *Talking Health: Conventional and Complementary Approaches*, London: Royal Society of Medicine Services.

Weed, Elizabeth (ed.) (1989) *Coming to Terms: Feminism, Theory, Politics*, London: Routledge.

Weeks, Jeffrey (1977) *Coming Out: Homosexual Politics in Britain from the Nineteenth Century to the Present*, London: Quartet.

—— (1985) *Sexuality and its Discontents: Meanings, Myths and Sexualities*, London: Routledge & Kegan Paul.

Weindling, Paul (1981) 'Theories of the Cell State in Imperial Germany' in Charles Webster (ed.) *Biology, Medicine and Society 1840–1940*, Cambridge: Cambridge University Press.

Weiner, Norbert (1961) *Cybernetics* (2nd edn), New York and London: MIT Press and John Wiley & Sons.

Weiss, Andrea (1992) *Vampires and Violets: Lesbians in the Cinema*, London: Jonathan Cape.

Wheeler, Sally and Selvy, Peter (1993) *Confronting Cancer: Cause and Prevention*, Harmondsworth, Middlesex: Penguin.

White, Evelyn C. (ed.) (1990) *The Black Women's Health Book: Speaking for Ourselves*, Seattle: The Seal Press.

White, Patricia (1991) 'Female Spectator, Lesbian Spectator' in Diana Fuss (ed.) *Inside/Out: Lesbian Theories, Gay Theories*, London: Routledge, pp. 142–72.

Wilber, Ken (1991) *Grit and Grace*, Boston, Massachusetts: Shambala.

Wilkie, Angela (1993) *Having Cancer and How To Live With It*, London: Hodder & Staughton.

Wilkinson, Sue and Kitzinger, Celia (eds) (1994) *Women and Health: Feminist Perspectives*, London: Taylor & Francis.

Williams, C. J. (ed.) (1992) *Introducing New Treatment for Cancer: Practical, Ethical and Legal Problems*, Chichester: John Wiley & Sons.

Williams, Raymond (1973) *The Country and the City*, St Albans, Hertfordshire: Paladin.

—— (1976) *Keywords: A Vocabulary of Culture and Society*, London: Fontana.

Williamson, Judith (1978) *Decoding Advertisements: Ideology and Meaning in Advertising*, London: Marion Boyars.

—— (1986) *Consuming Passions: The Dynamics of Popular Culture*, London: Marion Boyars.

—— (1995) Public Lecture on Cindy Sherman, 15 October, Manchester City Art Galleries.

Wilson, Alexander (1992) *The End of Nature*, London: Routledge.

Wilson, Elizabeth (1989) 'Tell It Like It Is: Women and Confessional Writing' in Susannah Radstone (ed.) *Sweet Dreams: Sexuality and Popular Culture*, London: Lawrence & Wishart, pp. 21–45.

Wilton, Tamsin (1995) *Immortal, Invisible: Lesbians and the Moving Image*, London: Routledge.

Winterson, Jeanette (1992) *Written on the Body*, London: Jonathan Cape.

Witz, Ann (1992) *Professions and Patriarchy*, London: Routledge.

Wright, Elizabeth (ed.) (1992) *Feminism and Psychoanalysis: A Critical Dictionary*, Oxford: Basil Blackwell.

Wynne, Brian (1987) *Risk Management and Hazardous Wastes: Implementation and the Dialectics of Credibility*, Berlin: Springer.

Yates, P. M., Beadle, G., Clavarino, A., Najman, J. M., Thomson, D., Williams, G., Kenny, L., Roberts, S., Mason, B. and Schlecht, D. (1993) 'Patients with Terminal Cancer Who Use Alternative Therapies: Their Beliefs and Practices', *Sociology of Health and Illness* 15(2): 199–216.

Young, A. (1980) 'The Discourse on Stress and the Reproduction of Conventional Knowledge', *Social Science and Medicine* 14B: 133–46.

Young, Robert J. C. (1995) *Colonial Desire: Hybridity in Theory, Culture and Race*, London and New York: Routledge.

INDEX

militaristic metaphors 172; stress
113–14
immunology 159–63
individualism 12–13, 193, 211,
220–1, 237
individuation 239, 257 (n5)
inequality 208, 223
infomedicine 191–2
information technology 158, 165,
229, 231
insights, cultural coding 173–6
Irigaray, Luce 199
isolation, trauma 16, 17
Issels, Joseph 165

Jacobsen, G. Crag 35, 36, 95
Jameson, Frederic 242
Johnson, Mark 50, 51, 52
Jones, Helen 212

Kelleher, David 227
Keller, Evelyn Fox 103, 208, 238,
239, 240
Kfir, Nira 246 (n6)
kinaesthesia 98, 254 (n1)
Kingman, S. 129
Kiple, Kenneth F. 142–3
Kirmayer, Lawrence J. 107, 119, 134,
186
Kitzinger, Celia 111
knowledge: disclosed 104–6;
legitimating 234–7; medical 52–7,
150; and perception 150–2; as
power 4; scientific 144; of self 149,
200, 237; specialised 102;
technological 233
Krauss, Rosalind 83, 86, 88
Kristeva, Julia: abjection 75, 77, 79,
80, 89; body 85–6; death 82; fear
83; homosexuality 253 (n20); skin
84, 254 (n26); taboo 74–5
Kuhn, Annette 99, 100, 140
Kuhn, Thomas S. 49
Kushi, Michio 246 (n2)
Kwinter, Sandford 159

Lacan, Jacques 122
Laing, G. P. 131
Lakoff, Georg 50, 51, 52
Lancet, The 128
Langley, F. 31, 32, 33, 58, 59, 91
laughter 116
Le Grand, Julian 212

legitimation, knowledge 234–7
lesbianism: abjection 77; desire 94;
as deviant 40, 63; feared 87;
hypersexual 73–4; narcissistic 82,
86; passing 67–8; reproduction 39,
81–2; taboo word 66, 252 (n2);
undifferentiated 78
LeShan, Lawrence 46, 115
life cycle, illness 243
lifestyle, health 217, 222–3
lifestyle medicine 213
Lock, Margaret M. 48, 107, 108
Loraux, Nicole 122
Lorde, Audre 190
love, healing quality 116
Love, Medicine and Miracles (Siegel)
186
Lupton, Deborah 209, 224
Lury, Celia 157, 231, 257 (n10)
lymphocytes 161
Lyotard, Jean François 200, 230–4,
242

McNeil, Maureen 207, 259 (n12)
McWilliams, Peter 125
Magli, Patrizia 122, 123, 125
mammography 156
Martin, Emily 143, 146, 160, 164,
165, 174
Martindale, Kathleen 248 (n22)
masculinity 10–12, 39
mastectomy 207
maternal body 85–6, 87
ME (myalgic encephalomyelitis) 188
medical anthropology 107
medical science 11, 48–9, 103, 104
medicine: anamnesic 196–7;
classificatory 52–4; clinical 52–3;
depoliticised 223–4;
deprofessionalised 214–15; elite
102; Galenic 115, 125, 142;
Hippocratic 142; lifestyle 213;
pathological 54; *see also*
biomedicine; doctor–patient
relationship
melancholia 125, 126
memory: in body 98, 99–100; cellular
information 148–9; photography
140–1; trauma 99–100, 118–19,
120; and writing 23, 242
memory loss 98–9
menstruation 146
Menzies, Isobel 258 (n4)